women's rights
human rights

women's rights
human rights

international feminist perspectives

edited by
julie peters and andrea wolper

routledge • new york london

Published in 1995 by

Routledge
29 West 35th Street
New York, NY 10001-2299

Published in Great Britain by

Routledge
11 New Fetter Lane
London EC4P 4EE

Library of Congress Cataloging-in-Publication Data

Women's rights, human rights : international feminist perspectives / edited by Julie Peters and Andrea Wolper.
        p.   cm.
    ISBN 0-415-90994-5 (hb) — ISBN 0-415-90995-3 (pb)
    1. Women's rights.   2. Human rights.   3. Women—Legal status, laws, etc.   4. Feminism.   I. Peters, Julie.   II. Wolper, Andrea.
    K644.Z9W665   1994
    323.3'4—dc20   94-15775
                                                             CIP

British Library Cataloguing-in-Publication Data also available

Contents

Acknowledgements

The editors wish to thank the women and men at universities and women's and human rights organizations who offered suggestions and referrals, and whose interest and assistance helped make this book possible. We thank our editor at Routledge, Cecelia Cancellaro, for her insightful handling of the project. Most of all, we extend our gratitude to Tamara Pulsts, who (with the help of Amnesty International USA Group #11) organized the 1992 conference at Columbia University that was the seed for the collection and whose continuing support has been instrumental in its creation.

Introduction
Julie Peters and Andrea Wolper

In India, a ten-year-old girl boards a flight for Saudi Arabia; her companion is a sixty-year-old businessman who has married the girl after purchasing her from her parents. In a U.S. suburb, a woman kept under "house arrest" is beaten if she tries to contact friends or relatives; her "jailer" is her husband. In a Sudanese village, a group of little girls is taken to an unfamiliar place where a woman cuts away their genitalia using an unsterilized piece of broken glass. In Peru, a woman is arrested after inquiring about her husband, who has not been seen since he was questioned by soldiers several days earlier. In Burma, a twenty-two-year-old woman and her eleven-year-old niece are taken into custody as they hurry home just after curfew; the young woman is raped by six soldiers, the eleven-year-old by seven—including the unit commander.

These are not rare or isolated incidents. Rather, they represent just a few of the innumerable atrocities inflicted on girls and women every day in virtually every country. Such occurrences are at the heart of the struggle over what constitutes women's rights as human rights, the physical territory of which, says feminist author and organizer Charlotte Bunch, is women's bodies.[1]

Gender-based abuse and discrimination may be sanctioned by society, made into law, or simply tolerated. Either way, under democracy and dictatorship, in times of war and times of peace, women's human rights are violated daily and often systematically. Women may be denied the right to vote or hold office. They may be subjected to rape and sexual abuse by soldiers, police, employers, family members. They may not be free to choose when or whom to marry or how many children to have and when to have them. The United Nations' *Universal Declaration of Human Rights* proclaims: "All human beings are born

1

free and equal in dignity and rights." Yet women's freedom, dignity, and equality are persistently compromised by law and by custom in ways that men's are not.

For decades, women's groups have focused on addressing women's civil and political rights. Organizations working at the grassroots level and on local, national, and international policy have drawn attention to gender-based abuses, among them: inequality of opportunity in education, employment, housing, credit, and health care; rape and domestic violence; reproductive freedom; the valuation of child care and domestic labor. Perceived as part of the women's rights movement and hence of a special-interest agenda, these issues have been considered marginal to international law's more "serious" responsibility for human rights. What the covenant makers have failed to see (as Hilary Charlesworth points out in her contribution to this collection) is that traditional human rights formulations are based on a "normative" male model and applied to women as an afterthought, if at all. The delineation of rights, it would seem, deals with state agents acting on behalf of (or against) a polity largely defined by men.

While human rights standards may be invoked to protect women (as when they are applied to violations such as the rape of women in detention) and human rights organizations may take action on behalf of individual women, human rights work has traditionally been concerned with state-sanctioned or -condoned oppression, that which takes place in the "public sphere," away from the privacy to which most women are relegated and in which most violations of women's rights take place. This focus has created an artificial legal and perceptual divide between crimes by state actors and those by nonstate actors, whether individuals, organizations, or even unofficial governments (a divide Donna Sullivan analyzes here).

Traditional human rights standards categorize violations in ways that exclude women, eliding critical issues. While men may care about reproductive freedom, their lives are not actually threatened by its absence; for women in areas of high maternal mortality (Rebecca Cook points out), full reproductive freedom may mean the difference between life and death. Likewise, while asylum law protects those with a "well-founded fear of being persecuted for reasons of race, religion, nationality, membership [in] a particular social group or political opinion," it rarely protects those persecuted for reasons of gender, as Pamela Goldberg explains. And while men may be the victims of private violence, such violence is not part of a pattern of gender-based abuse. Nor are they victims of the kinds of discriminatory family law discussed here by Marsha Freeman and Julie Mertus. The fact is that a woman need not be arrested or live in a war-torn area to be incarcerated and tortured. "Significant numbers of the world's population," writes Charlotte Bunch, "are routinely subject to torture, starvation, terrorism, humiliation, mutilation, and even murder simply because they are female. Crimes such as these against any group other than women would be recognized as a civil and political emergency as well as a gross violation of the victims' humanity."[2]

Recognizing that "it is not possible fully to separate the struggle for women's human rights from the struggle for women's equal rights" (as Elisabeth Friedman writes in her essay tracing those intertwined struggles), activists at the 1993 United Nations World Conference on Human Rights in Vienna proclaimed that it is no longer enough that existing human rights mechanisms merely be extended to women: *women's rights must be understood as human rights.* We must understand gender-based abuses as human rights abuses. That understanding must lead to the transformation of prevailing concepts of human rights, breaking open the now-defunct categories.

Conventional international rights instruments may in fact legitimize discrimination against women, as Natalie Hevener Kaufman and Stefanie Lindquist explain. The use of gender-neutral language as a way to insist on absolute equality fails to recognize the great weight of women's history, a history that makes it impossible for ostensible equality to mean *genuine* equality. Women may be granted equality of employment under the law, but in most cultures female workers are ghettoized into traditional "female" jobs, and most work both outside and inside the home, as Ilka Tanya Payan reminds us. Under such conditions, traditional concepts of "equal pay" or minimum wage become meaningless. Even state promotion of female employment may not always be to women's advantage: as Huda Seif points out, "Women's [labor] rights have historically been granted only in the service of the state's need for workers" and may be withdrawn when the socio-economy shifts. Women may be granted equal rights to freedom of expression, but, as Siobhan Dowd points out, such freedom has little meaning for those women who have been denied education, cannot read or write, or are effectively silenced in other ways. The story Carmel Shalev tells is illustrative: women praying and singing at the Western Wall in Jerusalem are denied access and labeled "provocateurs," not because they are violating any secular or religious law (or even challenging the segregation of men and women) but simply because they are disturbing to the men praying there—as well as to custom.

International law has begun to recognize that the establishment of structures for the prevention of discrimination is as valuable as the legal censure of discrimination. The *Convention on the Elimination of All Forms of Discrimination Against Women* (the Women's Convention) is a major step toward laying out not only passive provisions forbidding discrimination but also active provisions—what Kaufman and Lindquist refer to as "corrective language"—for remedying historical inequality. The essays in this collection show that the prosecution of crimes against women and the promotion of corrective measures are inextricably intertwined. Both are necessary to the rectification of discrimination, particularly in countries that fail to recognize their own complicity in de facto discrimination. If the Women's Convention has been rendered virtually impotent by the addition of reservations antithetical to its spirit and intent, it is nonetheless a major step— indeed, a first step—in the promotion of corrective legislation. The recognition of the necessity of such legislation is crucial to the directions the movement for women's human rights is taking, and will take, in the next decades.

The purpose of this collection is to map those directions while addressing the ramifications of critical events and issues—among them, the rapes in former Yugoslavia and the attempt to see that a War Crimes Tribunal responds to them, which Rhonda Copelon analyzes; trafficking in women and the spread of AIDS among female sex workers, which Hnin Hnin Pyne examines; female genital mutilation, which Nahid Toubia discusses; and reproductive rights and coercive methods of "population control." The essays here trace some of the roads leading from the Vienna Conference to the 1995 Fourth World Conference on Women in Beijing and beyond, showing how gender-based violations have largely gone unnoticed and articulating new agendas for dealing with them. They highlight the critical debates taking place in the discussion of rights and in international organizing: Why are women's rights not commonly classified as human rights? Why are violations of women's human rights excluded from traditional human rights programs? Who should define human and civil rights and how should they be defined? Are existing international agreements sufficient for guaranteeing the rights of women and girls and for ending violence and discrimination? Can legislation protect women from culturally sanctioned discrimination and abuse?

The examination of women's rights as human rights may finally serve as a litmus test for the question that human rights advocates and governments must face in the twenty-first century: Does the right to preserve cultural and religious practices take precedence over human rights norms? If so, is the very concept of international (universal) rights inappropriate in a multicultural world in which values and practices differ from place to place? Were universal human rights standards merely a dream of the final phases of imperialism, the post-war West's attempt to cling to an idea of the world remade in its own image?

Arati Rao and Ann Elizabeth Mayer make detailed cases here against granting exemption from international norms to state actors who claim that such norms coerce multiculturalism into a false unity. Their arguments are reinforced by the fact that there is surprisingly little disagreement among the contributors about the kinds of international mechanisms needed for ensuring women's human rights. As editors, we sought heterogeneity of viewpoint and found more unanimity than we had expected. Here, the concept of universal women's human rights (which may sound dangerously close to concepts that treat "woman" as an essential, uniform, and unchanging category) is reformulated as a wide-ranging and flexible set of standards, the product of a gathering of women's voices. That thirty-six contributors (lawyers, activists, scholars, urban women, rural women) representing twenty-one nationalities can agree on so many things suggests that women worldwide can formulate norms that nevertheless acknowledge different conditions (e.g., class based or racial) and that allow for cultural multiplicity. For example, while a South African Black woman's experience of oppression is radically different from that of a South African White woman, as Brigitte Mabandla's essay makes apparent, they nevertheless experience in common some forms of discrimination.

The collection, then, reiterates some of the important lessons of history: that states' laws do not account for the diversity of regional or cultural communities within them (indeed, most of today's nation-states are artificial constructs of the nineteenth century); that groups with a common interest may surmount national or regional differences to agree on a collection of principles. The kind of grassroots organizing that Maria Suarez Toro advocates is necessary to the establishment of an international agenda that not only genuinely reflects women's lives but that also recognizes simultaneously cultural differences and the commonality of women as a group, a commonality that may transcend national boundaries. States' codes are no more inherently contextual than international codes. When considering local, national, or international rulings, one must ask questions about context: What is the status of the speaker? In whose name is the argument from culture advanced? To what extent have the social groups primarily affected participated in the formation of the cultural practices being protected? As Arati Rao writes, "culture is not a static, unchanging, identifiable body of information" but "a series of constantly contested and negotiated social practices."

For those who resist the "universalizing" tendency of international human rights, the reiterations of the collection—the recurrence of issues from different perspectives—may provide a warning against placing too much emphasis on the recognition of radical difference. Violence against women, discriminatory family law, restriction of women's reproductive rights, persecution on the basis of sexual orientation (which Gloria Careaga Pérez and Julie Dorf discuss in the world context), and (perhaps most important) repressive cultural expectations are indeed global, and it is not hard to see these various forms of abuse and discrimination as part of a continuum of domination. While genital mutilation is generally considered primarily an African problem, cultural norms of sexual desirability in other regions (as Nahid Toubia points out) encourage women to mutilate their bodies through poisonous breast implants and other kinds of dangerous plastic surgery. Genital mutilation, trafficking in women, dowry death, rape, domestic violence, the frightening punishments that Akram Mirhosseini describes for women who violate the dress code in Iran—all are part of a global pattern of violence against women, a pattern supported by economic, employment, and educational discrimination; by sexual harassment; and by the demeaning representation of women. Like these, the selective abortion of female fetuses in India, China, and elsewhere (as Indira Jaising and Zhu Hong explain) is a manifestation of the general devaluation of women. The rapes in former Yugoslavia, as Jasmina Kuzmanović argues, are part—albeit an extreme part—of a tradition of silencing women. The point is not to create hierarchies or equivalencies of abuse but to recognize the structural interrelatedness of the various manifestations of gender discrimination.

Attempts to categorize violations will never be tidy. The overlapping of categories in this collection reflects the complex interrelatedness of the issues. If Sima Wali's paper, for example, is about the specific problems of women refugees, it is also about sexual violence, health, and a panoply of other issues critical to the women's human rights agenda. Designating a section "Regional Reports" does not, of course, preclude later discussion of certain far-reaching issues from within the context of a particular region, just as each of the regional reports addresses issues that are dealt with elsewhere in the collection: Koki Muli's overview of women's human rights abuses in Kenya necessarily deals with such issues as family law, violence and health, and labor; Liza Largoza-Maza's discussion of the abuse of Philippine bar girls, mail-order brides, and factory and domestic workers necessarily deals with such issues as sexual exploitation, domestic violence, and the (nation's) developing economy.

The essays in the first section—an overview of the issues, a history of the movement for women's human rights, and an examination and explanation of existing international mechanisms (in Elissavet Stamatopoulou's critique of the United Nations)—serve as the necessary backgrounds to the rest of the collection and respond to basic questions about the definitions, origins, and applicability of women's human rights. The regional reports suggest the ways in which a range of issues may be linked both intra- and interregionally, highlighting both regional differences and cross-regional recurrences. We couldn't begin to attempt full global coverage but instead tried to offer a varied representation that could suggest the interrelationship of issues.

The section on "Gendered Law, 'Public' and 'Private'" offers theoretical legal background, identifying gender imbalance in existing human rights structures and instruments, analyzing the ways in which existing laws are effectively (male) gendered, and establishing the theoretical grounds for feminist international law. The papers here address, among other things, the artificial distinction between the "public" and "private" spheres, dealing with the treatment of states as unique actors in human rights law, when in fact most violations of women's human rights are by nonstate actors. "Cultural Difference" analyzes the argument for exemption from human rights law on the grounds of cultural integrity. Together, these two sections address two critical issues: the need for *women's* human rights law; and the need for *international* women's human rights law.

Among the issues usually treated as private matters that cannot be regulated by international norms, violence against women and women's health are particularly critical. The essays in "Violence and Health" argue for the recognition of these as human rights issues and explore the ways in which the subordination of women's health to historic notions of femininity, sexuality, and reproductive responsibility (as well as to monetary interests) leads to the violation of women's bodily integrity. While Lori Heise's paper addresses directly the intersection of violence with health issues, most papers in this section reveal the relationship between health and violence as well as the chronic denial to women of the most fundamental of human rights: the right to possess one's own body.

The section on "Development and the Socio-Economy" shows the ways in which women are economically marginalized, whether through discriminatory practices (for instance, in credit extension or property rights), division of labor, or even global development policies. While Nadia Youssef suggests some of the ways in which legal strategies may be used to serve women in developing regions and protect women's development rights, Rhoda Howard questions altogether the utility of a development model as a basis for ensuring women's economic rights where powerful cultural forces keep women marginalized. The papers in the last section, "The Persecuted, the Voiceless," deal with the multiple forms of such marginalization, and suggest the relationship between gender-based persecution and more subtle ways of silencing women. Persecution (for lesbianism, for membership in a women's organization, simply for being a woman) and marginalization (through lack of education, political underrepresentation, cultural intolerance leading to self-censorship, denial of asylum and, in effect, forced exile in refugee camps) are powerfully effective tools for rendering women silent, invisible.

Women have been remaking history during the last century. We have shifted traditional assumptions about our roles and capabilities, rewritten the texts, and taken up positions in the halls of power. There *has* been a revolution, and it has been for the better. Many of its benefits, however, have yet to touch the majority, and all of us continue to experience forms of gender discrimination. Coming together, we expand the dialogue and continue to define women's human rights while building a global network. As this network grows and gathers strength, we renounce our victimization and celebrate our victories— those of us, that is, who have the luxury of doing so. For this is a luxury, one allowed only to those who are free from daily violence, torture, and humiliation. For the rest, the implementation of feminist law may mean the difference between life and death, as so many of the essays here remind us.

Note

1. Bunch, Charlotte "Women's Rights as Human Rights: Toward a Re-Vision of Human Rights," *Human Rights Quarterly* 12 (1990): 491.
2. *Id.,* 486.

Backgrounds

1

Transforming Human Rights from a Feminist Perspective

Charlotte Bunch

The transformation of human rights from a feminist perspective is crucial to addressing global challenges to human rights in the twenty-first century. This should be seen in the context of the growth and evolution of women's movements internationally in the past two decades. Women are taking leading roles in redefining social concepts and global policy issues in areas such as development, democracy, human rights, world security, and the environment. This means not just looking at what have been called "women's issues"—a ghetto, or separate sphere that remains on the margins of society—but rather moving women from the margins to the center by questioning the most fundamental concepts of our social order so that they take better account of women's lives.

In seeking to transform global policies in areas like development and human rights so that they better incorporate and respond to women's lives, we are also demonstrating that women's issues are not separate but are neglected aspects of these global agendas. Indeed, ignoring women's experiences and views has kept society further away from the common solutions so badly needed in many of these areas.

Feminist analysis begins with the recognition that each of us views societal concepts and institutions from a different lens depending on our consciousness and our place in society. Starting with female life experiences as the point from which to examine human rights, certain questions become important: Who has been excluded from exercising the rights of citizenship and how have women been affected by limited forms of democracy? What has been the impact on women of narrow definitions of human rights? Why have so many degrading life experiences of women not been understood as human rights issues?

11

Gender must also be analyzed in relation to other factors such as nationality, race, and class in order to discern the multiple forms of human rights abuse that women suffer. Women are asking what changes in human relations and in social systems are necessary to bring not only women in but also the voices of all who have been excluded from the benefits of human rights, democracy, and development. The exclusion of any group—whether on the basis of gender, class, sexual orientation, religion, or race—involves cultural definitions of the members of that group as less than fully human. That definition of certain people as less human, as not deserving human rights or full participation in society, becomes the basis upon which violence against them is tolerated and sometimes even state supported. Further, as long as any group can be denied its humanity, we are all vulnerable to human rights abuse.

Women's Rights as Human Rights

The lack of understanding of women's rights as human rights is reflected in the fact that few governments are committed, in domestic or foreign policy, to women's equality as a basic human right. No government determines its policies toward other countries on the basis of their treatment of women, even where aid and trade decisions are said to be based on a country's human rights record. Among nongovernmental human rights organizations women are rarely a priority and women's human rights are viewed as special interests, while violations that affect smaller numbers of people are considered "general." This separation of women's rights from human rights has perpetuated the secondary status of women and highlights the importance of recognizing specific women's human rights concerns.

Women's human rights are violated in a variety of ways. Sometimes, of course, women suffer abuses (such as political repression) in ways that are much the same as those inflicted on men. But since the dominant image of the political actor in our world is male, the problem for women is visibility. Most women's experiences of human rights violations are gendered, and many forms of discrimination or abuse occur because the victim is female. Women whose rights are being violated for reasons other than gender (as political prisoners or members of persecuted ethnic groups) often also experience a particular form of abuse based on gender, such as sexual assault. The women's human rights movement has focused primarily on abuses where gender is a primary or related factor because these have been the most invisible and offer the greatest challenge to the human rights movement.

The United Nations *Universal Declaration of Human Rights,* adopted in 1948, defines human rights broadly and symbolizes a world vision of respect for the humanity of all people. While not much is said about women, Article 2 does entitle all to the rights and freedoms set forth in the Declaration without distinction of any kind, including sex. Further, when read from the perspective of women's lives, many violations of women's rights such as rape and battering can readily be interpreted as forbidden under existing clauses such as "No one shall be subject to torture or to cruel, inhuman or degrading treatment or punishment." The problem is that little elaboration of these rights has been made from the point of view of women, and therefore we have no significant body of international human rights law and practice in this area. Thus the dominant definitions of human rights and the mechanisms to enforce them in the world today are ones that pertain primarily to the types of violation that the men who first articulated the concept most feared. These definitions have tended to exclude much of women's experiences (and that of many nonelite men as well) because these groups have not been well represented in human rights discourse.

Human rights, however, like democracy and all vibrant visions, are not static, nor are they the property of any one group. While these concepts began in a particular historical moment and were defined in terms of the needs of a limited sector of the population, their dynamism and ongoing relevance stem from the fact that more people are claiming them and, in the process, expanding the meaning of "rights" to incorporate their own hopes and needs. Much of the creativity of the human rights movement over the past forty years has come from expanding the concept to address areas such as racial discrimination, disappearances, socio-economic rights, and the collective right to a sustainable environment. So, too, women are transforming the concept of human rights to address the degradations and violations that are a fundamental threat to our human dignity and right to life, liberty, and security of person.

Because those Western-educated propertied men who first advanced the cause of human rights most feared the violation of their civil and political rights in the public sphere, this area of violation has been privileged in human rights work. They did not fear, however, violations in the private sphere of the home because they were the masters of that territory. Public civil rights are certainly important to women, who are even more often denied them since women's access to the public sphere is curtailed in many ways. Yet for most women and many men, the violations that daily threaten our human rights are not so narrowly confined. Much of the abuse of women is part of a larger socio-economic and cultural web that entraps women, making them vulnerable to abuses that cannot be delineated as exclusively political or solely caused by states. The indivisibility of rights and the inclusion of the so-called second generation (or socio-economic) human rights to food, shelter, and work (clearly delineated as part of the UN *Universal Declaration of Human Rights*) is therefore vital to addressing women's concerns fully.

The assumption that states are not responsible for violations of women's rights in the private or cultural sphere ignores the fact that such abuses are often condoned or even sanctioned by states even when the immediate perpetrator is a private citizen. The distinction between private and public is a dichotomy largely used to justify female subordination and to exclude human rights abuses in the home from public scrutiny. Yet human rights activists readily pressure states to prevent other forms of abuse, such as slavery and racial discrimination, that also occur in the private sphere at the hands of private actors and have often been proclaimed cultural traditions or matters of national sovereignty.

When women are denied democracy and human rights in private, their human rights in the public sphere also suffer, since what occurs in "private" shapes their ability to participate fully in the public arena. For example, in some countries state policies deny women the right to travel or leave the country without approval from their fathers, their husbands, their brothers, or even their sons. Few of those who have protested the refusal of governments to allow people to leave their countries at will have recognized this form of violation. Other women, whether they live in the North or the South, cannot exercise their right to freedom of assembly by attending political meetings or participate in development projects without fear of being beaten or locked up by their partners. Such violations are reported regularly, yet there is no outcry in the name of human rights about the denial of these women's right to political participation, to assembly, to free speech, and citizenship.

Excluding sex discrimination and violence against women from the human rights agenda also results from a failure to see the oppression of women as political. Female subordination runs so deep that it is still viewed as inevitable or natural rather than as a politically constructed reality maintained by patriarchal interests, ideology, and institutions. The physical territory of this political struggle is women's bodies. The importance of control over women can be seen in the intensity of resistance to laws and social changes that put control of women's bodies in women's hands: reproductive rights; freedom of sexuality, whether heterosexual or lesbian; laws that criminalize rape in marriage; and so on. Abusing women physically maintains this territorial domination and is sometimes accompanied by other forms of human rights abuse such as slavery (forced prostitution), sexual terrorism (rape), or imprisonment (confinement to the home).

The real questions are: Who defines legitimate human rights issues and who decides where the state should enter and for what purposes? Women's voices have been missing from these decisions for too long. Good governance demands that women from diverse groups participate in developing such policies. In order to respond to the brutal and systematic violation of women globally, governments and the human rights community must move beyond male-defined norms, a move that requires examining gender biases and acknowledging the rights of women as human rights. Governments must seek to end the politically and culturally constructed wars on women, rather than continuing to perpetuate them. Every state has the responsibility to intervene in the abuse of women's rights within its borders and to end its collusion with the forces that perpetrate such violations in other countries.

Gender-Based Violence: A Human Rights Paradigm

Gender-based violence is not the only form of human rights abuse that women suffer, but it is one in which the gendered aspect of such abuse is often the most clear. While many forms of gender-based violence are, in fact, general human rights violations, male-oriented biases have tended to recognize only the gender component of certain cases and hence failed to identify them with clear human rights violations whose victims are male. Battery of women, for instance, is a form of torture that often includes imprisonment in the home, whether enforced physically or psychologically through fear and terrorization. The practice of locking up women in order to prevent them from being unfaithful while their husbands are traveling has caused a few countries to recognize the need for laws to make confinement of a wife a crime. Women are held involuntarily in slavery for prostitution and pornography, and even domestic servants are sometimes beaten, raped, and locked up in their bosses' homes (as, for instance, in the cases of Asian women in Kuwait and Chicana women in Los Angeles).

Compulsory pregnancy both kills women and forces them into involuntary labor; arranged marriages and enforced heterosexuality deny women's physical integrity and their right to marriage by choice; to escape, some women have resorted to suicide or prostitution. Women face terrorism in the form of sexual assault on the streets and in jobs where sexual harassment is a condition for receiving a paycheck.

Rape has been recognized by the rapporteur of the United Nations on torture as a form of torture when it is performed by police or by other agents of the government, and has begun to be understood as a war-crime in some situations (for instance in Bosnia). This is an important step, but rape is a human rights violation even when it is performed by private actors. Rape, like other forms of torture and terrorism, is used to keep women out of certain places. For example, gang rapes often occur because a woman enters a place, such as a bar, that men consider their territory. If a woman exercises her right to go into a bar and have a drink, as men do, the response may be sexual terrorism. The purpose of these human rights violations is to keep women in their places by making them afraid. Few women have not been in fear of sexual violence in some place at some time, and it would be difficult to find a woman who hasn't shaped her life in some way to avoid this form of terrorism.

Female infanticide and malnutrition of girls are forms of female genocide. The World Health Organization reports that in most developing countries girls are fed less and are taken to the doctor less often than boys. From the outset, girls die and are physically and mentally maimed by inequitable distribution of resources. A dramatic photo of Bangladeshi twins, a boy and a girl, shows a plump and healthy boy next to an emaciated sister. Amartya Sen, an Indian male economist at Harvard, has done statistical surveys showing that somewhere between 80 to 100 million women are missing in the world today. By comparing statistical ratios of males and females in various regions, he calculates that there should be at least that many more women alive today, especially in Asia. These are the *desaparecidos* the "disappeared" of the women's human rights movement. Who demands government accountability for the genocide of these 100 million women?

These are only a few examples of the female human rights violations that could be examined through the lens of the various treaties on torture, slavery, and other aspects of human rights abuse. What they have in common is that they are forms of torture in the lives of millions of women throughout the world. In an effort to focus attention on, and ultimately put an end to, these abuses, the women's caucus at the United Nations World Conference on Human Rights in Vienna in June of 1993 demanded that gender-based issues like these should be put on the table whenever the UN Treaty Committees meet to monitor and seek enforcement of their treaties' provisions.

But the work of seeking to transform human rights to take better account of women's lives must proceed without waiting for permission from some authority from above. When the mothers and grandmothers of the Plaza de Mayo in Argentina stood up in the midst of one of the most brutal dictatorships and protested the disappearance of their children, there was no concept of disappearance as a human rights issue. When they stood in the Plaza and said by their actions: "We know that the rights of these people have been violated and we will not remain silent about it," they did not need to wait for the human rights community to say that such disappearances were a human rights violation. So, too, must we speak of the violations against women that have been hidden for too long.

Challenging prevailing concepts of, and reinterpreting the movement for, human rights from a feminist perspective is not merely a matter of semantics. It is about the lives and deaths of individual women everywhere, every day. At the World Conference on Human Rights, women put these issues squarely on the world's doorstep. Yet even as the international human rights community has begun to recognize gender-based violations as pervasive and insidious forms of human rights abuse, we must work further to see that concrete actions against such practices are taken. Human rights instruments and mechanisms provide avenues for challenging the systemic abuse of women, and governments can be made to take gender-based violations more seriously by being held accountable for the implementation of laws against them and for the sensitivity of agencies handling these issues. Only through community responsibility and state accountability, day by day, place by place, will we counter the massive violation of women's human rights in the world.

2

Women's Human Rights: The Emergence of a Movement

Elisabeth Friedman

> The concept of human rights, like all vibrant visions, is not static or the property of any one group; rather, its meaning expands as people reconceive of their needs and hopes in relation to it. In this spirit, feminists redefine human rights abuses to include the degradation and violation of women. The specific experiences of women must be added to traditional approaches to human rights in order to make women more visible and to transform the concept and practice of human rights in our culture so that it takes better account of women's lives.
>
> —Charlotte Bunch, "Women's Rights as Human Rights"

It's the Year of Women at UN rights congress
> —*Dallas Morning News* (6/14/93)

Women Seize Focus at Rights Forum
> —*New York Times* (6/16/93)

Women Take Reins—World sees more leaders, more calls for justice
> —*Los Angeles Times* (6/30/93)

In the three years between Bunch's inspirational call and the clear response from the 1993 United Nations World Conference on Human Rights in Vienna, Austria, a global movement, claiming hundreds of thousands of members in over one hundred countries, has coalesced in promotion of women's human rights.[1] Where did it come from?

Although it is not possible fully to separate the struggle for women's human rights from the struggle for women's equal rights, this paper traces some of the origins of the women's human rights movement.

18

No single essay can do justice to the magnitude and complexity of the organizing efforts that bore fruit at Vienna and continue to advance women's human rights. This essay focuses primarily on the process leading up to the World Conference on Human Rights, in a necessarily suggestive, not comprehensive, manner. To begin what must be a broader research effort, I have interviewed advocates from regional networks, women's human right experts in health and legal matters, representatives from human rights organizations, and Global Campaign coordinators; their contributions have been supplemented by primary and secondary sources on women's human rights. Admittedly, this paper—pieced together in a short time by a woman from, and residing in, the United States—represents only a partial picture of the movement.[2]

Like other movements for women's rights, the women's human rights movement has evolved from women organizing on local, national, regional, and international levels around issues that affect their daily lives. One special component of this movement is women's entry into the political "space" opened by the United Nations;[3] women have taken advantage of the opportunities presented by international meetings—such as the World Conference on Human Rights and those that took place during the UN Decade on Women—to organize among themselves while transforming the official agenda.

The Women's Human Rights Movement

The movement for women's human rights comprises women's rights activists' efforts to use the human rights framework to promote the achievement of women's rights in the interrelated areas of political, civil, economic, social, and cultural rights.[4] Such advocates have recognized that the time has come to move from an exclusive focus on elaborating alternative programs within women's organizations to placing women's issues on mainstream agendas. Women's human rights activists have come to recognize the power of the international human rights framework, which lends legitimacy to political demands, since it is already accepted by most governments and brings with it established protocols.

The process of including women transforms agendas: In this case, the realities of women's lives afford lessons for human rights work in general. The promotion of women's human rights bears on the question of whether the current hierarchy of rights, with civil and political rights at the pinnacle, is justifiable. Rhonda Copelon, codirector of the International Women's Human Rights Law Clinic of City University of New York, argues that "there is tremendous potential in the women's movement to put political, civil, social, economic, and cultural [rights] together, as well as to be a force for a much more powerful understanding of human rights as indivisible."

This claim for indivisibility brings another enormous challenge to the traditional framework of human rights law, which has generally focused on the promotion of rights in the "public," or political, arena. Promoting women's human rights—whether that means including women in job training, defending their right to bodily integrity, or insisting on their education—clearly involves efforts within areas of life considered to be "private." Calling for government accountability in these areas requires a considerable reorientation of human rights law.

The lessons from women's lives point to the fact that women's human rights are denied, and also reclaimed, in particular ways. As such, the notion of a universal approach to human rights work cannot be assumed but rather must be negotiated. Mallika Dutt, associate director of the Center for Women's Global Leadership, explains that "one of the biggest problems with universality as it has existed in the past is the process which led to that universal articulation, [which] meant that a lot of people did not participate. . . . Statements of universality must reflect the complexity of what happens to people."

One of the major issues that women's human rights advocates have used to demonstrate how human rights law has excluded women—as well as the importance of women's inclusion—is violence against women. It is, according to Charlotte Bunch, director of the Center for Women's Global Leadership,

> the issue which most parallels a human rights paradigm and yet is excluded. You can see in violence all the things the human rights community already says it's against: it involves slavery, it involves situations of torture, it involves terrorism, it involves a whole series of things that the human rights community is already comitted to [fighting, but which] have never been defined in terms of women's lives.

Violence against women throws into sharp relief the changes needed in human rights law in order to make it truly inclusive of women's experiences. Violations of women's rights are often perpetrated by "private agents"—members of women's communities, from family members to coworkers—and not the "governmental agents" generally targeted by human rights law. Traditionally, human rights law has been used to show government responsibility for abuse and to demand government redress. However, advocates for women's human rights have made a clear case that governments, while not directly responsible for private-agent abuse, can be seen as condoning it—through inadequate prosecution of wife abuse, sexual harassment, rape, etc.—and thus be held accountable.

This issue is of vital importance to women all over the world. Maria Suarez, a cofounder and producer of Feminist International Radio Endeavor (FIRE) in Costa Rica, notes that violence against women, far from being of concern only to women from developed countries, was in fact brought to the international agenda by women from developing countries who "had in our minds, our hearts, and our history, and in our bodies and our lives the violence that we have suffered from being imprisoned, from being disappeared, from being shot." In her work *Battered Dreams*, Roxanna Carrillo of the United Nations Development Fund for Women (UNIFEM) describes how violence not only causes physical harm but also prevents women from full participation in development. Despite vast differences in the way violence is manifested, be it as domestic battery or rape during wartime, the omnipresence of violence in women's lives provides them with a unifying agenda. Niamh Reilly, program associate with the Center for Women's Global Leadership, explains that violence is "a way of linking women, standing outside of the predefined chasms and fissures and divides [of politics]" without denying specific local manifestations. Thus, although violence against women is far from the only issue to be addressed, it is, according to Suarez, "an entry point for broadening and reconceptualizing" the women's human rights agenda.

Women's Rights as Human Rights: Regional Development in an International Context

Although the transformation of the human rights agenda is recent, it is deeply rooted in the story of women's organizing in different regions around the world. The cases described here are examples of some of the many forms this organizing has taken.

In Latin America, the perpetration of human rights abuses under the many dictatorial regimes of the twentieth century has resulted in a history of human rights organizing with massive involvement on the part of women. Perhaps the best-known example is the *Madres de la Plaza de Mayo* ("Mothers of the Plaza de Mayo"), a group of mothers who came together during the height of Argentina's *guerra sucia* ("dirty war") to demand the return of their children, who had been "disappeared" by the regime.[5] Although the women identified themselves primarily, as housewives, their bravery soon placed them at the center of the political opposition.

> It was the way in which motherhood became political, the way in which women had to break the separation between the private and the public and make their concerns a public issue. These were the women who were in charge of the children, who were in charge of the livelihood of their husbands, of their brothers, and so on, and once they were disappeared, [these women] politicized motherhood. It also meant that there was a reconceptualization of the struggle for human rights because motherhood and what happened in the house stopped being a private issue. (Suarez 11/11/93)

However, a change in the political situation did not bring an end to women's struggles. Despite Latin American women's expectations that democratization would fully include their needs and rights, their issues were marginalized in the restoration of politics as usual, with its usual actors: men. For example, democratic transition processes never addressed ending violence against women during peace or war—not surprising, since women rarely hold decision-making positions during such times.

To counteract this neglect, some women employed an old strategy in a new way: they began to use the human rights framework to advance women's rights. Instead of claiming rights as *women,* they claimed the human rights of *half of humanity.* Failure to "respect and recognize women as human" (Suarez 11/11/93) then caught the attention of those who otherwise might not have thought about women's rights.

In Pakistan, human rights law became a basis for women organizing for different reasons. Hina Jilani, founder of AGHS Law Associates in Lahore, tells how two factions existed in the women's movement: one that wanted to fight for women's rights within the framework of religious injunctions and another that sought a secular basis for struggle. Jilani and others, concerned that trying to reinterpret religious law "created controversies and no resolutions," turned to the norms of international human rights law. "We felt that these were the standards that you wanted to make the basis [of women's rights], by saying that we don't want religion as the basis, we want equality and social justice in accordance with internationally accepted standards."

While Latin American and Pakistani women's organizing were stimulated by their particular political contexts, the international arena provided spaces for other women's activism. Though women's involvement in the UN stems from its inception,[6] the United Nations Decade for Women (1975–1985) was a watershed both for placing women on the international intergovernmental agenda and for facilitating women's cooperation, a process that would expand to include non-gender-specific meetings in the 1990s. While women participated in the official delegations and gatherings of the General Assembly at the three meetings of the Decade (in Mexico City in 1975, Copenhagen in 1980, and Nairobi in 1985), their participation in the Non-Governmental Organization (NGO) Forums that accompanied each official meeting was equally important, if not more so. There, women from different countries met and were able to exchange strategies and develop ongoing working relationships.[7]

Women also took advantage of the directives stemming from the Decade. They urged their governments to turn rhetoric into reality by promoting women's involvement in national concerns. Women reminded their governments to fulfill the promises made during the Decade by altering discriminatory laws and establishing ministries or offices of women's affairs.

One of the most effective tools for promoting women's equality that came out of the Decade was the Convention on the Elimination of All Forms of Discrimination Against Women (The Women's Convention, or CEDAW), which laid out in detail the duties that states have to promote women's equality in all areas of life, from family to workplace to government.[8]

> CEDAW was fairly important in bringing women into the "rights talk" arena. Trying to get your government to ratify CEDAW is a political process that makes you see the ramifications of this quite extensive and encompassing document. Once your government has signed, it's a social contract that they're making with the women in the country. . . . [i]t gives you that tool, that leverage to say OK, this is the normative context within which women's status has to be dealt with—and it's a human rights document, so automatically you are in the basket of human rights. (Clarke 10/22/93)

Women also established international networks to promote CEDAW. The International Women's Rights Action Watch (IWRAW) was started in 1985 as a result of discussions at the Nairobi meeting that closed the Decade. An international group, headed by Arvonne Fraser (now a U.S. delegate to the United Nations' Committee on the Status of Women), decided that an international organization was needed to monitor the relatively new Convention. Thus IWRAW helps the Commission that oversees CEDAW with research as well as connects local women's activists through the reporting process.[9]

The Institute for Women, Law and Development also got its start at the Nairobi meeting. Inspired by her work in Central America promoting women's legal services, director Margaret Schuler had traveled around the world looking at different models of women's rights promotion in 1984. Her findings led to the "Third World Forum for Women and Development," planned by a team of women from different regions, that was held at the NGO forum in Nairobi. Because of the tremendous interest generated at the meeting, Schuler, in consultation with other international women's rights advocates, established an organization to link women seeking to promote women's human rights through campaigns to educate them in legal matters.[10] Three principal networks evolved: the Latin American Committee for the Defense of Women's Rights (CLADEM), the Asia-Pacific Forum on Women, Law and Development (APWLD), and Women in Law and Development in Africa (WiLDAF).

Florence Butegwa, the regional coordinator for WiLDAF in Zimbabwe, noted in an interview how much of the organizing around African women's legal issues began as a result of women's participation at the Nairobi conference. Such action was sorely needed in Africa, where women can find themselves caught in the conflicts between customary and codified law, with the former often legislating discrimination against women, particularly in family affairs. At forums like the one sponsored by IWLD, women were able to find out how lawyers and community activists were navigating within traditional belief structures and changing laws in other countries.

By the mid-1980s, women were sharing information across regions and gaining exposure to the human-rights framework, establishing the groundwork for the women's human-rights movement. Facilitating this process were many local groups and other international organizations, such as CHANGE in England, MATCH International and the International Centre for Human Rights and Democratic Development in Canada, GABRIELA in the Philippines, Women Living Under Muslim Laws in France, and the Global Fund for Women in the United States.

Human Rights as Women's Rights: Integrating International Human Rights Organizations

Toward the end of the 1980s, the women's human rights movement received help from an obvious source—the mainstream human rights movement. Dorothy Thomas, director of Human Rights Watch's Women's Rights Project, explained in an interview that "since the articulation of the human rights norms and their broader and broader ratification and enumeration over the years, [there's been] an emergence of a global human rights movement that has an increasingly central role to play in the relationships among nations." Several advocates add that the decline of unifying ideologies in the wake of the Cold War led to a search for new ones:

> [People have a need] to identify with a movement that crosses national boundaries, has some common values, and a sense that . . . what you are about is more than just [what happens] in your own country. I think that the human rights concept has come to stand for that more because the other things that did have been breaking down. So that concept has taken on a greater importance in the world, which makes it more important for women to claim it and be in on it. (Bunch 10/29/93)

But such linkage was not always easy. Before 1989, little specific attention was paid to women's human rights within any of the major human rights groups. Pressure from within and without created awareness in these institutions, generating women's human rights activism within the human rights movement. According to Suzanne Roach, coordinator of Amnesty International's (AI) International Women's Network and AIUSA's National Women's Committee, AI started to work on women's human rights in the late 80s, when staff and membership realized that women were systematically underrepresented in their research. In early 1989, U.S. staff convened a formal working group, which consulted with women's organizations that had a history of looking at women's human rights issues, as well as with women from other countries.

AIUSA was not the only section of the organization that had become concerned with women's human rights, as was made clear at the 1989 meeting of the International Council, the highest executive body of Amnesty International. There the Council passed a resolution that at every level of its work, from membership development to research to publications, the organization should improve and increase its efforts to protect women's human rights. An International Women's Network was established, as were groups focused on women within national sections of AI. Their research found that from the common experience of women forced to trade sex for food for their children within refugee camps, to the high incidence of rape of women in police and military custody, to the systematic vengeful abuse of female relatives of dissidents, there is much work to be done on behalf of women within the mandate of AI.[11]

To give a sense of the task at hand, consider the example of one Amnesty mission to Peru. In the course of their investigations of the human rights situation in the country, the delegation asked a military commander whether soldiers were known to commit rapes.

> "Yes, of course." That was followed up with the statement that when you have men who are headquartered away from their homes for a long time under difficult circumstances, they need to have their needs met somehow. There was not even the sense that this person should take care and deny [this]. When they raised the question of torture, of course *that* was denied. But there wasn't even the sense that [rape] was something that should be looked at askance. (Roach 11/17/93)

According to director Thomas, the most important factor in the formation of the Women's Rights Project of Human Rights Watch was women's rights groups' use of human rights methodology. Groups in many countries sought to broaden the base for their own work as well as to find mechanisms for holding their governments accountable for abusive patterns. At the same time, women's rights activists within the United States began to pressure Human Rights Watch to pay closer attention to abuses of women's rights abroad. Men and women inside the organization also became aware of the neglect of women's concerns and the need to examine them in a more systematic way. As a result, staff drafted a proposal for a women's rights project, which subsequently was approved.[12]

The Women's Rights Project has played and continues to play a vital role in the development of the women's human rights movement. As Thomas explains, "our niche . . . is that we do documentary fieldwork of abuses of women's human rights and demonstrate state responsibility for those abuses under international human rights law"(11/10/93). This is an essential task, as human-rights law cannot be applied unless both the violations and the violators have been identified. The work of the Women's Rights Project also advances the movement by helping women within specific countries learn to document abuse, thus teaching them that recourse is possible. In addition, this documentation can be used to convince those responsible for making human rights policy of the need to create one sensitive to gendered aspects of human rights abuse. Gendered policy is crucial to the advancement of women's human rights, as it institutionalizes and systematizes attention to women's concerns.[13]

The Global Campaign for Women's Human Rights: Taking on the World (Conference)

As women's rights activists throughout the world increasingly turned to human rights law and forged connections with mainstream human rights groups, the exclusion of women from international human rights norms and laws, as well as the possibility of using those norms and laws to advance women's rights, became clearer. One key group that helped articulate this possibility was the Center for Women's Global Leadership (CWGL), which was organized in 1989 with a focus on women, human rights, and violence. With the guidance of international advisors, the Center sponsored Women's Leadership Institutes with the purpose of bringing together women from every region interested in exploring the linkages among these issues. At the first of these Institutes, in 1991, the then-upcoming UN World Conference on Human Rights (WCHR) was determined to be an initial focus for activism. The Center then served as the coordination point for the Global Campaign for Women's Human Rights.

One of the Campaign strategies developed at the first Leadership Institute was "16 Days of Activism Against Gender Violence," a planned annual endeavor using local actions to call attention to violence against women as a human rights issue. The campaign takes place during the sixteen days that link November 25th, the International Day Against Violence Against Women, with December 10th, Human Rights Day.[14]

In 1991, this period served to launch a worldwide petition drive, initially cosponsored by the International Women's Tribune Centre (IWTC), the CWGL, and the International YWCA. The petition stated that, as the Universal Declaration of Human Rights protects women, the World Conference should "comprehensively address women's human rights at every level of its proceedings" and recognize gender-based violence "as a violation of human rights requiring immediate action."

The petition "took off like a rocket," according to Anne S. Walker, director of the IWTC, who faxed it around the world. Copies were returned to the IWTC in languages staff could not recognize and signed with fingerprints. Reilly of the CWGL remembers receiving batches of them from U.S.-based organizations that had received the petition from overseas. The petition drive lasted until the World Conference, with batches of 75,000 periodically sent to the UN to urge Conference organizers to include women's issues on their agenda. It eventually garnered over 300,000 signatures in 123 countries and 20 languages.[15] Over 800 groups also signed on as cosponsors of the petition, which was officially presented to the WCHR in June 1993.

The petition drive was an extremely effective recruiting tool for the movement, as it helped spread the concept of women's rights as human rights across the globe. Roxanna Carrillo describes why the petition was so potent:

> It was so broad and simple, but so full of meaning that people could relate to it. The petition was really crucial in getting people involved and interested. It was also a way of teaching people, of providing information. People just took it and translated it into whatever issue was most pressing for the group of people they were working with. (10/28/93)

The "16 Days" campaign continued in 1992, when it was observed in over fifty countries. Actions included marches against violence against women, educational panels, photographic exhibitions, and protest rallies. Another phase of the Global Campaign was launched to hold local and regional hearings on women's human-rights violations, documentation of which was brought to the WCHR and sent to the UN Commission on Human Rights.

Clearly, the Center for Women's Global Leadership could not have generated such worldwide interest on its own; it tapped into the ongoing regional organizing that was taking place around the World Conference. As the WiLDAF report on its participation explained, the World Conference provided an important opportunity in four respects: (1) to assess the status of women's human rights in particular countries;

(2) to explore the human rights framework and critique its inadequacy in addressing violations of women's human rights; (3) to mobilize at the national, regional, and international levels to demand that these violations be recognized and responded to by the international community and state governments; and (4) to work with other women's rights and human rights NGOs to promote common action.[16]

Therefore, in addition to participating in the "16 Days" campaign, petition drive, and hearings, women became involved in the regional preparatory meetings for the WCHR. Sensitive to the frequency with which governments slight or ignore women's issues, many advocates sought alternative ways to get on the agenda. To increase the representation of women's human rights perspectives at the World Conference, women used a mechanism called the "satellite meeting." Such meetings, if recognized by the UN Secretariat, could generate reports, recommendations, or statements that would be included in the official documentation of the WCHR.

This mechanism proved appropriate for the Latin American organizers. Through their experience in organizing for human rights and women's rights, these women were well aware of the pitfalls of relying on others' agendas, in this case those of the official regional preparatory meeting. They held a satellite meeting of women representing sixty-nine Latin American networks to draft their list of demands, which then served as a common basis for lobbying during the official regional conference. In this way, "we strategized to organize our issues in a way that would be autonomous but that would also be capable of making alliances, negotiating, and interacting with all the other sectors of society that are involved in the issue" (Suarez 11/11/93). The women named it *La Nuestra* ("Our [Meeting]") to emphasize that it offered women's *own* perspectives. It was effective: the final Latin American Declaration incorporated a paragraph stating that violence against women should be considered a human rights violation.

Women in Africa also used the satellite mechanism effectively, even though there was insufficient time to prepare for the regional preparatory meeting. In early 1993, they held five meetings (four subregional and one regionwide) at which they created a platform from which to lobby at the Conference, thereby gaining experience in intraregional networking.[17]

The satellite meeting was also valuable in promoting international coordination. The Center for Women's Global Leadership held the International Women's Strategic Planning Meeting in February 1993 to bring together women from every region in preparation for the

Conference. Among other organizing tasks the Planning Meeting issued a set of recommendations on women's human rights.

Women's strategic use of UN mechanisms did not stop with the satellite meetings. Aware that the recommendations were not going to appear in the draft document (put together at the official preparatory conferences) to be considered by the General Assembly at the World Conference, UNIFEM facilitated the attendance of a Global Campaign team at the last preparatory conference for the WCHR in April of 1993. "We came there and just took the place by storm. We took over. And they realized very quickly that the energy and the ideas and the organizing were coming from the women" (Carrillo 10/28/93). As a result, recommendations concerning women's human rights were included in the draft to be considered at the World Conference.

The hard work and extensive cooperation resulted in the "seizure" of the 1993 UN World Conference on Human Rights by women's human rights advocates. By far the most organized and vocal of the NGO participants, women promoted their issues at the NGO Forum and the official meeting. Over sixty of the workshops, seminars, and lectures presented at the Forum specifically addressed women's human rights. The Global Campaign's buttons declaring that "Women's Rights Are Human Rights" were seen on many official delegates' lapels. By far the most visible manifestation of this declaration was the Global Tribunal on Violations of Women's Human Rights.

The Tribunal's purpose was to present cases that documented human rights abuses against women and demonstrated clearly the failure of existing human rights mechanisms to protect and promote women's human rights. It was a day-long event, with panel discussions on five areas of violation: abuse within the family, war crimes against women, violations of women's bodily integrity, socioeconomic human rights abuses, and political participation and persecution. Thirty-three women from many countries told their dramatic stories to an audience of over a thousand. At the close, four distinguished judges issued a series of joint recommendations.

These, together with the recommendations made by women's rights groups, were included in *The Vienna Declaration and Programme of Action*. There were, however, significant omissions, pointing to the continued need for women's activism. Appropriately gendered language was not found throughout the document, nor was there any mention of transcending the public/private dichotomy so as to make states accountable for all violations of women's human rights. Finally, though the document contained many positive statements, it did not sufficiently address the problem of ensuring compliance with its recommendations.

From Vienna to Beijing: You Can't Let That Energy Sit Still![18]

From the groundswell of women's mobilization around human rights issues at the local level, to the inclusion of women's human rights within the *Vienna Declaration,* a global movement for women's human rights has definitively taken shape. Nahid Toubia, the first woman surgeon in Sudan and a current associate at the Population Council, notes how the language of women's rights as human rights moved very quickly into the national and regional levels at a pace that far exceeded that of any previous movement on behalf of women internationally. She attributes this speed to the fact that, by the early 1990s, women had laid substantial groundwork and, moreover, benefited from the astonishing rate at which communication now takes place.[19] Many of the groups and networks that became active during this process are now preparing to continue their strategic use of the UN by targeting upcoming world events: in 1994, the Year of the Family and the World Conference on Population and Development in Cairo; in 1995 the fiftieth Anniversary celebrations for the UN, the UN World Summit for Social Development in Copenhagen, and, of course, the Fourth World Women's Conference in Beijing. Already another global petition drive has begun, this time to demand that the UN make a report at the Beijing meeting on progress made in advancing women's human rights.

But as the planning goes forward, there are still challenges to be met. Dorothy Thomas outlines three key ones. The first is to move beyond mere visibility for women's human rights to actual accountability for abuse. Maria Suarez points to a lesson to be learned from the *Madres de la Plaza de Mayo:* it is essential to keep the pressure on by inundating the appropriate authorities with documented cases of women's human rights abuse. The second challenge is to avoid falling into "the trap of establishing some kind of parallel universe for women in the human rights area" (Thomas 11/10/93). Women's issues must be considered at every level of the UN, within every committee, convention, and assembly. Finally, one of the most difficult challenges ahead is to continue organizing cross-culturally, remaining sensitive to the needs and desires of women from every region of the world:

> In order to insure that the process is a dynamic one, reflective of the diversity, as well as the consensus, of women in an international framework, you have to have mechanisms and you have to have discussion about the basis on which certain agendas are set, and strategies for advancing those agendas determined. (11/10/93)

Referring to Amnesty International's efforts to promote women's human rights, Suzanne Roach affirms this need:

> One of the central commitments coming out of the Draft Declaration from Vienna is to integrate women into the human rights mechanisms of the United Nations. . . . One of the things we need to focus on is making sure that the voice of women themselves and the experience of women themselves and the reinterpretation of women's human rights done by women themselves become present there. (11/17/93)

Notes

1. At least 300,000 people from 123 countries signed the petition to demand that the World Conference on Human Rights address women's human rights. See text for a description of the petition drive.

2. There is no escaping the limitations of such a situation; for further information, see Kerr (1993), Schuler (1993), and Tomasevski (1993).

3. This is not unique to the movement for women's human rights. Miller (1991) discusses how, throughout their history of organizing on women's issues, Latin American women have made strategic use of such international and national spaces.

4. The need for a gendered analysis of, and women's inclusion within, the human rights framework has been under discussion by academics for over a decade. See for example Hoskin (1981), Eide (1986), Eisler (1987), Engle (1992), and Nesiah (1993).

5. For more information on the *Madres* organizing, see Navarro (1989) and Feijoó (1991).

6. See Cook (1987).

7. See Ashworth (1982), Tinker and Jaquette (1987).

8. See Convention on the Elimination of All Forms of Discrimination Against Women, UN DPI/993-98035 (reprinted February 1993).

9. IWRAW issues a quarterly publication, *The Women's Watch*, as well as other information concerning CEDAW and the status of women.

10. For more information, see Schuler (1992, 1993).

11. The results of this research can be found in AI's 1990 publication *Women in the Front Line.*

12. Thomas points out that the project would not have gone forward without the financial commitment of a few individual donors who earmarked funds specifically for work on women's human rights.

13. Smaller human rights groups, such as the International Human Rights Law Group and the Lawyer's Committee on Human Rights, have also been actively pursuing policy changes.

14. November 25th was declared the International Day Against Violence Against Women by the first Feminist *Encuentro* ("encounter" or "meeting") for Latin America and the Caribbean in Bogota, Colombia, in 1981. The date was chosen to commemorate the brutal murder in 1960 of the Miraval sisters by the Trujillo dictatorship in the Dominican Republic. December 10th marks the anniversary of the 1948 Universal Declaration of Human Rights. This period also includes December 1, World AIDS Day, and December 6th, the anniversary of the 1989 shooting massacre of fourteen women engineering students in Canada by a man shouting "You're all fucking feminists!"

15. Anne S. Walker explains that although this was the official count of signatures sent to the Global Campaign by June 1993, many more petitions were sent directly to the UN and remain uncounted.

16. See Butegwa (1993):2.

17. For more information on regional organizing, see Butegwa (1993), Suarez and Facio (forthcoming), and UNIFEM (1993).

18. Meera Singh, Programme Officer, IWTC.

19. Several advocates mentioned how important the FAX machine is in allowing for quite inclusive and frequent communication regarding the drafting of documents, passing on petitions, etc.

The research for this paper was made possible through the generous support of the Shaler Adams Foundation. The author would like to thank its director, Margaret Schink, for her encouragement; Martin Friedman and Derek Scissors, for their editorial and logistical assistance; and Mallika Dutt, for her guidance. A special thanks is due to the women who agreed to be interviewed for this article, as it would have been meaningless without their perspectives.

Works Cited

Publications

Amnesty International. 1990. *Women in the Front Line.* New York: Amnesty International.

Ashworth, Georgina. 1982. "The United Nations 'Women's Conference' and International Linkages in the Women's Movement." *Pressure Groups in the Global System,* edited by Willetts, 125–147. London: Frances Pinter.

Bunch, Charlotte. 1990. "Women's Rights as Human Rights: Toward a Re-Vision of Human Rights." *Human Rights Quarterly* 12:486–498.

Butegwa, Florence, ed. 1993. *The World Conference on Human Rights: The WiLDAF Experience.* Zimbabwe: WiLDAF.

Carrillo, Roxanna. 1992. *Battered Dreams: Violence Against Women as an Obstacle to Development.* NY: UNIFEM.

"Convention on the Elimination of All Forms of Discrimination Against Women." UN DPI/993-98035.

Cook, Blanche Wiesen. 1987. "Eleanor Roosevelt and Human Rights: The Battle for Peace and Planetary Decency," *Women and American Foreign Policy,* edited by Crapol, 67–90. New York: Greenwood.

Eide, Asbjørn. 1986. "The Human Rights Movement and the Transformation of the International Order." *Alternatives* 9:367–402.

Eisler, Riane. 1987. "Human Rights: Toward an Integrated Theory for Action." *Human Rights Quarterly* 9:287–308.

Engle, Karen. 1992. "International Human Rights and Feminism: When Discourses Meet." *Michigan Journal of International Law* 13:517–610.

Feijoó, Maria del Carmen. 1991. "The Challenge of Constructing Civilian Peace: Women and Democracy in Argentina." *The Women's Movement in Latin America,* edited by Jane Jaquette, 72–94. Boulder, CO: Westview.

Hosken, F.P., ed. 1981. "Symposium: Women and International Human Rights." *Human Rights Quarterly* 3.

International Women's Rights Action Watch. *The Women's Watch.* Minneapolis: Humphrey Institute of Public Affairs, University of Minnesota.

Kerr, Joanna, ed. 1993. *Ours By Right: Women's Rights as Human Rights.* London: Zed.

Miller, Francesca. 1991. *Latin American Women and the Search for Social Justice.* Hanover, NH: University Press of New England.

Navarro, Marysa. 1989. "The Personal is Political: *Las Madres de Plaza de Mayo.*" *Power and Popular Protest,* edited by Eckstein, 241–258. Berkeley: Univ. of California Press.

Nesiah, Vasuki. 1993. "Toward a Feminist Internationality: a Critique of U.S. Feminist Legal Scholarship." *Harvard Women's Law Journal* 16:189–210.

Schuler, Margaret, ed. 1992. *Freedom from Violence: Women's Strategies from Around the World.* New York: UNIFEM.

Claiming Our Place: Working the Human Rights System to Women's Advantage. 1993 Washington, DC: IWLD.

Schuler, Margaret, and Sakuntala Kadirgamar-Rajasingham. 1992. *Legal Literacy: A Tool for Women's Empowerment.* NY: UNIFEM.

Suarez, Maria, and Alda Facio. Forthcoming. *Resistir, Sostener, y Avanzar.*

Tinker, Irene, and Jane Jaquette. 1987. "UN Decade for Women: Its Impact and Legacy." *World Development* 15(3): 419–27.

Tomasevski, Katarina. 1993. *Women and Human Rights.* London: Zed.

UNIFEM. 1993. "A Grassroots View on Women's Rights." *UNIFEM News* 1(2): 1, 12–13.

Interviews by Author

Bunch, Charlotte. 1993. Director, Center for Women's Global Leadership, Rutgers University. October 29, Center for Women's Global Leadership, New Brunswick, NJ.

Butegwa, Florence. 1993. Regional Coordinator, WiLDAF (Women in Law and Development in Africa). October 22, Association for Women in Development Conference, Washington, DC.

Carrillo, Roxanna. 1993. Executive Assistant to the Director, UNIFEM (United Nations Development Fund for Women). October 28, UNIFEM offices, New York, NY.

Clarke, Roberta. 1993. Coordinator, Women and the Law Project, Caribbean Association for Feminist Research and Action (CAFRA), Trinidad and Tobago. October 22, Association for Women in Development Conference, Washington, DC.

Copelon, Rhonda. 1993. Codirector, International Women's Human Rights Law Clinic, CUNY Law School. October 29, CUNY Law School, Flushing, NY.

Dutt, Mallika. 1993. Associate Director, Center for Women's Global Leadership, Rutgers University. October 28, Norman Foundation offices, New York, NY.

Heise, Lori. 1993. Visiting Associate, Center for Women's Global Leadership, Rutgers University. October 29, Center for Women's Global Leadership, New Brunswick, NJ.

Jilani, Hina. 1993. Founder, AGHS Law Associates, Lahore, Pakistan. October 22, Association for Women in Development Conference, Washington, DC.

Reilly, Niamh. 1993. Program Associate, Center for Women's Global Leadership, Rutgers University. October 29, Center for Women's Global Leadership, New Brunswick, NJ.

Roach, Suzanne. 1993. Coordinator, Amnesty International's International Women's Network and AIUSA's National Women's Committee, Amnesty International, New York. Telephone conversation, November 17.

Rodriguez, Marcela. 1993. Director, Office of Women's Affairs, Buenos Aires, Argentina. October 22, Association for Women in Development Conference, Washington, DC.

Schuler, Margaret. 1993. Director, Institute for Women, Law and Development (IWLD). October 23, Private Residence, Washington, DC.

Singh, Meera. 1993. Programme Officer, International Women's Tribune Centre (IWTC). October 29, IWTC offices, New York, NY.

Suarez, Maria. 1993. Coordinator, Feminist International Radio Endeavor (FIRE), Costa Rica. Telephone interview, November 11.

Thomas, Dorothy Q. 1993. Director, Women's Rights Project, Human Rights Watch, Washington, DC. Telephone interview, November 10.

Toubia, Nahid. 1993. Associate of the Ebert Program in Reproductive Health, Population Council. November 29, Population Council offices, New York, NY.

Walker, Anne S. 1993. Director, International Women's Tribune Center. October 29, IWTC offices, New York, NY.

3

Women's Rights and the United Nations
Elissavet Stamatopoulou

Introduction

Until the turning point of the 1993 World Conference on Human
Rights in Vienna, few issues received as little political attention at the
United Nations as the human rights of women. Now, thanks to the
efforts of non-governmental organizations (NGOs), academics, and
other advocates, the Conference itself can claim the placement of
women on the human rights agenda as one of its clearest victories.

The weaknesses of the United Nations and of the international
community as a whole (including states and NGOs) have been primarily in two areas: (a) at the conceptual level, their failure, until recently,
to declare all women's human rights concerns as part of international
human rights law; and (b) at the operational level, their failure to
integrate women's human rights into the mainstream human rights
agenda, thereby marginalizing the issue in terms of monitoring and
implementation and in terms of national institution building.

Such neglect raises many questions: Is discrimination against women
so deeply embedded in history and tradition that it cannot be tackled
with the urgency human rights monitoring imposes? (It should be
noted that, while one might make the same argument about racism,
the elimination of racial prejudice is in fact part of the human rights
agenda.) Is it simply too overwhelming to face the fact that the human
rights of half of humanity are systematically violated? (And yet we
have made the human rights of children a priority.) Does the violation
of women's human rights cut across international, political, ethnic,
religious, or other lines to such a degree that no state or political
grouping of states considers the issue particularly threatening—and

thus "politically" interesting? Have the human rights NGOs them-selves perpetuated the sexist rift by not paying adequate attention to the violation of the human rights of women, especially to violence against women? Have the women's NGOs relied too heavily on the specialized and often marginalized women's institutions to further their cause, meanwhile neglecting to enter the politically more powerful human rights mainstream?

Conceptual Level: Women's Rights are Human Rights

The principle of nondiscrimination on the basis of sex is clearly enshrined in international law. Starting from the *United Nations Charter*[1] and the *Universal Declaration of Human Rights*,[2] the principle found its way into the two main International Covenants: the *International Covenant on Economic, Social, and Cultural Rights*[3] and the *International Covenant on Civil and Political Rights*.[4] In addition to the principle of nondiscrimination, a number of other provisions of great importance to women are also contained in these instruments.

The *Universal Declaration of Human Rights* calls for equal rights as to marriage, which it stipulates "shall be entered into only with the free and full consent of the intending spouses."[5] It also calls for equal pay for equal work,[6] and for the protection of motherhood.[7] The *Covenant on Economic, Social and Cultural Rights* states that all workers must be provided with "fair wages and equal remuneration for work of equal value without distinction of any kind, in particular women being guaranteed conditions of work not inferior to those enjoyed by men, with equal pay for equal work."[8] It, too, provides for the protection of motherhood, and calls for paid maternity leave or leave with adequate social security benefits.[9] The *Covenant on Civil and Political Rights* prohibits the use of the death sentence on pregnant women,[10] provides for equality between men and women during mar-riage and at its dissolution,[11] and for the right to participate in public life without discrimination[12] while declaring, finally, that equality before the law and the principle of nondiscrimination are enforce-able rights.[13]

A number of other international treaties are devoted to issues affect-ing specific aspects of women's lives. These include: the *Discrimination (Employment and Occupation) Convention*,[14] the *Convention against Discrimination in Education*,[15] the *Equal Remuneration Convention*,[16] the *Slavery Conventions*,[17] the *Convention on the Suppression of the*

Traffic in Persons and of the Exploitation of the Prostitution of Others,[18] the *Convention on the Nationality of Married Women,*[19] the *Convention on the Political Rights of Women,*[20] the *Declaration on the Protection of Women and Children in Emergency Armed Conflict,*[21] and the *Convention on the Rights of Migrant Workers and Members of their Families.*[22]

Finally, in 1979, the principle of nondiscrimination on the basis of sex, as well as other women's rights, became the object of a specific treaty, the *Convention on the Elimination of All Forms of Discrimination against Women* (CEDAW, or "the Women's Convention," since "CEDAW" is also used to refer to the Committee to Eliminate All Forms of Discrimination Against Women).[23] Article 1 of the Convention defines discrimination against women as "any distinction, exclusion or restriction made on the basis of sex which has the effect or purpose of impairing or nullifying the recognition, enjoyment or exercise by women, irrespective of their marital status, on a basis of equality of men and women, of human rights and fundamental freedoms in the political, economic, social, cultural, civil or any other field." States parties to the Convention are bound to take all the necessary legislative, judicial, administrative, or other appropriate measures to guarantee women the exercise and enjoyment of human rights and fundamental freedoms on the basis of equality with men.

This far-reaching legal instrument, however, has been saddled with reservations (the majority of which undermine its very purpose), despite the fact that Article 28, paragraph 2 stipulates that "a reservation incompatible with the object and purpose of the present Convention shall not be permitted." As of June 20, 1994, 40 of the 133 ratifying states had made 91 reservations, most of them on religious or cultural grounds, seriously weakening the conceptual framework of the Convention. In 1991, an effort by the United Nations Sub-Commission on Prevention of Discrimination and Protection of Minorities to seek an advisory opinion at the International Court of Justice was stifled at birth, and the draft resolution withdrawn.[24]

The 1993 World Conference on Human Rights in Vienna was a step forward, in that a call was made for the elimination of the gender bias that can arise between the rights of women and, *inter alia,* religious extremism.[25] The Vienna Programme of Action also recommended addressing the reservations to the Convention, calling for their continued review by the expert body established to supervise implementation of the Convention[26] and urging states to withdraw reservations that are contrary to its object and purpose or that otherwise are incompatible with international treaty law.[27]

Clearly, from the point of view of international law, women's rights *are* human rights. However, dominant legal theory is only just beginning to recognize as human rights some rights claimed by the women's movement. The Third World critique of international law and insistence on diversity may well have prepared the philosophical ground for feminist critiques.[28] This is especially true for demonstrations of violence against women, whether in the public or private sphere. Reinterpretation of human rights law from a women's perspective must lead to the recognition that violence against women, in the family and in the community, in peacetime and in war, is an affront to women's physical and moral integrity and to their dignity as human beings. The artificial barriers between the "private" and the "public" spheres have to be removed, and the shield of silence that protects cultural, religious, or other traditions and prejudices must be broken, so that acts such as the beating and raping of women (whether within or outside of the family), widow burning, and sexual mutilation, are clearly recognized and averted or punished for what they are: human rights violations. The precedent of the *Convention on the Rights of the Child* is significant in this respect.[29]

The dilemma that women's NGOs faced when lobbying on violence against woman vis-à-vis CEDAW was whether to request a revision of the Convention or to opt for an interpretation of the Convention in the form of a General Comment.[30] The advantage of the first option was its legally binding nature, but the concern was that too few states parties to the Convention would ratify and that the conceptual spectrum of the Convention would thus be limited. The second option, then, was judged preferable and, in 1992, the Committee to Eliminate All Forms of Discrimination Against Women (CEDAW) issued a General Comment in which it concluded that the prohibition of violence against women was indeed covered under the Convention and that states should report on measures they were taking to combat such violence.[31]

Not long after, in response to strong non-governmental pressure, the Commission on the Status of Women finalized a *Draft Declaration on the Elimination of Violence Against Women,* which the General Assembly adopted in December 1993.[32] The Declaration is a significant addition to the legal definition of the human rights of women. Article 1 defines "violence against women" as "any act of gender-based violence that results in, or is likely to result in, physical, sexual, or psychological harm or suffering to women, including threats of such acts, coercion or arbitrary deprivation of liberty, whether occurring in public or private life." Article 2 states that "violence against women" encompasses, but is not limited to:

(a) Physical, sexual and psychological violence occurring in the family, including battering, sexual abuse of female children in the household, dowry-related violence, marital rape, female genital mutilation and other traditional practices harmful to women, non-spousal violence and violence related to exploitation;

(b) Physical, sexual and psychological violence occurring within the general community, including rape, sexual abuse, sexual harassment and intimidation at work, in educational institutions and elsewhere, trafficking in women and forced prostitution;

(c) Physical, sexual, and psychological violence perpetrated or condoned by the State, wherever it occurs.

The last provision is particularly interesting because it holds the state responsible for failing to demonstrate due diligence in averting or punishing violence against women that occurs in the public *and* the private sphere.

While we can conclude that, since 1991, significant strides have been made toward recognizing the human rights of women under international law, much remains to be done, including withdrawal of reservations to the Women's Convention; the establishment of a complaints procedure under the Convention, thereby empowering the Committee to examine individual complaints and ensuring that governments report to it on issues of violence against women; implementation of the norms contained in the *Declaration on Violence against Women* (which does not have the binding force of a treaty) through effective international monitoring;[33] and the development of further international standards on the elimination of all forms of sexual exploitation.

Operational Level: International Human Rights Monitoring

The Commission on Human Rights

The original mandate of the Commission on Human Rights includes "the prevention of discrimination" on the basis of sex.[34] In 1946, the

Economic and Social Council (ECOSOC) also decided to establish a Sub-Commission of the Commission on Human Rights to deal with the status of women. At its first session, however, the Sub-Commission recommended that it be elevated in status to a Commission; the fact that the ECOSOC agreed seemed a real achievement at the time. Over the years, the agendas, mechanisms, and political weight of the Commission on Human Rights and the Commission on the Status of Women have developed quite differently, and there appeared to be—until the Vienna Conference—a tacit agreement that all women's issues, including human rights, were to be dealt with by the Commission on the Status of Women, although the prevention of discrimination on the basis of sex was never removed from the mandate of the Commission on Human Rights.[35]

Since the early 1970s, the Commission on Human Rights has developed an impressive number of mechanisms for monitoring gross violations of human rights.[36] By 1993, the Commission had appointed thirteen country Rapporteurs/Representatives and developed ten thematic mechanisms to address summary or arbitrary executions, enforced or involuntary disappearances, arbitrary detention, torture and other cruel or degrading treatment or punishment, religious intolerance, mercenaryism, sale of children, freedom of expression, and internally displaced persons. The Commission on Human Rights has developed into a high-profile decision-making body of fifty-three members that may hold (apart from its regular annual session) extraordinary sessions in cases of emergency. It dispatches more than thirty fact-finding missions annually, and deals with thousands of individual cases through its different monitoring procedures.[37] Moreover, it has established a program of technical assistance for human rights and democratic institution building and for the promotion of human rights awareness.[38] More than 150 NGOs in consultative status with ECOSOC attend the Commission's sessions, and many others, without such status, follow the sessions and press for their respective causes. From the role of a low-key promoter of human rights in its early years, the Commission has by now become a protector of human rights.

This impressive expansion of the Commission of Human Rights, however, has done almost nothing to draw attention to the human rights of women. The Commission has, of course, dealt with women victims of disappearance, torture, religious intolerance, and so on, but has not paid attention to issues of particular concern to women, such as rape, forced marriage, transboundary trafficking of women, "honor" crimes against women, genital mutilation, and other abuses. The oft-cited omission of rape as a form of torture or inhuman, cruel or degrading treatment—not only from the country-specific reports but also, until recently, from the report of the Special Rapporteur on Torture—is just one example of this neglect. The rape of women in former Yugoslavia was hardly mentioned in the early reports of the Special Rapporteur until women's NGOs demanded that it be taken seriously. Under the weight of these events, the hesitation to recognize rape as a war crime has at last begun to dissipate.[39] In an aide-mémoire dated December 3, 1992, the International Committee of the Red Cross stated that rape may be considered a case of "wilfully causing great suffering or serious injury to body or health." Moreover, the massive and systematic practice of rape and its use as an instrument of "ethnic cleansing" qualify it to be defined and prosecuted as a crime against humanity.[40] Still, in areas of armed conflict around the world, mass rape continues to be practiced on a daily basis, and there is no response from any of the UN monitoring bodies.

Three marked exceptions to the pattern of neglect of women's human rights in the UN mainstream should be mentioned:

(a) The Special Rapporteur on Traditional Practices affecting the Health of Women and Children is a Rapporteur of the Sub-Commission on Prevention of Discrimination and Protection of Minorities (of the Commission on Human Rights), mandated *inter alia* to submit a plan of action for the elimination of harmful traditional practices affecting the health of women and children such as female genital mutilation, preference for male children, nutritional taboos, and other harmful practices.[41]

(b) Since 1974, the Working Group on Contemporary Forms of Slavery of the Sub-Commission has examined reports submitted by states parties to the Slavery Conventions and has been considering information and recommendations from NGOs on situations ranging from prostitution to widow burning, forced marriage, and other similar phenomena. (This Working Group, however, is not a monitoring body and its recommendations are not always heeded by its parent body, the Sub-Commission.)

(c) In 1992 the Sub-Commission, in light of a growing momentum toward the integration of women's human rights, adopted a resolution by which it reaffirmed that the rights of women are inalienable human rights and must be treated as such by United Nations bodies, including the Commission on Human Rights.[42] In 1993 the Commission on Human Rights adopted a resolution entitled

"Integrating the Rights of Women into the Human Rights Mechanisms of the United Nations." The appointment of a Special Rapporteur[43] in 1994 was a historic step toward the integration of women's human rights into the mainstream of the UN's major human rights body.

The Commission on the Status of Women clearly has not developed the political profile of the Commission on Human Rights. Instead, it has often been placed in a precarious situation by its parent body, the ECOSOC,[44] and has not been allowed to establish any meaningful procedure for dealing with allegations of violations of women's human rights. It is highly significant that since the 1960s the Commission has shifted its concern from the legal status of women to their role in national development.[45] In 1973, the main unit in the United Nations Secretariat responsible for women's issues was transferred from the (then) Division of Human Rights to the Centre for Social Development and Humanitarian Affairs in the Department of Economic and Social Affairs. From then on, United Nations bodies (including the General Assembly) examined women's issues under the economic and social development agenda, and the human rights angle was marginalized. Even the Committee on the Elimination of Discrimination Against Women was viewed by some as a de facto subsidiary of the Commission on the Status of Women, although legally it is a body of independent experts supervising the implementation of a human rights treaty.

The Human Rights Treaty Bodies

Apart from CEDAW, there are two main human rights treaty-monitoring bodies explicitly mandated to deal with the human rights of women: the Human Rights Committee (CCPR), which supervises the *International Covenant on Civil and Political Rights;* and the Committee on Economic, Social and Cultural Rights (CESCR), which supervises the *International Covenant on Economic, Social and Cultural Rights.* Although neither Committee has paid particular attention to women's human rights, some steps in the right direction should be noted. The Committees have focussed on family-related rights and the rights to vote, stand for election, and participate in public life.[46] In 1989, the CCPR adopted a General Comment on Article 2 of the *Covenant on Civil and Political Rights* regarding the principle of non-discrimination.[47] After analyzing the basic thrust of this principle, the

Committee pointed out that states parties should, if necessary, take affirmative action in order to diminish or eliminate conditions that cause or help perpetuate discrimination prohibited by the Covenant.

Now that these two Committees' roles have been strengthened, it is particularly crucial that they receive from governments' and NGO's information that will allow them to make pronouncements and recommendations on the full spectrum of women's human rights in each country. It should be added that the overall political "weight" attached to the work of the CCPR and CESCR has been higher than that of CEDAW.

Advisory Services and Technical Assistance in the Field of Human Rights

While in several so-called "new democracies" the position of women in fact deteriorates,[48] policy makers of old democracies promoting institution building rarely view the equal status of women as a matter of concern. But efforts of ensuring human rights and strengthening democratic institutions must fully integrate women and women's issues if they are not to lose their significance. The United Nations is faced with a great challenge in this area, and human rights training and education have become central to its human rights program. To that end, the UN Centre for Human Rights (which is supported by a Voluntary Fund established in 1987),[49] has provided technical assistance to more than forty states, while some forty more await its services. Activities range from drafting legislation to strengthening the judiciary conducting training for officials working with the administration of justice, enhancing or establishing national human rights commissions, providing electoral assistance, and assisting NGOs dealing with human rights.

The Advisory Services, Technical Assistance and Information Branch of the Centre for Human Rights gradually has been incorporating women's human rights issues into its publications and programs. Needs-assessment missions take particular account of and incorporate measures designed to ensure the status and human rights of women. Training courses and seminars in the administration of justice now contain a practical component that focuses specifically on the human rights of women. A training course for lawyers and judges, for example, addresses issues relating to women as victims of violent crime (particularly sexual assault and domestic violence), women in the criminal justice system, women in the legal profession, and gender bias in the courtroom.

Conclusion

Women's human rights issues have been kept out of the mainstream of international (and frequently national) debates for a number of reasons. First, the creation of the specialized bodies for addressing women's issues within the United Nations has had the negative effect of "allowing" the mainstream human rights bodies to absolve themselves of this responsibility, resulting in the treatment of women's human rights as "lesser" rights. Next, since most states (even those with otherwise serious ideological and political conflicts) permit or condone discrimination on the basis of sex, abuses of women's human rights are not integral threats to peace, territorial integrity, or international relations. During the Cold War, human rights considerations were confined to the battle between East and West; the failure to see the oppression of women as a political issue resulted in the exclusion of sex discrimination and violence against women from the human rights agenda.[50]

The desire on the part of states to keep women out of the "serious political" human rights mainstream led in 1973 to the institutional divorce of the women's unit from the (then) Division of Human Rights. (The Division had shown no particular interest in keeping the unit.[51]) This institutional rift deepened the conceptual and political rift between "women's issues" and human rights issues. At international forums, states (represented almost solely by men) hardly noticed the paradox. But NGOs have a share in the responsibility for this situation. Until recently, mainstream human rights NGOs did not focus their work on the human rights of women and generally did not provide information on such issues to the United Nations human rights bodies.

After the World Conference on Human Rights, the international community had great expectations for the implementation of the *Vienna Declaration and Programme of Action* regarding women by the United Nations human rights bodies and mechanisms and the United Nations Centre for Human Rights. Whether these bodies will be able to live up to those expectations depends on political will, human and financial resources, and the responsibility of states. Apart from its promise of institutional renewal and reform, the Vienna Declaration nevertheless indicates a new awareness, a new ethos that, in the last analysis, may be guarded by the perpetual vigilance and outrage of the women—and men—who fight for human rights.

Notes

The views expressed here are those of the author and do not necessarily represent the United Nations. As an official of the United Nations Centre for Human Rights, I have often had difficulty explaining the Centre's failure to place the human rights of women as a high priority. For my understanding of this question, I am grateful to two women, Sol Nahon and Margaret Bruce, who years ago worked at the (then) United Nations Division of Human Rights on women's issues and who shared with me a wisdom which I could have never found in documents.

1. United Nations, *Charter of the United Nations and Statute of the International Court of Justice,* DPI/511, 3, article 1, para. 3.

2. United Nations General Assembly, Resolution 217A (III), 10 December 1948, 3rd session, article 2. Reprinted in the United Nations publication, *A Compilation of International Instruments,* E.XIV.1, vol. 1 (pt. I) p. 2, article 2.

3. General Assembly Resolution 2200A (XXI), 16 December 1966, 21st Session, reprinted in the United Nations publication, *A Compilation of International Instruments,* E.XIV.1, vol. 1 (pt. I), p. 9, article 2, para. 2, and article 3.

4. Idem, p. 21, article 2, para. 1, and article 3.

5. *Supra* n. 2, article 16.

6. Idem, article 23, para. 2.

7. Idem, article 25, para. 2.

8. *Supra* n. 3, article 7, subpara. (a).

9. Idem, article 10, para. 2.

10. *Supra* n. 4, article 6, para. 5.

11. Idem, article 23.

12. Idem, article 25.

13. Idem, article 26.

14. General Conference of the International Labor Organization (ILO), 42nd Session, 25 June 1958. Reprinted in the United Nations publication, *A Compilation of International Instruments,* E.93.XIV.1, vol. 1 (pt. I), p. 96.

15. General Conference of the United Nations Educational, Scientific and Cultural Organizations, 14 December 1960. Reprinted in the United Nations publication, *A Compilation of International Instruments,* E.XIV.1, vol. 1 (pt. I), p. 101.

16. General Conference of the ILO, 34th Session, 29 June 1951. Reprinted in the United Nations publication, *A Compilation of International Instruments,* E.93.XIV.1, vol. 1 (pt. 1), p. 117.

17. The *Slavery Convention* was signed on 25 September 1926; the Protocol amending the *Slavery Convention* was approved by General Assembly Resolution 794 (VIII) of 23 October 1953; the *Supplementary Convention on the Abolition of Slavery,*

the Slave Trade and Institutions and Practices Similar to Slavery was adopted by a Conference of Plenipotentiaries by Economic and Social Council Resolution 608 (XXI) of 30 April 1956. All these conventions have been reprinted in *A Compilation of International Instruments*, E.93.XIV.1, vol. 1 (pt. I), pp. 201, 206, 209.

18. General Assembly, Resolution 317 (IV), 2 December 1949, reprinted in the United Nations publication, *A Compilation of International Instruments*, E.93.XIV.1, vol. 1 (pt. I), p. 233.

19. General Assembly, Resolution 1040 (XI), 29 January 1957, reprinted in the United Nations publication, *A Compilation of International Instruments*, E.93.XIV.1, vol. 1 (pt. I), p. 607.

20. General Assembly, Resolution 640 (VII), 20 December 1952, reprinted in the United Nations publication, *A Compilation of International Instruments*, E.93.XIV.1, vol. 1 (pt. I), p. 104.

21. General Assembly, Resolution 3318 (XXIX), 14 December 1974, reprinted in the United Nations publication, *A Compilation of International Instruments*, E.93.XIV.1, vol. 1 (pt. I), p. 167.

22. General Assembly, Resolution 45/158, 18 December 1990, 45th Session, reprinted in the United Nations publication, *A Compilation of International Instruments*, E.93.XIV.1, vol. 1 (pt. II), p. 550.

23. General Assembly, Resolution 34/180, 18 December 1979, 34th Session, reprinted in the United Nations publication, *A Compilation of International Instruments*, E.93.XIV.1, vol. 1 (pt. I), p. 150.

24. Personal information.

25. United Nations Department of Public Information, *The Vienna Declaration and Programme of Action*, June 1993, DPI/1394-39399, August 1993, p. ii, para. 38, p. 54.

26. Idem, para. 39, p. 55.

27. Ibid.

28. Hilary Charlesworth, Christine Chinkin, and Shelly Wright, "Feminist Approaches to International Law," *American Journal of International Law* 85(4) (1991): 644.

29. General Assembly, Resolution 44/25, 20 December 1989, 44th Session, reprinted in the United Nations publication, *A Compilation of International Instruments*, E.93.XIV.1, vol. 1 (pt. I), p. 174. See in particular articles 9, 18, 19, and 20.

30. Personal information.

31. CEDAW, General Recommendation No. 19, 11th Session, UN Doc. CEDAW/C/1992/L.1/Add. 15.

32. A/RES/48/104.

33. It would be premature at this stage, I believe, to call for a convention on violence against women. The experience of the Special Rapporteur of the Commission on Human Rights in monitoring the 1981 *Declaration on the Elimination of All Forms of Intolerance and of Discrimination Based on Religion or Belief* showed that it is not always productive to go through the long and expensive process that convention drafting requires, a process that may prompt states, for fear of the binding nature of conventions, to weaken standards contained in a declaration.

34. Economic and Social Council (ECOSOC), Resolution 5(I), 16 February 1946, 1st Session, p. 163, UN Doc. Annex 8.

35. It is interesting that in 1987, when discussions were held on the restructuring of the ECOSOC, an attempt to delete women from the mandate of the Commission on Human Rights was immediately turned down by states with the obvious justification that the Commission must deal with the human rights of all people. (Informal meetings, personal information.)

36. The first such procedure was established by ECOSOC Resolution 1503 (XLVIII), 48th Session, p. 0, UN Doc. E/4832/Add. 1 (1970).

37. 1993 report of the Commission on Human Rights, UN doc. E/1993/23.

38. For the most recent account of activities under the technical assistance program, see UN Doc. E/CN.4/1994/78.

39. Theodor Meron, "Rape as a Crime Under International Humanitarian Law," *American Journal of International Law,* 87(3) (July 1993): 426.

40. Idem, 426–27.

41. Resolution 1993/33 of the Sub-Commission on Prevention of Discrimination and Protection of Minorities, UN Doc. E/CN.1994/2.

42. Resolution 1992/4 of the Sub-Commission on Prevention of Discrimination and Protection of Minorities, 43rd Session, UN Doc. E/CN.4/1993/2.

43. Commission on Human Rights Resolution 1994/45, E/1994/24.

44. Laura Reanda, "Human Rights and Women's Rights: The United Nations Approach," *Human Rights Quarterly* 3(2) (1981): 24–25.

45. Idem, 25.

46. Since 1992, the CCPR has been considering each report and making country assignments. This would have been inconceivable during the Cold War years, when only general (not country-specific) comments were made. Similarly, the CESCR has been strengthened since 1985, when it became a body of independent experts, and has tackled its work more creatively, including making plans for the drafting of an optional protocol that would set up an individual complaints procedure.

47. General Comment 18(37), UN Doc. CCPR/C/21/Rev.1/Add.1(1989).

48. See, for example, "Hidden Victims: Women in Post-Communist Poland," *News from Helsinki Watch, Women's Rights Project* 4(5) (March 12, 1992).

49. Commission on Human Rights, Resolution 1987/38, 10 March 1987, UN Doc. E/CN.4/1988/40.

50. Charlotte Bunch, "Women's Rights as Human Rights: Towards a Re-Vision of Human Rights," *Human Rights Quarterly* 12(4): 491.

51. Private information.

Regional Reports

4

Violence Against Women: The Indian Perspective

Indira Jaising

The persistence in India of cultural practices that discriminate against girls and women means not only the abuse of but, finally, the deaths of countless women. The girl child faces a hostile environment even in the womb. The male-dominated system of high technology, rather than offering relief, has contributed to the intensification of discrimination against women. Parents can now detect the sex of a fetus within the first trimester, and, upon learning that the sex of the unborn child is female, many women choose or are forced to abort. Although the evidence is not fully available, one study showed that 7,997 of 8,000 fetuses aborted were female, and another showed that 40,000 female fetuses were aborted in Bombay in 1984 alone. Some states, including Maharashtra, have passed laws requiring that technicians who conduct such tests register themselves, and introduced regulation of the use of amniocentesis and sonograms. At this point, however, legislation sufficient to deal with the problem has yet to be drafted on a national level, and selective abortion of female fetuses continues in many regions.

If a girl child is lucky enough to be born, she experiences discrimination in her infancy. Girl children are fed less and for shorter periods and are not given foods like butter or milk, which are reserved for boys. Studies have shown a 12 percent mortality rate among infant girls under a year old, and an 8 percent mortality rate among girls under five years old. While boys are sent to school, girls often stay home to look after younger siblings and to help with household chores. Even those girls who do receive some education must, at the same time, do washing and cleaning, as these are taboo chores for males. But only a little over half of all girls are enrolled in primary school, as compared with about 80 percent of boys, despite the fact that the education level of mothers is inversely linked to infant mortality.

Most Indian girls are married between the ages of 16 and 20, although some are married at significantly younger ages. Marriage is almost always arranged by parents or brothers. The young bride must be obedient to her elders, loyal to her husband and his family, and never discuss her marital problems with outsiders. The model wife is taught that she must be ready to sacrifice her life for the honor of her husband and his family name. Even educated and well-placed professional women submit, for instance, to wife beating, implicitly an acceptable form of control.

A major impediment to the human rights of women in India is the fact that laws relating to marriage, divorce, adoption, and inheritance are based primarily on religious law and tradition, with different laws for Hindus, Muslims, and Parsis. Any demand for equality based on sex is met with resistance on the grounds that such demands amount to interference with the right to freedom of religion. For example, under Hindu law, daughters and sons do not have equal rights to joint family property. A daughter is not a member of the coparcenary (an institution that holds ancestral property in the male line for three generations), and therefore has no right to claim partition of ancestral property.

The absence of any legislation relating to the right of the women to residence in the matrimonial home or to an equitable distribution of matrimonial assets on the dissolution of the marriage makes it legally possible for a husband to drive his wife out of her home. Divorce is taboo, and divorced women are treated as pariahs who, it is assumed, have failed to meet their husbands' needs. There are no viable alternatives to remaining in an abusive marriage—no group support, no support from relatives, no resources for a woman to live on her own. The longstanding demands of the women's movement for a general civil law against domestic violence have gone unmet. Judges are reluctant to grant injunctions restraining violent spouses from causing harm or injury to their wives.

Sexual abuse of girls and women in families is common, but rarely reported. If a girl is raped, both she and her family are considered to have been shamed. Only rarely have rape cases come to public notice. It is common for the police to be bribed, and those families that do report a rape to the police are liable to be ridiculed and, finally, intimidated into dropping the case. Among those cases that are tried, convictions can be won, but the process takes an average of eight years, and sentences are low. Despite the fact that serious sexual harassment is rampant in India, it usually goes unreported because women fear that complaining will attract negative attention. Although section 509 of the Indian Penal Code provides for prosecution of harassment, only a handful of cases are recorded; most are dismissed for lack of evidence. In one case, Rupan Bajaj Deol, a female senior officer at Indian Administrative Services (IAS), filed a formal complaint against the Director General of Police, K.P.S. Gill. The Indian government took no action against Gill, and the high court merely dismissed her case, stating that the government could claim privilege against disclosure of police records. In some parts of India, sexual abuse is institutionalized in the practice of offering teenage girls as *Devdasis*: girls (usually from poor families) who are officially "dedicated" to Hindu gods and goddesses and then sexually exploited; most of them end up as prostitutes.

Marriage, too, can be dangerous, even for well-educated and employed women. One of the most dramatic forms of violence against women in India is what has come to be known as "dowry deaths." "Dowry" is defined as any property given or agreed to be given at the time of the marriage in consideration for, or in connection with, the marriage. The institution of dowry was legislatively abolished by the Dowry Prohibition Act starting in 1961, but the giving and accepting of dowry persists. Dowry death, also known as bride burning, occurs when a wife and her family cannot meet the demands of her husband and/or his family for additional money or property or when a husband wishes to gain an additional dowry by remarrying. He and his family begin physically and psychologically abusing his bride, and the abuse, if it does not drive the wife to suicide, nevertheless often ends in her death by burning, with the husband claiming that the wife caught fire while cooking on a kerosene stove. More than 5,000 dowry deaths occur every year, and that number has been rising. Many cases are not reported, but it is difficult to prosecute those that are since—even if police do not believe a "cooking accident" to have been the cause of death—police can be easily bribed not to register the complaint. If brought to court, the cases tend to linger for months or even years, and the accused are usually acquitted due to lack of evidence. Most remarry soon after, receiving an additional dowry.

Although the profile of women in India is changing and women, particularly in the middle classes, are gainfully employed (many sustaining and supporting their immediate families), marriage continues to be considered the most desirable goal. Parents, therefore, are ready and willing to offer dowry on the occasion of their daughters' marriages. In 1984, the Dowry Prohibition Act was amended to introduce more stringent punishment for the giving and taking of dowry, and in 1986, the Indian Penal Code was amended to address the offense of dowry death. Section 304B states that when the death of a woman is caused by any burns or bodily injury or occurs under other than normal circumstances within seven years of her marriage, and when it is shown that shortly before her death she was subjected to cruelty or harassment by her husband or any relative of her husband for or in connection with any demand for dowry, such death shall be called "dowry death" and the husband or relative shall be deemed to have caused her death. By thus shifting the burden of proof, convictions have been made possible.

In 1983 yet another offense, that of cruelty by the husband or his relative, was introduced into the penal laws. Section 498A of the Indian Penal Code states that the husband or any of his relatives who willfully subject a woman to such abuse as is likely to drive a woman to commit suicide or cause grave injury or danger to her life, whether mental or physical, or who harasses the woman with a view to coercing her to meet any unlawful demand for dowry, is guilty of cruelty. The offense is punishable with a term of imprisonment that can extend up to three years. Special units dealing with violence against women have been set up by the police in all major cities to entertain complaints by women under this section. This particular provision of law has worked to the advantage of women and is perhaps the only legal mechanism available to help them to cope with violence. Although conviction rates are unavailable, the existence of this provision acts as a deterrent against wife abuse and is often used to bring about a settlement between spouses.

But there are other forms of violence against women from which the law offers no protection. Large-scale police brutality against women is a relatively recent phenomenon, but it is spreading fast. The rape of women in custody is rampant, particularly in the states of Punjab and Kashmir, where police forces have a free hand. Women accused without grounds of harboring terrorists are beaten and tortured before they are questioned. Women disappear and die in custody daily. Unfortunately, the Indian government has so far refused to accept that there is a problem, despite detailed reports submitted by Amnesty International and civil rights groups. Of the 412 reported custody deaths of men and women, judicial inquiries were made into only 62, resulting in only three convictions.

Although rarer, the custom of *Sati,* which involves the burning or burying alive of a widow along with the body of her deceased husband, persists. The practice, ostensibly intended to honor the devoted wife, was abolished in the last century, but the dramatic *Sati* of Roop Kanwar in 1987 shocked the nation, and the Central Government felt obliged to enact the Commission of *Sati* (Prevention) Act in 1987. The Act prohibits the glorification of *Sati,* and includes prohibition of observing any ceremony or engaging in any processions in connection with *Sati;* supporting, justifying, or propagating the practice of *Sati;* arranging any function to eulogize the person who has committed *Sati;* or the creation of any trust or collection of any funds, or the construction of a temple or place of worship with a view to perpetuating the honor or memory of any person who has committed *Sati.* The Constitutional validity of this Act has been challenged in the Supreme Court of India on the ground that it violates the right of freedom of religion. The outcome of this challenge is yet to be seen.

In the end, demographics provide what is perhaps the most telling indication of the status of women: the persistence of an adverse sex ratio, which declined from 934 females per 1,000 males in 1981 to 927 females per 1,000 males in 1991. And while bride burning, rape in police custody, and *Sati* are shocking and visible forms of violence against women, the more silent and invisible forms of oppression that women face every day are as troubling. Fortunately, there have been strong women's movements to counter discrimination. Sewa of Ahmedabad, which works for self-employed women; the Chipko movement of Garhwal, which saved the Himalayan forests from destruction and also helped preserve ecological diversity; and the antiliquor movement of Andhra Pradesh are all examples of positive women's action for change. In the same vein, the government has initiated measures for the empowerment of women, including the enactment of laws providing that one-third of all local-government elected bodies consist of women; the establishment of a national commission for women; and the establishment of a credit fund for women.

An essential step for combating the oppression of women would be absolute public acknowledgment—governmental as well as societal— of the existence of widespread abuse and discrimination at every level of Indian society, both in India and in Indian communities abroad. Next, all girls must be sent to school, and the curriculum should include education in the equality of the sexes, beginning in the primary schools. Support groups should be established to help rape victims, the sexually exploited, harassed, and physically abused. But women must be empowered not only by cultural changes, which may be slow in coming, but also by enforced statutes. The government must work to eliminate corruption at all levels—in law enforcement, the legislature, and the judiciary—so that those laws that are enacted may be enforced. Only then can the subcontinent address the fundamental human rights issue of violence against women. As long as cultural assumptions about the inferiority of women continue to exist, equality for women and freedom from discrimination based on sex will remain distant dreams.

5

Legacies of Invisibility: Past Silence, Present Violence Against Women in the Former Yugoslavia

Jasmina Kuzmanović

I met Marijana in a hospital in Zagreb. Her doctor told me she had arrived from Bosnia three days earlier. Though our interview was difficult, seventeen-year-old Marijana was beyond tears: dry, tense little face, child's body. She didn't exactly tell me what had happened; I had to coax the words out of her, one by one. One day in April, Serb irregulars came to the village near Tesanj, in Central Bosnia, where Marijana, a Muslim-Croat, lived with her family. Marijana, her mother, and her seven-year-old sister were tending their vegetable garden. The soldiers raped Marijana and her mother there, then loaded Marijana on a truck, along with twenty-three other women from the village. This was the last time she saw her mother or her sister. Raping continued on the truck. The soldiers took the women to an improvised camp in the woods that operated as a military brothel. Women between the ages of twelve and twenty-five were kept in one room and raped daily. Marijana became pregnant in the first month. After four months, the soldiers let her and seven other visibly pregnant women go. Marijana says, "They told us to go and have our Serbian babies."

Marijana's face was empty, and she had trouble speaking. The only time she became agitated was when asked about the delivery. "I will not give birth," she said with hard determination. That conviction seemed to be the only thing keeping her on this side of the precarious line of mental health. But her doctor told me they would not be able to perform an abortion, since Marijana had long since passed into the second trimester of pregnancy. Nobody in the hospital had dared to tell that to Marijana.

When I think about Croatia and former Yugoslavia's painful present and totalitarian past, I remember Marijana. Why is it, I wonder, that people identify totalitarianism as a part of the past, when only a year ago I talked to a victim of totalitarianism? She might not have called it totalitarianism, but then oppression has a curious effect on people's speaking ability, and when I met her, Marijana could speak only in monosyllables.

In this war, women are the most silent victims. That men are victims is obvious: they are drafted, they fight, they die. But one thing that characterizes the war in Bosnia is its brutality toward the weakest members of society. In the hinterland of Dubrovnik, almost all the inhabitants fled, deserting their homes. Only some older people remained, hoping they wouldn't be hurt. Toni Car, a doctor who had been treating these people before the war, managed to visit them during the occupation, under the agency of the International Committee of the Red Cross. Several women over the age of seventy-five confided that they had been raped by Serbian and Montenegrin soldiers. It is difficult to substantiate crimes like rape, since the patriarchal structure prevents victims and their families from telling. All of these women begged Car not to tell anyone nor even to speak of it to their families. The women's feeling of shame was deeper even than their hurt or anger.

But this is not the first time in the history of the region that women have chosen or been forced to remain silent. In earlier years, the victims of totalitarianism, it seemed, were always men: men who spoke their minds in favor of the supremacy of the Soviet Union and hence "Stalinists," dealt with by the young communist state in the way "Stalinists" deserved. Post-1948 gulag-style camps were made by men, for men. But it is easily forgotten that not all the prisoners were men; there was also a women's prison camp in the Yugoslav "Gulag," the infamous *Goli Otok* (Naked Island), a piece of rock off the northern Adriatic where political prisoners were kept from the late 1940s until recently. One of those prisoners was a friend's mother, at the time a young teacher in Rijeka. She and her husband, a local journalist, were taken away one night. Separated from her husband, my friend's mother spent the rest of the night with dozens of other women who had been arrested and with whom she was taken to Goli Otok. Until the moment of her death some years ago, she didn't know whether she had been taken because of who she was or because of who her husband was, whether she was a "Stalinist" in her own right or merely the wife of a Stalinist. For young intellectual women, the former position often ended up disappearing into the latter.

During these times, Croatian literary life involved a political and cultural paradox: publishers in Croatia could not publish dissident

Yugoslav writers like Vlado Gotovac, but were able to publish dissident writers like Kundera, Havel, Skvorecky, and Hrabal from other Eastern European countries because they spoke of life under Soviet occupation. But the literature played a cruel joke on the censors, because these books, in other ways, also spoke about us—although not quite, it seemed, about all of us. Men were in these works: male playwrights and novelists wrote about male heroes, survivors, prisoners. Women were hardly part of the picture. In fact, among all the published memoirs and works of fiction by those who had served time in the prison camps, not one was written by a woman.

Shortly before his death in the late 1980s, the writer Danilo Kis made a television serial in which he interviewed Jewish survivors of Goli Otok. Here, for the first time, women victims of totalitarianism spoke publicly about their experiences. Yet the overwhelming majority of the women who were taken to the prison in the late '40s and early '50s—hundreds of them, it is estimated—have remained silent. Some of them surely have died by now and, in most cases, their neighbors, friends, sometimes even relatives, do not know of their histories in the camps. In fact, it was only as a grown woman that my friend learned that her mother had been imprisoned. On the day of their release, prisoners were always told to remain silent about what had transpired in the camp, but such warnings were hardly necessary. Even in the early '80s, when my friend told me about her mother, she asked me not to tell anyone else; after all these years, the story still carried pain, fear, shame, and even the feeling of danger. To tell such a story is like coming out of the closet.

After the 1950s, Yugoslavia entered an era in which the subtler oppression of the ordinary one-party state could take hold. By then, women had been pushed out of the political arena, so over the course of more than thirty years only a few were imprisoned for political crimes. From that time on, rather than being viewed as the direct victims of oppression, women slid into the anonymous role of *wives* of the oppressed.

Born into a Croatian Jewish family, Olga Hebrang married a Jew shortly before World War II. Although her husband, young son, and entire family disappeared in concentration camps, Olga herself survived. She fell in love with a high-ranking communist official who was at the same time a Croatian patriot. They married and had three children. Shortly after the war, Olga's second husband was indicted for treason, was taken away, and disappeared during the investigation. Olga was arrested soon after, imprisoned for two years, then painfully reunited with her children; she subsequently endured years of pressure, poverty, and humiliation.

The fate of Olga's second husband became the subject of hot national debate in the late 1980s, and Olga became the center of media attention. If she had been born male, perhaps she would have written a book about her experiences. But being what she is, Olga gave just one interview, the central figure of which was her husband. That she had been a victim in her own right was of no interest. Her perceived value was as the wife of her husband. There were many other wives besides Olga, though less famous ones. During the first free elections in Croatia, the media and the publishing houses were full of stories about political prisoners, dissidents, the oppressed, or the blacklisted. They had gone to prison, they had suffered, and now, avenged martyrs, they had returned. Invariably, they were male.

Life in prison was hard for those men. But so was life at home for their wives, who were exposed to a unique type of state harassment, which targeted them at home, at work, even through their children. When I attempted to interview several of them, they all declined to tell me about those years of oppression. "There is nothing special in my story. I made no special choice in leading the kind of life I led," explained one of them. She made it clear that it was her husband who was the real and only victim, that her sacrifices were negligible compared to his.

If one were to learn about our region's recent history only by studying documentary and fiction works from and about the period, one might conclude that women—if there were any included—hardly suffered during the years of oppression. Of course, there have been a few cinematographic exceptions: Martha Meszaros's and the late Larisa Shepitkova's films, for example. Even then, however, works from that period like *Letters to Olga* (Václav Havel's letters from prison to his wife) and other lesser-known works by or about women will never be entirely understood by those who have not experienced totalitarianism. And anyway, in fiction as in faction, the old rule usually holds firm: It is always *Letters to Olga,* and never *Olga's Letters.* Talking to various Olgas, years later, one most often discovers they were too busy surviving to find the time to write letters.

In her hospital bed in Zagreb, Marijana is only one inheritor of a long history of female victims of oppression. Survivors from forty years ago have rarely voiced their testimony. Now comes a generation of teenagers even more hurt and, it seems, even more voiceless. Lost voices, lost lives, scarred destinies. This time, the women are slightly more visible, but for now, only articles, analyses, papers *about* Marijana can be written. If she survives, she may find the strength—and, someday, enough distance—to tell her story herself. So far she remains, like many others, a voiceless face. It should be imprinted like a watermark on every piece of paper about women: Marijana with an empty face.

6

The Medium Term Philippine Development Plan Toward the Year 2000: Filipino Women's Issues and Perspectives

Liza Largoza-Maza

When the U.S. bases leave, we will still be prostitutes servicing not only the Americans but also the multinationals.

—A former Olongapo bar girl

This statement accurately describes the direction in which the former American military bases in the Philippines are going, transformed in pursuit of the *Medium Term Philippine Development Plan* (MTPDP, or Philippines 2000) from exclusive "rest and relaxation" preserves of the U.S. military into a big brothel for multinationals.

The MTPDP is the Ramos government's economic blueprint for attaining the status of a newly industrializing country (NIC) by the year 2000, following in the footsteps of Asian neighbors like Taiwan, South Korea, Singapore, and Thailand. This plan envisions the establishment of regional agroindustrial estates with export processing and tourism as the main economic activities. The plan conforms to the set of conditions laid out by the current Structural Adjustment Program (SAP) of the International Monetary Fund (IMF) and the World Bank (WB). This is a refurbished version of the old balanced agroindustrial development strategy (BAIDS) that, during the Marcos dictatorship, similarly kowtowed to the dictates of the IMF/WB under an earlier SAP.

The sources of financing for the MTPDP are foreign investments, foreign loans, and the income from trade, which includes nontraditional export items like garments, electronics, and labor power. Foreign investments and foreign loans have so far come in trickles. Revenue from the garment and electronics industries (of which more than 80 percent of the work force are women) and remittances sent home by overseas contract workers and migrants (of which more than 50 percent are women) currently prop up the economy and fuel Ramos's MTPDP. Women are proving to be the very backbone on which the government is relying to subsidize the ambitious Philippines 2000 plan.

Nevertheless, Ramos' export-oriented/import-dependent, debt-driven economic program will further intensify the exploitation of Filipino women as a source of cheap, docile labor and as sexual commodities. According to research conducted by the Center for Women's Resources in Quezon City, the continuing displacement of farming communities (caused by the frenzied conversion of agricultural lands to industrial estates) and the encouragement of foreign investors and tourism "leave women vulnerable to exploitation as low-paid workers in export processing firms or as poorly paid contractual workers doing homework" (Taguiwalo and Angosta-Cruzada). The study gives as an example that workers in a Metro Manila-based firm producing winter gloves for export receive only $1 for every dozen leather gloves sewn. In Cebu, women involved in the production of paper wrappers for coils of mosquito repellent each net an average of 21¢ per day by working at home in groups of three and finishing one-hundred paper wrappers a day. The average daily wage in the Philippines is P118 (about $4.20 U.S.). The average daily cost of living for a family of six (the size of the average family) is P286 (about U.S. $10.20). Children, as well as both parents, may have to work in order to earn enough to maintain the family.

With business comes pleasure. The MTPDP integrates sex tourism into the overall scheme to attract foreign investors, using women as lures. In Cebu, the number of female prostitutes has doubled since the city launched a campaign to attract investment. From March 1992 to June 1993, the number of registered commercial sex workers increased from 1,557 to 2,189. In Laog City, where direct international flights from Taiwan bring in Taiwanese businessmen, prostitution also increased, and in another town in Central Luzon, there was an observable increase in the number of prostitutes working in beer houses and clubs along the highway.

For an increasing number of women, the only option other than prostitution is to migrate to other countries as brides, contract workers, or sex workers. In a country where 70 percent of the population lives below the poverty line, where 20 percent of the population (landlords, big businessmen, and bureaucrats) controls 52 percent of the national income, and where women continue to be marginalized in a development process that favors the rich, women will continue to migrate in large numbers to foreign countries to seek the proverbial greener pastures. Scattered throughout 132 countries, most of the Filipinas that have migrated abroad in the last ten years have found work as domestic helpers, chambermaids, entertainers, nurses, or prostitutes. Marginalized in low-status jobs and as migrants who do not enjoy the rights of citizens in the receiving countries, they are particularly vulnerable working in the private sphere of the home, where they live and render services beyond the reach and foreknowledge of entities that could provide them with needed assistance and protection.

When the floodgates of labor export were opened, trafficking of Filipino women abroad for prostitution became a systematized, large-scale operation. Migration for work, the mail-order bride system, and direct recruitment for the global entertainment industry were the channels. Filipino women in these situations frequently experience violence and other forms of abuse. In Japan, where about 90 percent of Filipinas work as entertainers, the women become easy prey to the Yakuza underworld of drugs and prostitution. In Australia, fifteen Filipinas have been murdered by their husbands since 1980.

Filipina migrants contribute greatly to propping up the Philippine economy through their tax remittances to the Philippine government, which (if one includes those paid by Filipino male migrants) total an average of $3 billion. This is almost equal to the amount the Philippine government pays in interest on foreign loans. Thus, after centuries of "development," women are still playing the centuries-old role of *pambayad utang*: payment for loans incurred. During the Spanish colonial period, the *encomienda* was an administrative unit set up to facilitate and systematize the exacting of tributes and taxes from the Filipino people. Included in the "payments" was forced and unpaid labor for the Spanish conquistadores, and women were included to meet production quotas, do unpaid labor as farm workers, and render free menial services in the convents. In many instances, women were forced to render sexual favors to Spanish friars and officials. Filipino peasant families were often forced to surrender their daughters to *hacienda* owners and landlords to work at jobs as payment for unpaid loans. This practice continues in some parts of the country today under the feudal-patriarchal tenancy system. Even the government uses women to repay foreign loans (now amounting to more than $30 billion and expected to reach $40 billion by the year 1998) by expropriating the income generated by women and allocating these to loan payments. (About 40 percent of the national budget is allotted annually to debt servicing.) The country lives off the exploitation of Filipino women's labor and their sexual commodification, both in the Philippines and abroad.

Since the early 1980s, women have been mobilizing to change their situation, and on all fronts—from legal reforms to armed revolution—women are weaving an agenda for liberation. Women were at the forefront of the anti-Marcos struggle from 1983 through 1986; that activism gave birth to GABRIELA, a coalition of women's organizations in the Philippines, that addresses women's issues comprehensively, from economic and political rights to sociocultural rights, reproductive rights, and the right to development; from the issue of the U.S. bases and nuclear power plants to rape, domestic violence, and prostitution; from U.S. imperialism and the stranglehold of multinational companies to militarization to Filipino "comfort" women. The coalition of (mostly grassroots) women's organizations continues to create various strategies for the development of the mass movement for women's liberation that is also integral to societal liberation. These strategies include organizing, research, and education; legislative action, campaigns, and mobilization; welfare and crisis intervention; and local and international networking.

Since 1986, new women's organizations and institutions have been formed, expanding the breadth and scope of the Philippine women's movement. These include women's research, resource, and study centers; crisis centers; community-based women's clinics and daycare centers; women's legal services; and women's socio-economic projects.

The development of the dynamic women's movement in the Philippines is a sign of hope amidst the myriad problems facing the Filipina today. At the core of this movement are the grassroots organizations representing women who have long been on the margins—the workers, peasants, urban poor, and indigenous women who are claiming their right to live as humans with dignity and freedom.

Bibliography

Eviota, Elizabeth. 1992. *The Political Economy of Gender: Women and Sexual Division of Labour in the Philippines.* London and New Jersey: Zed.

Medel-Anonuevo, Carol. 1992. "Feminist Reflections on the International Migration of Women." *Lila. Asian Pacific Women's Journal* 1. Manila: Institute for Women's Studies.

Medium Term Philippine Development Plan 1993–1998 (Philippines 2000). 1993. Manila: National Economic and Development Authority (NEDA).

Taguiwalo, Judy, and Elizabeth Angosta-Cruzada. 1993. "The Ramos Administration Medium Term Philippine Development Plan (Philippines 2000): Prospects for Filipino Women." *Piglas Diva* 6:2. Manila: Center for Women's Resources.

Women's News Watch (May 28, 1993). Manila: Isis International.

7

Women in South Africa and the Constitution-Making Process

Brigitte Mabandla

1. The Situation of Women in South Africa

The life experiences of the majority of Black women in South Africa starkly show that, for them, oppression rests on the intersection of race and class with gender. As in most countries, South African society is patriarchal. Religious and traditional norms relegate women to an inferior position in both society and family. Institutionalized racism exacerbates the oppression of Black women by further encroaching upon their rights. Thus, the historic denial of civil and political rights to Black people, coupled with the historic oppression of women as a gender and as a class, has meant that Black women occupy the lowest rung of the social ladder. In both rural and urban areas, their situation is grim.

In rural areas, the poorest areas of the country, the majority of African households are headed by women. With very little formal employment available, most families survive largely by subsistence farming and by producing artifacts; these activities supplement earnings sent back by family members who work in the mines or in domestic service in urban areas. Needless to say, African women make up the majority of urban domestic workers.

Conditions in urban areas are no better. With unemployment running as high as 40 percent in some cities, most women are unemployed and live in abject poverty. Those who are fortunate enough to find work are primarily in domestic service and in the clothing industry, where in some cases conditions resemble those of sweat shops. Following the abolition of pass laws, many people made their way to urban areas, where they were met by conditions of poverty similar to those they were attempting to escape and found themselves living in over-crowded informal settlements. Once again, it is women who make up the majority of this population.

2. The Constitution-Making Process and the Question of Gender

Attempts by South African women to inform the post-Apartheid constitution-making process began even before the negotiation process took off in earnest. In 1990, for example, a series of workshops was held on the Charter for Women's Rights and ways in which it could be built into a post-Apartheid constitution. These workshops culmi-nated in a conference at the University of Western Cape, where women of various political affiliations, professions, and classes focused primar-ily on the status of the Charter vis à vis a post-Apartheid constitution. The Women's Coalition, which emerged toward the end of 1991, is an integral part of this movement.

The Coalition, formed to campaign solely for women's rights, brought together women from political parties and organizations and from special-interest groups (rural women, the disabled, rape crisis workers, religious groups, women from the trade unions). The ensuing nationwide campaign was the first of its kind in the history of South Africa. As the debate it generated gathered momentum, not only were the South African media forced for the first time to focus in significant ways on women's concerns, but there was also an increased demand for women activists to address communities and various civic bodies. The leadership of both discussions and organizations was diverse, drawing largely from rural women's organizations. The activism of rural women—who contend not only with Apartheid but also with customary law in its harshest form—brought into question the future of customary law in a post-Apartheid state founded on a democratic and nonsexist constitution.

Women were not the only sector, however, seeking to influence the outcome of the constitution-making process on gender issues. A determined conservative lobby called for the constitutionalization of women's subordination. The thrust of this conservative lobby varied, with some factions arguing against abortion rights and others mobiliz-ing for the retention of male authority in the home. African traditional-ists, for example, lobbied the Negotiations Forum for the entrenchment of the institution of chieftainship in the post-Apartheid constitution and argued openly against the equality clause in the chapter on fundamental rights. Consequently, the relationship between customary and constitutional law in a constitutional state came to be one of the most disputed issues in the negotiations. This touched on yet another sensitive issue in the South African context: the relationship between traditional rule and customary law.

Historically, colonial conquest undermined and sought to distort traditional norms and institutions by curtailing the power of chiefs and making their functions subservient to colonial interests. Administratively, the institution of chieftainship was subject to White authority. The Governor-General, for instance, was the designated Supreme Paramount Chief. Eventually, additional methods of control were devised, with the ultimate effect that chiefs, who had come to be seen as puppets of the Apartheid regime, were unpopular during the struggle against Apartheid. Those chiefs who resisted manipulation and co-optation— thereby resisting Apartheid—were either demoted or removed from office, and in some cases, tortured. In areas of strong resistance, the Apartheid regime recruited collaborators whom they installed as chiefs.

Apart from local administration, the major function of the chiefs was to administer customary law. Customary law, distorted along Calvinistic lines by colonial powers and interpreted by chiefs who were arms of the colonial administration, helped to hold women firmly in a subordinate position within the African family.

In the later years of Apartheid, some chiefs, in an attempt to break away from the system, organized themselves into the Congress of Traditional Leaders of South Africa (CONTRALESA) to become part of the Mass Democratic Movement (MDM). Still, in the recent context of constitutional negotiations, the interests of the chiefs and those of women (when the focus was on human rights) at times seemed to be in conflict and thus were a source of tension. CONTRALESA's stated policy included the promotion of nonracialism and nonsexism while seeking to reclaim the dignity of the African people through the constitutional recognition of traditional institutions. However, in the debate on the equality clause, chiefs negotiating as representatives of CONTRALESA argued against the clause's application to African women living under traditional rule. Women opposed this proposal and managed to force negotiators to recognize the constitutional right to equality of all South African women, including those living under traditional rule. While recognizing that traditional rule and the institution of chieftainship cannot be wished away, women insisted that traditional rule conform to human rights standards and that these standards encompass women's concerns.

It was not just the chiefs who took a regressive view on the human rights of women and the equality clause. A group of professional women presented the negotiators with a memorandum recommending a two-year moratorium on the application of the equality clause to women living under traditional rule. This indicated a serious failure to determine a conceptual framework for a women's agenda. Most feminists, recognizing that South African women's oppression is premised on the conjunction of race and gender, opposed the memorandum. Although this incident indicated that we had not yet found a way to put theory into practice, the feminist position holds that ways to transcend arguments in favor of "traditional" roles of women based on customary law can be found.

Negotiations can be seen as having been favorable to women if one recalls that, until the beginning of the negotiation process, women (even White women, who have had voting rights since 1933) were underrepresented in power and decision-making structures. Prior to the historic election in April 1994, very few members of Parliament were women; now South Africa is among the leading ten countries in terms of sizable representation of women in parliamentary bodies. In the parliament of the Government of National Unity, women make up 15 percent of Senate members and 24 percent of National Assembly members. The majority of these women come from the African National Congress (ANC), which, in drawing up its list of candidates, reserved a quota of 33 percent for women. Furthermore, by the time South Africa went to the polls in April 1994, women's collective action had won them the right to participate in negotiations. Following a demonstration in which women took to the streets to demand inclusion, the Planning Committee ruled that all parties (each represented by four participants) should have a female negotiator and a female advisor to the Negotiations Council. Women negotiators and advisors organized themselves into a women's caucus to address issues of concern to them. Zola Skweylya, an ANC negotiator, conceded that without the participation of women, gender-specific issues would not have been addressed. In addition to negotiating the constitutionalization of women's rights, women successfully lobbied for the establishment of a Sub-Council on the status of women within the framework of the Transitional Executive Council (TEC). The establishment of the Sub-Council was an indication that gender issues had become a national concern, since TEC Sub-Councils addressed only the most important issues in the transformation process, issues such as security, finance, and international affairs. The central task of the Sub-Council on the Status of Women was to ensure the creation of a climate conducive to women's claims for civil and political rights. It also laid the foundation for the active participation of women in the Government of National Unity.

The struggle for women's advancement in South Africa has only just begun. The immediate challenge is to ensure not only that women continue being visible actors in the GNU and future governments but also that their presence in government and in finalizing the constitution yields meaningful and enduring gains for women throughout the country.

8

After the Revolution: Violations of Women's Human Rights in Iran

Akram Mirhosseini

During the second half of the nineteenth century, at the time of the Ghajar Dynasty, women in Iran began a struggle for rights, establishing schools for girls, and publishing newspapers and periodicals for women. Although the clergy and others denounced the schools and called for their immediate closure, women's resistance was sufficient to withstand such pressure and to continue to stress the centrality of women in society. After the Constitutional Revolution of 1907, women's rights were expanded. In 1936, Reza Shah declared the emancipation of women and abolished traditional women's attire. In 1963, women received the franchise; in the ratification of the Family Protection Act, polygamy and the sole right of men to divorce were banned, and women were given custody of children, while laws enforcing the husband's power over the wife's right to work or to travel were not enforced.

Just fifteen days after the 1979 Islamic Revolution,[1] the Family Protection Act was abolished. Polygamy once again became accepted practice, divorce became the unique right of men, and the legal age for marriage was declared to be nine years old for girls (with Khomeini asserting that a girl should have her first menstrual period in her husband's house, not her father's).

According to the Islamic Penal Code, a woman's worth is half that of a man: A woman's testimony in court is worth half that of a man; women inherit half as much as men. "The Law of Retribution and Punishment" prescribes that, in the case of murder, *Dieh* (blood money—the compensation paid to the family of the victim) is half for a murdered woman what it is for a murdered man (fifty camels or one hundred cows for a woman as opposed to one hundred camels or two hundred cows for a man).

Women are not permitted to marry foreigners without written permission from the Ministry of the Interior. Without it, such marriages (or those with only religious registration), according to Ahmad Hosseini, the Ministry's Director General for the Affairs of Foreign Citizens and Immigrants, will not be legally recognized. Married women may not work or travel abroad without written permission from their husbands.[2]

Men, who may be polygamous, are permitted to have up to four wives and an unlimited number of concubines. A married woman must be at all times willing to meet her husband's sexual needs, and if she refuses, she loses the right to shelter, food, and clothing. A husband, father, or brother has the right to kill his wife, daughter, or sister—and go unpunished—if he finds her committing an "immoral" or "unchaste" act (such as having sex with a man not her husband). Divorce is the indisputable right of men, according to Islamic Republic Canon Law, unless there is a statement to the contrary in the marriage contract. Women get custody of children only if there is no father or grandfather living. Where a marriage is dissolved, even if the father has died, a woman may have custody only of daughters under seven years old and sons under two years old.

In the process of "purification" during the early days of the revolution, the majority of women in government positions (even those highly trained and specialized) were fired. Khomeini and the mullahs in the mosques insisted that the physical and mental weakness of women made them incapable of taking up certain jobs, and the female gender was from then on omitted from employment announcements. For those lucky enough to be employed, opportunities for promotion were few, and there were practically no women in managerial or supervisory positions.[3] The regime fired more than 40,000 women working as elementary and high school teachers, and banned the employment of women in government altogether for a certain period of time. During the five years preceding the revolution, 13 percent of women had been employed; after the revolution, this fell by 50 percent and reached as low as 6.2 percent female employment during the first five years of the regime. According to the Ayatollah Mutahari (one of the principal ideologues of the Islamic Republic): "The specific task of women in this society is to marry and bear children. They will be discouraged from entering legislative, judicial, or whatever careers may require decision making, as women lack the intellectual ability and discerning judgement required for these careers."[4]

Strict sexual segregation of teachers and students at all levels has resulted in the closure of many schools for girls due to a lack of female teachers, overcrowding of classes, and a decline in standards.[5] In rural areas in particular, this has meant essentially that girls are denied education.[6] From the beginning of the regime, women have been excluded from 79 out of 157 courses of study in the university: 55 courses out of 84 in technology and mathematics, 7 out of 40 in natural sciences, and 17 out of the remaining 33. Only 50 percent of the women who passed the entrance examination in medicine have been allowed to attend. Women have been banned from all four fields of agriculture. In the faculties of letters and humanities, only 10 of 35 courses are available to women, and women are not allowed to study archaeology, the restoration of historic monuments, handicrafts, graphics, visual communications, or cinematography. They are banned from the central Art Institute. In industrial design, there is the maximum quota of 20 percent women. In most fields, women are denied scholarships and not allowed to leave Iran for postgraduate study.

Segregation extends to women's representation in the arts, even in cultural products that have traditionally placed women at the center. During the first six years of the revolution, no actress played in an Iranian film because the authorities often refuse to approve films with women. In the five movies presented in the Fajr Festival of 1988, women were portrayed as second-class citizens.[7] Iranian women athletes were not allowed to participate in the Olympic games in Barcelona in 1992. In the opening ceremonies, the authorities forbade even a non-Iranian woman to carry the placard with the name of Iran.

The veil and the Islamic dress code are central to the segregation of women. In an effort to confine women to the home, Khomeini declared that the 1936 authorization of freedom of dress for women was null and void, and that the veil and Islamic attire (*Chador*) were compulsory for women. "From now on," he declared on March 6, 1979, "women have no right to be present in the governmental administration naked. They can carry on their tasks provided they use Islamic dress." Many women attempted to demonstrate, but mercenaries were brought in to suppress the demonstrations.

In April 1991, the Office of Disciplinary Forces for Greater Tehran, which is run by the Guardians of the Islamic Revolution, issued a communiqué in which all traders and shopkeepers were asked not to sell goods to women who were not wearing full Islamic attire, and shopkeepers and people responsible for government offices, hospitals, cinemas, and other public places were asked to keep such women from entering their premises. Women became subject to searches at the entrances to government offices to see if they had cosmetics or thin stockings, and, if so, were usually arrested. According to the Iranian News Agency (IRNA) and to Reuters cables, on two days alone (the 22nd and 23rd of April 1991) the Guardians of the Islamic Revolution Komitehs, along with other forces such as the "RAD" and "TAEMIN," arrested eight hundred women for nonobservance of the dress code.[8]

In 1986, special camps had been established for women caught not observing the dress code. It became normal procedure for Revolutionary Guards to collect women from the streets and then take them to the Committees, where the women usually had to blackmail the guards (often for exorbitant amounts) if they didn't wish to be subjected to ill treatment. Only then were the women dispatched to the camps.

Clause number 102 of the Islamic Penal Code now provides that the penalty for women who do not adhere to the dress code is between 34 and 74 lashes with a whip. But the actual penalties are much more varied. There are cash penalties for the use of lipstick (2,000 Rials), for the use of rouge (1,500 Rials), for showing one's hair (10,000 Rials), for putting on transparent stockings (3,000 Rials), and for open cloak buttons (4,000 Rials). But, just as commonly, women who do not adhere to the dress code are punished with acts of extreme cruelty: their feet may be put in a gunny sack full of mice and cockroaches, their faces splashed with acid or cut with razor blades.

These are not rare or eccentric penalties, but have been enacted with great frequency. Even in a town as small as Roudsar in Northern Iran, a woman's face was severely slashed in public. A thirteen-year-old girl named Sara Vafaie committed suicide by throwing herself out of the fifth floor window of the building in which she had been trying to hide from the *Bassijis* (authorities responsible for enforcing the dress code). On August 15, 1991, the Prosecutor-General, Abolfazl Musavi-Tabrizi declared that "anyone who rejects the principle of the *Hijab* [dress code] is an apostate and the punishment for apostasy under Islamic law is death."[9]

It is considered meritorious to rape women prisoners, especially virgin girls (who will thereby be barred from heaven), whether they are imprisoned for violating the dress code or have been accused more generally of being against the regime. This is regular practice, and often takes place as a punishment in public, sometimes in front of children. A woman who was arrested in 1981 for allegedly being a Mohahedin sympathizer was imprisoned for two-and-a-half years, during which time she was raped repeatedly and so severely that she had to be hospitalized for a year and a half and undergo surgery for intestinal damage.[10] The wife of a leader of the Organization of Revolutionary Workers of Iran was reportedly arrested in 1983 and sentenced to ten years in prison; her son, who was six months old at the time of the arrest, remained in prison with his mother until he reached school age.[11] In 1991, a woman was stoned to death after having been accused of having relations with a Guardian of the Islamic Revolution.[12] In another case, a woman was arrested after refusing the sexual advances of the prison Procurator; in prison, she was flogged and forced to witness the torture of other prisoners.[13] On June 15, 1991, in a street near Vali-Ahd-Place, several women were reportedly shot by Revolutionary Guards for protesting against the obligation to wear Islamic dress.[14]

There are also, of course, cases in which women are summarily executed without an explicitly gender-specific reason. Sussan Hosseinzadeh-Arabi, for instance, was detained in 1981 (at the age of nineteen) in Rasht, the city of her birth, and executed there eight years later without having had a trial. Mahin Jahangiri was imprisoned in 1981 (at the age of twenty-six) and, after a little over a month in prison, executed without trial.[15] Thousands and thousands of women have been imprisoned, flogged, shot, hanged, or stoned to death under invented charges (accused of offending against Islam and Allah) and in accordance with the religious judicial system.

Resistance would seem to be impossible. On July 26, 1991 in downtown Isfahan, for instance, the Revolutionary Guards harassed, beat, and arrested a group of women on the charge that they were improperly veiled. A number of people attempted to free the women from the Guards, but they were shot and wounded, and 355 people were arrested. Opposition and disobedience became so widespread that suppressing it was named the first priority for the policy makers of the National Security Council of the clerical regime.

Yet women continue to resist, both passively and actively, individually and in groups. We Iranian women know that we are equal to men (politically, economically, and socially), and we are determined to bring back our historic rights and to safeguard them despite ever-increasing pressures. The most important result of the repression and degradation of women is that women have become more alert and better organized and learned how to fight for their freedom and rights both within the family and in society. In spite of all the barbarity, women in Iran have not stopped challenging the regime. Aware of our duties, inspired by our thousand-year-old history, we will continue our fight.

Notes

1. Draft resolution presented to the *Majlis* (Islamic Parliament) in May 1991. Although unmarried women are legally permitted to travel, in practice the authorities create serious obstacles, particularly for female students who have won scholarships to study abroad.

2. The Constitution of the Islamic Republic of Iran mentions nothing about the equality of men and women, and Article 19, which deals with other issues of equality, is silent when it comes to gender. Where Article 20 asserts the equality of men and women, that equality is identified as contingent on the observance of Islamic Canon Law. Article 115 states that the President of the country should be elected a man out of all God-fearing and dedicated men, excluding women from the rank not only of President but also of *Vali-e-Faghih* (leader of a muslim nation). Article 163 specifies that women are not qualified to be judges.

3. Ministry of Culture and Islamic Guidance, report. My principal sources are: the report of the Special Representative of the Commission of Human Rights of the United Nations to the Islamic Republic of Iran (UN Doc. E/CN.4/1992/34, Geneva, 2 January 1992); official newspapers (the *Salam, Ettelaat, Resalat,* and *Kayhan*); independent newspapers (the *Iran Tribune Journal,* the *International Herald Tribune*); and reports in the House of Representatives of Iran.

4. Ayatollah Mutahari, "The Question of the Veil."

5. *Resalat* (official newspaper), June 23, 1986.

6. There are now 16 million people in Iran who are not literate, of whom 5.7 million are men and 10.3 million are women. Of rural Iranian women, 89 percent are illiterate, according to the 1992 report of the Special Representative of the United Nations Commission of Human Rights.

7. *Kayhan* (official newspaper), March 21, 1987. Ministry of Culture and Islamic Guidance.

8. Rinaldo Galindo Pohl, Special Representative of the United Nations Commission on Human Rights in the Islamic Republic of Iran, report of January 2, 1992, cites cables between April 22 and April 29th.

9. Ibid.

10. Ibid., p. 17.

11. Ibid., p. 23.

12. Ibid., p. 17.

13. Ibid., p. 17.

14. Ibid., p. 21.

15. Ibid., p. 22.

9

"Help Me Balance the Load": Gender Discrimination in Kenya

Koki Muli

Mbaikye in the Kamba language means "help me balance the load." When I was growing up in the rural parts of Kenya, I often heard women ask each other, "*Mbaikye.*" Women would never ask men. I grew up thinking it a taboo to ask a man to balance your load, and one day I asked my grandmother whether this was the case. She told me that men merely treat it as a taboo.

Even where Kenyan law bars discrimination, traditional practice accepts and tolerates the inferior position of women. Chapter 5, section 70 of the Kenyan Constitution guarantees fundamental human rights and freedoms to every individual irrespective of her/his race, tribe, place of origin residence or other local connection, political opinion, color, creed, or sex. But section 82, which prohibits the enactment of any law that is discriminatory either in itself or in its effect, defines discrimination in all other contexts except that of gender or sex. The failure to proscribe discrimination based on gender is a significant omission in the Constitution. This silence ensures that, where such gender discrimination occurs, no existing law can challenge it. As a result, attempts to remove discriminatory laws in Kenya have proven impossible.

For instance, in both 1976 and 1979, a male-dominated parliament rejected the Marriage Bill, which would have given women equal status with men in matters relating to marriage and divorce.[1] Of the four systems of family law in Kenya (Christian or statutory, Hindu, Islamic, and African customary), two allow male polygamy (but not female). Where bigamy and adultery are crimes, they are rarely subject to prosecution. Under African customary law, marriages are not registered, and where parties must prove the existence of the marriage, they often have to swear affidavits in order to do so.

Because African customary law gives the man a decisive advantage over the woman, many middle- and upper-class men prefer to marry under customary law, or to enter into what is commonly known as "trial marriage." If the trial marriage works to the man's satisfaction, the decision to convert it to Christian or statutory marriage is left solely to his discretion.

Under African customary law, in many types of marriage the woman is not necessarily a consenting party. Often, in Islamic, Hindu, and African customary marriages, the parents of both parties arrange the marriage. Girls are still married off to generate income to educate the male family members. The payment of dowry for the bride, central to African customary and Islamic marriages and widely practiced in Christian statutory marriages, means that husbands regard their wives as part of their property. Under section 91 of the Constitution, a Kenyan man who marries a foreigner is able to pass on his citizenship to his foreign wife, but a Kenyan woman who marries a foreigner cannot do the same.

While a husband can sue his wife for adultery, the wife cannot similarly sue her husband. The husband also has the right to "discipline" his wife under customary law, which often means serious domestic violence. If reported, such violence—illegal, but widely tolerated—is usually treated as the husband's prerogative. When women are raped, whether in marriage or outside of it, the law treats them not as victims but as prosecution witnesses on whom the burden of proof lies. Women who report domestic violence of any kind to the police are often sent home to fetch their husbands. Women who attempt to take legal action are likely to be deserted, which means losing their means of subsistence and hence of providing for their children.

Divorce under both African customary and Islamic laws can be extrajudicial; one party can unilaterally bring about the divorce without any requirement that a court hear the dispute. While officially gender neutral, the result is de facto discrimination against women, who have no recourse to independent hearings of their cases. In the case of divorce, women married under Islamic and African customary laws are almost never entitled to marital property and are rarely provided with a maintenance. After the breakup of a marriage, a woman is usually left with little more than her personal belongings and is expected to return to her father's care.

The persistence of customary law in many rural parts of Kenya means that only a few middle- and upper-class women can own property. In a system in which property ownership is the only way to acquire more property, women generally lack tangible security with which to secure loans from banks and other financial institutions in order to buy property. The Registration of Titles Act is still largely based on the African customary system of land ownership, in which only a man and his family or clan own land in the area in which they live. Only under very special circumstances can women have land registered under their names. And while women constitute 80 percent of the labor force in the agricultural sector, which is the mainstay of Kenya's economy, extension services, financial credit, and farming technology are all geared toward men. All payments from cash crops are made to land-owners: men.

The domestic services of housewives are not quantified in monetary terms or counted as part of a woman's contribution toward the purchase of matrimonial property. Such work (let alone physical, emotional, and moral support) is not recognized under the law as a contribution to the welfare of the home or the matrimonial property, and the fact that a woman may have resigned from paid employment to work for the family is considered irrelevant. As the majority of women are employed in the informal and often nonremunerative sector, legislation still fails to protect them.

The Employment Act of 1969 is regarded as the core of Kenya's labor legislation. While the law may appear gender neutral, in fact sections of it tend to discriminate against women in employment. Section 28 prohibits the employment of women and children between the hours of 6:30 p.m. and 6:30 a.m., for instance, and prohibits women from working in mines or underground. Section 56 gives the Minister of Labor free power to prohibit the employment of women in any trade or occupation he (and it is always a he) might choose to specify. Married men, under the Act, are entitled to house allowances (for payment of rent), but married women are not.

Eighty percent of Kenya's population live in rural areas; more than half of that percentage are women. This is because most men have moved to cities and towns to work or look for paid employment. When the men move to the cities, they rarely come back to stay in the rural areas, except perhaps when they retire. Women are left behind to take care of children and household, some receiving little support from their husbands and others none at all. They engage in agricultural activities to generate food and money. In areas where the land is fertile and the climate good, people grow cash crops as well as subsistence food crops. In areas where cash crops are grown, the men who have not migrated to the cities form a high percentage of the farmers.

Women do most of the farming; men do most of the marketing. In less fertile areas, women mostly do subsistence farming and keep domestic animals, and often need to supplement their incomes by working as agricultural laborers, keeping chickens for sale, or brewing traditional beer.

The commercialization of land and labor, and the preference given to men by the government in a variety of distributive functions, have, on the whole, marginalized women even further. But such marginalization has meant the growth of women's groups throughout Kenya, which have found ways of confronting economic and social powerlessness. They have promoted access to land use (even though the groups may not be able to own land), dug wells, contributed money to buy and install storage tanks to preserve water and prevent soil erosion, planted trees and grass, dug gullies, and taught one another better methods of farming. They have grouped themselves for income-generating activities: growing trees in nurseries, cutting and selling firewood, making and selling pottery and handicrafts, keeping and selling poultry and the products of domestic animals. The money earned is shared; given to members as loans; used for small projects like building a nursery school, clinic, church, dispensary, or social/community hall; used for adult education (agricultural training, formal education for the illiterate, education in the law and rights, political process); or used in larger enterprises like public housing or public transportation. Although women in rural areas have organized themselves in progressive self-help groups to better their lives and those of their daughters, there is still a long way to go toward redefining power relations in the family structure, in the equalization of access (to educational resources, information, economic strategies, and decision-making bodies), and in the de-schooling of the mind. There is a long way to go before the load is balanced.

Note

1. *Weekly Review* (August 1991), the source of some of the statistics and other data in this essay.

10

Women's Human Rights in the United States: An Immigrant's Perspective

Ilka Tanya Payan

The United States is known as the land of opportunity, replete with educational and economic possibilities, unlimited freedom, and the full protection of civil and human rights and liberties. The United States also likes to be known as the world's watchdog and considers itself exempt from human rights monitoring.

As we reach the end of the millennium, it is true that most U.S. laws are technically nondiscriminatory, including some that specifically provide for the protection of human rights as understood in the *International Covenant on Civil and Political Rights*. There are, however, glaring exceptions: the death penalty (permitted in some states), which is administered inequitably and which may be applied even to the mentally retarded and to those who were underage at the time their capital crimes were committed; the absence of freedom of expression and association for homosexuals in the military.

But the official story that all may partake of the plethora of economic and educational opportunities does not match the reality of their radically unequal distribution. The promise of equal protection under the law does not match the reality of the ways economic, ethnic, and gender differentials determine the quality of legal representation that defendants receive, their opportunities for bail, and the length of time they must serve. It does not match the reality of the ways such differentials result in the low rates of prosecution of rape and domestic violence or the absence of full police protection in poorer urban areas. If one were to monitor such areas in the United States for violation of the *Covenant on Economic, Social and Cultural Rights,* which the United States has ratified, the United States would be found to be a serious violator, with, for instance, high malnutrition, illiteracy, and unemployment rates. That the United States has failed to ratify the *Conven-*

tion on the Elimination of All Forms of Racial Discrimination, the *Convention Relating to the Status of Refugees,* or the *Convention on the Elimination of All Forms of Discrimination Against Women* is merely one indicator of the failures of the government to offer full human rights protection.[1]

Women and children are the primary victims of this failure. Since the 1980s, the Equal Protection Clause of the 14th Amendment ("No state shall . . . deny to any person within its jurisdiction the equal protection of the laws . . .") may have been used to bar discrimination against women, but the country still refuses to pass the *Equal Rights Amendment,* which would officially grant women equal rights under the Constitution.[2] Little has been done (except in the most privileged milieus) to rectify not only the long history of discrimination against women in the United States but also the intensification of gender differentials in situations of economic hardship.

It is easy to forget that women were granted the franchise in the United States as late as 1920, which means that some women alive today could not legally vote when they reached the age of majority.[3] It is easy to forget that it was only in the 1970s that Congress began to pass laws against sex discrimination in education; that Title IX of the *Civil Rights Act* of 1964, which forbids sex discrimination in public schools, specifically allowed several forms of discrimination when it was initially passed in 1972; and that the *Equal Educational Opportunities Act* of 1974 failed to mention deliberate segregation by sex.[4] It is easy to overlook the fact that, although Title IV of the *Civil Rights Act* allows the U.S. Attorney General to sue schools and colleges for sex discrimination policies,[5] the Attorney General has rarely done so. Most of all, it is easy for those men and women privileged with education and opportunity to forget the nearly insurmountable cultural barriers against which most women in the United States must struggle if they are to reach the level at which they might begin to benefit from the equal protection of the law.

This struggle is intensified in the case of immigrant women like me. During my childhood in the Dominican Republic, surrounded by my grandmother, two sisters, and (during summers) by my father's nine other daughters, his wife, and his mistress, men were nearly invisible. We lived in a world of women, but not a woman's world: we had all the responsibilities and knew nothing of rights. My grandmother, who had raised me and my sisters from infancy after our mother's death (supporting us by distributing milk to the poor and by selling home-made pastries, lottery tickets, and gasoline from her house), believed that in New York, where my uncle and aunt lived, we could get a better education and be guaranteed a better economic future. In 1956, at the age of thirteen, I began my journey into "America"—a world of myriad opportunities and endless possibilities, though not for a thirteen-year-old immigrant Latina with limited English skills.

I soon realized that my eighth-grade public school education in the Dominican Republic had been superior to that which I was receiving in the ninth grade at New York City's George Washington High School. In the Dominican Republic, I had had courses in chemistry, physics, zoology, world history, civics, biology, anatomy, trigonometry, and English. In New York, I learned the names of automobile parts and how corn is grown and harvested. Geography and geometry classes covered material I had studied in the third and fourth grades; my Spanish teacher spoke the language poorly, and English classes were elementary, even for me.

When, at fourteen, I began to show an interest in boys, my uncle taught me to drink liquor so that I would not be seduced without my consent. That was the only form of sex education I received. There was no discussion of contraception, either in school or at home, although there was a great deal of talk of the holiness of virginity and marriage. The condom (as word or object) was taboo.

In my junior year of high school, when the students were asked to select a specific course of study that, we were told, would determine our futures, my teacher and uncle urged me to choose a secretarial, rather than an academic or general, diploma since, as I was reminded, I was a Spanish girl whose family needed my financial help, and who would eventually get married anyway. As a role model, I was to look to my cousin, a bilingual secretary with Hoover Vacuum Cleaners; surely I could do as well as she had.

Indeed I did, despite the fact that I had stubbornly insisted on getting an academic diploma. To my frustration and disappointment, however, I was unable to enter college, as I could not afford tuition. In order to enroll at the tuition-free City College of New York, resident aliens like me were required to file with the Immigration and Naturalization Service sworn statements of our intention to become U.S. citizens. But becoming a citizen would mean I would no longer be Dominican so, as an act of patriotism, I went to work as a salesgirl at Woolworth's. During the next eighteen years, I supported myself, my grandmother for a time, my two sisters, and my daughter (after her birth in 1964) by working at various secretarial jobs.

As a bilingual executive secretary at The *New York Times*—in reality performing the duties of top salesmen in the international advertising department—my repeated requests to join the sales force (which had only one woman on it) were ignored. I was still in a world of women, and still had no notion of rights. No one had ever mentioned to me the existence of Title VII of the *Civil Rights Act,* the *Equal Pay Act,* the *Age Discrimination Act* of 1967. Without education, I had no access to equal protection.

The women's movement has, particularly since the 1970s, helped to transform sex discrimination laws, eliminating many of the earlier discriminatory provisions in areas like education, credit, and housing. These are important advances. But they are not enough to combat the more subtle (but perhaps more insidious) failure to ensure basic equal rights for all women: in education and employment, in credit and housing, in family law. While there have been some major attacks on discriminatory employment practices, and while meaningful and better-paid positions have opened up for some women, women continue to be largely confined to the lower rungs of the employment ladder. It is not merely that women are still paid less than men for doing the same work but that, for the most part, women do not *do* the work that men do. The number of women in Congress may have increased in 1993 (though it is still far short of the 52 percent that would constitute proportional representation), but most women hold lower-level and hence badly paid jobs. The mere granting of equal pay for equal work will not touch these women's lives.

If *all* women in the United States are to enjoy equal rights, judges and legislators must take seriously both national civil rights legislation and the equal rights provisions in the human rights treaties we have ratified. They must require employers to integrate jobs, increase the wage levels of traditionally "female" (and hence undervalued) jobs—including those in the domestic sector (childcare, housework, care for the aged, and so on) for which workers must be granted the same benefits as workers in the nondomestic sector.

If my personal history gave me experience of educational and employment discrimination, it also gave me experience of de facto discrimination in housing, family law, and credit, which occurs even when such discrimination is formally illegal. To elaborate: since my own public-school education had been abysmal, I was determined to send my daughter to private school. To do so on my secretary's salary (which barely sufficed to cover food and rent, and included only meager benefits), we had to live in a "poor" neighborhood. When I sought a subsidized apartment, I found that there were gender-based restrictions on the number of rooms available to families. While a mother and son would be given a two-bedroom apartment, a mother and daughter would get a one-bedroom apartment. On paper the law was gender neutral: opposite-sex parents and children would be given two-bedroom apartments, same-sex parents and children one-bedroom apartments. What the law failed to recognize was that, since many more women than men are below the poverty level, and a still larger proportion are heads of single-parent households, families with girls were likely to be crammed into far smaller quarters than families with boys.

I lied on the housing application, and Genevieve Gazon, my daughter, became "Gene" Gazon, my son. No one expected my ex-husband to have any part in caring for our daughter. Although he had been ordered to pay a measly 50 Dominican pesos ($50 U.S.) in child support, after nine years of nonpayment there was no mechanism in place that would force him to pay. At one point, when my daughter went to live with him in the Dominican Republic (because at the time I could no longer afford her private school education), he sent her back after three months.

The rent for our subsidized apartment was actually higher than that for our previous apartment, and without child support or a high-paying (read: "male") job, I could not get a loan to pay for my daughter's education. The *Equal Credit Opportunity Act* of 1974 made it officially illegal arbitrarily to deny credit to women. But, without education myself, I had no knowledge of the Act and, even if I had, it might not have helped me, since creditors' prejudices continue to make it more difficult for women than for men to obtain credit and more difficult still for poor women who are heads of household. To obtain a tuition loan to pay for my daughter's schooling, I lied again, this time inflating my salary.

These experiences helped motivate me to learn about the law in order to protect myself and others from such discrimination. With neither money nor an undergraduate degree, I was able to register only at the unaccredited, tuition-free People's College of Law. I received my J.D. and passed the California bar in 1981, and was admitted to a U.S. District Court and a U.S. Appeals Court.

Also in 1981, the year I turned thirty-nine, my health was compromised, unbeknownst to me. After graduation, the summer before taking the bar exam, I was exposed to the HIV virus, which I did not discover until five years later. As an immigrant woman living with HIV, I have a profound personal investment in my professional dealings with complex political issues: restrictions on immigrants with AIDS; the lack of proper education about and services for HIV-positive women; discrimination against women in health care generally. The lack of funding for research in women's diseases, for instance, or the relatively fewer hospital resources committed to women's care are further instances of the ways in which government policies and social norms do not come close to promoting the Constitution's guarantee of equal protection for women.

I question why it still seems so difficult for women in this country, especially women with limited resources, to achieve any visible, meaningful levels of equality in, for example, government, the military, financial institutions, scientific institutions—those entities that invariably determine the policies that shape our lives and the lives of our children. Are we women too timid to aspire to the promises of the Constitution, to demand full liberty and equality, to engage in "the pursuit of happiness"? If we consider women's rights to be *human* rights, then we must work to make the reality of our lives match the ideals laid out by the rights standards that international law extends to all human beings.

Notes

1. The United States, of course, tends to attack other countries (with some justification) for cynically ratifying conventions with which they have no intention of complying. The U.S. failure to ratify is usually attributed to the seriousness with which it treats the covenants and the fear of incompatibilities between them and states' laws. But one would expect, then, that, in order to move U.S. law toward conformity with international norms, legislators and judges would invoke the covenants in the formulation of U.S. law or the rendering of decisions—a very rare occurrence.

2. The *Equal Rights Amendment,* which proclaimed that "equality of rights under the law shall not be denied or abridged by the United States, or by any State on account of sex," was first proposed in 1923, gained political momentum, was approved by Congress in 1972, and was sent to the states for ratification. But by 1982, it had failed to be ratified by the necessary thirty-eight states.

3. Not only were women denied the right to vote, but some laws created separate and unequal status for the married woman. In 1848, such laws were condemned at the first Women's Rights Convention of Seneca Falls, New York, but it was not until seventy years later that the 19th Amendment to the Constitution was ratified, granting women the franchise.

4. *Education Amendments of 1972 Act* (200 U.S.C. & 1681 et seq.) According to Susan Deller Ross and Ann Brucher, "each of these laws [against sex discrimination] suffers from some defect." See *The Rights of Women,* rev. ed. (New York: Bantam, 1993).

5. *1964 Civil Rights Act,* 42 U.S.C. section 2000c–6.

11

Women in Israel: Fighting Tradition

Carmel Shalev

The Declaration of the Establishment of the State of Israel in 1948
stated its commitment to "freedom, justice and peace" and to "complete equality of social and political rights to all its inhabitants, irrespective of religion, race or sex." Indeed, for several decades the common
understanding was that gender equality prevailed in Israeli society,
exemplified by (the myth of) women's equal participation in *kibbutz*
life, the drafting of women into the military, and the token figurehead
of Golda Meir as Prime Minister. As elsewhere in the world, however,
recent years have brought a change of consciousness and an unveiling of
the reality of Israeli women's lives.[1] The universal issues of gender—the
unequal distribution of political, economic, and physical power—
appear in local form: the underrepresentation of women in governmental, political, and financial decision-making bodies; segregation in the
workplace, the devaluation of women's labor, and the feminization
of poverty; the bodily abuse of women and their subordination through
domestic violence, rape, sexual harassment, and pornography.

The gap between the ideology of equality and the reality of gender
may be explained best by what Wendy Williams has called "the cultural
limits of the equality principle."[2] At certain points we may find that
the idea of equality is unpalatable to ordinary people, beyond the pale
of consensus. These are the raw nerves of the social construction of
sex that, when tickled, arouse ridicule; the primal roots of gender roles
that, when exposed, invoke a protest of incredulity and irritation.

The agenda for the advancement of gender equality in contemporary
Israel can be gleaned from topics of recent legislation. In 1991, a
domestic violence act was introduced, providing for immediate court
separation orders to protect the victim of violence, even if other matrimonial proceedings have been initiated. In 1992, the income tax ordinance was amended, substituting an optional gender-neutral taxation

model for the old male-breadwinner, head-of-household model; a social welfare act for single-parent families was passed; and employers were required to continue payment of certain employment benefits during the period of statutory maternity leave. 1993 saw the precedent-setting enactment of affirmative action legislation with regard to the appointment of members of boards of directors in government-owned corporations; private health plans were subjected to an antidiscrimination standard and required to extend coverage to physical injury resulting from domestic violence and sexual and other assault; and a parental right to be absent from work in case of a child's sickness was recognized.

Current legislative initiatives address various issues, including affirmative action mechanisms to increase women's political representation within a state-financed party system, comparable pay for labor of comparable worth, and minimum sentencing standards and special testimonial proceedings in crimes of sexual violence. Finally, it is worth mentioning an initiative to establish a governmental agency vested with appropriate powers and resources to oversee the enforcement of existing laws that ensure gender equality.

Yet none of these advances touch upon the cultural limits to equality that are specific to contemporary Israeli society. All the initiatives mentioned above mean incremental progress for women's human rights. But there are two matters in which the very possibility of rational discourse and debate is limited: women in the military, and the religious law pertaining to marriage and divorce.

In Israel, women's conscription in the military, like men's, is mandated by statute.[3] Unlike men, however, women are excluded from combat and the more prestigious military occupations, and the statute prescribes a double standard with respect to the age of conscription, length of service, and the right to adult education. In addition, exemptions from the draft are sex differentiated, so that married women, pregnant women, and mothers are completely exempted from regular service as well as from reserve duty. The result is that, despite the universal draft, the army as an institution is central to perpetuating traditional sex roles.

Its double standard, of course, stems from a worldview ordaining the primal division of labor between the male warrior and the female childbearer. Thus, secondary legislation contains a list of occupations to which female soldiers may be assigned (often secretarial and decorative positions, or social work)[4] which corresponds to the traditional model of women in the service of men. Although the rules state that a woman may volunteer for any other occupation, in actuality this is not the case; for example, women may not gain admission to pilot training in the Air Force.[5] Following the recommendations of a 1978 Commission on the Status of Women, more occupations have been opened gradually to women, but many are still closed even to volunteers.

Not surprisingly, the privileges accorded to women in the form of special treatment have a detrimental effect. Women's shorter term of service is often invoked to justify their exclusion from occupations requiring fairly long training periods. The leadership and vocational opportunities available to male soldiers are not available to women, and exclusion from combat creates a glass ceiling that obstructs the advancement of women who choose a military career. In all of Israel, there is not one woman with the rank of general (which requires field-operations experience). Young men are expected to sacrifice their lives in the defense of their country, but young women must be protected from rape and sexual torture in captivity. The relatively inferior position of women in the military means that they would seem dispensable were a universal draft no longer necessary. In a country where the military serves as a finishing school, where army veterans are compensated economically for their years of service (e.g., in housing loans and job placement), and where military experience can be a springboard into key positions in civilian, financial, and political life, women would pay a heavy long-term price for their exemption from the draft.

A correlation between militarism and pronatalism is historically evident.[6] In Israel, demographic concerns related to the collective trauma of the Holocaust (as well as to the statistics of population growth among Arabs in Israel and surrounding countries) connect with a Jewish tradition of strong family ties. Voluntary childlessness is virtually nonexistent in Israeli society, which boasts the highest per capita consumption of reproductive technology. For historical reasons, the laws of marriage and divorce—the very constitution of the family—are governed by religious law and custom and administered by religious courts: Jewish law for Jews, Islamic law for Moslems, and Christian law for Christians. This legal scheme was inherited from the Ottoman Empire's nineteenth-century policy of nonintervention in local traditions and of preserving multireligious autonomy,[7] but it adds another layer of apparently unquestionable patriarchy to Israel's legal and social culture.

For example, the world according to Jewish law (*halakha*) is divided into two spheres, the public and the private. Man's place is in the public sphere of political government and the market economy, while woman's place is in the private sphere of domesticity. This is dictated by woman's fragile nature as well as by the imperative of female modesty. Thus, according to the *halakha,* women are disqualified from becoming rabbis. And since only rabbis may officiate at marriages and sit as judges on the rabbinical courts (*dayanim*) in cases of divorce, women subsequently are incompetent, under Israeli law, to fill such public functions. The same applies to women in Moslem and Christian communities.

Furthermore, the substantive Jewish laws of marriage and divorce are pervaded by a double standard that is patently discriminatory. The woman's role in the ceremonies of both marriage and divorce is wholly passive. While the matrimonial relation defines separate duties and rights that ostensibly balance each other, it is the wife who owes a duty of obedience to the husband. Divorce is a legal act of the couple rather than a *res judicata,* as in civil systems, except that the power of the husband to bind the woman to the marriage is greater than that of the woman because of the unequal consequences of adultery. If, on remarriage, there is any doubt as to whether the former husband consented freely to the divorce, the court may consider the marriage not to have been dissolved, and the wife may be considered to have committed adultery.

Under biblical law, the rule of monogamy applied only to women, whereas men were entitled to practice polygamy. A rabbinical decree in the eleventh century applied the standard of monogamy to men, but for them the consequences of diverting from that standard are less severe. Thus, even today, if a wife refuses to grant her husband a divorce or is incompetent to do so, the husband might be given special permission to marry another woman. On the other hand, if it is the husband who refuses the divorce, the woman remains bound in marriage. The differentiated consequences of adultery are especially important. First, the child of an adulterous woman is punished, by the stigma of bastardy (*mamzerut*), for her mother's sin. Such a child may not marry a Jew, nor may her offspring for ten generations. Since there is no civil marriage in Israel, she is thus effectively excommunicated from Jewish society. Second, the adulterous woman herself is sanctioned twice: on the one hand, her husband may not continue to live with her and must divorce her; on the other hand, she is forbidden to marry her lover. Hence, the grave predicament of the *agunah* (the woman who is unable to get a divorce because her husband arbitrarily refuses to grant it, or has abandoned her and disappeared, or is simply incompetent), who is prevented from rehabilitating herself by establishing another family.[9] Since divorce is not possible, in effect, without mutual consent, and since the juridical weight of the husband's will is heavier than the wife's, his bargaining position in the divorce negotiations is stronger than hers. In other words, she is more vulnerable to extortion and to the threat of his arbitrary refusal to grant a divorce.[10]

Because of the religious law of marriage and divorce, Israel signed the 1979 *Convention on the Elimination of All Forms of Discrimination Against Women* with reservation as to Article 16, under which states parties undertake to eliminate discrimination against women in all matters relating to marriage and family relations. The inequality of religious law in this respect has also been one of the major obstacles to the enactment of a comprehensive bill of human rights. Despite the existence of a strong and clear constitutional jurisprudence of individual liberties in case law, a charter of rights is considered essential to the consolidation of a written constitution.

In 1992 two chapters were added to the project of piecemeal basic legislation—"Basic Law: Human Dignity and Liberty," and "Basic Law: Freedom of Occupation"—introducing for the first time a mechanism for the judicial review of ordinary legislation. A 1993 attempt to complete the list of rights thus guaranteed constitutional protection floundered in face of a stormy debate surrounding the principle of equality and the proposed proviso that its inclusion would "not affect any legal prohibition or permission relating to marriage or divorce."[11] Feminists of different strains took the position that a notion of equality that excluded the family would be not only false but also damaging. Legitimation of the hegemony of religious marriage and divorce in a constitutional document would entrench the discriminatory patterns of gender, undermining the fabric of justice and fairness in the most fundamental of human relations.[12]

Of course, the force of tradition is such that its cultural customs are not merely tolerated for the most part but also embraced with nostalgic affection. For most people, the fantasy of wedding white probably overrides feminist discomfort with religious divorce law. Given that constitutional changes rely upon a broadly based consensus, cultural limits on equality reinforce the status quo.

A recent Israeli Supreme Court decision on women's right to religious worship provides a nice metaphor for those cultural limits.[13] Two groups of women wished to hold prayer services at the Western Wall, reading from the *torah* scroll and wearing traditional prayer shawls. The official in charge (on behalf of the Ministry of Religious Affairs) refused to permit them to do so, claiming that it would deviate from the custom of the place. The petitioners were also labelled "provocateurs," because they had arrived on several occasions in organized form singing out loud, and they were blamed for the somewhat violent reaction of orthodox men and women who objected to "the violation of their feelings."[14] The Supreme Court dismissed the women's petition for permission to exercise their freedom of religious worship and of expression, recommending that the government establish a commission to examine the matter in depth and reach a solution that would simultaneously uphold freedom of access to the Wall and minimize offense to religious feelings.

No provision in religious law actually prohibits the conduct of the petitioners: there was no attempt to challenge the segregation of male and female worshippers at the Wall. Yet the appearance of women organized as a group to pray out loud in a public and holy place was taken by the religious authorities as an outrageous act of rebellion and a usurpation of the male claim to exclusive communion with the sacred powers. The Supreme Court failed to condemn the restriction of the petitioners' liberty, probably because there was a lack of consensus about the seriousness of their claim to equality. For most people, it seemed an absurdity; the symbolic meaning of the claim was lost at the outer limits of the culture. But this is precisely where radical actions and ideas emerge to point the way to the possibility of a different world.

Notes

1. See *Calling the Equality Bluff: Women in Israel*, edited by Barbara Swirski and Marilyn Safir (New York: Teacher's College Press, 1993).

2. Wendy Williams, "The Equality Crisis: Some Reflections on Culture, Courts and Feminism," *Women's Rights Law Reporter* 7 (1982): 175.

3. The *Defence Service Law* (Consolidated Version), 5746–1986.

4. The *Defence Service (Women's Occupations in Regular Service) Regulations*, 5712–1952.

5. A recent amendment to the *Defence Service Law* inadvertently removed the statutory authorization to digress in secondary legislation from the principle of equality and to differentiate between male and female soldiers. As a result, the exclusion of women from occupations for which they are personally qualified might well be challengeable in court. This could instigate a reevaluation of the role of women in the military.

6. See *Behind the Lines: Gender and the Two World Wars*, edited by Higonnet, Margaret R, and Jane Jenson, Sonya Michel, and Margaret C. Weitz (New Haven, CT: Yale Univ. Press, 1987).

7. Nor did the rule of the British Mandate intervene in this scheme. See sections 47 to 65 of the *Palestine Order in Council,* 1922.

8. Section 2 of the *Marriage and Divorce (Registration) Ordinance,* 1919. Section 3 of the *Dayanim* Law, 5715–1955.

9. This predicament does not apply only in cases of adultery; no matter how long or for what reason they have been separated, if a husband refuses to sign a *get* (divorce document), his wife will never be free to remarry.

10. See for example, Pnina Lahav, "The Status of Women in Israel—Myth and Reality," *Am J Comp L* 22(107) (1974): 119–124.

11. Cf. section 5 of the *Women's Equal Rights Law,* 5711–1951.

12. Cf. Susan Moller Okin, *Justice, Gender and the Family* (Basic Books 1989).

13. HC 257/89, 2410/90 *Hoffman et al. v. Officer of the Western Wall,* judgment delivered on January 26, 1994.

14. Note that section 2 of the *Protection of Holy Places Law,* 5727–1967 makes it a criminal offence to do "anything likely to violate the freedom of access of the members of the different religions to the places sacred to them or their feelings with regard to those places."

12

The Testimony of Women Writers: The Situation of Women in China Today

Zhu Hong

The marriage of convenience between a market economy and the socialist state in China has borne many strange offspring, one of which is the revived and intensified degradation of women. The official press overflows with stories about women who have "made" it, about the opportunities that have opened up for women in the New Era of Reform. This phenomenon is in fact an open acknowledgement of the existing double standard: for every single successful female entrepreneur, there must be at least ten thousand male ones, yet there are no stories about men who made it, since men's success is considered the norm.

Gender images have always been used as national symbols in the discourse on China—foot-binding for the backwardness and weakness of China, rape as a symbol of foreign aggression, prostitution for the corruption of the old society before Liberation (1949) and, finally, the wiping out of prostitution and reform of prostitutes after Liberation as a symbol of the national moral regeneration under communist rule.

What is particular to women as women in the new market economy is not the market opportunities that affect men and women alike, but the revived reification of women, with prostitution again often cited as a symbol. As one report says, "Prostitution is once again an entrenched facet of urban life in many of the prosperous and free-wheeling cities along China's coast."[1] According to this report, more than 580,000 people have been detained for prostitution, which is rapidly spreading to rural areas. Another main area of abuse is widespread pornography: streets in secluded areas are often lined with publications wallowing in explicit sex and lurid illustrations, perpetuating the image of women as sex objects.

The abduction and sale of women as sex slaves is another abuse that has reached monstrous proportions. Relying mainly on officially released figures from the police or women's organizations at local levels, a report states that 48,100 women have been kidnapped from various parts of the country and sold into six counties within the municipality of Xuzhou in Jiangsu province since 1986.[2] China has about 2,000 counties.

Flagrant abuse persists in the area of reproductive rights. One of the first campaigns that swept the country after Liberation was the antiabortion campaign, in which promoters of birth control—notably President Ma Yinchu of Peking University—were denounced as ideological enemies. Thus it was that women were first denied the right to abortion then later *forced* to abort. Recently, the government announced a plan for the avoidance of undesirable births, in essence a more precisely targeted campaign for forced sterilization and abortion. Modern technology, such as the ultrasound scanner, is used for the selective abortion of female fetuses, which has led to an imbalance in the female/male ratio of births: "Last year we had only one girl born in the village—everybody else had boys," a peasant was quoted as boasting.[3] The population problem was regarded as just one of China's many crises, and little regard was given, even in the much-acclaimed critical study *Hills of China*, to how the solutions to those crises affect women.[4] Only recently, at an international conference on women's issues at Peking University, did the delegates raise the question of the physical and psychological damage caused to women by forced abortion.[5]

Under certain circumstances, China's new affluence actually reduces the status of women and deprives them of choice. For instance, according to a report in *The New York Times,* Mrs. Yang of the much-vaunted Daqiuzhuang model village "doesn't have to hold down a job because her husband makes so much money." She spends her time playing mah-jong, watching one of her three televisions, or talking on one of her two telephones.[6]

The most telling sign of gender inequality in the new era is the way women are "challenged" in the workplace. One recent study pointed out that women's ability to adapt to the market economy will determine their "survival and their relative status in the society." Figures show that in professional jobs, women employees number only half of men, while in managerial positions, the ratio of female to male is 1:9. Employment figures also show men moving more quickly into professional jobs, while increases in women's employment are overwhelmingly in agriculture and service sectors.[7] This leads to the vicious cycle of girls being taken out of school (since it is believed there is less reason to invest in their education), which in turn makes them less competitive in the job market. Thus, it is overwhelmingly women who have to endure the pains of reform. "Women's Rights—a Casualty of Reform"[8] is a recurring theme in present-day discourse; as one article put it, "With Focus on Profits, China Revives Bias Against Women."[9]

One of the positive effects of the current policy is the growing articulation of women's issues. There are many centers for women's studies in the main universities, and scholars and social workers are trying to contend with the new reality. But women writers, though they do not necessarily identify themselves as *feminist* writers, have the advantage of literary images and the unlimited possibilities of language to give the most vivid, most emotional articulation to women's problems and to reach a wide readership. Even within the limited works available in English translation, the achievement of women writers is quite impressive.

Zhang Jie's novella *The Ark* is the first work in contemporary Chinese writing to expose the patriarchal nature of Chinese society and give voice to the theme "How difficult it is to be a Woman!"[10] She describes the frustrations and humiliations of professional women, including sexual harassment on the job. In a short story called "Where did I Miss You?" Zhang Xinxin protests how male standards are imposed on women, who are then rejected by men because they are not "feminine" enough. Many writers also protest against the pressure put on women to marry.[11]

The suffering by women of forced abortions is another important subject in writing by women. Both Tang Min, in "Bearing the Unbearable,"[12] and Lu Xin'er, in "The Sun is Not Out Today,"[13] bear witness to the suffering and humiliation that women have to undergo when they are processed like objects and looked at with contempt for "unplanned" pregnancies. In her *Series on Chinese Women*, Dai Qing describes the cruelty of a society that treats rape victims as irreparably damaged goods.[14] The insistence on female chastity is an anomaly at odds with the "modern attitude" of many men. Zhang Jie's "What's Wrong With Him"[15] is a biting satire of men who demand virgin brides. Zhang describes a bridegroom who sued for divorce after missing the red spot on his wedding night: his bride

> dreamed that she had grown larger, thinner. Turned into a huge hymen, so thin it rustled in the wind. She ought to take a scalpel

and cut it into bits two centimeters square to sell to women whose husbands were no use, to guarantee that at one puff they would break. She could make a fortune that way and the divorce rate would drop.[16]

The ultimate symbol of sexual/political victimization is the writer Yu Luojin, "fallen woman" and "enemy of the state" all rolled into one. Both her parents had been labelled enemies of the state in the 1950s; and her elder brother Yu Luoke was executed as a criminal for his writings against Mao Zedong's theory of class struggle. Yu herself was in labor camp for writing "incorrect" thoughts in her diary, and ultimately had to sell herself into marriage in order to survive. After two divorces and three marriages, Yu Luojin had become the ultimate social outcast. In the autobiographical *A Chinese Winter's Tale*,[17] the account of her brother's execution by firing squad and the description of marital rape on her own wedding night are intertwined to highlight the sexual/political nature of the double outrage. The book was roundly denounced by the official press and Yu Luojin is now in political asylum in Germany.

On a more positive note, in revolt against the conventional practice of relegating women to the background, or else imaging them as the moon reflecting male glory, there is a recent upsurge of writing using the metaphor of the sun for women. Nine prominent women writers are putting together a Television series to be called *The Sun Woman* and, as a critic has pointed out, "Women's self-identification as the sun is a new consciousness" for many women in China today.[18]

Notes

1. *Washington Post,* March 12, 1992.

2. *The Sale of Women—A Factual Report,* Hong Kong, 1989, p. 13

3. Nicholas D. Kristof, "Peasants of China Discover New Way to Weed Out Girls," *New York Times*

4. For extracts, see *New Ghosts, Old Dreams* Gereme Barmé, ed. (New York: Random House, 1992), p. 165.

5. See *Beijing Daxue Xuebao* 1993.

6. *New York Times,* January 10, 1992, xx.

7. "On Female Adaptability to the Market Economy," *Xinhua Wenzhai* 10 (1993).

8. See *China Now* 128 (Spring 1989).

9. See *New York Times* July 30, 1992.

10. Zhang Jie, *The Ark* (Beijing and San Francisco: Panda Books/China Books, 1987), p. 201.

11. See for example Zhang Jie's "Love Must Not be Forgotten," in *Love Must Not be Forgotten* and Xu Naijian's "Because I'm Thirty and Unmarried," *One Half of the Sky* (London: Heineman, 1987).

12. See *China Now* 128 (Spring 1989).

13. See *The Serenity of Whiteness: Stories By and About Women in Contemporary China* Zhu Hong, ed. (New York: Ballantine, 1992).

14. *Zhongguo Nuren Xilie* (Liaoning People's Publishing House, 1988).

15. See *As Long as Nothing Happens, Nothing Will* (London: Virago, 1988).

16. Zhang Jie, "What's Wrong With Him?" *As Long as Nothing Happens, Nothing Will* (London, 1988).

17. Yu Luojin, *A Chinese Winter's Tale* (Hong Kong: Renditions, 1987).

18. *Shijie Ribao* (January 1994).

Gendered Law, "Public" and "Private"

13

Human Rights as Men's Rights
Hilary Charlesworth

Although there is no doubt that the apartheid of gender is considerably more pervasive than the apartheid of race, it has never provoked the same degree of international concern or opprobrium. The international community usually couches discussion of the advancement of women in terms of the acquisition and implementation of rights particular to women. While this is certainly an important and valuable project, it can also obscure some basic elements contributing to the oppression of women. My central argument is that the current international human rights structure itself and the substance of many norms of human rights law create obstacles to the advancement of women. Because the law-making institutions of the international legal order have always been, and continue to be, dominated by men, international human rights law has developed to reflect the experiences of men and largely to exclude those of women, rendering suspect the claim of the objectivity and universality of international human rights law. Until the gendered nature of the human rights system itself is recognized and transformed, no real progress for women can be achieved.

There are problems in speaking about women and their experiences in a global context. Obviously, differences of class, wealth, race, and nationality will lead to differing power relationships among women. Some feminists of color and women from developing nations have questioned attempts to universalize a particular understanding of feminism, charging White Western feminists with inappropriately assuming that their particular concerns are shared worldwide.[1] But patriarchy and the devaluing of women, although manifested differently within different societies, are almost universal. As Peggy Antrobus, Director of the Women and Development Program at the University of the West Indies, told the 1991 World Women's Congress for a Healthy Planet in Florida:

Although we are divided by race, class, culture, and geography, our hope lies in our commonalities. All women's unremunerated household work is exploited, we all have conflicts in our multiple roles, our sexuality is exploited by men, media, and the economy, we struggle for survival and dignity, and, rich or poor, we are vulnerable to violence. We share our "otherness," our exclusion from decision making at all levels.[2]

Certainly no monolithic "women's point of view" can be assumed, but it is also important to acknowledge commonalities across cultures. In analyzing other cultures, we must interrogate our own assumptions and tools, acknowledge the partialness of our perspective, and regard women from other cultures with, in Maria Lugones's words, "loving perception" rather than as objects for theory.[3]

The International Legal Structure

The structure and institutions of the international legal order set up under the United Nations reflect and ensure the continued dominance of a male perspective. In the primary subjects of international law—nation-states and, increasingly, international organizations—the invisibility of women is striking. Power structures within governments are overwhelmingly masculine: very few states have women in significant positions of power, and even in those states that do, the numbers are extremely small. Women are either unrepresented or underrepresented in the national and global decision-making processes. The global average of women's representation in parliaments is less than 10 percent.

International organizations have the same problem. Their structures replicate those of states, with women restricted to insignificant and subordinate roles. Wherever, in international institutions, major decisions are made concerning global policies and guidelines, women are almost completely absent, despite the often disparate impact of those decisions upon women.[6] This is of course the case in the Secretariat of the United Nations and its specialized agencies, despite the terms of Article 8 of the Charter, which states:[7] "The United Nations shall place no restriction on the eligibility of men and women to participate in any capacity and under conditions of equality in its principal and subsidiary organs." Although over 40 percent of Secretariat staff are women, very few women are in management positions.[8] Since the

1985 Nairobi conference, there have been some improvements in this respect.[9] It has been estimated, however, that at the current rate of change it will take until the year 2021 for women to hold half of the United Nations professional jobs.

The silence and invisibility of women is also a feature of those bodies with special functions in creating and progressively developing international law. Only one woman has sat as a judge on the International Court of Justice,[10] and no woman has ever been elected to the International Law Commission. Although the question of human rights has typically been regarded as an appropriate area in which attention can be directed towards women, women are still vastly underrepresented in the specialized United Nations human rights bodies. Apart from the Committee on the Elimination of Discrimination Against Women, all of whose members are women, in 1993 there was only one woman (out of eighteen members) on the Committee on the Elimination of Racial Discrimination, two (out of eighteen) on the Economic, Social and Cultural Rights Committee, three (out of eighteen) on the Human Rights Committee, and two (out of ten) on the Committee against Torture.[11] Strikingly, the only occasion on which imbalance in gender representation was ever the subject of an official criticism was when the Economic and Social Council called on states parties to nominate both men and women for election to the Committee on the Elimination of Discrimination Against Women.[12]

Why is it problematic that all the major institutions of the international legal order are peopled by men? What is the value of insisting on the need for significant representation of women? Long-term male domination of all bodies wielding political power nationally and internationally means that issues traditionally of concern to men are seen as *general* human concerns; "women's concerns," by contrast, are regarded as a distinct and limited category. Because men generally are not the victims of sex discrimination, domestic violence, or sexual degradation and violence, for example, these matters are often relegated to a specialized and marginalized sphere and are regulated, if at all, by weaker methods. Unless the experiences of women contribute directly to the mainstream international legal order, beginning with women's equal representation in law-making forums, international human rights law loses its claim to universal applicability: it should be more accurately characterized as international *men's* rights law.

The United Nations system has already accepted the importance of balanced representation among nations of differing political and economic structure and power in all aspects of its work. It is acknowledged that the international legal system cannot simply reproduce the concerns of a particular set of states—that its effectiveness depends precisely on its reflection of truly global interests. Although women make up more than half of the world's population, this sensitivity has never been extended to the accommodation of alternative gender perspectives, producing an impoverished, ineffective, and lopsided jurisprudence.

The Substance of International Human Rights Law

Many generally applicable international human rights principles are inherently biased against women. An important aspect of international human rights law is that, like many national legal systems, it operates primarily in the public sphere, that is, within the world of government, politics, economics, and the workplace, areas traditionally associated with men. Its contrast is the private sphere of home, hearth, and family, the traditional province of women, which is generally regarded as outside the scope of both national laws and international human rights laws. And yet the most pervasive harm against women tends to occur within the inner sanctum of the private realm, within the family.

The following examples of what I suggest are male "human" rights principles are drawn from each of the so-called generations of rights. The priority to be enjoyed by each generation of rights has, of course, been a matter of great controversy, the North typically giving prominence to the first generation of civil and political rights, the South emphasizing the importance of the second and third generations. It is striking, however, that the three generations have in common the exclusion of the experiences of women.

First Generation Rights

The primacy traditionally given to civil and political rights by developed nations is directed toward protection of men within public life, in their relationship with government. But this is not the arena in which women most need protection. The operation of a public/private distinction at a gendered level is seen most clearly in the definition of those civil and political rights concerned with protection of the individual from violence.

An example of this, often regarded as the most important of all human rights, is the right to life set out in Article 6 of the *International Covenant on Civil and Political Rights*. The right is concerned with the arbitrary deprivation of life through public action. But protection from arbitrary deprivation of life or liberty through public action, important as it is, does not address the ways in which being a woman is in itself life threatening and the special ways in which women need legal protection to be able to enjoy their right to life. From conception to old age, womanhood is full of risks: of abortion and infanticide because of the social and economic pressure in some cultures to have sons; of malnutrition because social practices give men and boys priority with respect to food; of less access to health care than men; of endemic violence against women in all states. Yet the right to life is not regarded as extending to these threats to women's lives.

A similar myopia can be detected in the international prohibition on torture. A central feature of the international legal definition of torture is that it takes place in the public realm: it must be "inflicted by or at the instigation of or with the consent or acquiescence of a public official or other person acting in an official capacity."[13] Although many women are victims of torture in this "public" sense,[14] by far the greatest violence against women occurs in the "private," non-governmental sphere. This is left untouched by the international definition of torture.

In a wide range of cultures, significant forms of violence against women such as wife murder, battery, and rape, are, through (for example) nonprosecution or comparatively lower sentencing practices, treated less seriously than other violent crimes.[15] One reason for the official toleration of violence against women worldwide is the both explicitly and implicitly held view that it is a "private" matter, not within the proper scope of national criminal justice systems.[16] And yet if violence against women is understood not just as aberrant "private" behavior but as part of the structure of the universal subordination of women, it can never be considered a purely "private" issue: the distinction between "public" and "private" action in the context of violence against women is a not a useful or meaningful one. Yet it is by no means clear that the traditional rules of state responsibility can be invoked to hold states internationally accountable for legal and social systems in which violence and discrimination against women are endemic and in which such actions are trivialized or discounted.

The traditional construction of civil and political rights, then, obscures the most consistent harms done to women. While recent developments such as the United Nations' *Declaration on the Elimination of Violence Against Women*[17] indicate international concern on this issue, they do not directly challenge the inability of human rights law generally to respond to injuries sustained constantly by women worldwide. Apart from a brief preambular reference, the Declaration does not define violence against women as a human rights violation, but presents it implicitly as a discrete category of harm, on a different (and lesser) plane than serious human rights violations.

Second Generation Rights

It might be thought that "second" generation rights—economic, social, and cultural rights—by their nature transcend the dichotomy between public and private spheres of life and thus offer more to women's lives. But the definition of these rights, set out in the *International Covenant on Economic, Social and Cultural Rights,* indicates the tenacity of a distinction between public and private worlds in human rights law.[18] The Covenant does not touch on the economic, social, and cultural contexts in which most women live, since the crucial economic, social, and cultural power relationship for most women is not one directly with the state but with men—fathers, husbands, or brothers—whose authority is supported by patriarchal state structures. For example, the definition of the right to just and favorable conditions of work in Article 7 is confined to work in the public sphere. Marilyn Waring has documented the tremendous amount of economic activity by women that is rendered invisible precisely because it is performed by women without pay and within the private, domestic sphere.[19] Article 7's guarantee to women of "conditions of work not inferior to those enjoyed by men, with equal pay for equal work" thus sounds rather hollow in light of the international myopia with respect to the extent and economic value of women's work.

Moreover, notions of cultural and religious rights can often reinforce a distinction between public and private worlds that operates to the disadvantage of women: culture and religion can be seen as spheres protected from legal regulation even though they are often the sites for oppression of women by men. While the right to gender equality, on the one hand, and religious and cultural rights, on the other, can be reconciled by limiting the latter,[20] in political practice cultural and religious freedom tend to be accorded much higher priority nationally and internationally.

Third Generation Rights

The philosophical basis of group rights rests on a primary commitment to the welfare of the community over and above the interests of particular individuals. It might seem that such rights would hold particular promise for women, whose lives typically center more on the family, the group, and the community than the individual. There has been much controversy over the legal status of such rights, but, from a woman's perspective, they are, in fundamental ways, little different from the first and second generations of rights, since they too have developed in an androcentric way.

The theoretical and practical development of third generation rights has, in fact, delivered very little to women. The right to development, for example, is both defined and implemented internationally to support male economic dominance.[21] The subordination of women to men does not enter the traditional development calculus: "development" conceived as economic growth is not concerned with the lack of benefits or disadvantageous effects this growth may have on half of the society it purports to benefit. Indeed, the position of many women in developing countries has deteriorated over the last two decades: women's access to economic resources has been reduced, their health and educational status has declined, and their work burdens have increased.[22] The generality and apparently universal applicability of the right to development as formulated in the UN *Declaration on the Right to Development* is undermined by the fundamentally androcentric nature of the international economic system, which accords far greater value to work conducted in the public (male) sphere than to women's work in the private sphere. The problematic nature, for Third World women, of current development practice cannot of course be attributed solely to the international legal formulation of the right to development. But the rhetoric of international law both reflects and reinforces a system that contributes to the subordination of women. More recent UN deliberations on development have paid greater attention to the role of women.[23] However, these concerns are usually presented as quite distinct (soluble by the application of special protective measures) rather than as crucial to the notion of development itself.[24]

So, too, the right to self-determination, allowing "all peoples" to "freely determine their political status and freely pursue their economic, social and cultural development," has been invoked and supported recently in a number of contexts and ultimately to the disadvantage of women. The oppression of women within groups claiming the right of self-determination has never been considered relevant to the validity of such claims or to the form self-determination should take. In this sense, the right to self-determination is relevant only in the most public of contexts: male political life. The right to self-determination attaches to "peoples"—entities defined ethnically or culturally—even if half the persons who make up the "people" have little or no power in the community.[25] In many cases (the Afghani Mujihadeen and "liberated" Kuwait are well-documented examples), the oppression of women within the self-determining unit is ignored. In practice, then, the "people" to whom the right of self-determination attaches are men.

Strategies for Change

Most United Nations work relating to the advancement of women is centered on the Commission on the Status of Women and the *Convention on the Elimination of All Forms of Discrimination Against Women.* The Commission and the Women's Convention have provided a valuable, if underresourced, focus for women's interests in the international system, but, ironically, the creation of a specialized branch of women's human rights law has also allowed its marginalization. "Mainstream" human rights bodies have tended to ignore the application of general human rights norms to women.

I have argued that both the process and substance of international law is gendered, and thus is partial in its effectiveness and authority. It is important, as a strategy for the advancement of women, to ensure that women's voices and experiences are included in the definition of all human rights norms. The United Nations' concern for balanced geographical and ideological representation should be extended to gender: The critical importance of having equality of representation of women in all international lawmaking forums must be recognized and acted on so that international law can claim truly global applicability. Training in equal opportunity issues should be mandatory for both state representatives and civil servants in international forums. Effective affirmative action programs need to be designed for the United Nations Secretariat to counter its resistance to gender equality. A commitment to gender-inclusive language in all United Nations work (especially in human rights instruments) is a good way of starting the task of reducing the overtly masculine culture of international lawmaking.

Most fundamentally, the boundaries of "mainstream" international law must be reoriented to incorporate women's experiences. One method of doing this in the context of human rights law is to challenge the gendered dichotomy of (and to reshape doctrines based on) public and private worlds. The expert committees established under the major human rights treaties should be encouraged to consider issues of gender in their work, and to use techniques, such as the issuing of general comments, to broaden the traditionally androcentric scope of rights.

The Second World Conference on Human Rights held in Vienna in 1993 responded to the well-organized lobbying by women's groups by declaring that "the full and equal enjoyment by women of all human rights" be a priority for national governments and the United Nations. It urged that women's rights be integrated into the mainstream of United Nations activity. The effect such encouragement will have is as yet uncertain. Although there remains much to be done within the deeply androcentric United Nations, redefining the traditional scope of international human rights law so as to acknowledge the interests of women may lead international actors to pursue change that will allow for the reimagination of gender difference.

Notes

1. E.g., Maria Lugones and Elizabeth Spelman, "Have We Got a Theory for You," *Women's Studies International Forum*, 6(6): 573.

2. Peggy Antrobus, paper presented to the World Women's Congress for a Healthy Planet, Miami, FL, November 8–12, 1991.

3. Maria Lugones, "Playfulness, World Traveling and Loving Perception," *Hypatia* 2(2): 3. See also Isabel Guning, "Arrogant Perception, World-Traveling and Multi-cultural Feminism: The Case of Female Genital Surgeries," *Columbia Human Rights Law Review* 23 (1991–92): 189; Annie Bunting, "Theorizing Women's Cultural Diversity in Feminist International Human Rights Strategies," in *Feminist Theory and Legal Strategy*, edited by Anne Bottomly and Joanne Conaghen (Oxford, UK and Cambridge, MA: Blackmell, 1993), p. 6.

4. United Nations, *Women in Politics and Decision-Making in the Late Twentieth Century* (Dordrecht, Netherlands: Martinus Nijhoff, 1992). UN Sales No. E.91.IV.3.

5. Ibid.

6. See Hilary Charlesworth, Christine Chinkin, and Shelley Wright, "Feminist Approaches to International Law," *American Journal of International Law* vol. 85 (613): 623 n. 60 (1991).

7. Charter of the United Nations, Article 8, 1945.

8. The Secretary-General's report, *Review and Appraisal of the Implementation of the Nairobi Forward-Looking Strategies for the Advancement of Women,* UN

Doc. E/CN. 6/1990/5, indicates that between 1984 and 1988 the total increase in the representation of women in professional and management positions in the UN was 3.6 percent, to a total of 21 percent of professional staff. At the senior management level in 1988, however, only 4 percent of staff were women (Id., pp. 84–86).

9. In 1985 the Secretary-General appointed a Coordinator for the Improvement of the Status of Women for twelve months. This position was subsequently extended.

10. Mme. Suzanne Bastid was Judge ad hoc in *Application for Revision and Interpretation of the Judgment of 24 February 1982 in the Case concerning the Continental Shelf (Tunisia/Libyan Arab Jamahiriya)*, [1985] ICJ Rep. 4.

11. See A. Byrnes, "The 'Other' Human Rights Treaty Body: The Work of the Committee on the Elimination of Discrimination Against Women," *Yale Journal of International Law* 14 (1):8 n. 26 (1989). The Sub-Commission on Prevention of Discrimination and Protection of Minorities has six women out of twenty-six members.

12. Hilary Charlesworth, Christine Chinkin, and Shelley Wright, op. cit., p. 624.

13. United Nations, General Assembly *Convention Against Torture and Other Cruel, Inhuman or Degrading Treatment or Punishment,* General Assembly Resolution 39/46, Art. 1 (1), (December 10, 1984). UN Doc. A/RES/39/46(1984).

14. See, e.g., Amnesty International, *Women in the Front Line: Human Rights Violations Against Women* (London: Amnesty International, 1991). Even given the limited international definition of torture, recent research suggests that the torture of women receives considerably less attention than the torture of men. See International Human Rights Law Group, *Token Gestures* (Washington, DC: International Human Rights Law Group, 1993), which examines the work of the United Nations Special Rapporteur on Torture. The report argued that the Special Rapporteur failed adequately to investigate and condemn many well-documented cases of systematic torture of women.

15. See, for example, Margaret Schuler, ed., *Freedom from Violence: Women's Strategies from Around the World* (New York: Unifem, 1992).

16. See Americas Watch, *Criminal Injustice: Violence against Women in Brazil* (Washington, DC: International Human Rights Law Group, 1991); and Dorothy Thomas and Michele Beasley, "Domestic Violence as a Human Rights Issue," *Human Rights Quarterly* 15 (1993): 36.

17. UN Doc. E/CN.6/WG.2/1992/L.3 (3 September 1992).

18. Shelley Wright, "Economic Rights and Social Justice: A Feminist Analysis of Some International Human Rights Conventions," *Australian YearBook of International Law,* 12 (1992): 242.

19. Marilyn Waring, *Counting for Nothing* (Sydney: Allen and Unwin, 1988).

20. See Donna Sullivan, "Gender Equality and Religious Freedom: Toward a Framework for Conflict Resolution," *New York University Journal of International Law and Politics* 24 (1992): 795.

21. This argument is more fully pursued in Hilary Charlesworth, "The Public/Private Distinction and the Right to Development," *Australian YearBook of International Law* 12 (1992): 190.

22. See United Nations, *World Survey on the Role of Women in Development* 19–20 (New York: United Nations, 1986).

23. E.g., *Analytical Compilation of Comments and Views on the Implementation of the Declaration on the Right to Development Prepared by the Secretary-General*, UN Doc E/CN.4/AC.39/1988/L.2, paras. 59–63; *Report Prepared by the Secretary-General on the Global Consultation on the Realization of the Right to Development as a Human Right*, UN Doc E/Cn.4/1990/9, paras. 15, 42, 51, 52, 59.

24. The section of the Secretary-General's report dealing with "Obstacles to the Implementation of the Right to Development as a Human Right," for example, mentions failure to respect the right of peoples to self-determination, racial discrimination, apartheid, foreign occupation, restrictions on transfers of technology, and the consumption patterns of industrialized countries as serious barriers to the realization of the right to development; it contains no reference to sex discrimination. Idem., paras. 27–35. Compare the detail of Article 14 of the Women's Convention. UN Doc. A/RES/34/180(1980).

25. See C. Chinkin, "A Gendered Perspective to the International Use of Force," *Australian YearBook of International Law* 12 (1992): 142.

This paper is a revised version of an address to the Third Committee of the United Nations General Assembly, New York, on 27 October 1992. An expanded account of the argument in the paper is to be published in *The Human Rights of Women: National and International Perspectives*, ed. Rebecca Cook, Univ. of Pennsylvania Press (forthcoming).

14

Critiquing Gender-Neutral Treaty Language: The Convention on the Elimination of All Forms of Discrimination Against Women

Natalie Hevener Kaufman
Stefanie A. Lindquist

I. Introduction

Since the inception of the women's movement, feminist activists have focused on establishing rights and opportunities for women equal to those enjoyed by men. Rights have an intimate connection with feminism as a social and political movement, both nationally and internationally. In international treaty law, feminists have pressed for the recognition of women's rights as equal to the rights available to men.[1]

In this tradition, the *Convention on the Elimination of All Forms of Discrimination Against Women* (the "Women's Convention" adopted by the United Nations in 1979) refers repeatedly to the ensuring of women's rights "on a basis of equality with men." In this sense, the Women's Convention is dominated, albeit with some important exceptions, by what we will refer to as "gender-neutral" language (Hevener 1983, 1986). Gender-neutral provisions observe the principle that men and women are to be treated equally in order to ensure that gender will no longer operate as a basis for the allocation of benefits and burdens in society (Hevener 1987, 78). Those important exceptions involve "corrective language," which has three advantages over gender-neutral language: (1) it addresses situations that do not victimize men as they do women; (2) it allows for a woman-centered solution without reference to male action; and (3) it can prescribe active public policy to achieve fairness rather than passive elimination of discriminatory laws and norms.[2]

This essay evaluates the gender-neutral language of the Women's Convention in light of recent feminist critiques of the focus on "rights" in the women's movement. In so doing, it describes the reasons that rights language, or gender-neutral treaty provisions, may not address problems that women, in telling their own stories, identify as salient. Finally, this essay proposes particular criteria to evaluate treaty provisions and applies them to the Women's Convention, examining the strategies the Convention language reflects as it attempts to advance the status of women.

II. A Feminist Evaluation of Rights Discourse

a. Rights and the Imbalance of Power

In both the domestic and international arenas, rights discourse has come under considerable criticism in recent years by feminists and others who challenge the "myth of rights," both in the women's movement and in politics at large. That critique has focused on the inability of legal rights to alter the underlying structure of domination within society. In general, it has been observed that "even if [rights] sometimes work for one person or one situation, it is far harder for rights to alter the structures of institutional power and behavior that shape individual actions" (Stone 1988, 273). Indeed, while rights claims can help develop political consciousness and help define social movements, "the formal acquisition of a right, such as the right to equal treatment, is often assumed to have solved an imbalance of power. In practice, however, the promise of rights is thwarted by the inequalities of power [between men and women]" (Charlesworth, Chinkin, and Wright 1991, 635). Thus, not only may the promise of equality through gender-neutral laws be thwarted by actual power differences, but, as Catherine MacKinnon has observed, the pursuit of equality may also conceal "the substantive way in which man has become the measure of all things" (1991, 82).

At the core of the rights issue, in both national and international law, is the fact that legal rights do not stand alone; they are embedded in the dominant social and cultural milieu. As a result, the interpretation of rights guaranteed by an international treaty occurs at the intersection of the legal system and the social system. When judges interpret applicable law in individual cases, the law is "read" in the subjective, social realm. There, the interpretation of the legal "right" becomes subject to the dominant cultural paradigm—an engendered, socially constructed world, where women's experience is seldom recognized. When the interpretation is undertaken by a man (which it often is) or by a woman who has been socialized to accept the male elite's norms and interests as her own, the law is subjected to the interpretation of a judge whose approach to the law constructs women's lives from a male-centered perspective (cf. Jones 1993, 189). The experience of Shahieda Issel, a South African activist, clearly exemplifies this phenomenon: "The colonel had assaulted me so terribly that my leg was broken. But the police [blamed me]. . . . In court, police officer Van der Merwe said of me: Your Honor, this lady claims to be a lady, but she is no Lady at all" (Russell 1989, 72).

The history of judges' interpretation of laws affecting women in the United States demonstrates that the "objective" application of law is a socially constructed enterprise. Critical legal theorists drive this point home through evaluation of such cases as *General Electric Company v. Gilbert*,[3] in which Justice Rehnquist's majority opinion asserted that the exclusion of pregnancy-related disabilities from an employer's health insurance plan did not have a disparate effect on women since pregnancy was an "extra" disability that only women suffered. The exclusion of pregnancy ensured the equality of the plan with respect to men (see Williams 1991, 23). By using men as the measure against which to determine the "equality" of the plan's coverage, Justice Rehnquist revealed the inherent male-oriented bias in his reasoning; according to his reasoning, pregnant women could be viewed as "pregnant persons," while men, along with nonpregnant women, were simply "nonpregnant persons."[4]

b. Rights and the Search for Consistency

The United States Supreme Court's *Gilbert* opinion may be viewed as a manifestation of the "reverence for consistency" found in the common-law tradition. In speaking of her search for a "unified and coherent theory of equality" by which to assess the equality provisions of the Canadian Charter of Rights and Freedoms, Diana Majury explains:

> Proponents of the various equality models seemed to agree (some explicitly, some implicitly) that one must adopt a single model of equality and use it exclusively. Within the common law legal system, consistency is considered to be of paramount importance. Given this reverence for consistency, it is generally considered unthinkable to go into court to argue that equality means one thing in one situation and something different (often inappropriately characterized as contradictory) in another. (1991, 327)

As Majury recognizes, attempts to subject all issues involving women's difference to the same "consistent" equality analysis can lead to reasoning like that employed by the United States Supreme Court, which forces some women into the category of "pregnant persons" and men into the category, of "nonpregnant persons."

This search for consistency is fostered by the nature of legal education itself, which trains lawyers to view the world as structured by rules of logical coherence. Lawyers learn to look for hierarchical and logical relationships and thus become desensitized to arguments that challenge a hierarchical view of society. In this way, legal education denigrates flexibility and contextual values. Duncan Kennedy observes that "law school teaching makes the choice of hierarchy and domination ... look as though it flows from and is required by legal reasoning rather than being a matter of politics and economics" (1990, 45). The conservative influence of legal education is then brought to bear when individual cases are presented for judicial resolution. As a consequence, the search for equal rights may result in distorted (from a woman's perspective), yet logically consistent, case outcomes.

c. Rights and Political Action

The acquisition of rights, of course, may be of considerable value in certain circumstances. Anyone who witnessed the battle over the Equal Rights Amendment in the United States can attest to "the substantial symbolic freight" of rights for women (see Rhode 1989, 68–72). Many of the provisions in the Women's Convention that use gender-neutral language play this symbolic role, which is an essential first step to beginning the difficult work of changing the distribution of burdens and benefits in a society.

Nevertheless, a strategy based solely on the acquisition of equal legal rights using current "male" rights as a standard may provide benefits for women that are more symbolic than actual. In some contexts, moreover, this strategy may have pitfalls. Although legal rights do not necessarily translate into actual equality of opportunities within a given society, the successful acquisition of rights may lead to decreased activism within a social movement if activists come to believe that the battle has been won.

The recognition that equal rights often fail to reflect the realities of women's lives (and are often hampered by the very legal system designed to enforce them) thus highlights the shortcomings of universal treaties phrased predominantly in gender-neutral language. The failure to respond to women's voices, combined with the inherent bias of those empowered to interpret, apply, and enforce law has the potential to severely undermine the efficacy of laws written in gender-neutral language.

d. Rights and Women's Diverse Voices

At the international level in particular, cultural differences between parties to human rights treaties like the Women's Convention compound the difficulty of determining whether equal rights guarantees will translate into actual equality of opportunity and outcome for women, since the conception of equal rights and the balance of power between men and women may differ across national boundaries.[5] Indeed, the likelihood of judges' ignorance or failure to recognize women's experience is more than probable, in part because men often dominate legal and judicial institutions. In the International Court of Justice, for instance, as of 1991 there has been only one female justice (Charlesworth, Chinkin, and Wright 1991, 623). Regardless of the acquisition of certain rights, societies, their governments, and courts may view the claim of discrimination as "reasonable and objective differential treatment" under prevailing social norms (Cook 1990, 818).

Indeed, "rights" language itself often does not reflect the manner in which women actually conceptualize their unique concerns regarding such issues as child care or rape. As the U.S. Supreme Court's *Gilbert* opinion makes clear, women's concerns are often impossible to articulate in the inflexible language of equality. For this reason, Majury notes that "women's narratives generally do not speak in terms of equality" (1991, 335). For example, women's concern for their children is unconnected to an equality standard. Ruth Mompati describes the concerns of women in her South African federation without reference to equality: "Working with all women in the federation enabled us to realize that there were no differences between us as mothers. We were all women. . . . We all wanted to bring up our children to be happy and to protect them from the brutalities of life" (Russell 1991, 114). Women are concerned with controlling their own lives and providing for their families, but they are not generally preoccupied with ensuring that their level of control "equals" that of men. Rather, an equality framework superimposed by law may serve to distort the realities of women's lives.

The effectiveness of rights discourse needs special investigation given the diversity of cultural norms that make up the international system. Because women across national boundaries are usually silenced through their exclusion from public spheres of decision making, we have little reason to believe that formal legal documents reflect their conceptualization of a just society. Because of the incommensurability of rights language across different cultures, treaties that grant equal rights dependent upon governmental implementation are less likely to provide the kind of help that women need most.

A brief review of the reservations to the Women's Convention by individual parties illustrates this point. Egypt's reservation to the Convention's grant to women of equal rights concerning the nationality of children is based upon the "customary" practice of women, who agree, on marrying an alien, that their children will have the father's nationality. Other nations, including Egypt, have acceded to the Women's Convention subject to the more broad-based reservation that accession not conflict with the laws on personal status derived from the Islamic *Sharia*.

III. Analyzing the Language of the Women's Convention

Many ratifying nations, then, use the claim of cultural difference to justify reservations to the Women's Convention. But the gender-neutral language of the convention facilitates a more subtle form of injustice. Article 1, for instance, defines the goal of the treaty in gender-neutral terms:

> Any distinction, exclusion or restriction made on the basis of sex which has the effect or purpose of impairing or nullifying the recogni-

tion, enjoyment or exercise by women, irrespective of their marital status, *on a basis of equality of men and women,* of human rights and fundamental freedoms in the political, economic, social, cultural, civil or any other field. (emphasis added)

The treaty thus relies heavily on legal equality as a method of achieving justice for women. In light of the various concerns with such a framework described in Part II of this paper, we have developed criteria for examining and evaluating gender-neutral treaty provisions from a feminist perspective and offer some observations on the provisions most likely to achieve feminist objectives and on why they might do so.

Phrased in the form of questions, the criteria or guidelines are set forth below. In developing these criteria, we rely in part on the adoption of corrective language as a method of addressing the shortcomings of gender neutrality. Corrective provisions are designed to address a specific practice that oppresses women but not men or that is of much greater importance to women than to men. The active character of corrective language is necessary to respond to the political and economic reality of women's disempowerment in most contemporary societies, a disempowerment that cannot be addressed effectively through the "level playing field" approach encoded in the gender-neutral language of equal rights.

a. Women Speaking in Their Own Voices

First, does the provision advance the ability of women to speak and define their own power in their own voices? Provisions that merely provide women with an equal opportunity under the law to enunciate their unique concerns within male-dominated institutions cannot automatically alter patterns of historical disempowerment. For example, Articles 2, 3, and 7 of the Women's Convention require that women be granted equal access to organizations. These provisions may desegregate historically male organizations, but at a cost to newly emerging female organizations. Women's organizations are a necessary part of the process of women's acquisition of genuine political power, a critical antecedent to effective participation in integrated organizations. As one South African woman remarked in support of separate women's political organizations:

I feel women are doubly oppressed. . . . Most men feel that women should play a subordinate role. I have been at a number of workshops where men object heavily to women being there. They think our role is in the kitchen. . . . I support the need to have separate women's organizations at this time, and I have participated in the United Women's Congress. I feel that women have problems which can't be addressed in a broader organization. It's not that we want to be alone. It's merely that women need to get the confidence to speak up. (Russell 1989, 79)

A corrective provision would respond by clearly recognizing that single-sex organizations may constitute a need that is greater for women than for men, i.e., *not* on an equal basis with men. Article 14, paragraph (e), of the Women's Convention provides a good example of such a corrective provision. It specifically requires parties to ensure rural women the right "to organize self-help groups and co-operatives in order to obtain equal access to economic opportunities through employment or self-employment."

b. Escaping the Male Standard

Does the treaty language imply that man is the measure and the standard for establishing appropriate, fair, and reasonable behavior or treatment? Equality is a blunted instrument for women in a world in which the male standard provides the measure. Indeed, the title of the Women's Convention itself arguably presupposes a male standard to the extent that it calls for the elimination of discrimination against women, attempting to bring women into the male world through the removal of legal constraints.

For example, there is no place for maternity benefits in a male-centered society. Since men are precluded from such benefits, it can be argued that maternity benefits constitute a special right prohibited by a strict equality standard. Yet for women, these benefits may be a high priority. Emma Mashinini, a South African organizer, feels that her "greatest joy" has been her union's achievements for women workers. "We were the first union in South Africa . . . to have an agreement that protects women's maternity rights. . . . [w]omen cannot now lose their jobs or be demoted because of pregnancy" (Russell 1991, 187).

Gender-neutral language would have evaded this issue entirely or attempted to deal with it in terms of a male medical analogue like prostate disease. The Women's Convention uses the language of correction rather than equality to address the maternity leave issue. In Article

11, paragraph 2, states are required to take steps to prohibit sanctions against women who marry or become pregnant and to provide maternity leave with benefits, including the protection of job seniority.

c. Protecting Against Hostile Interpretations

Are there safeguards built into the treaty to ensure that the provisions will not be used against women? Because the worldview of the male elite is so often the starting point of legal interpretation, it is important to ensure that gender-neutral laws not be interpreted in a manner contrary to women's interests. Will the premise of strictly and consistently equal legal treatment result in the elimination of needed opportunities for women (single-sex organizations, for instance) or of actual advantages for women (maternity leave, for instance)? As has been documented in the adjudication of no-fault divorce and child custody cases in the United States, equality can be a double-edged instrument if it is used to punish women for failing to conform to the conventional norms expected by men.[6]

The Women's Convention shows some sensitivity to this potential problem in its provision for single-sex organizations for rural women, as well as in its maternity leave provisions. In addition, the treaty allows for a full range of corrective strategies that would safeguard measures that might otherwise be eliminated in a "purely equal rights" approach. Article 4, paragraph 1, for example, provides for parties to adopt temporary special measures that deviate from equal treatment in order to achieve de-facto equality.

d. Remedies for Specific Injustices

Does the treaty construct remedies and clearly indicate steps that must be taken to redress problems that solely or almost exclusively affect women? Here the concept of equality may not be particularly relevant or necessarily helpful.

Article 16, paragraph 1, of the Women's Convention, for example, provides a blanket call for the equality of men and women "in all matters relating to marriage and family relations." The long, culturally diverse list of practices that effectively treat women as objects or property cannot be adequately addressed by such a vague invocation to equal treatment. Many of these practices are considered so "normal," "natural," and "inevitable" that only clear rejection of the specific practice will help real women and their daughters. Practices that range from child marriages to trafficking in women to child pornography are often justified through appeals to *rights,* rights that men have designed to protect their freedoms to private commerce, free speech, and cultural integrity.

For example, one interpretation of bride price is that the woman and her family are honored by the payment of money by the groom. Mavivi Manzini of South Africa explains how insidious the practice can, in actuality, be: "*Lobola* (bride price) [is one of the] practices [that] serve men and oppress women. . . . A man who has given *lobola* to his wife's parents regards her as his property with whom he can do anything because he has bought her" (Russell 1989, 131).

The corrective language of earlier treaties on this subject may sometimes prove more effective than equality language (see Hevener 1983, 32–33). But one corrective provision in the Women's Convention is an advance over even the corrective language found in the earlier *Convention on the Elimination of Discrimination in Education.* According to Article 10 of the Women's Convention, states are required to act affirmatively to ameliorate female dropout rates and to organize programs to assist girls and women who have left school prematurely.

e. Establishment of Active Public Policy

Does the treaty require that direct and active public policy address the concerns of women, or does it limit parties' obligations to a series of passive steps? Does the language of the treaty suggest that changes in the law are tantamount to changes in society? Many Western legal systems rest on the assumption that "freedom from" governmental interference is the ultimate test of justice; in these systems it is presumed that removal of barriers against women is sufficient, and that programs specifically geared toward helping women, especially in the economic and social arenas, would be unnecessary and contrary to good public policy. Many women, for example, have expressed the need for active public policy on the issue of health care for themselves and their children, which, they argue, should be an integral part of the definition of a just society. Spokeswomen for this position may consider health care laws based on the relative position of men as irrelevant and the removal of formal barriers, or the ending of sexual discrimination, as equally unsatisfactory solutions.

The language in Article 12 of the Women's Convention moves from a "remove the barriers" approach to one embracing an active public program. Paragraph 1 of Article 12 opens with gender-neutral language requiring states to eliminate discrimination against women in health care and to provide access to them on an equal basis with men. Paragraph 2 reflects an awareness of the inadequacy of formal equality by stating "*Notwithstanding the provisions of paragraph I of this article,* States Parties shall ensure to women appropriate services in connexion with pregnancy, confinement and the postnatal period" (emphasis added).

Conclusion

The equal rights approach, then, is an important but partial strategy in the struggle for improving the status of women nationally and internationally. The criteria identified above provide a framework in which to evaluate the use of gender-neutral laws. If treaties designed to address the concerns of women are to have a dramatic and positive impact on women's lives, they must be sensitive to the social, economic, and political disempowerment of women throughout the world. Given the cultural diversity within and among nations, international agreements that include provisions aimed at specific wrongs (measures that acknowledge the differential status and treatment of women and that require active and engaged public policy programs) are far more likely to improve the lives of real women and girls. The Women's Convention has, to a great extent, incorporated such provisions into its otherwise gender-neutral framework. But the ultimate test of such conventions will be the ability of grassroots women's groups to use these instruments to bring about change. The most important measure of their success should be the extent to which they enable women to interpret, apply, and enforce laws of their own making, incorporating their own voices, values, and concerns.

Notes

1. Riane Eisler observes that separating women's rights from human rights may be seen to serve "systems maintenance functions in male dominant or patriarchal societies" (Eisler 1987, 289–91).
2. The discussion of corrective language that follows represents a significant change over the definition of this category described in Hevener (1983, 9–12).

3. 429 U.S. 125 (1976).

4. *Gilbert,* 429 U.S. at 135 (quoting *Geduldig V. Aiello,* 417 U.S. 484, 496–97 n.20 [1974]).

5. Indeed, legal rights "have a special resonance in [U.S.] culture," but other cultures do not necessarily share that commitment (see Rhode 1991, 342).

6. See Rhode 1989, chap. 7.

Works Cited

Charlesworth, H., C. Chinkin, and S. Wright, 1991. "Feminist Approaches to International Law," *American Journal of International Law* 85:613–43.

Cook, R., 1990. "International Human Rights Law Concerning Women: Case Notes and Comments," *Vanderbilt Journal of International Law.* 23:779–818.

Eisler, R. 1987. "Human Rights: Toward an Integrated Theory for Action," *Human Rights Law Quarterly* 9:287–308.

Hevener, N. Kaufman. 1983. *International Law and the Status of Women.* Boulder, CO: Westview.

"An Analysis of Gender Based Treaty Law: Contemporary Developments in Historical Perspective," 1986. *Human Rights Law Quarterly* 8:70–88.

Jones, K.B. 1993. *Compassionate Authority: Democracy and the Representation of Women.* New York: Routledge.

Kennedy, D. 1990., "Legal Education as Training for Hierarchy." *The Politics of Law,* edited by D. Kairys. New York: Panthcon.

MacKinnon, C.A. 1991. "Difference and Dominance: On Sex Discrimination." *Feminist Legal Theory,* edited by K. T. Bartlett and R. Kennedy, Boulder CO: Westview.

Majury, D. 1991. "Strategizing in Equality." *At the Boundaries of Law,* edited by M.A. Fineman and N.S. Thomadsen. New York: Routledge.

Mitchell, J. "Women and Equality." *Feminism and Equality,* edited by A. Phillips. New York: New York Univ. Press.

Rhode, D. 1989. *Justice and Gender: Sex Discrimination and The Law.* Cambridge: Harvard Univ. Press.

"Feminist Critical Theories." 1991. *Feminist Legal Theory: Readings in Law and Gender,* edited by K.T. Bartlett and R. Kennedy. Boulder, CO: Westview.

Russell, D. 1989. *Lives of Courage: Women for a New South Africa.* New York: Basic Books.

Stone, D.A. 1988. *Policy Paradox and Political Reason* Glenview, IL: Scott, Foresman.

Williams, W.W. 1991. "The Equality Crisis." *Feminist Legal Theory,* edited by K. T. Bartlett and R. Kennedy. Boulder, CO: Westview.

15

The Public/Private Distinction in International Human Rights Law

Donna Sullivan

International human rights law and practice only faintly reflect the reality of the grave human rights abuses suffered by women. This article examines how the exclusion of many violations of women's human rights from the work of international institutions and non-governmental organizations has been maintained by demarcations of public and private life and by international law defining state responsibility for violations by private persons. These questions are considered with reference to gender-based violence.

The legitimating function of international law means that the content of human rights norms has political, as well as legal, dimensions. Human rights discourse is a powerful tool for affecting political processes at the national and international levels. Gender-specific abuses have yet to be fully integrated into that discourse or into human rights jurisprudence. One factor contributing to this silence is the historic focus within international law on violations committed directly by the state against individuals. Within this conceptualization of the law as a constraint on the power of the state, many abuses against women have not been acknowledged as human rights violations because they are committed by private persons rather than by agents of the state.

This focus on violations committed by the state is attributable to several factors. First, international law evolved as a set of rules intended to regulate relations among states and remains centered on the state. Second, civil and political rights hold a privileged position in human rights law and practice despite formal recognition by the international community of the interdependence and indivisibility of economic, social, cultural, civil, and political rights. Civil and political rights remain at the forefront of efforts by intergovernmental bodies like the United Nations to protect human rights and of efforts by major human rights organizations to expose violations. The liberal ideology underlying much of civil and political rights discourse views the law principally as a means of regulating state intervention in private life, generally without acknowledging the role of the state itself in constructing the separation of public from private life.

Certain violations of civil and political rights by private individuals or groups, including various forms of discrimination, clearly fall within the scope of state responsibility as defined by international instruments or international and regional jurisprudence. The dominance of civil and political rights discourse has nonetheless entailed a preoccupation with constraints on the power of the state rather than an emphasis on its affirmative duties to ensure rights. Systemic gender inequality has been addressed primarily within the framework of development policy rather than the affirmative human rights obligations of states.

Third, international norms concerning the life of the family call on the state to protect the institution of the family and enshrine the right of privacy in the family.[1] Both the duty to protect the family and privacy rights discourage direct state intervention in the life of the family. Because the family is the site of many of the most egregious violations of women's physical and mental integrity, any blanket deference to the institution of the family or privacy rights within the family has disastrous consequences for women.

These three factors—the state-centered nature of international law, the dominance of civil and political rights discourse, and deference to the institution of the family—account for much of the emphasis placed on direct violations of civil and political rights by the state and corresponding neglect of gender-specific abuses in private life. The challenge is not to shift the focus away from gross violations of civil and political rights by the state but, first, to broaden the normative framework to include the abuses suffered by women that do not fit this paradigm because they occur at the hands of private individuals; and then to develop effective international monitoring and implementation mechanisms in this area. The distinction between public and private life in international law is one of the principal theoretical barriers to this effort.

Two aspects of the public/private distinction should be considered in this context. First are the political, legal, and social processes by which the public and private domains are constructed. The second is the theoretical distinction in international law between conduct that can be attributed to the state, and for which the state will therefore be held responsible by the international community, and the conduct of private persons that does not implicate the international obligations of the state.

The demarcation of public and private life within society is an inherently political process that both reflects and reinforces power relations, especially the power relations of gender, race, and class. In this process, particular activities are recognized as defining the public realm and others as characterizing the private realm. For example, in many societies, participation in formal structures of governance and in public sector employment are viewed as quintessentially public activities, and relations in marriage and child rearing are defined as the core of private life. Feminists have long emphasized the gendered nature of this division. Economic, social, and political power adheres in the public realm, to which women have limited access and over which they have limited control. The law constructs and sustains power relations within private life through both active regulation of private life (by such means as social welfare and taxation systems) and by the failure to regulate other conduct in private life.

Although the demarcation of public and private realms is a gendered process, gender does not operate in isolation from other factors in the construction of public and private life. The parameters of "public life" are not uniform even within a single national setting. Demarcations of the public domain may vary among different classes, among different racial or ethnic groups, among different regions within a country, and between urban and rural environments. The shared feature of the public/private distinction in different contexts is the attribution of lesser economic, social, or political value to the activities of women within what is defined as private life.

In addition, the boundary between public and private life has long been permeable when the state seeks to exercise control over disempowered communities. In the United States, for example, the notion of the sanctity of the family has not protected women of color from sterilization abuse or other coercive reproductive health policies. Police power is routinely exercised against poor and working class families without the deference to family privacy that often characterizes law enforcement interactions with middle class and wealthy families. Race, class, ethnicity, and sexual orientation all shape the definitions of what constitutes a family entitled to protection against state intervention and condition the extent to which that protection is available.

Moreover, there are important normative exceptions to the general principle favoring nonintervention in the life of the family. International norms affirm a countervailing principle of gender equality in marriage and family life. In particular, article 16 of the *Convention on the Elimination of All Forms of Discrimination Against Women*[2] (Women's Convention) obligates states parties to take affirmative steps to ensure the equality of women and men in marriage and in parental responsibilities. Article 16 contemplates the restructuring of the gender relations of power within the family. Precisely for that reason, it is subject to a large number of reservations by states parties.[3] The guarantee of equal rights as to marriage, during marriage, and at its dissolution is established in the *Universal Declaration of Human Rights* and the *International Covenant on Civil and Political Rights*.[4] Far-reaching exceptions to the general reluctance to regulate the life of the family are also established in the *Convention on the Rights of the Child,* which explicitly requires the state to protect children from all forms of physical or mental violence, injury, or abuse while in the care of parents, guardians, or others charged with care of the child.[5]

State Responsibility in International Law

The international law of state responsibility holds states accountable for the acts or omissions of their agents and organs. Acts of violence against women committed by agents of the state thus directly engage state responsibility. Treaty-based and customary law also impose state responsibility for violations of certain rights by private persons if the state has condoned or acquiesced in the abuses.[6]

In addition, several treaty-based norms explicitly apply to private persons and require states parties to take measures to secure compliance with international obligations by non-governmental actors. The Women's Convention bars discrimination by private persons or organizations.[7] It also obligates states to take measures to eliminate social and cultural practices that constitute discrimination or that perpetuate stereotyped gender roles.[8] The Convention thus requires the state to take affirmative steps to protect women against discrimination by nonstate actors and to modify gender relations in private life.

The Committee on the Elimination of Discrimination Against Women (CEDAW), the expert body that monitors compliance with the Convention, has adopted a "general recommendation" making clear that the Convention prohibits gender-based violence as a form of discrimination.[9] Although CEDAW's general recommendations are not binding interpretations of the Convention, they do provide important guidance as to the meaning of its provisions. General recommendation number 19 emphasizes that the prohibitions of gender discrimination and gender-based violence are not restricted to acts by or on behalf of governments, but extend also to acts by private persons.[10]

Other human rights treaties also impose duties on the state to prevent and respond to breaches of certain rights by private persons. The *International Covenant on Civil and Political Rights,* the *European Convention for the Protection of Human Rights and Fundamental Freedoms,* and the *American Convention on Human Rights* all require the state to ensure, as well as to respect, the rights set forth. Emerging jurisprudence under these instruments has interpreted the obligation to ensure rights as entailing affirmative duties on the state to take the steps necessary to enable individuals to exercise their rights—marking a growing recognition of a duty on the part of the state to protect human beings against violations of their fundamental rights.

Authoritative interpretations of these conventions have outlined the scope of the state's duty to protect the rights not to be arbitrarily deprived of one's life and to integrity of the person.[11] Those interpretations make clear that a state violates its affirmative duty to secure these rights if it does not: establish adequate legal protections against violations by its agents or nonstate actors; make good faith efforts to investigate violations when they occur and seek to punish those responsible; and provide reparations to victims.

The opinion of the Inter-American Court of Human Rights in the *Velasquez Rodriguez* case sets out a framework for an analysis of state responsibility centered on affirmative duties to protect against violations.[12] In *Velasquez Rodriguez,* which concerned disappearances in Honduras, the Court stated that the duty to ensure rights implies the state's duty to organize the government apparatus, and all the structures through which public power is exercised, in such a way that they are capable of ensuring the full and free enjoyment of human rights.[13] As a consequence, states must take reasonable steps to prevent, investigate, and punish violations, and ensure the victim compensation.

With regard to violations committed by private actors of the rights to life or to physical and mental integrity, international and regional human rights treaties may hold the state accountable for its failure to exercise due diligence to prevent such violations or to respond to them as required by the treaty in question. In addition, a state's failure to punish repeated or notorious breaches of the rights to life and physical integrity breaches its obligations under customary law.[14] This focus on the failure to protect victims offers a framework for establishing state responsibility for gender-based violence by nonstate actors, but its application to particular forms of violence has yet to be developed.

Violence against women in the family has been at the center of the theoretical debate over state responsibility for gender-based violence by nonstate actors. The norms shielding the family from direct state intervention and the law of state responsibility have intersected to limit recognition of domestic violence as a human rights violation. There are recent positive developments in this area, however.

On December 20, 1993, the United Nations General Assembly adopted by consensus the *Declaration on the Elimination of Violence Against Women*.[15] The Declaration is the first international instrument to express international political consensus that states have human rights obligations to prevent gender-based violence and to redress the harm caused. The aims of the Declaration are to answer the "need for a clear and comprehensive definition of violence against women, [and] a clear statement of the rights to be applied to ensure the elimination of violence against women in all its forms" and to establish a "commitment" by states and by the international community to eliminate violence against women.[16] The Declaration crystallizes a political and moral commitment to end gender-based violence, but does not fully clarify the scope of state obligations to eliminate gender-based violence or the content of the category of violations termed "violence against women." These issues require further examination against the backdrop not only of the Declaration but also of the Women's Convention and general human rights instruments that prohibit gender discrimination and/or guarantee the physical and mental integrity of the person and other rights abrogated by gender-based violence.

Article 1 of the Declaration defines violence against women as "any act of gender-based violence that results in, or is likely to result in, physical, sexual or psychological harm or suffering to women, including threats of such acts, coercion or arbitrary deprivation of liberty, whether occurring in public or private life." Article 2 enumerates specific forms of violence that fall within this definition under the categories of violence in the family, violence "within the general community," and violence "perpetrated or condoned by the State, wherever it occurs." This emphasis on the site of violence, rather than on the nature of the harm suffered by women or whether it is directly or indirectly imputable to the state, reflects the programmatic nature of the Declaration.

The Declaration does not fully clarify the standard to be applied in defining state responsibility for violence by nonstate actors, however.

The definition of violence and the examples identified in Article 2 clearly encompass violence by nonstate actors within the family and in public life. Article 4 directs states to pursue a "policy of eliminating violence against women" and specifies strategies governments should adopt to eradicate it, including such specific measures as counseling; health and social services; and general preventive, punitive, and remedial measures. Efforts to eliminate violence against women are thus framed as policy initiatives rather than as measures pursuant to human rights standards. Article 4(c) also directs states to "exercise due diligence to prevent, investigate and, in accordance with national legislation, punish acts of violence against women, whether those acts are perpetrated by the State or private persons." The reference to "national legislation" undercuts the normative force of this provision and the right to reparation is omitted.

The Declaration is nonetheless a significant step toward building the normative framework applicable to violence against women. It underscores the connections between gender-based violence and women's subordination in public and private life. This link is more explicitly developed in CEDAW's general recommendation number 19, which interprets the Women's Convention to prohibit violence against women in the family, including battering, rape, mental suffering, and other violence perpetuated by traditional attitudes concerning women's subordinate status. The Committee has specified measures states should take to combat domestic violence, including criminal penalties, where necessary, and civil remedies; the abolition of the honor defense; and services to ensure women's safety and security.

Beyond Criminal Justice Responses

Women's human rights advocates have argued that, under general human rights law, state responsibility for domestic violence can be established where the state fails to enact and enforce criminal penalties against such violence. This approach is generally consonant with emerging international jurisprudence concerning the state's duty to ensure the rights to life and security of the person, as outlined above, but it raises questions concerning whether the standard of due diligence requires a broad-based failure by the state to protect and/or whether the prohibition of gender discrimination coupled with the right to a remedy for violations of the integrity of the person are sufficient bases for imposing state responsibility. In addition, establishing the necessary factual record presents serious practical difficulties, in light of the extent to which the state and society conceal domestic violence.

Analyses that rely on the failure to criminalize, investigate, and prosecute domestic violence as the principle means for establishing state responsibility should be further examined. The appropriateness of criminal penalties should be assessed in the context of particular social and political systems. Activists in a number of countries have stressed the need to evaluate the effectiveness of criminal justice approaches in deterring violence in the family within particular national legal and social systems, and their impact on women's needs for economic and social support.

Moreover, any analysis of the use of criminal penalties as a response to domestic violence must consider whether effective restraints on the exercise of police power are in place. Human rights organizations have reported patterns of rape and other sexual abuse by law enforcement officials in a number of countries. In addition, histories of police violence against communities of people of color in the United States and the United Kingdom, for example, mean that women in those communities often cannot rely on law enforcement officials for protection in cases of domestic violence. Indeed, in a number of cases women of color have themselves become the targets of police violence when they sought that protection. If the failure of the criminal justice system to protect against violence in the family is considered as the key to establishing state responsibility, broader questions about the use of the criminal justice system as a means of repression must be addressed. The state's duty to take effective measures against domestic violence must be defined to include civil remedies and reparations (compensation and rehabilitation) and preventive measures in the fields of education and social services.

Finally, there is a critical need to place gender-based violence within the context of women's structural inequality, as a means of breaking down the distinction between public and private life that operates to exclude gender-based violence from the human rights agenda. An analysis of women's structural inequality should be substituted for the current "mainstream" preoccupation with the public/private distinction. This requires advocates to take on an economic, social, and cultural rights agenda as such, as well as to attempt to recharacterize civil and political rights. Advocates should call for national and international measures to ensure basic economic, social, and cultural rights.

In addition, economic discrimination against women within the labor force, the informal sector, and the family, and development policies that hamper or deny women's access to economic resources, all reinforce violence against women. Within the family, the denial of access to household resources, and gender discrimination in the distribution of household resources (including the preference for male children in many societies that may result in inferior nutrition, medical care, and education for female children), place women and girls at risk of violence. Eliminating the structural inequality that reinforces gender-based violence thus requires steps to ensure the underlying rights and to end discrimination with regard to those rights.

Notes

1. See, e.g., *Universal Declaration of Human Rights* (Universal Declaration), arts. 12, 16(3), G.A. Res. 217, UN Doc. A/810, at 71 (1948); *International Covenant on Civil and Political Rights*, (ICCPR), arts. 17(1), 23(1), December 16, 1966, 999 U.N.T.S. 171.

2. Women's Convention, G.A. Res. 34/180, December 18, 1979, UN GAOR, 34th Sess., Supp. No. 46, UN Doc. A/34/46 (1979).

3. See generally, *Declaration, Reservations, Observations and Notifications of Withdrawal of Reservations Relating to the Convention on the Elimination of All Forms of Discrimination Against Women: Note by the Secretary-General*, UN Doc. CEDAW/SP/1992/2 (1992).

4. See, Universal Declaration, *supra* n. 1, art. 16(1); ICCPR, *supra* n. 1, art. 24(4).

5. *Convention on the Rights of the Child*, G.A. Res. 44/25, 44 UN GAOR, Supp. (No. 49), UN Doc. A/44/49, art. 19.

6. See, e.g., *Convention Against Torture and Other Cruel, Inhuman or Degrading Treatment or Punishment*, G.A. Res. 39/46, December 10, 1984, U.N. GAOR, 39th Sess., Supp. (No. 51), UN Doc. A/39/51, art. 1(1).

7. Women's Convention, *supra* n. 2, arts. 1, 2(c) and (f), and 5.

8. Idem, art. 5.

9. For the text of general recommendation No. 19, see UN Doc. HRI/GEN/1, p. 74 (1992).

10. Idem, p. 75.

11. For discussion of the scope of duties under human-rights treaties and customary law to prevent, investigate, and punish violations of the integrity of the person, see Diane Orentlicher, *Settling Accounts: The Duty to Prosecute Human-Rights Violations of a Prior Regime*, Yale Law Journal 100: 2537, 2566–73 (1991).

12. *Velasquez Rodriguez v. Honduras*, Inter-American Court H.R. (ser. C) No. 4, Judgment of July 29, 1988.

13. Idem, paras. 172, 174.

14. See Restatement (Third) of the Foreign Relations Law of the United States (1987).

15. G.A. Res. 48/104 of December 20, 1993. For the text as adopted, see UN Doc. A/C.3/48/L.5 (1993).

16. Idem, Preamble, para. 12.

16

State Discriminatory Family Law and Customary Abuses

Julie Mertus

The mythical haven of the nuclear family plays an important role in many societies; this unit, characterized by a legally married adult man and woman accompanied by children, floats in a separate, "private" sphere informed by religion, culture, and tradition, free from governmental interference.[1] Under the cloak of the separate sphere ideology, states maintain that they are incapable of dealing with domestic violence, child brides, and other inequities in marriage. The private life of the family must be respected, the state argues, and government must stay out. Yet, "far from being an enclave, the family is vulnerable to the state, and the laws and social policies that impinge upon it undermine the notion of separate spheres."[2] The state, however, only intrudes upon family life to the extent that such interventions serve larger political and social goals.

The State's Interest in Family Law

Family law, while not the only factor, is an important mechanism through which the state can maintain or disrupt existing family arrangements and influence women's ability to participate fully in the social and political spheres. Women's obligations in societies are often defined in terms of their obligations in the family. By prescribing women's role in society—as reproducer, producer, or a combination of the two—and by regulating women's access to wealth—particularly the rights to property ownership and inheritance—family laws profoundly affect women's social and economic status, influencing everything from women's access to education and health care to their rates of fertility and mortality.

When increased participation of women in economic and political activity would advance desired economic change, the state often promotes family reforms in order to reduce the control of families over women and to induce women into the labor force.[3] By contrast, where political and economic developments indicate that the state would benefit from higher fertility rates and low rates of women's participation in the formal labor sector, the state tightens social and legal policies toward women, further limiting their function to reproduction and related familial duties.[4] The unifying factor here is an instrumentalist approach toward women and the family—one that supports only the images of women that strengthen state goals.

Family law is complicated in many regions by the potential application of contradictory religious and/or customary laws and civil laws.[5] At times, states may refrain from redressing inequalities between religious law and civil legislation on the grounds that such restraint best respects culture and tradition and/or is most consistent with the state's secular ideology.[6] But states sometimes directly advance a religious legal code when doing so is deemed necessary and/or desirable, repressing the internal contradictions and interpretive difficulties usually present in religious law.[7]

Types of State Interventions

"Human rights norms postulate the right of everyone to marry and to found a family . . ."[8] but, at the outset, nearly all states restrict access to legally sanctioned family life through marriage regulation, defining acceptable and unacceptable forms of union and the social and political cost of unacceptable unions. Often, states further regulate the composition of the family through laws pertaining to reproductive freedom, including access to contraception, abortion, artificial insemination, and through economic inducements to bear—or not bear—children.

Family laws also often regulate rights and responsibilities within family units by, for example, specifying the responsibilities of family members to each other and respective rights upon dissolution (through divorce, death, abandonment, or migration). The content of these laws varies widely in different places, as Valentine Moghadam notes:

> In many cases female family members are understood, if not legally required, to be care providers (to children, to in-laws, and to parents).

In other cases, a father is legally required to provide for his family. In yet other cases there are social policies creating extra-family supports: day care, homes for the aged or infirm, nursing help, and so on. There may or may not be legal codes pertaining to domestic violence, child abuse, wife battering, or spousal rape.[9]

However constructed throughout the world, family laws and practices tend to perpetuate a patriarchal structure in which women are subordinated to men and in which male economic and decision-making powers are enhanced. In contemporary China and Korea, for example, the social systems foster patriarchy by institutionalizing women's economic and social dependence on men. A woman's worth is measured largely in relation to the man to whom she is appended, be he a father, a husband, or a son.[10] As in many societies, the women and girl children of the family are perceived as having little or no value and, as such, are the last to receive medical care, food, and education.[11]

Across cultures, the social organization of tribes or communal groups is usually based on blood ties through the male kin, and women have been subordinated through restrictive codes of behavior, gender segregation, and ideologies linking family honor to female virtue.[12] Men have been granted the right to make all important decisions for women, unilaterally determining when they shall marry and divorce, when and how often they shall bear children, and whether they shall be educated and permitted to work outside the home. To varying degrees, all societies employ legal measures and social practices designed to protect the superior position of men.

A Look at Selected Problem Areas

While a comprehensive summary of all family issues raising potential human rights concerns is beyond the scope of this essay, the following survey illustrates the global scope and varied nature of many of these concerns.

Consent to Marriage and Divorce

In many countries, marriages are still arranged by families, without the woman's consent. In Ethiopia, for example, women are used without their consent as a means of barter in a practice known as "exchange marriage," a system whereby a man who wishes to marry arranges with another man to exchange sisters.[13] In many Mediterranean countries, by law and by practice, women have little or no choice of mate. Likewise, families in several regions of the world promote "cousin marriages"—usually the union of second or third cousins—in order to safeguard control over property. The Maleki interpretation of Islamic law, prevalent in Northern Africa, for instance, favors arranged marriages within the extended patrilineal kin group.[14]

Through various devices, states may also restrict women's right to remarry. For example, Article 987 of the Civil Code in the Republic of China provides that "after the dissolution of her first marriage, a woman is prohibited to remarry within six months, unless within that period she has already given birth to a child."[15] Similarly, in many countries throughout the world, men have a unilateral right to divorce, while women's right to divorce, if it exists at all, is dependent upon the husband's consent.[16]

Marital Age

Families that arrange marriages for their girl children often do so before the girls reach puberty. In addition to the question of whether these young girls can and do consent to such marriages, this practice also raises the problem of early birth rates, which frequently are coupled with early marriages. Girls between the ages of 11 and 13 who give birth when they are not fully mature can suffer permanent injury to their health, and their maternal mortality rate is three times greater than that of the 20–24 year age group.[17] To combat this danger, many countries have enacted marital age laws. In some Middle Eastern countries, for example, the legal age of marriage is fifteen, higher in countries like Syria, Bangladesh, and Tunis.[18] A novel approach to the marital age problem is found in Syria, Jordan, and Morocco, where laws specify the minimum gap in ages between spouses. For example, Jordanian law proscribes marriages between women under the age of 18 and men more than 20 years older.[19] Despite the host of legal reforms addressing marital age, families in many countries continue to marry off their daughters at a young age.

Polygamy

While the laws of some countries in which polygamy is considered acceptable allow women to use their marital contracts to restrict their husbands' right to take additional wives, in most cases the decision ultimately rests with the husband.[20] Today, as one commentator has noted, polygamy is increasingly becoming a class phenomenon:

> Only a rich man can permit himself such a commitment. . . . As for the middle classes, they live mainly in towns, and urban living conditions have led them increasingly to adopt the nuclear family structure. What limitations there are on polygamy thus seem to flow more from economic conditions than from any reforming zeal aimed at reducing the inequalities suffered by women.[21]

Thus, polygamy continues to be practiced wherever men can afford it.

Instead of prohibiting polygamy outright, some countries attempt to regulate it.[22] In Bangladesh, for example, husbands who wish to take on additional wives must notify the Arbitration Council under the *Muslim Family Laws Ordinance*.[23] Yet few men obey the law, rendering these provisions and other legal mechanisms far from effective. And in Ethiopia, where the civil code explicitly forbids polygamy, polygamy is nevertheless practiced among both Christians and Muslims.[24]

Marriage Payments

The age-old practice of giving marriage payments of cash or kind at the time of marriage has been prevalent in numerous cultures, from Portugal and Spain (where such systems no longer exist) to India, Africa, and the Middle East (where they continue to function).[25] Cross-culturally, three systems are most prevalent: (1) dowry—property brought to the marriage, provided by the family of the bride; (2) dower—property brought to the marriage, provided by the family of the groom; and (3) bridewealth—property offered by the family of the groom to the family of the bride.[26]

Marriage payments were originally intended as a source of economic security for women in case of divorce or other emergency, as they were generally intended to be held for the woman's use upon dissolution of the marriage. In practice, however, the male kin exercise control over the dower. Thus, marriage payments often actually work against women's interests: the very idea that women carry a price advances the notion that women are property to be bought and sold.

Dowry Murders

Recently, a spate of vicious dowry murders have occurred among Hindu families in India. Husbands feel justified in killing their wives when the wives' families fail to deliver material goods as a continuing dowry payment.[27]

> The demands of in-laws, which sometimes escalate after marriage, leaves [*sic*] newly married daughters virtual hostages against payments by their parents. The young women are harassed by the in-laws with whom they must live, and are neglected by their own parents if they complain. Both families collude in the murders; one to find a new more lucrative hostage; the other to be free from harassment and expense.[28]

Many families do not accept the practice. Still, family members who try to press charges after a dowry murder have been beset by a host of legal difficulties from being ignored or scorned during the investigatory stage, to being prevented or dissuaded from presenting effective testimony.[29]

Various forms of violence are associated with dowry in Bangladesh as well.[30] In response, Bangladesh passed the *Dowry Prohibition Act* in 1980, making the giving of property or any other valuable security upon marriage an offense punishable by imprisonment and/or fine. In addition, the Bangladesh *Cruelty to Women Ordinance* of 1983 provides for capital punishment of a husband and his family for murdering or attempting to murder a woman to obtain a dowry.[31] Still, husbands may ignore both laws with impunity as it is difficult to prosecute a case successfully under their provisions.[32]

Domestic Violence

Domestic violence, like rape, is seriously underreported, but available statistics hint at the magnitude of the problem. Seventy percent of all crimes reported to the police in Peru are of women beaten by their partners.[33] In Japan, wife beating is the second most frequent cause of divorce initiated by women.[34] In Brazil, until 1991 wife killings were considered to be noncriminal "honor killings"; in just one year, nearly eight hundred husbands killed their wives.[35] Similarly, in Colombia, until 1980 a husband legally could kill his wife for committing adultery.[36] In the United States, the Federal Bureau of Investigation has estimated that a woman is beaten every eighteen seconds.[37] And in most regions of the world, including many states in the United States, husbands are free to rape their wives without fear of legal reprisal.[38]

Child Custody

The laws of many regions of the world grant the father the right to custody and control over the children. For instance, under *shari'a*, which (to varying degrees) regulates family law in Muslim countries, even when children live with their mother, fathers are considered the legal guardians and maintainers.[39] Women lose custody of their children altogether when the boys are seven and girls are nine, or when boys reach puberty or girls reach a marriageable age. In contrast, custody decisions in some U.S. courts have been made on the assumption that custody and control of children should be granted to the so-called biological mother, thus forcing the father or guardian of the children to prove that the best interests of the children mandate an alternative placement. At the same time, U.S. courts have held that a "nonbiological parent" who is nevertheless a "psychological parent" cannot even make a case for visitation rights.[40]

Citizenship

The area of citizenship is one in which a great conflict exists between religious and customary law, on the one hand, and civil law, on the other. In Sri Lanka, for example, while civil laws grant women equal access to citizenship, religious laws may assign a woman (and her children) citizenship only on the basis of the husband's status.[41] Another problem, typical of many countries, is found in Gabon, where a woman must renounce her citizenship upon marrying a foreigner; if she is subsequently divorced, she cannot regain her original Gabonese citizenship.[42]

International and domestic courts have at times been receptive to women's challenges to discriminatory citizenship provisions. In 1992 in Botswana, Unity Dow, a Botswana national married to an American, successfully challenged a Botswana law declaring that a father's nationality determines children's citizenship. In 1984, at the request of Costa Rica, the Inter-American Court on Human Rights issued an advisory opinion providing that the right accorded to women to acquire the nationality of their husbands was "an outgrowth of conjugal inequality" and that legal solutions "which favor only one of the spouses . . . constitute discrimination".[43] Similarly, in 1979 the United Nations Human Rights Committee found against a Mauritian law that restricted the right of residence of foreign husbands but not of foreign wives.[44]

Credit, Loans, and Entitlements

States limit women's access to credit and loans through overt restrictions on their ability to obtain credit and/or through requirements that loans be given only to or with the consent of the "head of the household," i.e., the husband or eldest son.[45] For example, in Sri Lanka, women governed under a system of customary law known as *Tesawalamai* have been denied the right to contract property without the consent of their husbands.[46]

The assumption that men are the supporters and heads of households also reinforces many state policies pertaining to entitlements and housing. In fact, few countries have changed their laws in order to eliminate sex prejudice in this area, instead requiring at a minimum that a married woman prove that she is a breadwinner before she may claim any state benefits, while not requiring a man to offer any such proof.[47] Globally, such policies hinder women's access to equal resources.[48]

Property Ownership and Inheritance

Married women are doubly jeopardized in property ownership rights.[49] As women, they often cannot own and inherit property; as *married* women, whatever rights to property they might otherwise have are stripped away.[50] Under customary law in Africa, for example, "in terms of real property, where this is communal or clan property, a woman has no right to exercise ownership rights over it. Under customary law all the property acquired by the spouses, except personal goods, belong to the husband who is entitled to retain all of it at the dissolution of the marriage."[51] In Rwanda, for instance, a married woman cannot enter into contracts, buy or sell property (including land), or even open a bank account without the authorization of her husband.[52]

Similarly, many countries either deny women the right to inherit, render their claims secondary to those of male kin, or treat their claims in other subordinate and discriminatory ways.[53] Some women have brought successful court challenges to laws pertaining to inheritance and property ownership. For example, in 1986, the UN Human Rights Committee held that Peruvian legislation, which allowed only husbands to represent marital property in the legal system, was discriminatory.[54]

Concluding Remarks

In different contexts and to varying degrees, nearly all states have used the institution of marriage and family to mold the role of women to suit the states own needs. Given the great impact of family law on women's lives, states have an obligation to address injustices in the family. Yet women organizing to combat the problems illustrated above encounter a dilemma, for, torn between political expediency and justice, states will never choose justice until they are pressured into believing that justice is politically expedient.

Notes

1. Rebecca Cook has called this an "ideally perceived family, based upon middle class standards of westernized countries." Rebecca Cook, "The Family as a Basic Unit of Social Order," 8th Commonwealth Law Conference, Ocho Rios, Jamaica, Sept. 7–13, 1986.

2. Valentine M. Moghadam, *Modernizing Women* (Boulder, CO: Lynne Rienner, 1993), p. 104.

3. The 1978 personal status law in Iraq (the Ba'th Party) provides one illustration of this phenomenon. Suad Joseph, "Elite Strategies for State-Building: Women, Family, Religion and the State in Iraq and Lebanon," in *Women, Islam and the State*, ed. Deniz Kandiyoti (London: Macmillan, 1991), pp. 176–200. For another example in Soviet Central Asia, see Gregory J. Massel, *The Surrogate Proletariat: Muslim Women and Revolutionary Strategies in Soviet Central Asia, 1919–1929* (Princeton, NJ: Princeton Univ. Press, 1974). See generally, *Promissory Notes: Women in the Transition to Socialism*, ed. Sonia Kurks, Rayna Rapp, and Marilyn Young (New York: Monthly Review, 1989); Kumari Jayawardena, *Feminism and Nationalism in the Third World* (London: Zed, 1986); Maxine Molyneux, "Socialist Societies: Progress Toward Women's Emancipation?" *Monthly Review* (3) (July–August 1982): 56–100.

4. For an example of this phenomenon in Palestine, see Nahla Abdo-Zubi, *Family, Women and Social Change in the Middle East: The Palestinian Case* (Toronto:

Canadian Scholars' Press, 1987), pp. 29–30. For other examples in Eastern Europe, see Ann Snitow, "Feminist Futures in the Former East Block," *Peace and Democracy News* 7(1) (Summer 1993). See also Nira Yuval-Davis and Floya Anthias, eds., *Women-Nation-State* (London: Macmillan, 1989).

5. For example, the Civil Code of Ethiopia recognizes three types of marriages: (1) civil marriage, which is celebrated before an officer of civil status; (2) religious marriage, which is celebrated according to the religious rite of the religion of one or both of the parties; (3) customary marriage, which is celebrated according to the custom of the community to which the spouses belong. To complicate matters further, in addition to the civil code, the law of marriage in Ethiopia is covered by many different customary laws, including but not limited to: (1) the *Fetha Negast,* a work combining both spiritual and secular matters, applied mainly to Christians of the Ethiopian plateau; (2) the *shari'a,* the religious law of Ethiopian Muslims; and (3) the *gada,* the sociopolitical system of the Ormo people of Ethiopia. Daniel Haile, "Law and the Status of Women in Ethiopia," African Training and Research Centre for Women, Addis Ababa, Ethiopia (1980), pp. 1, 3. For another complicated illustration from Sri Lanka, see Ministry of Health and Women's Affairs, "Status of Women (Sri Lanka)" (March 1993), p. 1.

6. According to Rani Jethmalani, India adopts such an approach in refusing to reconcile the differences between its very egalitarian state constitutional provisions and its religious laws. Rani Jethmalai, "India: Law and Women," in *Empowerment and the Law: Strategies of Third World Women,* ed. Margaret Schuler (Washington, DC: O.E.F. International, 1986), pp. 60, 61. See also Helen L. Vukasin, " 'We Carry A Heavy Load,' Rural Women in Zimbabwe Speak Out: Part II 1981–1991," Zimbabwe Women's Bureau (1992). Another roadblock to advancing women's status in marriage is education about legal reforms, and illiteracy generally. Idem.

7. For example, as Mounira Charrad points out, differences in family legislation between Tunisia, Morocco, and Algeria—all Islamic countries—can be attributable to variations in the balance of power between the state and local communities and the goals of the state. Mounira Charrad, "State and Gender in the Maghrib," *Middle East Report* 163 (March–April 1990): 19, 20.

8. Katarina Tomasevski, *Women and Human Rights* (London: Zed, 1993).

9. Valentine, M. Moghadam, *Modernizing Women,* supra n. 2, p. 104.

10. Shen Mei-Chen, "The Sex Discrimination of Current Family Law in the R.O.C. and the Strategies for Change in the Future," paper presented at the Asian Conference on Women, Religion and Family Laws, December 16–20, 1987, Bombay, India; Tai-Young Lee, "Korea: Customs and Family Law Reform," in *Empowerment and the Law: Strategies of Third World Women,* ed. Margaret Schuler (Washington, DC: OEF International, 1986), p. 306; Judith Stacey, *Patriarchy and Socialist Revolution in China* (Berkeley: Univ. of California Press, 1983). For an essay on recent changes in family law in Korea (which nonetheless notes that the "head-of-household" provisions privileging men remain intact), see Sung-Ja Chang, Soon-Young Chung, and Sun-Hye Kang, *Status of Women in Korea* (Korean Women's Developmental Institute, 1991), pp. 54–56.

11. See Amartya Sen and Sunil Sengupta, "Malnutrition of Rural Children and the Sex Bias," *Economic and Political Weekly* 18 (1983): 855–63.

12. For a discussion of the link between female virtue and family honor, see David Mandelbaum, *Women's Seclusion and Men's Honor: Sex Roles in North India, Bangladesh and Pakistan* (Tucson: Univ. of Arizona Press, 1988); Fatima Mernissi, *Beyond the Veil: Male-Female Dynamics in Modern Muslim Society* (Bloomington: Indiana Univ. Press, 1987); Fatna A. Sabbah, *Women in the Muslim Unconscious,* trans. Mary Jo Lakeland (New York: Pergamon, 1984).

13. Daniel Haile, "Law and the Status of Women in Ethiopia," unpublished paper, African Training and Research Centre for Women, Addis Ababa, Ethiopia (1980), pp. 7–8.

14. Mounira Charrad, "State and Gender in the Maghrib," *Middle East Report* 163 (March–April 1990): 19–24.

15. Shen Mei-Chen, "The Sex Discrimination of Current Family Law in the R.O.C. and the Strategies for Change in the Future," a paper presented at the Asian Conference on Women, Religion and Family Laws, December 16–20, 1987, Bombay, India, pp. 10–11.

16. For the situation in India, see Rani Jethmalai, "India: Law and Women," in *Empowerment and the Law: Strategies of Third World Women,* ed. Margaret Schuler (Washington, DC: OEF International, 1986), pp. 60, 63; in Bangladesh, Rabia Bhuiyan, "Bangladesh: Personal Law and Violence Against Women," in *Empowerment and the Law: Strategies of Third World Women,* ed. Margaret Schuler (Washington DC: OEF International, 1986), pp. 48, 49; Juliette Mincer (Michael Pallis, translator) *The House of Obedience: Women in Arab Society* (London: Zed, 1982), pp. 64–68.

17. Halima Embarek Warzazi (Special Rapporteur), *Study on Traditional Practices Affecting the Health of Women and Children,* Final Report, UN Doc. E/CN.4/Sub.2/1991/6, July 1991, para. 30.

18. In Bangladesh, *The Child Marriage Restraint Act Ordinance* of 1984 raised the marriageable age of females from 16 to 18 years of age and of males from 18 to 21. Rabia Bhuiyan, "Bangladesh: Personal Law and Violence Against Women," in *Empowerment and the Law: Strategies of Third World Women,* ed. Margaret Schuler (Washington DC: OEF International, 1986), p. 50. See also Naila Kabeer, "Subordination and Struggle: Women in Bangladesh," *New Left Review* 168 (March/April 1988): 95.

19. Jamal J. Nasir, *The Status of Women Under Islamic Law* (London: Graham & Trotman, 1990), pp. 7–8.

20. The reasons for tolerating polygamy range from economic justifications to romantic ones. Compare "Malaysia: States Differ on Approaches to Polygamy," *Far Eastern Economic Review* (August 22, 1991): 18, with Melford E. Spiro, *Kinship and Marriage in Burma: A Cultural and Psychodynamic Analysis* (Berkeley: Univ. of California Press, 1977), p. 251.

21. Juliette Mincer (Michael Pallis, translator) *The House of Obedience: Women in Arab Society* (London: Zed, 1982), p. 63.

22. For a summary of reforms in Muslim countries, see John L. Esposito, *Women in Muslim Family Law* (Syracuse, NY: Syracuse Univ. Press, 1982), p. 84.

23. Rabia Bhuiyan, "Bangladesh: Personal Law and Violence Against Women," *Empowerment and the Law: Strategies of Third World Women,* ed. Margaret Schuler (Washington, DC: OEF International, 1986), p. 49.

24. Daniel Haile, "Law and the Status of Women in Ethiopia," unpublished paper, African Training and Research Centre for Women, Addis Ababa, Ethiopia (1980), p. 6.

25. See, e.g., *Initial Report of Guinea* (reporting on compliance under the *International Covenant on Civil and Political Rights*), UN Doc. CCPR/C/6Add.11 of November 25, 1986 (noting the existence of dowry); Daniel Haile, "Law and the Status of Women in Ethiopia," unpublished paper, African Training and Research Centre for Women, Addis Ababa, Ethiopia (1980), p. 5 (noting the existence of bride price in Ethiopia). A system akin to the dowry is practiced in some parts of Japan; however, the gift accompanying the bride in Japan is regarded as a trousseau, rather than a dowry, because the items are usually for the bride's personal use. See Joy Hendry, *Marriage in Changing Japan: Community and Society* (Rutland, VT: Charles E. Tuttle, 1981), pp. 165–66.

26. Melford E. Spiro, *Kinship and Marriage in Burma: A Cultural and Psychodynamic Analysis* (Berkeley: Univ. of California Press, 1977), pp. 192–209 (noting various types of marriage payments in Burma). Although dower and bridewealth are alike in that the groom's side is the property giver, they differ importantly because in the dower the property is brought to the marriage (and usually becomes part of the conjugal estate of the newlyweds), while in the bridewealth the property is offered to and becomes the possession of the family or lineage of the bride. Idem.

27. Usha Bhowmik, "The Dowry System in the Context of the Present Social Order and the Need for a Social Structure Based on Equality, Liberty and Peace," unpublished manuscript, Bombay, India; (cited in Janice Wood Wetzel, *The World of Women: In Pursuit of Human Rights* (New York: MacMillan, 1993), p. 165).

28. Janice Wood Wetzel, *The World of Women, supra* n. 27, p. 164. See also Hanna Papanek, "India's Dowry Murders Mark Rise in Violence Against Women," *The New York Times,* February 11, 1989.

29. Rani Jethmalai, "India: Law and Women," in *Empowerment and the Law: Strategies of Third World Women,* ed. Margaret Schuler (Washington, DC: OEF International, 1986), pp. 60, 62.

30. Rabia Bhuiyan, "Bangladesh: Personal Law and Violence Against Women," *Empowerment and the Law: Strategies of Third World Women,* ed. Margaret Schuler (Washington, DC: OEF International, 1986), p. 48.

31. Idem.

32. Idem, p. 50.

33. Janice Wood Wetzel, *The World of Women, supra* n. 27, p. 161.

34. Idem.

35. James Brooke, "Honor Killing of Wives is Outlawed in Brazil," *New York Times,* March 29, 1991.

36. Magdala Velasquez Toro, "Colombia: Legal Gains for Women," in *Empowerment and the Law: Strategies of Third World Women,* ed. Margaret Schuler (Washington, DC: OEF International, 1986), pp. 71, 73.

37. Janice Wood Wetzel, *The World of Women, supra* n. 27, p. 161.

38. Idem.

39. John L. Esposito, *Women in Muslim Family Law* (Syracuse, NY: Syracuse Univ. Press, 1982), p. 37.

40. One court considering a lesbian custody case termed this parent the "non-biological stranger." *Alison D. v. Virginia M.,* 77 N.Y.2d 651, 569 N.Y.S.2d 586 (1991).

41. See, e.g., a discussion of such a conflict in Sri Lanka, in Sri Lanka Ministry of Health and Women's Affairs, "Status of Women (Sri Lanka)" (March 1993), pp. 2–3.

42. *Implementation in Africa of the Convention on the Elimination of All Forms of Discrimination Against Women,* UN Doc. E/ACA/CM.13/27 (1987), para 33.

43. *Advisory Opinion of the Inter-American Court on Human Rights of 19 January 1984,* Series A, Judgment and Opinions, No. 4, paras. 64 and 68.

44. United Nations, Human Rights Committee, Communication No. R.9/35. In this case, a group of twenty women successfully challenged the *Mauritian Immigration (Amendment) Act* (1977) and the *Deportation (Amendment) Act* (1977) that granted an unrestricted right of residence to foreign wives of Mauritian nationals but restricted the right of residence of foreign husbands. The Human Rights Committee found the law to be in violation of the *International Covenant on Civil and Political Rights* (ICCPR) in that it constituted sex discrimination and violation of Mauritian women's right to found and protect a family.

45. For the head of household system in Korea, see Tai-Young Lee, "Korea: Customs and Family Law Reform," *Empowerment and the Law: Strategies of Third World Women,* ed. Margaret Schuler (Washington, DC: OEF International, 1986), p. 306.

46. Savitri Gooneskere, "Sri Lanka: Legal Status of Women," *Empowerment and the Law: Strategies of Third World Women,* ed. Margaret Schuler (Washington, DC: OEF International, 1986), pp. 52, 56. See also Sri Lanka Ministry of Health and Women's Affairs, "Status of Women (Sri Lanka)" (March 1993), p. 1; Anberiya Hanifa, "Contemporary Family Laws Applicable to Muslims of Sri Lanka," paper presented at Asian Conference on Women, Religion and Family Laws, December 1987, Bombay, India.

47. Katarina Tomasevski, *Women and Human Rights* (London: Zed, 1993), p. 35. See also A. M. Brocas, *Women and Social Security, Progress Towards Equality of Treatment* (Geneva, Switzerland: International Labour Office, 1990), p. 30.

48. See "Nairobi Forward-Looking Strategies for Advancement of Women," UN Doc. A/CONF.116/28, 15 September 1985, para. 295.

49. See Submission by UNESCO, in *Respect for the Right of Everyone to Own Property Alone as Well as in Association With Others and its Contribution to the Economic and Social Development of Member States,* Report of the Secretary-General, UN Doc. A/45/523, 22 October 1990, p. 43.

50. For the situation in India, see Rani Jethmalai, "India: Law and Women," *Empowerment and the Law: Strategies of Third World Women,* ed. Margaret Schuler (Washington, DC: OEF International, 1986), pp. 60, 67; and Chandermani Chopra, "India: Women and Property Rights," *Empowerment and the Law: Strategies of Third World Women,* ed. Margaret Schuler (Washington, DC: OEF Interna-

tional, 1986), p. 84; for Ethiopia, see Daniel Haile, "Law and the Status of Women in Ethiopia," unpublished paper, African Training and Research Centre for Women, Addis Ababa, Ethiopia (1980), pp. 29–31; for the Republic of China, see Shen Mei-Chen, "The Sex Discrimination of Current Family Law in the R.O.C. and the Strategies for Change in the Future," a paper presented at the Asian Conference on Women, Religion and Family Laws, December 16–20, 1987, Bombay India, pp. 12–13; for Nepal, see Prativa Subedi, *Nepal Women Rising* (Katmandu: Women's Awareness Center, 1993); for Muslim family law generally, see John Esposito, *Women in Muslim Family Law* (Syracuse: Syracuse University Press, 1982), pp. 39–48.

51. "Comparative Study of National Laws on the Rights and Status of Women in Africa," UN Doc. ECA/ATCRW/3.5(ii) (b)/89/3 (1989), p. 9. For a comment on changes in the law related to marital property in South Africa, see June Sinclair, "South Africa: Marriage, Property and Money," *Journal of Family Law*, 26(1) (1987–88): 187–95.

52. *Implementation in Africa of the Convention on the Elimination of All Forms of Discrimination Against Women*, UN Doc. E/ACA/CM.13/27 (1987), para 51.

53. For example, despite changes in the law in Japan, the male son usually enjoys a greater right to inheritance. Joy Hendry, *Marriage in Changing Japan: Community and Society* (Rutland, VT: Charles E. Tuttle, 1981), p. 97.

54. United Nations, Human Rights Committee, Communication No. 202/1986. As early as 1963, the Economic and Social Council (ECOSOC) recognized that discrimination in inheritance laws is incompatible with the principle of equal rights for women. United Nations Economic and Security Council Resolution 888D (XXXIV) of July 16, 1962.

The author would like to thank Nadine Taub, Mahnaz Afkhami, Shahla Haeri, Anika Raman, Marsha Freeman, and Regan Ralph for their comments and suggestions, and to acknowledge the last-minute research assistance of Fania Washington, Jean Lee, and the staff of the International Women's Tribune Centre.

17

The Human Rights of Women in the Family: Issues and Recommendations for Implementation of the Women's Convention

Marsha A. Freeman

Human rights begin at home. The rationale given most often for denial of human rights to half the world's population—women—is preservation of family and culture. But preservation of family and culture need not, and should not, be pursued at the expense of human rights. The *Convention on the Elimination of All Forms of Discrimination Against Women* (the Women's Convention) defines equality within the family as well as the role of the state in promoting an equitable balance between preservation of family units and protection of individual family members. A multilateral treaty (ratified as of December 1993 by 130 countries), the Women's Convention establishes international standards of equality between women and men in a context that includes the historical fact of change in families and in society.

The essential premise of nondiscrimination, stated in the *Universal Declaration of Human Rights* in the Women's Convention . . . and in all the multilateral human rights treaties, is that human rights shall not be denied on the basis of membership in a particular racial, ethnic, or religious group and, particularly, on the basis of sex.[1] The essence of human rights is respect for human dignity and for the human capacity to make responsible choices, regardless of gender or geography.

The substantive provisions of the Women's Convention describe the significant areas in which women must be accorded the right to make choices. Two of the most important are marriage and family law (Article 16)—because women's roles, responsibilites, and recognized capacities within the family are frequently limited by law and by culture and affect the exercise of their capacities outside the family as well; and nationality (Article 9), because it defines the essence of women's relationship with the state. The foundation of all the rights outlined in these articles is legal personhood-legal capacity, as stated in Article 15. While other human rights instruments allude very generally to this right, the Women's Convention spells it out, stating that women shall be equal with men before the law and shall have full legal capacity equal to that of men.

Women's Human Rights and Legal Capacity

The Women's Convention is based on the premise that achievement of women's human rights—their essential right to personal liberty and fundamental freedoms—requires recognition of their legal and de facto capacity to conduct themselves as responsible adults. The centrality of legal rights as a goal was debated at length during the drafting of the Convention. As the document developed, it was clearly designed to foster improvement of women's status through a legal rights approach rather than through a social welfare approach. Most of the sixteen substantive articles obligate states parties to take appropriate measures, *including legislation,* to ensure equal rights and opportunities for women in all areas that governments have the power to regulate.[2]

Legal capacity connotes adulthood in all its aspects, from appearing in court on one's own behalf to making decisions about bearing children. The concept rests on the distinction between those who are acknowledged to have the knowledge and judgment to make legally enforceable decisions and those who are not. In many countries and cultures, adult women still are not seen as people with full capacity to make responsible decisions. They remain legal minors, unable to own property, obtain credit on their own, or make legally effective decisions affecting their children, such as consent to medical procedures.

Beyond its classic *de jure* meaning, capacity also refers to the ability to accept and to exercise the responsibilities of adulthood in one's society and to perceive oneself and be perceived as an adult. Nationality and family law are two of the most important areas in which this recognition is essential. Equal nationality rights acknowledge women's relation to the state as full adult citizens. Equality in the family is a matter of fully recognizing women's personal and economic contributions, as responsible adults, to family well-being, without confining them solely to roles within the family.

The law and the language of capacity are positive methods of addressing equality issues. They focus on ability, action, and inclusion. Elimination of discrimination against women, and implementation of the principles of the Women's Convention, ultimately rely on the recognition of women's legal and de facto capacity in every aspect of life. Articles 9, 15, and 16 of the Women's Convention state the principles that are fundamental to that recognition.

Article 15

In providing for women's full legal capacity, Article 15 of the Women's Convention obligates all governments to ensure that women can exercise the full range of rights necessary to function as responsible adults in society. It states simply that women shall have equality with men before the law, full legal capacity and the same opportunities as men to exercise that capacity, and equal rights pertaining to property. Women are to have equal rights to make contracts, and contracts limiting women's legal capacity are to be deemed null and void. The article also confirms women's human right to liberty of the person in specifically stating that women shall have equal rights to movement and to choice of residence and domicile.

Historically, in the common law and in European legal systems, legal capacity has been denied to children, the mentally impaired, and women, on the grounds that they are not in a position to protect themselves against those who might take advantage of their lack of knowledge and judgment. While children and mentally impaired persons as a matter of fact can be found to lack the judgment and/or knowledge to make decisions of legal consequence, women have been deemed legal minors solely because of their sex. In the last hundred years, many countries' laws have evolved formally to recognize women's legal capacity, although in many places male consent is still required (formally or informally) for some transactions, such as obtaining bank loans. Men still frequently have the right to manage family property as, for example, in Chile, where most marriages are on a "conjugal association" (community property) basis, in which the husband has the sole right to manage the property.

Article 15: Directive Language

While most of the substantive articles of the Convention require states parties to "take all appropriate measures" to eliminate discrimination in particular areas, Article 15 states that states parties "shall" accord the rights of legal personhood. The obligation is clear, the measures indicated unequivocally; if and when such measures are enacted, they provide the legal basis for women to take their place economically and politically as adults in the community, in the family, in society at large.

Article 15(2): Contracts, Property, and Majority

Under Article 15(2), states parties must provide women with the same opportunities as men to exercise all aspects of legal capacity. At the most basic level, this means that the age of majority should be the same for women as for men and that women of legal age should be able to undertake contractual obligations and administer property in their own right. In essence, this provision requires states parties to recognize women as citizens with economic interests.

The language of Article 15(2) also implies that women should be able to inherit property on an equal basis with men, and this is confirmed by the language of Article 16(1) (h). Legal capacity to "administer property" refers to the ability to own as well as to manage, and administration of property includes administration of estates; along with equal rights to inheritance, this last issue remains a matter of controversy throughout the world, as many religious and customary legal systems are based on assumptions that property must be retained in male hands, and statutory systems reflect the traditions of male property control.

The existence of legal and cultural impediments to owning and managing property, however, is a major cause of women's poverty worldwide. A recent U.S. Agency for International Development (AID) inquiry found that legal status limited women's participation in approximately half of AID development projects. Land-title acts and practice frequently exclude women—particularly married women—from taking title to land, even in progressive redistribution schemes.

Marital property generally includes all the property accumulated by either (or any, in the case of polygamy) spouse during a marriage for use in maintaining the household and family. In many cultures, however, the wages or products of women's labor are used to support family needs, while men's income is used exclusively by and for men. In many countries, marital property is controlled by the husband only, either by law or by tradition. Some marital property regimes provide that all assets gained during marriage belong to the husband or his family.

In community property states, all property accumulated by a married couple belongs jointly to them and is divided equally between them upon divorce. Despite the presumed equality of ownership, however, management authority over the property frequently belongs to the husband. Where authority over marital property is joint by law, the balance of power between the spouses will determine the management issue. Even where the power over property is joint, the law may still provide, as it does in Botswana, that the husband remain head of household for purposes of domicile and guardianship of the children, thus weighing the balance of power in his favor.[3]

Article 15(2): Equal Treatment before Courts and Tribunals

"Equal treatment at all stages of procedure in courts and tribunals" (Article 15[2]) must be established in practice as well as by law. In many countries women still do not have the legal ability to appear in court in their own right nor is their testimony accorded equal weight to men's. But even where these issues have long since been resolved, the issue of women's treatment in the courts remains significant.

In the last ten years, a close examination of the treatment of women in the courts has been undertaken by women's law groups, state bar associations, and state and federal judiciaries in the United States and Canada and in a number of developing countries. The uniform conclusion of these studies is that, for economic and cultural reasons, the courts are at worst totally inaccessible to women and at best reflective of the discriminatory legacy of male-dominated legal systems and judiciaries. In all countries, women's relative poverty, socialization, and lack of education or knowledge of their rights frequently prevent them from asserting themselves to claim those rights.

In all countries, judges and court personnel frequently operate on the basis of biased assumptions about women's roles and capabilities and treat women in their courtrooms with less respect than they show men. In divorce cases, women are frequently not awarded the property and maintenance they should receive under the law because of misplaced sympathy for men's financial well-being. In countries in which women are supposedly protected by progressive domestic abuse laws, judges sometimes refuse to issue orders of protection and accuse women of exaggerating claims or provoking the abuse. Women lawyers report disturbingly frequent incidents of disrespectful behavior and even harassment, which affects their ability to obtain favorable outcomes for their clients. Female court personnel are subject to sexual harassment by judges, against whom they have no recourse, and even women judges report disrespectful behavior by male colleagues and court staff.

Women consistently have less access to the courts to press their legal claims, primarily for economic reasons. To meet the Article 15(2) obligation to accord women the same opportunity as men to exercise their legal capacity, states parties should make certain that any legal aid or legal literacy projects they establish are properly staffed to address women's needs.

Article 15(3): Contracts Limiting Legal Capacity

Article 15(3), which calls for the nullification of all contracts and other private instruments "directed at restricting the legal capacity of women," was the subject of considerable discussion during the drafting process. While there was some question about whether contracts covered by international law were included in the meaning of "contracts," states parties seemed to agree that private contracts between individuals are covered by this section, that it covers commercial as well as personal matters, and that any contract that restricts women's legal capacity should be void by law.[4] Despite these interpretations, however, it is clear that no state party has undertaken systematically to nullify by law contracts that limit women's legal capacity.

The prime example of a private contract that restricts legal capacity is the marriage contract, which may be a document negotiated by the parties or be implied. Where marriage contracts are implied, rights and duties between spouses, while not overtly stated by law or private contract at the time of marriage, become apparent at the time of dissolution because failure to live up to the implied contract (adultery, abandonment, failure to support, failure to have children) becomes the basis of the dissolution.

Article 15(4): Freedom to Choose Residence and Domicile

Although freedom of movement is universally recognized as a basic human right, women's right to move freely is frequently restricted by law and by culture. For women, the legal right to choose one's residence and/or domicile is usually restricted by marriage. In some countries, such as Iraq, a woman can never choose her domicile, as it must be either that of her father or that of her husband. In many countries—Madagascar, Iraq, and Kenya, for example—the law requires that the husband determine the domicile for the family, although in Kenya the wife can establish her own domicile as well. In Senegal, a wife can challenge the husband's choice of domicile if she "believes it will result in physical or moral danger to the family." While it may seem impractical for married couples to have separate domiciles, it is nonetheless discriminatory to insist that domicile be determined by the husband. Moreover, since some married couples do live apart, requiring that the wife's domicile be that of her husband not only is impractical but also can create hardship for her and for the couple's children.

Article 9: Nationality

The basic legal relationship between the individual and the state lies in the concept of nationality. The state grants to its citizens certain rights and protections, and the citizens in turn are expected to have certain loyalties to the state. In the contemporary world of nation-states, a stateless person lacks both the right to live in a particular place and the positive rights, such as education and political participation, granted by a state to its citizens.

Because nationality is so fundamental, it is essential that it be granted on a nondiscriminatory basis. The language of Article 9, like that of Article 15, is prescriptive and unequivocal, stating that states parties "shall grant women equal rights with men" in matters of their own and their children's nationality. Discrimination regarding nationality is primarily an issue for married women, as governments traditionally have considered married women's nationality to be related to, and frequently subsumed in, that of their husbands. One of the first international instruments to deal specifically with women's human rights was the *Convention on the Nationality of Married Women* (opened for signature January 29, 1957; entered into force August 11, 1958), which, by requiring that states not discriminate against women in granting nationality to their citizens, clearly establishes that states' sovereignty interests may be overridden by the international human rights principle of nondiscrimination.

Nationality laws generally discriminate against women by limiting their rights in situations in which men's nationality rights are not limited. A common form of discrimination is the failure to extend to women the legal ability to confer on foreign husbands certain rights (such as the right of residency or the right to become a citizen after a relatively short residency period) that men can confer on their foreign wives. If a woman's decision to marry a foreign national results in her losing citizenship or his having an uncertain right to reside in her country, her fundamental freedom to marry and found a family is restricted.

Nationality is integral to women's exercise of personal liberty and freedom of movement. If a woman's nationality or that of her children is dependent upon her husband's, her ability to make adult decisions as to residence, travel, her children's welfare, or even marriage is severely limited. In Saudi Arabia, women are not permitted to leave the country without the written permission of father or husband (indeed, female visitors are not allowed into the country unless accompanied by a male family member). In Nigeria, married women cannot obtain passports without their husbands' permission; while this appears to be a customary, rather than a legal, practice, its eradication is as important to implementing Article 9 as any legal change.

Article 9(2): Nationality of Children

Article 9(2) provides that women and men shall have equal rights with respect to the nationality of children. This is a critical area in which many countries continue to discriminate. The standard discriminatory legal construction is that, under certain circumstances, only fathers can pass citizenship to their children. Kenya, Madagascar, and Rwanda, for example, provide that children of a marriage between a citizen and a foreign national are considered to be citizens of the father's country. Under such laws, in a marriage between nationals of different countries, the mother's citizenship is rendered meaningless as to her children. This not only discriminates against women but also makes the children potentially stateless, because laws on claiming nationality are not consistent from country to country, and the children may lose citizenship in one parent's country before they meet the residency requirements to gain citizenship in that of the other.

Laws that prohibit children born in wedlock from taking their mother's nationality severely restrict a woman's freedom of movement because she cannot decide to travel without considering that her children cannot travel with her on her passport. If she divorces, she cannot take her children out of the country, while her husband, who has the sole right to travel with them, can. Further, where children take only their father's nationality, their mother may not have an independent right to have them live with her because the children's right of residency frequently depends on the citizenship attributed to the children.

Article 16: Marriage and Family Law

Article 16(1) (a): Starting Out: Entry into Marriage
Article 16(1) (b): Rights to Consent

Because many limitations on equality in the family are based on religious or customary personal status laws, successful implementation of the Convention requires countries to ensure that individuals can marry under a civil marriage code designed on a basis of equality within the family. All couples should be allowed to marry under the civil code regardless of religion, race, or ethnicity. This allows them to have the choice of marrying without subjecting themselves to the inequities of other codes and avoids the serious legal problems that can arise when the spouses are from different religious or ethnic communities and therefore subject to different personal status laws.

For most women, marriage is a major life event that defines their economic and social roles and status, and confirms them as adults in their society. For too many women, however, marriage is more limiting than liberating. The premise of Article 16 is that marriage must be a partnership of equals in which each spouse has the opportunity to develop her or his capacities.

Article 16(1) (a) and (b) concern the goal of equality at the point of entering marriage. The key issue is choice: Do women have the same degree of choice concerning marriage as men do? In many countries marriages are arranged, and neither spouse has a great deal of choice; but there also are many circumstances in which women—particularly young girls—are forced by their families to marry men who have chosen them. In some cultures, levirate marriage (marriage of a widow to her husband's brother) is still practiced, and the question arises as to whether the widow is free to refuse.

The question of whether a woman can choose to enter into marriage is largely an economic and social one. Most countries report that men and women have equal rights as to entering marriage, but in some cultures in which it is assumed that all people will marry, a woman's decision not to marry, or her decision to live alone, can result in ostracism. Lack of employment opportunities for women, as well as comparatively low economic status, also play significant roles in the decision to marry. Laws granting equality in the process of entering into marriage fail to address these issues.

Polygamy raises significant questions about equality and choice. While historically under some forms of religious or customary law husbands consulted their wives before taking new ones, that practice is far less common today. In any case, polygamy is an inherently unequal practice because no legal system allows women to take more than one husband. Where dowry or bridewealth are standard elements of marriage transactions, wives usually have no legal right to transferred property. Under African customary law, the bridewealth must be returned to the husband's family in the case of a permanent separation; this can result in enormous pressure on the wife to stay in an abusive marriage, particularly if the bridewealth was in the form of cash or goods that are no longer available. Acceptance of the universality of international norms is a particularly significant issue with respect to Article 16. A large proportion of the reservations to the Convention pertain to this article, the general rationale being that it conflicts with personal status laws, which states parties will not readily challenge or alter.

Article 16(1) (c): Equality of Rights and Responsibilities During Marriage and At Dissolution

This general provision indicates that during marriage women and men should carry equal burdens of household and family responsibilities and have equal rights in family decision making. This encompasses all the issues discussed in this paper, and confirms the importance of women having full legal capacity, as they cannot fully undertake family responsibilities unless their capacity is recognized. The provision also underscores the difficulty of implementation, as division of responsibilities within families is essentially a matter of negotiation between the spouses. Cuba, for example, included in its 1975 *Family Code* a provision that men and women should share household responsibilities, but fifteen years later researchers found that couples were still struggling to define roles and expectations.

Equality with respect to dissolution of marriage is somewhat simpler to define and implement. Laws can be designed to provide for equitable treatment of the spouses, and judicial officers can be educated to deal fairly with women in the legal system. The most important legal issues that can be addressed through legislation are grounds and procedures for dissolution, property division and postdissolution financial support, and custody of children.

In many legal systems women must establish more dramatic grounds for divorce than men. Under Ugandan civil law, for example, men can divorce their wives on grounds of adultery, while wives must establish that their husbands have engaged in two or more marriage offenses (adultery and cruelty, for example) in order to obtain a divorce. In Uruguay, either spouse can initiate a divorce on grounds of adultery, but a man can divorce his wife on the basis of one incident, while a wife must establish flagrant misbehavior on the part of her husband. In Argentina, which has a relatively progressive divorce statute requiring only that either party show that a breakdown in the relationship has occurred, courts have accepted as evidence the wife's failure to keep house properly.

Divorce procedure is also unequal in some systems. Under Islamic law, a man can divorce his wife unilaterally by pronouncing *talaq* ("I divorce thee"), whereas wives can divorce their husbands only by establishing grounds. Under traditional Jewish law, which applies to Jewish citizens of Israel, a couple is not divorced legally unless the man signs a document of divorce (a *get*); not only is this practice essentially unequal, but abandoned wives sometimes cannot obtain the *get* and so are never free to remarry.

To achieve equality in property division, laws must provide that property accumulated by the efforts of either or both spouses during the marriage is "marital property" that must be divided equally upon dissolution. These laws must be applied to the valuation of a spouse's unpaid labor in the home, agricultural homestead, or family enterprise as contributing to the marital property. While it can take many years— even generations—to obtain and implement such laws, it is imperative that the effort be made, because without them women leave marriages with nothing to show for years of effort. The Tanzanian *Law of Marriage Act* (1971), for example, provides for the distribution of property upon divorce with regard to the contribution of each spouse, but the law was in effect for twelve years before the Court of Appeal (which is the highest court) ruled that a wife's unpaid household labor was to be considered a "contribution" to the marital property for purposes of distribution. The new Korean family code provides that property be distributed according to the contributions of the spouses, but household labor is considered to be a nonvalued "labor of love." CEDAW has stated that the valuation of women's unpaid labor is of major international importance.[5] In the context of marriage dissolution, it can be a matter not simply of economic equality, but of survival.

Postdissolution maintenance of former spouses is a very difficult issue in every legal system. The essential question—which is philosophical, rather than legal—is whether postdissolution maintenance payments can or should be used to compensate women for economic (employment and educational) opportunities lost because of marrying, for the labor they contribute to the family, and for the basic economic inequality in every society. An important related question is whether spouses who do not maintain their marriage should be tied indefinitely to each other by such an arrangement. Law concerning postdissolution maintenance payments to former spouses must be written to provide for equal treatment of men and women in evaluating the relevant circumstances.

Article 16(1) (d): Equal Rights and Responsibilities as Parents

This provision addresses the historical inequities in every legal system as to the distribution of rights and responsibilities between parents of minor children. In most systems, when children were born to married couples, fathers traditionally had sole rights to make decisions concerning them. Day-to-day responsibility for care and maintenance of the children, however, frequently rested with the mother.

Many countries have attempted to redress this imbalance of authority and responsibility by passing new laws that give both parents rights to make decisions for the family and particularly for the children. In the 1980s, for example, a number of Latin American countries changed their laws of *patria potestad* (authority over family decisions) to provide familial authority to both parents. However, even where legislation calls for equality in decision making, it cannot address inherent imbalances of power between spouses or force men to perceive their wives as equal partners worthy of respect.

One area in which law can make a difference is the allocation of responsibility for managing children's property. Where children inherit property in their own right, where they are given assets before they are of majority age, or where adult children die intestate without a spouse, management of their property rests with the parents. Laws concerning these situations should not be drafted on the assumption that men are better suited to manage property or administer estates.

Single-parent Families and Parental Rights and Responsibilities

Most statutes address parental rights assuming that the parents are married. But with the tremendous increase worldwide in the number of children living outside of traditional nuclear or extended family relationships, governments must design new systems to allocate responsibility for support of children. Traditionally, in all legal systems, children were supported by the parent with whom they lived. However, because most custodial single parents are women and because female-headed households are much more likely than two-parent or male-headed households to be poor, this method can have a negative impact on women's and children's economic status. Many countries now have child support (sometimes called maintenance) laws that require parents to pay for support of children who are not living with them, on the premise that every child should be supported financially by both parents. Since the child support laws apply to both parents, this is not clearly a sex discrimination issue, but a near-universal lack of enforcement indicates that judicial and administrative systems do not respond to women's actual needs and circumstances.

Many methods of child support enforcement have been tried in various countries. In Zimbabwe and other southern African countries, as well as in the United States, wages may be garnished to collect delinquent child support payments. Other methods include suspension of state benefits (such as education grants or licenses), liens against property, and liens against tax refunds. All of these methods are more productive where the infrastructure allows tracing of individuals, a high percentage of whom are in the wage economy. Incarceration as an enforcement mechanism is highly controversial; few judges want to use it, and opponents claim it is counterproductive because it prevents the nonpayer from working to gain the means to pay, while proponents point out that the threat even of weekend incarceration can have an impact.

Article 16(2): Minimum Age of Marriage and Registration of Marriage

The principle that children should be neither permitted nor forced into marriage as a matter of international law was established by the adoption in 1962 of the *Convention on Consent to Marriage, Minimum Age for Marriage and Registration of Marriages* (entered into force in 1964). While the premise would seem to be self-evident, the incidence of child marriage remains a significant problem. In 1989, the United Nations Population Fund reported in *State of the World's Population* that in Bangladesh, the average age of marriage for girls was 11.6 years. In Zambia, 11 percent of married women had been married between the ages of 12 and 14.

The Women's Convention does not offer a definition of "child" for the purposes of Article 16. To be consistent with other articles of the Convention as well as with the *Convention on the Rights of the Child,* particularly concerning legal capacity, "child" should be defined as a person below the legal age of majority.[6] However, since cultures frequently assign different ages of responsibility for different activities (such as 16 for driving and 21 for consumption of alcohol in many states in the United States), the appropriate age of marriage may be culturally determined as well. As a practical matter, the age of marriage should be, within the given social context, when an individual is likely to have completed at least minimum schooling and to be sufficiently mature physically to bear children safely. The designated age for this in Sweden and Guyana, for example, is 18 years. Arguably, any age lower than 16 has serious health and social consequences.

Registration of marriage is a critical issue for women because it offers a point at which the state can be involved in preventing discrimination against women in the family. Through registration, the state can enforce age of marriage, consent requirements, prohibitions against polygamy, and requirements of notice to prior wives. Registration requirements can also protect women in that certain rights may follow registered marriages: property may be held jointly by married persons, surviving spouses may inherit property, and certain financial benefits may accrue to spouses during and after the marriage.

Registration of marriage also provides a context for the state to allow civil marriages and to control the application of religious law. The state can decide, for example, that religious marriages are valid only if they meet state-imposed requirements. If a particular community traditionally practices child marriage, the state can refuse to recognize them while recognizing marriages between legal adults that are performed according to that community's rites.

The Women's Convention and States' Laws

Rare as it may be, courts do sometimes invoke international standards like those of the Women's Convention to rule against discriminatory state law. The most notable case to date has been *Dow v. Attorney General,* in which Unity Dow challenged as discriminatory (under the Botswana constitution and international law) the Botswana nationality law, which provided that children born in wedlock have only their father's citizenship. Because Dow's husband is American, two of the couple's children were deemed not to have Botswana citizenship. The children were allowed to reside in Botswana on Peter Dow's residency permit, which only he could renew. This resulted in significant hardship on the family when, in January 1991, after the permit had expired and there was some question about renewal, immigration authorities questioned the children's right to reenter the country after a family trip abroad. Further, the children would not be able to vote or receive the free university education to which all citizens were entitled.[7]

In the Court of Appeal opinion finding in Dow's favor, Justice Agudah noted that the *Convention on the Elimination of All Forms of Discrimination Against Women* "has created an international regime" that must be considered in interpreting the constitution and evaluating discrimination claims. He concluded, with the majority of the Court, that the law prohibiting women from passing their citizenship to their children constituted sex discrimination under the Botswana constitution as interpreted in light of international standards.[8]

This decision is significant. Coming from a common law court, which operates in the common law tradition of respect for precedent and for decisions in other common law countries, it provides a basis for similar decisions to be made. More critical, it underscores the importance of the Women's Convention as an international human rights instrument to be respected in national courts and sets a precedent for the future.

Notes

1. *Universal Declaration of Human Rights,* Article 2; *International Covenant on Civil and Political Rights,* Articles 2, 3; *International Covenant on Economic, Cultural and Social Rights,* Articles 2, 3.

2. The Convention is the only document to have emerged from the International Decade for Women that legally obligates governments to eliminate discrimination against women by granting them rights as well as opportunities. While under the Declaration, the Women's Convention, and all the multilateral human rights treaties governments have a positive obligation to eliminate discrimination, under the Women's Convention they also have a particular obligation to take special positive measures to do so: ratifying countries must report to the UN Committee on Elimination of Discrimination Against Women, a twenty- three–member expert group, on measures undertaken to eliminate discrimination as well as on obstacles to full Convention implementation.

3. A. Molokomme, in *Women and Law in Southern Africa*. Harare: Zimbabwe Publishing House, 1987.

4. See *Report of the Working Group of the Whole on the Drafting of the Convention on the Elimination of Discrimination Against Women*, A/34/60 (Annex) (2 March 1979), pp. 31–33.

5. United Nations, CEDAW, Tenth Session, Gen. Rec. No. 17X.

6. According to the *Convention on the Rights of the Child* (adopted 1989), a child is a "human being below the age of 18 years, unless, under the law applicable to the child, majority is attained earlier" (Article 1).

7. Lisa Stratton, "The Right to Have Rights: Gender Discrimination in Nationality Laws," *Minnesota Law Review* 77(1) (November 1992): 1.

8. *Attorney General v. Unity Dow*, Court of Appeal Civil Appeal No. 4/91 (Appeal Court of Botswana, July 1992), p. 83.

Parts reprinted with permission from International Women's Rights Action Watch.

Cultural Difference

18

The Politics of Gender and Culture in International Human Rights Discourse

Arati Rao

Can we have an international discussion of human rights in a world of cultural difference? While the topic of human rights has never been free from politics (in either its formulation or deployment), the cautionary call from "culture" has intensified in recent years. In United Nations debates, governmental declarations, newspaper editorials, and classrooms, the din of exhortation to greater sensitivity toward differences between cultural groups within countries (and to increased respect for societies elsewhere) has reached unprecedented levels. In international politics, the global spread of violent intergroup conflict has raised alarming questions about the relevance and effectiveness of a human rights–based approach to conflict resolution between culturally diverse actors. And yet, even those who recognize the importance of cultural sensitivity feel that recognition challenged, and even trampled, by an intuitive sense of horror and outrage in the face of human suffering.

The argument from "culture" is employed to serve a variety of interests. In international politics, the old insensitive and self-congratulatory voices have risen to a bullying shout today, overriding all who do not subscribe to an unchanged formulation of the established liberalism-based vision, with its emphasis on individualism and civil and political rights. (The end of the Cold War has given enormous economic and defense advantages to the Western powers, under the leadership of the United States.) At the same time, extreme and wide-ranging human rights violations, by both governments and extra-constitutional groups, have continued to be defended, and even justified, on the grounds of cultural difference. At the 1993 Vienna conference, for instance, countries as culturally dissimilar as China, Syria, and Malaysia relied on nations of cultural integrity in their criticism of various aspects of human rights doctrine.

The concept of human rights itself is a historically circumscribed and context-bound phenomenon. What is rarely analyzed, however, is the much publicized notion of "difference" itself. We seem content to acknowledge that difference exists where it is asserted, and we concentrate our energies on maintaining peace among supposedly different social groups. Indeed, an overly simple notion of the relationship between culture and human rights in our world of differences has emerged in a dichotomous form, with the universalists falling on one side and the relativists on the other (Donnelly 1989; Manglapus 1978; Pollis and Schwab 1980). Distinctions between "West" and "non-West"—which are murky at best—atrophy in the Self's construction of an inferior Other (Said 1979). When a government exempts itself from the perceived cultural hegemony of human rights doctrine, its supporters as well as its detractors participate in perpetuating a false oppositional dichotomy in which geopolitical borders are erased and a multitude of cultures are collapsed into two falsely unified packages, one bearing the stamp of human rights and the other lacking it. Hence the search for human rights in "Africa," in "Islam," and so on (Cobbah 1987; Sajoo).

I want to move away from these misleading constructions of culture to ask: What are the *politics* of any argument based on culture in human rights discourse today? In this essay, I question our easy acceptance of cultural differences as they are presented to us, and critically assess four major components of any claim made from culture. First, what is the status of the speaker? Second, in whose name is the argument from culture advanced? Third, what is the degree of participation in culture formation of the social groups primarily affected by the cultural practices in question? Fourth, what is culture, anyway?

When the representatives of (usually) Third World governments make the general cultural defense against the frequent and wearying interventions of (usually) Western governments, all parties seem to be engaged in international politics as usual. But where the defense is organized to "protect" the status of women (and the status quo of gender), we need to ask what effect the ensuing debate might have on women themselves. Will any departure from "tradition," which now will have to be measured against the rhetorical posing of a proprietary national leadership, further endanger their well-being? Will any suggested move away from culture-based gender oppression now be viewed as an embrace of Western scheming and arrogance? Will gender reform now have to be filtered through the same bureaucratic cadres of statist diplomats and *fonctionnaires* whose amenability to change is qualified by their dependence on governmental approval?

No social group has suffered greater violation of its human rights in the name of culture than women. Regardless of the particular forms it takes in different societies, the concept of culture in the modern state circumscribes women's lives in deeply symbolic as well as immediately real ways. Historically, women have been regarded as the repositories, guardians, and transmitters of culture. Women represent the reproduction of the community. Women usually are the primary caregivers in the family and therefore the earliest inculcators of culture in the child. Through their clothing and demeanor, women and girls become visible and vulnerable embodiments of cultural symbols and codes. In addition, the primary identification of the woman with the family and home, in a problematic separation of "public" and "private" spheres of existence, contributes to her secondary status in the very realm where her future is debated and even decided: the public.

A protective stance in governmental rhetoric is intertwined with the special agenda that states have developed to control (through incentives as well as force) women's reproductive capacities, to torture women, and to curtail women's freedom through specific social policies (Bryan, Dadzie, and Scale 1985; Bunster-Burrotto 1985; Mama 1989). On occasion, states eschew subtlety and tact and openly target women. "Calls for a 'White Australia' immigration policy or Jewish 'return' to Israel are supplemented at times of slack immigration or national crisis with active calls for women to bear more children so that no 'demographic holocaust' will take place" (Anthias and Yuval-Davis 1989, 8).

Thus, the very high stakes for all parties here, and the consequent intensity of the claims for exemption on cultural grounds, exacerbate the difficulty of dialogue on this issue. The resort to cultural explanations of women's status is usually defensive, combative, and specifically designed to placate an international audience consisting primarily of national political leaders and statist diplomats.

The international human rights movement cannot avoid reiterating at the policy level its conceptual gender biases, notably its relentless focus on the public sphere as the primary site of violations (without adequately addressing private social institutions, such as the family), its pronatalist treatment of gender and the family, and its organizing principle of intergovernmental interaction (Rao 1993). Thus, the statist framework of the human rights movement legitimates statist representatives—political leaders and diplomats—even as the movement defines states as the greatest violators of human rights.

Any appeal to public international law to address gender concerns involves an uphill struggle. "International organizations are functional extensions of states that allow them to act collectively to achieve their objectives" (Charlesworth, Chinkin, and Wright 1991). These authors argue that thus international law is, in concept and practice, a gendered system that privileges men and marginalizes women; they note the shameful underrepresentation of women in the United Nations, the overwhelmingly male distribution of judges on international courts, and the widespread obstacles to expanding women's involvement in international human rights bodies.

Consequently, mainstream human rights discourse continues to rely on the pronouncements of heads of states or high-ranking government ministers, and this often amounts to hearing the oppressor's voice in lieu of the victim's. In the United States, for example, when President Ronald Reagan's Assistant Secretary of State, Elliott Abrams, said: "In a field as complicated as human rights, differences in policy are to be expected, and should be treated as legitimate intellectual differences rather than as fundamental moral disagreements" (Drinan 1987, 100), we must ask how policy can become separated from morality in human rights—(that most moral of subjects)—or, for that matter, in politics. Where is the logical proof for the argument that complexity necessarily favors intellectual over moral differences?

Some defenses are long-lived and repeatedly deployed. For example, when Kenyatta writes that "it is unintelligent to discuss the emotional attitudes of either side of [female genital mutilation in Kenya], or to take violent sides in the question, without understanding the reasons why the educated, intelligent Gikuyu still cling to this custom" (Kenyatta 1953, 133), he seems to be making no more than a call for a sensitive and fair hearing. But when he defends the practice on the grounds that "it is important to note that the moral code of the tribe is bound up with this custom and that it symbolizes the unification of the whole tribal organization" (134), we are compelled to question the *politics* of such a claim, particularly when it is made by a male national leader on behalf of the social group most directly affected by the practice: women. Much-vaunted government reforms often are in reality little more than rhetorical flourishes, toothless legislation, and weak policy measures. It is only when women are placed at the center of the discussion that the gender complexity of the cultural argument emerges, dramatically calling into question the simplicity and finality of the politician's formulation and conclusion (Boulware-Miller 1985; Slack 1988). At all times, feminists must question their own reliance on cultural explanations of gendered social practices in the Third World and be suspicious of the defense of similar practices elsewhere (such as dangerous cosmetic surgery) on the grounds of seemingly culture-free concepts of individual autonomy and freedom of choice.

Women themselves have begun to be heard only recently, and then mostly in feminist undertakings. But feminist representation should not escape examination for its positionality, particularly where the feminist leadership is urban, well educated, middle class, and often government paid. Travel to international meetings is often, perforce, funded by governments, and, in the international arena, the goals of sympathetic feminist leadership are forced into the same statist mold as the goals of their unsympathetic bureaucratic colleagues, cramping possibilities for genuine gender reform and change. Since the responsiveness of the state to women's well-being remains debatable, we must remain critical of the relationship between governments and those women's groups permitted to flourish freely. While feminists courageously continue their battle on every front, including that of the state, there is no escaping the danger of dependency on (and influence by) established governments as long as the bulk of human rights dialogue is based on intergovernmental arrangements.

Accordingly, we must examine the resonance of the word "culture" at all levels of society, acknowledging that various groups have different degrees of participation in culture and that participation occurs in multiple contexts. When women's groups or individual women talk about culture, we must remind ourselves that there can never be a purportedly popular notion of culture that is unmediated by the positionality of the speaker; we must look at the claim for exemption on cultural grounds in relation to the axes of class, ethnicity, race, sexuality, age, and so on. We need to listen with care, but also with skepticism, to sweeping definitions of this thing called culture, forged as they are in a world of constantly expanding difference and complexity. Yuval-Davis and Nira Floya Anthias strike a cautionary note, for instance, in their reminder that there is no exclusive linkage of the national with the male: "Empirically, for example, it is clear that women themselves participate in the oppression and exploitation of women from other ethnic groups as well as from other economic classes" (Anthias and Yuval-Davis 1989, 2).

However, while women are neither purely victims nor purely beneficiaries of cultural politics, a recognition of their limited access to public defenses of cultural practices can help us to contextualize the greater politics of claims against rights on the basis of culture. Although women are no less (and, arguably, far more) immersed in cultural formation and reification than other social groups, talking about women-in-culture in international forums largely remains the prerogative of someone else.

In societies across the world, women's appropriation of culture has taken several forms, most visibly in the resistance to neocolonialism and hegemony and the affirmation of nationalism. In their resistance to very real conditions of transnational oppression, women, too, own this thing called culture. In this context, it is not impossible to talk about resistance and the potential for liberation inherent in the claim for culture, even as one criticizes restrictive cultural practices. But the issue is complicated by the debatable nature of the changes that nationalism facilitates in the status of women. The wide variety of notions about female abilities and social roles that emerged during the nationalist struggles often resulted in confused and contradictory goals in the politics of gender relations, and this legacy continues to play itself out in contemporary postcolonial societies (Jayawardena 1986). International feminist struggles are similarly affected. For decades, women around the world have had to locate and view each other past cultural blinkers, and courageously negotiate the heavily mined terrain of cultural nativism, before they can reach each other and begin working together.

Cultural sensitivity in the international arena is important; it is equally important to retain our awareness of intracommunity gender oppression and, in so doing, fully articulate the painful coexistence of multiple oppressions. For too long, gender has been subsumed by the call to nationalist self-assertion; for too long, gender equality has been asked to take a position secondary to other struggles; for too long, women have been required to choose between compartmentalized struggles for freedom. Feminist theory continues to unravel the inextricably connected oppressions of race, class, gender, sexuality, colonial experience, and the like, showing that (false) hierarchies of seemingly separable oppressions can only generate suspect and incomplete political strategies for attaining freedom and equality. That women often accept such misleading analyses of their predicament is insufficient reason to write off the possibility of uniting amidst their very real differences.

In any event, culture is not a static, unchanging, identifiable body of information, against which human rights may be measured for compatibility and applicability. Rather, culture is a series of constantly contested and negotiated social practices whose meanings are influenced by the power and status of their interpreters and participants. Furthermore, culture is only one constituent part of the complex web of power relationships that circumscribes our existence. As Arif Dirlik (1987) notes, "A critical reading of culture, one that exposes it as an ideological operation crucial to the establishment of hegemony, requires that we view it not merely as an attribute of totalities but as an activity that is bound up with the operation of social relations, that expresses contradiction as much as it does cohesion" (15).

Culture's reconstitutions have taken several ironic turns over the centuries. For example, the agents of colonialism helped to create "legends" and "folklore" (as in Maori New Zealand), to concoct "traditional" land tenure arrangements (as in Fiji), and to redefine gender roles in all colonized societies. Indeed, the formal legal systems of postcolonial countries are often informed by the rights-based legal ideology of the former colonial master. Local appropriation of a "culture" of such mixed pedigree is not problematic by itself; the truly problematic issue lies in the politics of the legerdemain that transforms historically contingent and shifting practices into implacable eternal verities.

We must acknowledge change, complexity, and interpretive privilege in cultural formation to avoid reductionism, essentialism, and rhetorical rigidity. This enables us to locate and condemn the particular historical formulations of culture that oppress women (such as the emphasis placed by male religious leadership on those passages in a religious text that permit wife beating) as well as to understand and support women's ability to wrest freedom from amidst these oppressive conditions (such as women's emphasis on other passages that advocate nonviolent and respectful treatment of wives).

Nor is a particular community's culture a single homogeneous entity. Furthermore, "high" culture and "low" culture are selectively deployed in so widespread a fashion that even proponents of human rights fall into the trap of relying on a confusion of "representative" cultural texts and practices, now leaning toward the self-serving and oppressive texts of privileged groups, now inclined toward folk practices (Pannikkar 1982; Renteln 1990). Furthermore, rapidly expanding technology and communications capabilities have greatly shrunk our world and exposed even the remotest parts of the planet to the consequences, if not the direct experience of, modernity. "Tradition" can no longer be reasserted without confronting the processes of secularization (Howard 1986, ch. 2). Even within the state-based framework of mainstream human rights, the culture defense sounds shaky when placed in the context of urbanization, industrialization, the rapidly expanding bureaucratic machinery and communication systems that enhance state control, and systems that link national economies to the international monetary system.

Accordingly, the notion of culture favored by international actors must be unmasked for what it is: a falsely rigid, ahistorical, selectively chosen set of self-justificatory texts and practices whose patent partiality raises the question of exactly whose interests are being served and who comes out on top. We need to problematize all of culture, not just the perceived "bad" aspects. When we limit our inquiry to egregious violations, we limit our capacity to ameliorate human pain to just that one instance of a "bad cultural practice." Without questioning the political uses of culture, without asking whose culture this is and who its primary beneficiaries are, without placing the very notion of culture in historical context and investigating the status of the interpreter, we cannot fully understand the ease with which women become instrumentalized in larger battles of political, economic, military, and discursive competition in the international arena.

Works Cited

Anthias, Floya and Nira Yuval-Davis, eds., 1989. *Woman-Nation-State*. New York: St. Martin's.

Boulware-Miller, Kay. 1985. "Female Circumcision: Challenges to the Practice as a Human Rights Violation." *Harvard Women's Law Journal* 8:155–77.

Bryan, Beverley, Stella Dadzie, and Suzanne Scafe. 1985. *The Heart of the Race: Black Women's Lives in Britain*. London: Virago.

Bunster-Burotto, Ximena. 1985. "Surviving Beyond Fear: Women and Torture in Latin America." *Women and Change in Latin America*, 297–325, ed. June Nash and Helen Safa, South Hadley, MA: Bergin and Garvey.

Charlesworth, Hilary, Christine Chinkin, and Shelley Wright, 1991. "Feminist Approaches to International Law." *The American Journal of International Law* 85:613–45.

Cobbah, Josiah. 1987. "African Values and the Human Rights Debate: An African Perspective." *Human Rights Quarterly* 9:309–331.

Dirlik, Arif. 1987. "Culturalism as Hegemonic Ideology and Liberating Practice." *Cultural Critique* 6 (Spring): 13–50.

Donnelly, Jack. 1989. *Universal Rights in Theory and Practice*. Ithaca, NY: Cornell Univ. Press.

Drinan, Robert F. 1987. *Cry of the Oppressed: The History and Hope of the Human Rights Revolution.* New York: Harper & Row.

Howard, Rhoda E. 1986. *Human Rights in Commonwealth Africa.* Totowa, NJ: Rowman and Littlefield.

Jayawardena, Kumari. 1986. *Feminism and Nationalism in the Third World.* London and Atlantic Highlands, NJ: Zed.

Kenyatta, Jomo. 1953. *Facing Mt. Kenya: The Tribal Life of the Gikuyu.* London: Secker & Warburg.

Mama, Amina. 1989. "Violence Against Black Women: Gender, Race and State Responses." *Feminist Review* 32 (Summer):30–48.

Manglapus, Raul S. 1978. "Human Rights Are Not a Western Discovery." *Worldview* 21 (10):4–6.

Pannikkar, Raimundo. 1982. "Is the Notion of Human Rights a Western Concept?" *Diogenes* 120:75–102.

Pollis, Adamantia, and Peter Schwab. 1980. "Human Rights: A Western Concept with Limited Applicability." *Human Rights: Cultural and Ideological Perspectives,* ed., A. Pollis and P. Schwab. New York: Praeger.

Rao, Arati. 1993. "Right in the Home: Feminist Theoretical Perspectives on International Human Rights." *National Law School Journal* (special issue on feminism and law) 1:62–81.

Renteln, Alison Dundes. 1990. *International Human Rights: Universalism versus Relativism.* Newbury Park, CA: Sage.

Said, Edward W. 1979. *Orientalism.* New York: Vintage.

Sajoo, Amyn B. 1990. "Islam and Human Rights: Congruence or Dichotomy?" *Temple International and Comparative Law Journal* 4 (1) (Spring): 23–33.

Slack, Alison T. 1988. "Female Circumcision: A Critical Appraisal." *Human Rights Quarterly* 10:437–86.

19

Cultural Particularism as a Bar to Women's Rights: Reflections on the Middle Eastern Experience

Ann Elizabeth Mayer

There are two basic positions that one can take on women's human rights: the universalist and the cultural relativist.[1] What does the universalist position entail? Simply put, it holds that "all members of the human family" share the same inalienable rights. This means that the international community has the right to judge, by reference to international standards, the ways states treat their own citizens and that states must reform their constitutions and laws where necessary to bring these into conformity with the international norms. According to the universalist position, all women are entitled to the rights set forth in international covenants and conventions such as the 1966 *International Covenant on Civil and Political Rights* and the *Convention on the Elimination of all Forms of Discrimination Against Women* (CEDAW), which has been in force since 1981.

Cultural relativists argue that members of one society may not legitimately condemn the practices of societies with different traditions, denying that there can be valid external critiques of culturally-based practices and claiming that no legitimate cross-cultural standards for evaluating the treatment of rights issues exist. Where Western criticisms of the treatment of women in the Middle East are concerned, cultural relativists object to universalist approaches on the grounds that they use criteria that are ostensibly international but that actually reflect the values of Western culture. Therefore, Western condemnations of discrimination against women in other regions are said to reflect an insensitive, ethnocentric approach to rights issues, which is linked to cultural imperialism.

This essay assesses one aspect of the implications of the cultural relativist argument: appeals to what might be called "Islamic particularism" to justify the denial of civil and political rights to Middle Eastern Muslim women. In what follows, it will be argued that according unquestioning deference to Middle Eastern governments that insist that cultural particularism requires the international community to tolerate those governments' discrimination against women constitutes a misguided application of cultural relativism.

Regarding the status of Muslim women, cultural relativists might maintain that the reasons for tolerating deviations from international norms are particularly strong, because many discriminatory features of Middle Eastern law are directly traceable to religious precepts. Thus, demanding respect for human rights could be equated with disrespect for indigenous religious norms set by Islamic law,[2] particularly after the 1990 issuance of the *Cairo Declaration on Human Rights in Islam* by the Organization of Islamic States, to which all Muslim countries belong. The declaration affirmed that all rights were subject to Islamic law, and it was notably lacking in provisions granting women equal rights with men or assuring them equal protection of the law.[3]

Application of international rights standards would have enormous impact on the legal systems of the Middle East because, in addition to customary norms that relegate women to a subordinate status, much of the discrimination against women depriving them of civil and political rights is *de jure*.[4] Even a selective listing of the types of discriminatory laws currently in force in Middle Eastern legal systems indicates that there would be a wide range of laws that would be potentially affected by rigorously adhering to norms of equality and equal protection. Laws commonly provide that the wife must obey her husband, that wives are not allowed to work outside the home without their husbands' permission, that men may take up to four wives, that Muslim women may not marry outside the faith, and that women are entitled to only one-half the inheritance share that men inherit in the same capacity. Depending on the country involved, one may find that women are compelled to wear concealing garments in public, that they are excluded from studying certain subjects, that they are deprived of the right to vote, that they are barred from the legal profession and the judiciary, that their testimony in court is excluded or valued at one-half the weight of a man's, that they are not allowed to travel without the permission of a male relative or unless accompanied by a male relative, or that they are not allowed to drive cars. Obviously, it would be hard to justify the retention of such laws if one took seriously international norms such as Article 2 of CEDAW, requiring all states "to pursue by all appropriate means and without delay a policy of eliminating discrimination against women," which would entail abrogating and revising laws that confer an inferior status on women.[5]

Claims that Islam justifies noncompliance with international norms regarding the rights of women have been raised in connection with debates over CEDAW. Although few Muslim countries have ratified CEDAW, among those that have, all have entered reservations to its substantive provisions, several on religious grounds. Bangladesh, Egypt, Libya, and Tunisia have invoked "Islam" as the reason for making reservations,[6] Egypt saying, for example, that it would comply with CEDAW's antidiscrimination provisions "provided that such compliance does not run counter to the Islamic *shari'a*."[7] From the fact that Egypt did not subsequently modify its laws discriminating against women after ratifying CEDAW, one could infer that Egyptian officials had concluded that reforms undertaken pursuant to CEDAW principles to give women equal rights would violate *shari'a* requirements.

Now, it is permissible to ratify international treaties subject to reservations, but the reservations are not supposed to be incompatible with the object and purpose of the treaty or convention involved.[8] Rather than ratify with reservations that effectively nullify its obligations under the treaty, a state should elect not to become party to a treaty in the first place. The reservations made by Bangladesh, Egypt, Libya, and Tunisia were so sweeping that critics have claimed that they are not compatible with the object of CEDAW, which is to free women from systematic subordination because of sex.[9]

Showing their concern for this issue, some states that were parties to CEDAW debated whether the reservations that had been entered were acceptable. When in 1986 these concerned countries wanted the Secretary-General of the United Nations to survey the parties to CEDAW as to their respective views on what reservations would be incompatible with the object of the convention, the proposal was denounced by some delegations as being anti-Islamic or amounting to a Western attack on Third World countries.[10] At the forty-first session of the General Assembly, delegations from Muslim countries denounced the West for "cultural insensitivity" in this matter.[11] In 1987 the CEDAW committee decided to recommend that the UN and specialized agencies study the status of women in Islamic law. The General Assembly squelched this proposal after Muslim countries asserted that the proposal of the CEDAW committee constituted religious intolerance and cultural imperialism.[12]

The result was that, faced with appeals to cultural particularism, the UN tolerated a situation where some Middle Eastern countries would be treated as parties to a convention whose substantive provisions they had professed their unwillingness to abide by. Implicitly, the UN acquiesced to the cultural relativist position on women's rights in the Middle East, allowing parties to CEDAW to invoke Islam and their culture as the defense for their noncompliance with the terms of the convention. This was paradoxical, since CEDAW Article 5 calls on parties to "modify the social and cultural patterns of conduct of men and women with a view to achieving the elimination of prejudices and customary and all other practices which are based on the idea of the inferiority or the superiority of either of the sexes or on stereotyped roles for men and women." That is, CEDAW was premised on the notion that, where cultural constructs of gender were an obstacle to the achievement of women's equality, it was the culture that had to give way—not that women's rights should be sacrificed in situations where their realization would require modifying local social and cultural patterns. In the UN, the ostensibly religious/cultural bases for Muslim countries' objecting to CEDAW principles remained unexamined; here they will be subjected to critical scrutiny.

In examining whether one should defer to pleas that "Islam" justifies denying women full rights, it would be well to ponder the significance of the general acquiescence of the international community to the gutting of CEDAW. In reality, the treatment of CEDAW suggests that there is nothing peculiar to Islam or Middle Eastern culture that stands in the way of realizing the norms of full equality for women that the treaty mandates. Of all human rights treaties, CEDAW has the distinction of having "the greatest number of reservations with the potential to modify or exclude most, if not all, of the terms of the treaty."[13] Where CEDAW was concerned, states were permitted to make their own determinations as to whether their reservations were incompatible with CEDAW, which stood in sharp contrast to the rule imposed regarding the *Convention on the Elimination of Racial Discrimination* (CERD), where a two-thirds vote by other parties can declare a state's reservations incompatible with the object of the convention.[14]

Muslim countries were not alone in registering reservations that undermined the treaty; countries as diverse as Belgium, Brazil, Canada, Cyprus, Jamaica, the Republic of Korea, Mauritius, and Thailand did so as well.[15] This is hardly surprising, given that the governmental actors in international forums consist for the most part of men, as, for instance, in most delegations sent to the UN. Therefore, the disparity between the treatment of reservations to CERD and those to CEDAW and the greater toleration for discrimination directed at women can be linked to a prevailing pattern of the exclusion of women from real influence in the UN system as well as from real influence in the institutions shaping international law more generally.[16]

Middle Eastern governments have made deliberate attempts to stifle dissenting women's voices when they could discredit the authenticity of the official constructs of Islamic/Middle Eastern culture that are used to rationalize the treatment of women. In this regard, the governments can exploit Western stereotypes of Islam. Western supporters of cultural relativist approaches seem disposed to believe that non-Western cultures are monolithic and immutable. In reality, intense conflicts and debates on rights issues rage within Muslim countries from Africa to Asia, particularly regarding the rights of women; there is no single monolithic cultural position on women's role in society and no unanimity of opinion about how Islamic requirements should apply to problems of contemporary societies. A substantial feminist literature has been produced by Muslim women in the Middle East that seriously challenges the patriarchal biases that infect the political systems in the region as well as the readings offered by male interpreters of the Islamic sources.[17]

It is inconvenient for Middle Eastern regimes attempting to legitimize their opposition to women's rights by appeals to Islam to be faced with domestic manifestations of feminist dissent, and there have been many instances in which regimes have tried to stamp out Muslim women's voices. The brutal repression by the postrevolutionary Iranian Government of women's protests against the retrograde version of Islam, which interprets the law in its most discriminatory form, is notorious. In Pakistan in 1984 the government violently suppressed women's protests over a new law reviving elements of Islamic evidentiary law that downgraded the value of women's testimony.[18] In Saudi Arabia, after women demonstrated in November of 1990 against the local ban on women driving—a ban that was officially justified as flowing from Islamic morality and principles—the government prohibited all future demonstrations by women.[19] In Egypt, the suppression of the prominent Arab Women's Solidarity Association (AWSA), a dynamic feminist association that advocated enhanced rights for women, provided a particularly interesting example of governmental determination to ensure that opinions of progressive Muslim women would not be heard—and the exploitation of Islam to justify the suppression.

AWSA was dissolved in June of 1991 by the Egyptian government, apparently because the regime disapproved of its political activities, although officially AWSA was dissolved for being in "perpetual violation of the law" and for "dissemination of ideas running counter to the position of the State."[20] There was considerable international criticism of this action,[21] but in May of 1992 the order dissolving AWSA was upheld on appeal, this time for a different reason: the court asserted that AWSA had offended the Islamic religion. According to the ruling, AWSA had "threatened the peace and political and social order of the state by spreading ideas and beliefs offensive to the rule of Islamic *shari'a* and the religion of Islam," had "violated the rule of law and public order and morality by the practice of political and religious activities through its magazine and publication," and had put out publications that "contained attacks against and aroused suspicions of the social and religious order, especially the conventions of marriage, divorce, and the (permitted) number of wives," constituting "attacks on state policy."[22]

Given this ruling, it would appear that in Egypt "state policy," "public order and morality," "the rule of law," "Islam," and specific elements of Islamic law according men superior rights all afford interchangeable rationales for suppressing feminist activism. One might then ask: if any or all of these rationales can be employed against a feminist group, how important is Islam to the government's position? And since the appeals to "Islam" only came belatedly, a year after the Egyptian government had originally dissolved AWSA for other reasons, one may wonder if the Egyptian government had concluded in the interim that "Islam" would be the most effective defense it could deploy before its international critics in its efforts to justify dissolving AWSA.

These (and other attempts to silence women) suggest that when governments assert that adherence to their culture and religion precludes the granting of equal rights to women, they actually fear being discredited by women in their own societies—women who are prepared publicly to take issue with them.

One should also bear in mind that the versions of Islam invoked by various UN delegations to justify reservations to CEDAW represent official constructs of Middle Eastern/Islamic culture that are in almost all cases imposed by undemocratic regimes, which raises doubts about whether they should be taken as representative of the societies they dominate. Historically, Middle Eastern Muslim cultures have not been monolithic creations imposed from above by the nation-state (the nation-state being a modern innovation recently borrowed from the West). The actual cultures of the Middle East have been produced by women as well as men and have shown innumerable variations. Local expressions of Islamic culture have not necessarily corresponded to the norms expounded by the Islamic jurists from the educated male elites of urban milieus, but have been greatly influenced by forces such as folk tradition, mysticism, and customs that women have participated in shaping. Is there, then, any reason to treat state-generated definitions of "culture" and "Islam" as authentic or definitive? And if the same states that have generated these artificial national models of "Islam" then subsequently insist that these very models compel them to deny rights to women, why should outsiders accept such rationales, particularly from states that have spotty records of adhering to Islamic law elsewhere?[23]

One may doubt whether these states actually believe in the authoritative character of the official constructs of Islamic culture that they put forward in international forums in their efforts to justify their refusal to undertake reforms to eliminate the legal barriers to women's equality. If the governmental constructs of culture were indeed normative and authentic, the elimination of legal barriers to equality could be taken without risk of upsetting the status quo. States could be confident that Muslim women would react by saying that, despite the fact that it had become legally permissible, they did not want to drive, vote, study law, disobey their husbands' commands, demand an equal share of inheritance, etc., because such things would be deemed contrary to authoritative cultural norms. In reality, it seems that governments appreciate all too well that the cultural model they rely on to rationalize discrimination against women has shaky authority and that Muslim women increasingly aspire to equality—which is precisely why Muslim men are obliged to have recourse to state-sponsored legislation and rough police measures designed to try to keep women in the place to which they were once confined by the strictures of living custom and tradition.

One should also consider that, where governmental constructs of the local culture and religion are deployed as bulwarks against international human rights norms and "alien" ideas of freedom, accepting these ultimately means that one is denying the people of the region the right to change culture, to challenge existing norms, and to assimilate new ideas. Such acceptance presumes a normative model of Middle Eastern culture to be a self-contained, static entity—one different from cultures elsewhere, whose historical records have shown that a culture almost always changes to accommodate modern norms of human rights.[24]

A comparison is illuminating in this connection. If we were to take seriously the claim that one can have the principle of male/female equality only in societies in which the local culture and religion have been geared to accept such an ideal, we would have to regard equal rights for women in the West as equally illegitimate, since the struggle to introduce feminist principles went against the grain of Western culture. One does not have to go back many decades to find outspoken, deeply ingrained Western cultural and religious resistance to feminist ideals combining with laws that subjugated women in many of the same ways Middle Eastern laws do today. Indeed, in the more retrograde quarters of the Western world, the notion of full equality for women is still being resisted and denounced for being subversive of the natural order of society and incompatible with religious values. However, cultural relativists do not seem to treat the norm of full equality for women as lacking cultural legitimacy in the West, which means that they must, at least implicitly, believe that Western culture is one that by its nature is destined to evolve and embrace new ideas, unlike non-Western cultures associated with Islam, which they presume are frozen in time somewhere in the darkness of the Middle Ages.

To assume that it is unnatural for Middle Eastern cultures to evolve is particularly odd given the aspirational character of international human rights principles, which set norms to be achieved and are designed to foster the evolution of laws in ways that enhance rights protections. One recalls that the *Universal Declaration of Human Rights* in its Preamble proclaimed itself "a common standard of achievement for all peoples and all nations" and that the *International Covenant on Civil and Political Rights* in its Preamble spoke of "the ideal of free human beings enjoying civil and political freedom." To claim that these international rights cannot be extended to the Muslim Middle East is tantamount to saying that the people in that region cannot aspire to a future in which such ideals could be realized—that they alone among the peoples of the world can never have more rights than they had in the past.

The cultural relativist might reply that there is a difference between the way feminist currents arose in the West and the way feminist standards are employed to judge the cultures and societies of the Middle East. As perceived by cultural relativists, Western feminism is a movement offering an indigenous critique of patriarchy, while demands that

Middle Eastern countries respect women's rights and freedoms come from the outside—an argument that on the surface might seem reasonable in light of governmental suppression of indigenous feminist views. External critiques of the treatment of women in the Middle East, then, are considered representative of ethnocentric Western attitudes and, ultimately, expressions of imperialism.[25] This notion warrants critical evaluation. Is it true that imperialism and colonialism are inextricably tied to demands for according women in the Middle East full equality in the areas of civil and political rights?

Associating any demands for enhancing the rights of Muslims with imperialism is odd because, in the main, the great powers in the age of imperialism took the position that it was only citizens of Western powers who deserved to have their rights protected according to Western standards, setting forth the precursors of today's international rights norms. Some confusion in this area is understandable, because one can cite certain instances in the past where imperialist powers did seek to control Muslim societies by driving a wedge between Muslim men and women, condemning traditional Islamic strictures, and offering Muslim women the relatively greater freedoms afforded by European laws. The tactics used by the Soviet Union to divide Muslim men and women in Central Asia provide a particularly striking example in this regard.[26] It is important, however, to examine the relevance of such historical examples in today's circumstances. Where is there at present a neoimperialist power that stands to advance its own political agenda by pursuing policies designed to promote enhanced rights and freedoms for Muslim women?

The United States may be the country that many cultural relativists and Middle Easterners have in mind when they—too casually—associate neoimperialist designs with the use of international human rights norms to judge or condemn the human rights records of Middle Eastern governments. However, given the antifeminist policies of the recent Reagan and Bush administrations, the United States has hardly been in a position to preach to others about women's rights or to condemn other states for their failure to ratify CEDAW or for reservations they have entered. The close American alliance with Saudi Arabia, which has one of the worst records in the world in its treatment of women, shows how little women's concerns have mattered to the architects of U.S. foreign policy.

It is significant that the strongest voice for women's rights in the controversies over reservations to CEDAW has been that of Sweden, yet it is hardly plausible to cast Sweden in the role of an imperialist power bent on subjugating Middle Eastern societies via its calls for adhering to norms of equal rights for women. In fact, the positive role Sweden has played in this regard comes from Sweden's genuine commitment to the principle of full equality for women, as evidenced in its feminist domestic policies, which allow women significant roles in public affairs.

After the 1993 Vienna conference on human rights, where deviations from international norms were justified with appeals to culture, Dorothy Thomas, a representative of Human Rights Watch, spoke of women's reactions:

> Women from every single culture and every part of the world are standing up and saying we won't accept cultural justification for abuses against us anymore. We are human, we have a right to have our human rights protected, and the world community must respond to that call and throw out any attempts to justify abuse on the grounds of culture.[27]

Thus, claims from diverse states and regions that the conventions interfere with their right to culture turn out to have the *same* consequence—denying women equal rights. If all such "particularisms" mean that violations of women's rights are excused and perpetuated, they are nothing more than disguises for the universality of male determination to cling to power and privilege. If constructs of a supposed Islamic particularism are no more than a universal claim for the subordinate status of women, they deserve to be treated with the same degree of skepticism as the other rationales that are being invoked by men for depriving women of their full human rights.

Notes

1. For a general introduction to this topic, see Douglas Donoho, "Relativism versus Universalism in Human Rights: The Search for Meaningful Standards," *Stanford Journal of International Law* 27 (1991):354–91. For a work sympathetic to universalism, see Jack Donnelly, *Universal Human Rights in Theory and Practice* (Ithaca, NY: Cornell Univ. Press, 1989); for one sympathetic to cultural relativism, see Alison Dundes Renteln, *International Human Rights: Universalism Versus Relativism* (Newbury Park, CA: Sage, 1990). A particularly stimulating analysis is provided in Rhoda Howard, "Cultural Absolutism and the Nostalgia for Community," *Human Rights Quarterly* 15 (1993):315–38.

2. For a general examination of the ways that Islam is used to justify deviations from international human rights standards, see Ann Elizabeth Mayer, *Islam and Human*

Rights: Tradition and Politics (Boulder, CO: Westview, 1991). For a critical appraisal of the use of cultural relativism in this way, see ibid., 9–21.

3. In an ambiguous formulation, Article 1(a) provides that all "men" are equal in terms of basic human dignity and basic obligations and responsibilities (not "rights"). Article 6, which deals with women, provides that "woman is equal to man in human dignity" (not "rights") and stipulates that she has rights as well as duties to perform. In context, the failure to provide for equal rights must be seen as an attempt to accommodate the existing discriminatory laws. For a general discussion of this declaration and its context, see Ann Elizabeth Mayer, "Universal versus Islamic Human Rights: A Clash of Cultures or a Clash with a Construct?" in *Michigan Journal of International Law* 15 (1994), 307–404.

4. For a survey of personal status laws affecting women see Jamal Nasir, *The Islamic Law of Personal Status*, 2d ed. (London: Graham & Trotman, 1990). For information on laws discriminating against women outside the area of personal status, one can consult reports of human rights organizations like Amnesty International or Middle East Watch, as well as the annual U.S. Department of State *Country Reports on Human Rights Practices*.

5. The CEDAW mandate has become particularly important in an era like the present when Islamic fundamentalism has augmented the discriminatory features of previous laws. For information on the retrograde impact of Iran's Islamic Revolution on the progress that had been made toward enhancing women's rights, see Farah Azari, *Women of Iran: The Conflict with Fundamentalist Islam* (London: Ithaca Press, 1983); Guity Nashat, ed., *Women and Revolution in Iran,* (Boulder, CO: Westview, 1983); Eliz Sanasarian, *The Women's Rights Movement in Iran: Mutiny, Appeasement, and Repression from 1900 to Khomeini* (New York: Praeger, 1982); Azar Tabari and Nahid Yeganeh, eds., *In the Shadow of Islam. The Women's Movement in Iran* (London: Zed, 1982). Pakistan is another example. See Khawar Mumtaz and Farida Shaheed, *Women of Pakistan* (London: Zed, 1987). The 1984 Algerian *Code of Family Law* represented a triumph for proponents of reactionary patriarchal ideas. See Nouredine Saadi, *La Femme et la Loi en Algerie* (Casablanca, Morocco: Le Fennec, 1991), pp. 43–80. Under the fundamentalist regime that seized power in the Sudan in 1989, women's rights have suffered serious setbacks. See "Sudan: Threat to Women's Status from Fundamentalist Regime," *News from Africa Watch,* April 9, 1990; "Women under Sudan's Fundamentalist Regime," *Middle East International,* August 3, 1990, p. 20.

6. Rebecca Cook, "Reservations to the Convention on the Elimination of All Forms of Discrimination Against Women," *Virginia Journal of International Law* 30 (1990): 687–703.

7. Ibid.: 688.

8. See Belinda Clark, "The Vienna Convention Reservations Regime and the Convention on Discrimination Against Women," *American Journal of International Law* 85 (1991): 282.

9. Ibid.: 299–302, 310–311, 313, 317, 320.

10. Ibid.: 284.

11. Ibid.: 287.

12. Ibid.: 287–88.

13. Ibid.: 317.

14. Ibid.: 287.

15. Ibid.: 298–302.

16. The implications of this exclusion have been critically appraised in an important recent article. See Hilary Charlesworth, Christine Chinkin, and Shelley Wright, "Feminist Approaches to International Law," *American Journal of International Law* 85 (1991):613–45.

17. In addition to the sources on Iran and Pakistan already cited, see Leila Ahmad, *Women and Gender in Islam: Historical Roots of a Modern Debate* (New Haven, CT: Yale Univ. Press, 1992); Nadia Hijab, *Womanpower: The Arab Debate on Women at Work* (Cambridge, UK: Cambridge Univ. Press, 1988); Fatima Mernissi, *The Veil and the Male Elite. A Feminist Interpretation of Women's Rights in Islam,* trans. Mary Jo Lakeland (Reading, MA: Addison-Wesley, 1991). Mernissi, *Beyond the Veil: Male-Female Dynamics in Modern Muslim Society* (London: Al Saqi, 1985); Freda Hussain, ed., *Muslim Women* (New York: St. Martin's Press, 1984); Naila Minai, *Women in Islam: Tradition and Transition in the Middle East* (New York: Seaview, 1981); Nawal el-Saadawi, *The Hidden Face of Eve* (Boston: Beacon, 1982).

18. Mumtaz and Shaheed, *Women of Pakistan,* pp. 106–107.

19. For an account of the incident, see Judith Ceasar "Big Saudi Brother," *Christian Science Monitor,* January 4, 1991, p. 18.

20. "Update: Dissolution of the Arab Women's Solidarity Association," *News from Middle East Watch,* December 1991.

21. Among other things, a brief was submitted on behalf of AWSA by American human rights activists. See Bert Lockwood and Kenneth Roth, *Dissolution of the Arab Women's Solidarity Association. Brief for the Urban Morgan Institute for Human Rights. University of Cincinnati College of Law and Middle East Watch and Women's Rights Project of Human Rights Watch as Amicus Curiae.* October 22, 1991.

22. "Egypt. Court Upholds Closure of Women's Organization," *News from Middle East Watch,* June 1992.

23. In areas where women's rights are not involved, Egypt has preserved its largely French-inspired legal system, refusing to reinstate Islamic law despite strong pressures from fundamentalist groups for the Islamization of all laws. See Rudolph Peters, "Divine Law or Man-Made Law? Egypt and the Application of the Shari'a," *Arab Law Quarterly* 3 (1988):231–53. The Egyptian government does not seem to feel compelled to follow Islamic law where this would require amputating the hand of the thief or eliminating interest charges from the economy.

24. For a thoughtful analysis of this subject, see Rhoda Howard, "Dignity, Community, and Human Rights," *Human Rights in Cross-Cultural Perspectives: A Quest for Consensus,* Abdullahi An-Na'im, ed. (Philadelphia: Univ. of Pennsylvania Press, 1992).

25. This is a refrain endlessly reiterated by the Iranian government and its ideological allies, who see in foreign condemnation of the way women have been treated since the Islamic Revolution an imperialist plot designed to undermine Iran's

independence and restore American domination—whence the castigation of Iranian women who rebel against the "Islamic" constraints placed on their freedoms as agents of imperialism. See, for example, Farah Azari, "The Post-Revolutionary Women's Movement in Iran," *Women of Iran. The Conflict with Fundamentalist Islam*, Farah Azari, ed. (London: Ithaca Press, 1983), pp. 194, 206.

26. See Gregory Massell, *The Surrogate Proletariat: Muslim Women and Revolutionary Strategies in Central Asia, 1919–1929* (Princeton, NJ: Princeton Univ. Press, 1974).

27. Hilary Bowker, "Women Succeed in Pressing for Rights Hearing at Vienna," CNN, June 22, 1993, available in LEXIS, ALLNWS file.

20

Popularizing Women's Human Rights at the Local Level: A Grassroots Methodology for Setting the International Agenda

Maria Suarez Toro

In approaching the subject of women's rights as human rights, almost all would agree that what is needed are not mere legal abstractions but, rather, concrete measures that emerge from and respond to the lives of women—real women, in all their diversity. While some would argue that the only way to give legitimacy to those claims that emerge from local situations and individual lives—and to redress recurrent wrongs against women—is through the use of international legal instruments, others contend that traditional assumptions about the roles of women and men can be challenged at the grassroots level, in communities, by members of those communities.

At the United Nations World Conference on Human Rights held in Vienna in June 1993, women who had been working for decades at the grassroots level came together with human rights activists, women from specialized agencies, and women in government to share information and create cohesive strategies. This was an important step toward the advancement of women's rights as human rights, in part because it showed that work at the international level may be based upon grassroots work and that grassroots work may use the power of international organizations without being drowned out by them. It showed that women from a vast variety of backgrounds could work together successfully within their differences. Because lobbying and advocacy at the international level are effective only insofar as they are grounded in the day-to-day experiences of women and reflective of the efforts of women's organizations working at local and national levels, grassroots groups must be recognized as critical components of the global movement.

For that reason, the movement for women's human rights faces a particular post-Vienna challenge that is, after all, the same one that brought many of us to the Conference: If we are to be successful in compelling the United Nations to move beyond declarations and into implementation, if we are to transcend the critique that international human rights norms coerce cultural variety into a false unity, we must make certain that international legislation reflects and supports advocacy that is taking place at the local and national levels. Despite advances made at the international level, most real gains for women have in fact been the result of women's struggles in their own communities. These struggles have been necessary for several reasons, not the least of which is that battles won in the international arena in the past have often had little impact on the daily lives of the women they were meant to serve. In the words of one Nicaraguan woman, "Equality before the law is not equality in life for women."

This is why we say in Central America that the *popularization* of women's human rights is an urgent need. "Popularization" is a process whereby we discover ourselves and each other as subjects of human rights; we recognize and claim our dignity by constructing human rights out of our own life experiences; and we seek to have those constructs reflected in national and international legislation. In this paper, I discuss from a Central American perspective the importance of work done at the grassroots level and its connection to work in the international arena. Although the Central American experience is in some ways unique, those of us working at both the local and the international levels have discovered that, from country to country, one finds many similarities in women's life experiences, needs, and methodologies for making change that go beyond difference.

The women's and human rights movements have used popular human rights education for decades; only recently, however, has a methodology for the reconceptualization of women's human rights and the construction of those rights out of women's daily lives begun to be systematized. In Central America, we wanted to develop a methodology that would emphasize the construction of a human rights doctrine based on our life experiences, a methodology that would transcend traditional conceptions of national and international human rights, using our own lives as the starting points; and that would simultaneously allow us to see the possibilities for the reconstruction of our own lives within a transformed society.

This methodology strengthened us as women, as human rights activists, and as feminists committed to building a movement at the grassroots level. We have been able to trace back and re-examine those situations that have characterized the denial of basic human rights in our lives, and this process has contributed to the rebuilding of personhood and the gaining of a sense of empowerment. We have come to have a better appreciation of women's roles as protagonists in society and in our own lives, as social, economic, and political actors in the development of civil societies. This work has been instrumental in allowing us to move beyond the limiting portrayals of women-as-victims. The affirmation and construction of our human rights, then, requires that we make our contributions and rights visible not only to others but also to ourselves. Education and the popularization of women's human rights must be a priority.

The extreme cost of political violence in Central America in recent years is no secret: Hundreds of thousands of people have been subjected to torture, rape, summary execution, and disappearance. Throughout, women have been at the forefront of efforts to defend our rights to life, liberty, sovereignty. By participating in, and frequently leading, these efforts, women have gained numerous skills. Most important, perhaps, is that we have learned about human dignity, our own strength, and our capacity to transform society. When things began to change for the better, however, we realized they were not necessarily changing for us. We also realized that the kinds of changes that would improve women's lives would never come about unless we took it upon ourselves to see that they did.

In the 1990s, we see clearly that efforts to enhance human rights in Central America—whether those of Nicaragua's Sandinista Revolution or the Chamorro government, the military confrontation in El Salvador or the peace process there, transitions toward civil government and electoral processes in Honduras and Guatemala, the process of the decolonization of Belize, the post–invasion government of Panama— have had little impact on the basic status of women. It is not surprising, then, that today women in Central America ask ourselves how it is possible that after so many years of struggle for human rights we are still subject to the same—if not greater—levels of exploitation, subordination, and discrimination. The reason for this situation is, perhaps, that not one of the experiments or struggles for social change has addressed the patriarchal foundations of our political, economic, and social structures, of our cultures, relationships, and socialization.

If we are to move forward, it is vital that we begin to understand that in many cases we have in fact been willing to set our own rights aside while we struggled for everyone else's. There are several reasons for this:

- We have been socialized to subordinate our own needs to the needs of others. A woman from Guatemala asked, "How can we aspire to have our rights in Guatemala when even the men have not yet achieved theirs?"
- Society as a whole does not recognize or accord legitimacy to our needs.
- The denial of women's human rights is socially, politically, and culturally accepted by men in general, and by most human rights organizations.
- Women's organizations have not always seen the relationship between human rights and the struggles in our daily lives; until the current decade, some women from CEFEMINA (a Costa Rican-based women's organization) took the position that dealing with women's human rights would "water down" feminism.

These and other factors contribute to the idea that women's rights are not human rights, rendering us effectively "invisible" and allowing violators to carry on with impunity. Clearly, we must look to local women's groups to develop strategies for moving beyond cosmetic socio-political reforms or there will always be oppression, conflict, repression, and social injustice. Further, the exclusion of/discrimination against women within the human rights movement itself must be addressed, and women must take active roles in the development of human rights platforms and strategies. It is of the utmost importance to reach women at the grassroots level and to facilitate methodologies and processes by which they can: articulate their issues and agendas; learn about formal (legal) mechanisms for prevention, protection, and defense; develop alternative, nonformal mechanisms of defense; and formulate various strategies for action.

The general objective of this methodology is to contribute to the construction of women's human rights using our daily lives, needs, and experiences as informative building blocks, so that civil society is transformed into a system deeply rooted in respect for, and the promotion and protection of, all rights, and the rights of all. To achieve this end, it is necessary to:

- identify those rights of greatest concern to women, particularly those for which there are as yet no protections in national and international legislation;
- identify those rights fought for and won by women in our daily lives, the result of our struggles, strengths, and mutual support;
- build a new pedagogy of human rights, in which women go through a process of appropriation and reconceptualization of international human rights instruments as "instruments of the people" that can respond directly to our specific needs; and
- develop concrete strategies for promoting, protecting, and preventing abuses of women's human rights, and for the qualitative transformation of our societies.

The methodology consists of several strategies. These include exercises in which women recall the first time their human rights were denied to them because they were women and the first time they were able to claim their rights, having recognized their own needs, dignity, and power. Next, it is essential that women at the grassroots level analyze international human rights instruments in order to discover whether they adequately reflect the needs and concerns of women. Finally, we can formulate actions and strategies for creating change in our daily lives and influencing local, national, and international policy. Since women's personal responses to taking action must not be overlooked, the methodology includes an exercise in which we articulate and process our resistance, fear, excitement, etc., and help one another move toward implementation of our actions.

This methodology and others created for the same purpose can become vital components of the global movement for women's human rights. At the grassroots level, it is a useful tool for enabling women to examine their own lives and experiences and to begin to understand those experiences as more than simply the facts of their lives, as part of larger social, political, and cultural constructs as well—as part of a global problem. By bringing women together in their own communities, by popularizing women's human rights, the methodology helps build and strengthen the women's movement at the local and, ultimately, national and international levels.

Women working at local and international levels must reach out to each other so that the experiences, discoveries, and agendas of one group can inform and influence the work of the other. In Vienna, women from diverse regions and with varied kinds of experience worked together to create a unified agenda for advocacy in the international arena. That they were able to do so is in itself a victory. But though Vienna may have brought the movement for women's human rights to a new threshold, it was only a stepping stone. The challenge for advocates of women's human rights remains: to contribute to the empowerment of women in everyday life; to make a *tangible* difference in women's lives by implementing the kinds of change they themselves choose; and to hold the United Nations and individual governments accountable for the needs and rights of women in their own very diverse communities and in the global governance. That challenge must be met at every level and in every possible venue.

Violence and Health

21

Gendered War Crimes: Reconceptualizing Rape in Time of War

Rhonda Copelon

Introduction

Historically, the rape of women in war has drawn occasional and short-lived international attention. It comes to light as part of the competing diplomacies of war, illustrating the viciousness of the conqueror or the innocence of the conquered. When war is done, rape is comfortably filed away as a mere and inevitable "by-product," a matter of poor discipline, the inevitable bad behavior of soldiers revved up, needy, and briefly "out of control."

Military histories rarely refer to rape, and military tribunals rarely either indict or sanction it.[1] This is the case even where rape and forced prostitution are mass or systematic, as in both theatres of World War II, which included the rape of German women by the conquering Russian army and the enslavement on the battlefields of 200,000–400,000 "comfort women" by the Japanese army.[2] It is even the case where open, mass, and systematic rape has ostensibly shocked the conscience of the world, as in the "rape of Nanking"[3] or the rape of an estimated 200,000 Bengali women during the war of independence from Pakistan.[4] Rape was ignored by the International Tribunals at Nuremberg and, although it was discussed in the Judgment of the Military Tribunal in Tokyo, it was not treated as a crime for which the Japanese Commander would be separately charged. In Bangladesh, amnesty was quietly traded for independence.

More recently, the rape of women in the wars in the former Yugoslavia—most often committed by Serbs against Bosnian-Muslim women as part of the campaign of "ethnic cleansing"—broke through media barriers and briefly captured international attention.[5] The rape of women in Bosnia-Herzegovina, however, appeared unique because the rape of women in history (as well as in the present) has been rendered invisible. Moreover, geopolitical factors—that the locale is Europe, that the conflict threatens to set off a new world war and that the agents are White men and the victims White (albeit largely Muslim) women—cannot be ignored when explaining the visibility of these rapes. By contrast, the routine rape of women in the civil wars and military dictatorships in Haiti, Peru, Liberia, and Burma (to name a few) goes largely unreported until women's voices are heard. [6] Nor does the international press report that mercenaries hired by an international agribusiness company rape 50 percent of the women of the indigenous Yuracruz people in Ecuador in order to "cleanse" the land of the Yuracruz people.

When the rapes in Bosnia-Herzegovina were revealed, feminists had already been working for decades on rape and gender violence.[8] It was also a moment in which women were organizing, regionally and globally, to put recognition of women's human rights on the agenda at the 1993 World Conference on Human Rights in Vienna. In this effort, violence against women—both official and personal—was a central issue. Thus the issue of the rape of women in Bosnia became part of the broader global feminist effort, less influenced by nationalist diplomacies,[9] at the same time that it advanced the feminist campaign by underscoring the gravity of ongoing gender violence just two hundred miles from the conference site. The Vienna *Declaration and Programme of Action* condemned gender violence generally and made special mention of "systemic rape, sexual slavery and forced pregnancy" in armed conflict.[10] The statute of the International Tribunal, created by the United Nations to prosecute war crimes in the former Yugoslavia, included widespread or systematic rape as an indictable offense.[11]

Nonetheless, the question today is whether the terrible war-time rape of women in former Yugoslavia will disappear into history or survive but be viewed as an exceptional case. Just as, historically, the condemnation of rape in war has rarely become an outcry against crimes of gender, so the mass rape in Bosnia captured world attention largely because of its association with "ethnic cleansing" or genocide. In a single week, a midday television talk show opened with, "In Bosnia, they are raping the enemy's women,"[12] and a leading Croatian-American scholar distinguished genocidal rape from "normal" rape, with very little reaction from the audience.[13] When women argued that rape is a weapon of war, rather than a by-product, they were referring to all its various purposes (e.g., to dilute ethnic identity, destabilize civilian populations, or reward soldiers). This assessment, however was accepted by the public only as regards rape as a vehicle of genocide.

The elision of genocide and rape in the focus on "genocidal rape" as a means of emphasizing the heinousness of the rape of Muslim women in Bosnia is thus dangerous. Rape and genocide are each atrocities. Genocide is an effort to debilitate or destroy a people based on its identity as a people, while rape seeks to degrade and destroy a woman based on her identity as a woman. Both are grounded in total contempt for and dehumanization of the victim, and both give rise to unspeakable brutalities. Their intersection in the Serbian (and, to a lesser extent, the Croatian) aggressions in Bosnia creates an ineffable living hell for women there. From the standpoint of these women, they are inseparable.

But to emphasize as unparalleled the horror of genocidal rape is factually dubious and risks rendering rape invisible once again. When the ethnic war ceases or is forced back into the bottle, will the crimes against women matter? Will their suffering and struggles to survive be vindicated? Or will condemnation be limited to this seemingly exceptional case? Will the women who are brutally raped for purposes of domination, terror, booty, or revenge in Bosnia and elsewhere be heard?

The situation presents an historic opportunity (indeed an imperative) to insist on justice for the women of Bosnia as well as to press for a feminist reconceptualization of the role and legal understanding of rape in war.

To do this, we must surface gender in the midst of genocide at the same time that we avoid dualistic thinking. We must examine critically the claim that rape as a tool of "ethnic cleansing" is unique, worse than, or incomparable to other forms of rape in war or in peace—even while we recognize that rape coupled with genocide inflicts multiple, intersectional harms.[14] This is critical if the horrors experienced by women in Bosnia are to be fully acknowledged and understood and if that experience is to have meaning for women brutalized in less-known theatres of war or in the by-ways of daily life.

Although there are significant concerns about the viability of the new International War Crimes Tribunal generally,[15] the rules that have been adapted articulate a commitment to sensitively and effectively prosecute sex crimes.[16] If the Tribunal functions and takes rape and the abuse of women seriously, it will be the first time—even if its actions are largely symbolic. The Tribunal also will be called upon to apply international law to rape in ways that could provide significant precedents for other situations.[17]

This essay examines the evolving legal status of rape in war with attention both to the particular context in which rape is occurring and to the general gender dimension, as well as to the tension between them. It focuses on two central conceptual questions: first, whether these crimes are fully recognized as war crimes under the Geneva Conventions—the cornerstone of what is called "humanitarian" law (i.e., the prohibitions that, by regulating war, also acknowledge it as permissible)—and, second, whether international law does, and should, distinguish between "genocidal rape" and mass rape for purposes other than genocide. In this regard, it examines the limitations of, and the potential inherent in, the concept of "crimes against humanity," as well as the relationship between gender and nationality/ethnicity in the crimes committed against women in Bosnia. The Conclusion suggests the relationship between everyday rape and rape in armed conflict or under military rule.

Rape, Forced Prostitution, and Forced Pregnancy As War Crimes

Although news of the mass rape of women in Bosnia was a significant factor in the demand for the creation of the International Tribunal, international law experts debated whether rape and other forms of sexual abuse are "war crimes" of the gravest dimension, subject to universal jurisdiction and therefore prosecutable before an international tribunal as well as in the courts of every country. The answer is not yet clear.

Rape and other forms of sexual assault have long been prohibited under national and international rules of war, and to prevent rape, the Geneva Conventions require separate quarters for women prisoners, as well as supervision and searches by women only.[18] But these crimes have been categorized as crimes against honor, not as crimes of violence[19] comparable to murder, mutilation, cruel and inhuman treatment, and torture.

Traditionally, rape has been condemned as a violation of a man's honor and exclusive right to sexual possession of his woman/property, and not because it is an assault on a woman.[20] Today, the mass rape in Bosnia is often referred to as the rape of "the enemy's women"—the enemy in this formulation being the male combatant and the seemingly all-male nation or religious or ethnic group. The victim is male, humiliated and emasculated by having failed as both warrior and protector. While this describes a significant patriarchal dimension of rape, it ignores the fact that women, too, are the enemy, and are raped as such.

The Geneva Conventions characterize rape as a crime against the honor and dignity of women.[21] But this too is problematic. Women's "honor" has traditionally been equated with virginity or chastity.[22] Loss of honor implies the loss of station or respect, reinforcing the social view—often internalized by women—that the raped woman is dishonorable. While the concept of dignity potentially embraces more profound concerns, the emphasis on honor obfuscates the fact that rape is violence against women—against women's body, autonomy, integrity, selfhood, security, and self-esteem, as well as standing in the community.

This failure to recognize rape as violence is critical to the traditionally lesser or ambiguous status of rape in humanitarian law. Under the Geneva Conventions, international crimes are those identified as "grave breaches."[23] On the level of discourse, this calls attention to the egregiousness of the assault. As a legal matter, only grave breaches are subject to universal jurisdiction under the Geneva Conventions, triggering the obligation of every nation to bring the perpetrators to justice and justifying the trial of such crimes before an international tribunal.

Under the Geneva Conventions, rape is not specified in the list of crimes considered grave breaches, which includes "willful killing, torture or inhumane treatment" and "willfully causing great suffering or serious injury to body or health."[24] Clearly these categories are broad and generic enough to encompass rape and sexual abuse. But if the egregiousness of rape is to be fully recognized, rape must be explicitly recognized as a form of torture.

When the Conventions were drafted, torture was largely understood as a method of extracting information. By contrast, today, as the historian Edward Peters writes, "It is not primarily the victim's information, but the victim, that torture needs to win—or reduce to powerlessness."[25] Recent treaties define torture as the willful infliction of severe physical or mental pain or suffering not only to elicit information but also to punish, intimidate, discriminate, obliterate the victim's personality, or diminish her personal capacities.[26] Thus, torture is now commensurate with willfully causing great suffering or injury. Increasingly its definition encompasses not only the inflicting of physical pain but also methods of humiliation and debilitation that work directly on the mind. In the contemporary understanding of torture, degradation is both vehicle and goal.[27]

Although largely ignored by human rights advocates,[28] the testimonies and studies of women tortured during dictatorial regimes and military occupations make clear that rape is one of the most common, terrible, and effective forms of torture used against women.[29] Rape attacks the integrity of the woman as a person as well as her identity as a woman. It renders her, in the words of Lepa Mladjenovic, a psychotherapist and Serbian feminist antiwar activist, "homeless in her own body."[30] It strikes at a woman's power; it seeks to degrade and destroy her; its goal is domination and dehumanization.[31]

The impact of rape is multiplied and becomes sexual enslavement when it is institutionalized as forced prostitution or linked with the threat, fear, and/or reality of pregnancy. The expressed intent to make women pregnant is an additional form of psychological torture; the goal of impregnation leads to imprisoning women and raping them until they are pregnant; the fact of pregnancy, whether aborted or not, continues the initial torture in a most intimate and invasive form; and the fact of bearing the child of rape, whether placed for adoption or not, has a potentially lifelong impact on the woman, on her liberty, and on her place in the community.

Because rape is a transportation of the intimate into violence, rape by acquaintances, by those who have been trusted, is particularly world-shattering and thus is a particularly effective method of torture and tool of ethnic cleansing.[32] In Bosnia, the fact that the rapists are, in many cases, former colleagues, neighbors, or even friends further exacerbates the trauma and degradation. There are reports that some Bosnian-Serbs are being recruited as rapists through methods commonly used in training torturers: exposure to and engagement in increasingly unthinkable violence and humiliation.[33]

Although rape and related crimes are widely accepted as grave breaches in the context of the former Yugoslavia, it is not clear that this acceptance applies to contexts in which rape is neither widespread nor linked to ethnic cleansing.[34] The statute establishing the jurisdiction of an International War Crimes Tribunal does not explicitly list rape, forced prostitution, and forced pregnancy in its definition of grave breaches, although it is implicit in the recognized categories.[35] But if, as a consequence of women's interventions, these are prosecuted as such by the International Tribunal, this will effectively amend or expand the meaning of grave breach. This emphasizes the importance, from a practical as well as moral perspective, of insisting that all rape in war, not only mass or genocidal rape, be understood as torture.

Genocidal Rape vs. "Normal" Rape: When Is Mass Rape a Crime Against Humanity?

"Crimes against humanity" were first formally recognized in the Charter and Judgment of the Nuremberg Tribunal. They are viewed as violations of mandatory customary norms that brook no exceptions. This means they do not depend on adherence to a treaty and are subject to universal jurisdiction. The statute of the International Tribunal lists rape as a crime against humanity, and the commentary mentions forced prostitution as an example of a related offense.[36] Local Council Law No. 10, which provided the foundation for the trials of lesser Nazis by the Allied forces, also listed rape, although no one was prosecuted for it.[37] While it is critical to have rape identified, the meaning of this designation and its import for other contexts in which women are subjected to mass rape apart from ethnic cleansing is not clear. The danger, as always, is that extreme examples produce narrow principles.

The commentary on this aspect of the jurisdiction of the International Tribunal signals this danger. It explains crimes against humanity as "inhumane acts of a very serious nature, such as willful killing, torture or rape, committed as part of a widespread or systematic attack against any civilian population on national, political, ethnic, racial or religious grounds."[38] Several aspects of this definition deserve comment.

On the positive side, the statute correctly encompasses violations that are widespread but not necessarily systematic. The law wisely does not require massive numbers but, rather, patterns of abuse. (This is particularly important vis-à-vis rape, since only a small percentage of women will ultimately come forward, and statistics therefore, conceal, rather than reveal, the significance of the pattern.) Moreover, rape need not be ordered or centrally organized for commanders to be held accountable: they are responsible for failing to take steps to prevent patterns of violence of which they were aware or should have been aware.[39] While it is politically and ethically important for the Tribunal to investigate and prove the chain of command, it is likewise important that the leadership be held legally responsible without such proof.

The important gender question is whether widespread or systematic rape, apart from genocide or ethnic cleansing, would qualify as a crime against humanity. The original concept of crimes against humanity recognized two separate and independent criteria: gross acts of violence and persecution-based offenses. The statute of the Tribunal listed rape alongside torture and, thus, might be understood as recognizing rape as a gross act of violence. But by merging the criteria of gross violence with persecution-based offenses, the commentary might be seen to limit prosecution to those rapes undertaken as a method of persecution on the specified grounds.

The latter narrow view, expressed in the popular distinction between so-called "normal" rape and genocidal rape, is unfortunately quite prevalent. This distinction contrasts the common and tolerable with the unique and heinous. It is proffered not as a typology but rather as a hierarchy. To thus exaggerate the distinctiveness of genocidal rape obviates the atrocity of common rape. Genocidal rape in Bosnia involves gang rapes, often in public or in front of children or partners. It involves imprisoning women in rape "camps" and raping them repeatedly. These characteristics are unfortunately not unique but rather common to most rape in war—rape for booty or to boost the morale of soldiers—just as they are to the use of rape as a form of torture and terror by dictatorial regimes.

The notion that genocidal rape is uniquely a weapon of war is also problematic. The rape of women is a weapon of war where it is used to spread political terror, as in the military repression in Haiti, and the civil war in Peru. It is a weapon of war where, as with the Russian rape of German women at the close of World War II, it is used against women to destabilize a society and break its resistance.[40] It is a weapon of war where, as in Bosnia and the indigenous Yuracruz homeland in Ecuador, it is part of a calculated effort to terrorize and shame women into fleeing their homes, and often their families and communities.

The rape of women as the "booty" of war, where permitted or systematized, is likewise a tactic or engine of war: it maintains the morale of soldiers, feeds their hatred and sense of superiority, and keeps them fighting. During World War II, the Japanese military industrialized and made invisible the enslavement of women as booty: women—mostly Korean, but also Filipino, Chinese, Indonesian and some Dutch—were deceived or disappeared into "comfort stations" where they were raped repeatedly, and moved from battlefield to battlefield to motivate and reward the Japanese soldiers. Genocide was not a goal, but it is believed that 90 percent of these women died in captivity. Among the known survivors, few if any were able subsequently to bear children.[41] For similar reasons, the United States military in Vietnam raped Vietnamese women and established brothels, relying on the women's desperate poverty and family pressures, rather than kidnapping, to fill them.[42]

While the testimonies of women from Bosnia reveal, in fact, an admixture of all these tactics, genocidal or ethnic cleansing rape as practiced in Bosnia has some aspects particularly designed to drive women from their homes or destroy their possibility of reproducing within and "for" their community.[43] Since war and propaganda have made enemies of neighbors, women are raped by men familiar to them, thus exacerbating the trauma, shame, betrayal, and impulse to flee. The second and more generally distinctive feature of genocidal rape is the focus on women as reproductive vessels. The commonly articulated goal to make Muslim women bear "Serbian babies" (as if the child is the product of sperm only) justifies repeated rape and aggravates the terror of—as well as the future stigma on—the women. Similarly, Bengali women were raped by the Pakistani army to lighten their race and produce a class of outcast mothers and children. Enslaved African women in the southern United States were raped as property to produce babies who were then bartered, sold, and used as property.[44]

While intentional impregnation is properly treated as a separate offense,[45] this should not obscure the fact that pregnancy is a common consequence of rape. In situations where women are raped repeatedly, most fertile women will become pregnant at some point. When the U.S. Navy took over Saipan, for example, one observer reported that virtually all the women who had been enslaved as "comfort women" by the Japanese army were pregnant.[46]

These distinctive characteristics do not, however, place genocidal rape in a class by itself; nor do they reflect the full range of atrocities, losses, and suffering that the combination of rape and genocide inflict. Bosnian-Muslim women are being presecuted based on multiple elemental aspects of identity: gender and ethnicity or religion. But the effect on women of rape apart from genocide may be no less life-shattering, given the enormity of the assault on a woman's integrity and personality and the unacceptability of a raped woman to the patriarchal community and, as a result, to herself. The crystallization of the concept of "crimes against humanity" in the wake of the Holocaust has meant that it is popularly associated wih religious and ethnic genocide. The categories of persecution, however, are explicitly open-ended, capable of expanding to embrace new understandings of persecution and of embracing persecution based on gender as a category of crimes against humanity.The problem is, of course, that historically gender has not been recognized as a category of persecution. The frequency of mass rape and the absence of sanction is sufficient evidence. In the Holocaust, the gender persecutions—the rape and forced prostitution of women as well as the extermination of gays—were obscured.[47] A parallel problem exists in the context of political asylum, which requires a well-founded fear of persecution but has not yet explicitly recognized gender as a source of persecution.[48] Expansion of the concept of crimes against humanity to include gender is thus part of the broader movement to end the historic invisibility of gender violence as a humanitarian and human rights violation.

Moreover, the particular goals and defining aspects of genocidal rape do not detract from, but rather underscore, the nature of rape as a crime of gender. Women are targets not only because they "belong to" the enemy but also because they keep the civilian population functioning and are essential to its continuity. They are targets because they too *are* the enemy; because of their *power* as women; because of hatred of their power including their sexual and reproductive powers; because men delight in the objectification and degradation of women.

The crime of forced impregnation—central as it is to genocidal rape—also underscores the gender component. Since in a patriarchy women are viewed as little more than vessels for childbearing, involuntary pregnancy is commonly viewed as natural, divinely ordained perhaps, or simply an unquestioned fact of life. As a result, the risk of pregnancy in all rape is treated not as an offense but as a sequela. Forced pregnancy has drawn condemnation only when it reflects an intent to harm the victimized race.

Since, in Bosnia, ethnically mixed families are common in certain areas, the issue is not so much about racial impurity as it is about the perpetrator's purpose and the victim's choice. The taunt that Muslim women shall bear Serbian babies is not simply an ethnic harm. The intent to impregnate is equally an assault on the reproductive self-determination of women; it marks the rape and rapist upon a woman's body and spirit and upon her life.

Finally, the fact that the rape of women is also designed to humiliate men or destroy "the enemy" to whom the women "belong" itself reflects the fundamental objectification of women. Women are the targets of abuse at the same time that their existence and subjectivity are completely denied. The persistent failure to acknowledge the gender dimension of rape and sexual persecution is thus a most effective means of perpetuating it.

In sum, the international attention focused on Bosnia challenges the world to recognize squarely that sexual violence against women in war is a form of torture. Widespread or systematic rape, forced prostitution, and forced pregnancy must be viewed as crimes against humanity not only when they are the vehicles of some other form of persecution but also independently, because they are invariably forms of persecution based on gender. Nor is it enough for the Tribunal statute simply to recognize rape as a crime; those responsible for rape and related crimes must be charged and prosecuted in accordance with bias-free standards and recognized procedure. This is essential if the women of Bosnia are to be understood as full subjects, as well as objects, of this terrible victimization, and if the international attention focused on Bosnia is to have meaning for women subjected to rape in other parts of the world.

Given the formidable pressure being brought to bear by women survivors and the women's movement globally, it may well be that some few men will be indicted and even tried before the International Tribunal or national courts—*if* impunity is not once again the price of peace. This would be precedent setting in international law and provide symbolic vindication of the untold numbers of women rendered homeless in so many senses by this war. It would strengthen the claims women in other countries can make on their governments to prosecute such criminals when they come within their territory and would enable victims and survivors to sue perpetrators for damages based on the incorporation of international law into national law.[49] But unless the gender dimension of rape in war is recognized, it will mean little for women where rape is not also a tool of genocide.

Conclusion

When women charge rape in war, they are more likely to be believed because their status as enemy, or at least as belonging to the enemy, is recognized and because rape in war is seen as a product of exceptional circumstances. When women charge rape in everyday life, they are disbelieved largely because the ubiquitous war against women is denied. Emphasis on the gender dimension of rape in war is critical not only to surfacing women as full subjects of sexual violence in war but also to recognizing the atrocity of rape in so-called times of peace.

This is not to say that rape is identical in the two contexts. There are differences, just as there are differences between rape for the purposes of genocide and rape in which women are considered booty. War tends to intensify the brutality, repetition, public aspect, and likelihood of rape. War diminishes sensitivity to human suffering and intensifies men's sense of entitlement, superiority, avidity, and social license to rape. But the line between rape committed during wartime and at other times is not so sharp. Gang rape in civilian life shares the repetitive, gleeful, and public character of rape in war. Marital rape, the most private of all, also shares some of the particular characteristics of genocidal rape in Bosnia: it is repetitive, brutal, and exacerbated by a profound betrayal of trust; it assaults a woman's reproductive autonomy, may force her to flee her home and community, and is widely treated as legitimate by law and custom.[50]

From a feminist human rights perspective, gender violence has escaped sanction because it has not been viewed as violence and because the public/private dichotomy has insulated its most common, private forms.[51] The recognition of rape as a war crime is thus a critical step toward understanding rape as violence. The next step is to recognize that rape that acquires the imprimatur of the state is not necessarily more brutal, relentless, or dehumanizing than the private rapes of everyday life, nor is violation by a state official or enemy soldier necessarily more devastating than violation by an intimate.[52]

Every rape is a grave violation of physical and mental integrity. Every rape has the potential to debilitate profoundly, to alienate a woman from her own body and destroy her sense of security in the world. Every rape is an expression of male domination and misogyny, a vehicle for terrorizing and subordinating women. Like torture, rape takes many forms, occurs in many contexts, and has different repercussions for different victims. Every rape is multidimensional, but not incomparable.

The rape of women in the former Yugoslavia challenges the world to refuse impunity to atrocity and to resist the powerful forces that would make the mass rape of Muslim women in Bosnia appear exceptional, thus neutralizing its meaning for women raped in different contexts. We must recognize situational differences without losing sight of the commonalties. To fail to make distinctions flattens reality; to rank the egregious demeans it.

Notes

Credit for extensive research into the historical and current understanding of war crimes and crimes against humanity is due to Krishna Stark and Ethan Taubes. I also appreciate

Celina Romany's and Marilyn Young's comments on the draft, as well as conversations with Jennifer Green, Vesna Kesic, Guadeloupe Leon, Sara Sharett, Ann Snitow, and Dorothy Thomas, among others.

1. See, e.g. Susan Brownmiller, *Against Our Will: Men, women, and Rape,* (New York: Simon and Schuster, 1975), pp. 31–113.

2. Attina Grossman, unpublished paper; and Lourdes Sajor, "Women in Armed Conflict Situations," MAV/1993/WP.1 (September 21, 1993) (prepared for Expert Group meeting on Measures to Eradicate Violence Against Women, UN Division for the Advancement of Women).

3. The "rape of Nanking" refers to the brutal taking of Nanking by Japanese forces, which involved several months of mass and open killing, looting, and rape. It is estimated that 20,000 women were raped in the first month. See Leon Friedan, *The Law of War, A Documentary History,* Vol. 2 (New York: Random House, 1972), p. 46.

4. Brownmiller, *supra* n. 1, pp. 78–86. Among the motives for these rapes was a genocidal one—to destroy the racial distinctiveness of the Bengali people.

5. Although the Serbian campaign against the Bosnian-Muslims is the most extensive, the hatred inflamed and the atrocities committed in the wars in the former Yugoslavia are far too complicated to describe as a one-way street. Croatian women were also targets. Moreover, from before the outset of the war, the Croatian government has sought to "cleanse" Croatia of Serbs and has waged a bitter war against Muslims in Bosnia in the effort to claim territory as Croatian. There are reports as well of rape and other at atrocities commited by Muslims. See Jeri Laber, "Bosnia: Questions of Rape," *New York Review of Books* (March 25, 1993), pp. 3–6; and Alexandra Stiglmayer, *Mass Rape: The War Against Women in Bosnia-Herzegovina* (Lincoln, NB: Univ. of Nebraska Press, 1994). There are some reports that men have been subjected to rape, which is also a crime of gender, but rape has been, as usual, overwhelmingly directed against women (telephone conversation with Patrick Cotter, January 1994.)

6. See, for example, America's Watch and Women's Rights Project, *Untold Terror: Violence Against Women in Peru's Armed Conflict* (New York: Human Rights Watch, 1992); Asia Watch and Women's Rights Project, *Burma. Rape, Forced Labor, and Religious Persecution in Northern Arakan* (Washington, DC: Human Rights Watch, 1992); Shana Swiss, *Liberia: Women and Children Gravely Mistreated* (Boston: Physicians for Human Rights, 1991). For other examples, see Shana Swiss and Joan E. Giller, "Rape as a Crime of War," *Journal of the American Medical Association* 270 (August 4, 1993): p. 612.

7. The routine rape of Haitian women identified as Aristide supporters was ignored in the periodic reports of the Inter-American Commission on Human Rights until the pressure of women forced the UN/OAS Observer Mission to conduct a special investigation. As a result of a brief investigation in Cité Soleil, a very poor and pro-Aristide section of Port-au-Prince, the Mission reported that "rape appear[s] to form an integral part of the political violence and terror" (UN/OAS Observer Mission, Communiqué, March 21, 1994). See also presentation of Guadalupe Leon, Panel on Military Violence and Sexual Slavery, 1993 UN Conference on Human Rights, NGO Parallel Activities, June 1993.

8. See Cynthia Enloe, "Afterword" in Stiglmayer, *supra*, n. 5, and Lourdes, Sajor, *supra*, n. 2.

9. National experience and divisions have, however, divided women and feminists. See Vesna Kesic, "A Response to Catherine MacKinnon's 'Turning Rape into Pornography: Postmodern Genocide,' " *Hasting's Women's Law Journal* 5(1) (Winter 1994) (written to refute Catherine MacKinnon, "Turning Rape into Pornography: Postmodern Genocide," in Stiglmayer, *supra* n. 5, pp. 73–81), and C. Carr, "Battle Scars: Feminism and Nationalism Clash in the Balkans," *Village Voice*, July 13, 1993, p. 25.

10. *Report of the Drafting Committee*, Addendum, Final Outcome of the World Conference on Human Rights, A/conf. 157/PC/Add. 1 (June 24, 1993) (hereinafter, "Vienna Declaration").

11. The full title is "International Tribunal for the Prosecution of Persons Responsible for Serious Violations of International Humanitarian Law Committed in the Territory of the Former Yugoslavia Since 1991," *Report of the Secretary-General, pursuant to para. 2 of the Security Council Resolution 808* (1993), S/25704 (May 3, 1993), para. 48 at 13. Discussion infra pp. 8–9.

12. CNN, *Sonya Live,* January 26, 1993.

13. Bogdan Denitch, panel held at CUNY Law School, May 22, 1993, sponsored by the Queens Coalition for Political Alternatives. Some feminists have also made this distinction. See MacKinnon, *supra* n. 9; Carr, *supra* n. 9.

14. On the significance of the intersection of categories of oppression, see Kimberle Crenshaw, "Demarginalizing the Intersection of Race and Sex: A Black Feminist Critique of Anti-Discrimination Doctrine, Feminist Theory, and Antiracist Politics," *University of Chicago Legal Forum* (1989), pp. 139–67. For examination of the particularities of ethno-gender violence, see Stiglmayer, "The Rapes in Bosnia-Herzegovina," *supra* n. 5, pp. 82–169; Azra Zalihic-Kaurin, "The Muslim Women," in Stiglmayer, *supra* n. 5, pp. 170–73; MacKinnon, "Rape, Genocide, and Women's Human Rights," in Stiglmayer, *supra* n. 5, pp. 183–196; Adrien Katherine Wing and Sylke Merchan, "Rape, Ethnicity, and Culture: Spirit Injury from Bosnia to Black America," *Columbia Human Rights Law Review* 25(1) (Fall 1993), 1–46; International Human Rights Law Group, *No Justice, No Peace* (Washington, DC: 1993).

15. More than one year after its creation, the Tribunal still has no Chief Prosecutor, the Deputy Prosecutor has just begun hiring a skeletal staff, the project is substantially underfunded, and only two of the eleven judges are women. The Tribunal is politically compromised by its ad hoc status, and the risk remains that formal impunity will again be the price of peace. Further, the power of the Tribunal is sorely limited; it cannot compel the appearance of the accused without the cooperation of a willing state. Thus, in relation to major figures who remain in or close to power in their countries, the Tribunal can generate only an international "wanted" list that will, at least, restrict the ability of the accused to travel internationally.

16. See International Tribunal for the Prosecution of Persons Responsible for Serious Violations of International Humanitarian Law Committed in the Territory of the Former Yugoslavia since 1991, *Rules of Procedure and Evidence,* UN Docs. IT/ 32 (March 14, 1994) and IT/61/Rev.1 (May 6, 1994). The rules clearly reflect the influence of feminist approaches to rape. See, e.g., rule 75 (protection of witnesses);

rule 79 (closed sessions); and, particularly, revised rule 96 (evidence in cases of sexual assault), which precludes requiring corroboration of the victim's testimony, precludes the defense of consent where violence, duress, detention, or psychological oppression are shown, and prohibits evidence of the prior sexual conduct of the victim. An extensive proposal for the treatment of war crimes was submitted to the Tribunal by the International Women's Human Rights Law Clinic at CUNY Law School, and the Harvard Human Rights Program.

17. The international legal meaning of rape is also under consideration in petitions before the Inter-American Commission on Human Rights concerning Haiti and Peru.

18. See, e.g., Yougindra Khusalini, *Dignity and Honour of Women As Basic and Fundamental Human Rights* (Boston: Martinus Nijhoff, 1982). Also, *Geneva Convention Relative to the Protection of Civilian Persons in Time of War,* common art. 3, 1(a) and (c), arts. 27, 76, and 97 (hereinafter referred to as Geneva Convention IV); *Protocol Additional to the Geneva Conventions of 12 August 1949, and relating to the Protection of Victims of International Armed Conflicts (Protocol I),* art. 76; *Protocol Additional to the Geneva Conventions of 12 August 1949, and relating to the Protection of Victims of Non-International Armed Conflicts (Protocol II),* art. 4. All of the conventions above reprinted in Center for Human Rights, *Human Rights: A Compilation of International Instruments,* Vol. 1 (pt. 2) (New York: United Nations, 1993), pp. 799–939.

19. Khusalini, *supra* n. 18; *Geneva Convention IV,* art. 27, para. 2; *Protocol II,* art. 4.

20. In the United States, the death penalty for rape was prevalent in the Southern states as a result of a combination of sexism and racism. See *Coker v. Georgia,* 433 U.S. 584 (1977).

21. Khusalini, *supra* n. 18, pp. 39–76.

22. See, e.g., America's Watch, *Untold Terror, supra* n. 6.

23. *Geneva Convention IV,* note 9, art. 147; *Protocol I,* note 9, arts. 11 and 85(3). The concept of "grave breach" applies only to international conflict and not to civil war. With respect to the question of whether the conflict in former Yugoslavia is international or internal, the UN has taken the position that the warring parties have agreed to abide by the rules governing international armed conflicts. United Nations, *Report of the Secretary-General, supra* n. 11, para. 25, p. 8.

24. *Geneva Convention IV,* note 9, art. 147; *Protocol I,* note 9, arts. 11 and 85(3).

25. Edward Peters, *Torture* (New York: Basil Blackwell, 1985), p. 164.

26. *UN Convention Against Torture,* art. 1; *Inter-American Convention Against Torture,* art. 2, reprinted in J. Herman Burgers and Hans Danelius, *The United Nations Convention Against Torture and Other Cruel Inhuman and Degrading Treatment or Punishment* (Boston: Martinus Nijhoff, 1988), Appendix.

27. Amnesty International, *Report on Torture* (New York: Farrar, Straus and Giroux, 1974). See Rhonda Copelon, "Recognizing the Egregious in the Everyday: Domestic Violence as Torture," *Columbia Human Rights Law Review,* 25(2) (Spring 1994): pp. 291–367.

28. It was not until 1991 that a mainstream human rights non-governmental organization recognized rape in detention or under military occupation as a form of torture.

Amnesty International, *Women in the Front Line* (New York: Amnesty International, 1991). In 1992, the UN Commission on Commission on Human Rights' Special Rapporteur on Torture did likewise. *Report of the Special Rapporteur P. Kooijmans, Pursuant to Commission on Human Rights Resolution 1992/32,* UN Doc. E/CN.4/1993/26 (15 December 1992), e.g., paras. 355, 371. For a discussion of the recognition of rape as torture by the United Nations Commission on Human Rights' Special Rapporteur on Torture, see *Token Gestures: 1, the UN Special Rapporteur on Torture* (Washington, DC: International Human Rights Law Group, June 1993). See also, Deborah Blatt "Recognizing Rape as a Method of Torture." *NYU Review of Law and Social Change* 19:821 (1992); and Theodor Meron, "Rape As a Crime Under International Humanitarian Law," *American Journal of International Law* 87:424 (1993).

29. See, e.g., Ximena Bunster-Bunalto, "Surviving Beyond Fear: Women and Torture in Latin America," *Women and Change in Latin America,* edited by June Nash and Helen Safa (Westport, CT: Bergin and Garvey, 1986), pp. 297–325; F. Allodi and S. Stiasny, "Women As Torture Victims," *Canadian Journal of Psychiatry* 35 (March 1990): 144–48; Inge Lunde and Jorge Ortmann, "Prevalence and Sequelae of Sexual Torture," *The Lancet* 336 (August 1990): 289–91. While not the subject here, the rape of men is also a devastating crime of gender, designed as it is to humiliate through "feminization."

30. Testimony before the Global Tribunal on Violations of Women's Human Rights, part of the NGO Parallel Activities, 1993 World Conference on Human Rights, Vienna, June 15, 1993.

31. See, e.g., Brownmiller, *supra* n. 1; Bunster-Bunalto, *supra* n. 29; Amnesty International, *Women in the Front Line, supra* n. 28.

32. See Amnesty International, *Report on Torture, supra* n. 27; Elaine Scarry, *The Body in Pain: The Making and Unmaking of the World* (New York: Oxford Univ. Press, 1985), p. 41; Judith Lewis Herman, *Trauma and Recovery* (New York: Basic Books, 1992); David Finkelhor and Kersti Yllö, *License to Rape: Sexual Abuse of Wives* (New York: Free Press, 1985); Diana E.H. Russell, *Rape in Marriage* (New York: Collier, 1982).

33. See Stiglmayer, *supra* n. 5. See also, e.g., Stanley Milgram, "Some Conditions of Obedience and Disobedience to Authority," *Human Relations* 18(1) (1965): 57–74. On the training of torturers, see Amnesty International, *Torture in Greece: The First Torturers' Trial 1975* (New York: Amnesty International, 1977); Mika Haritos-Fatouros, "The Official Torturer: A Learning Model for Obedience to the Authority of Violence," *Journal of Applied Social Psychology* 18(13) (October 1988): pp. 107–120.

34. UN Commission on Human Rights, *Rape and Abuse of Women in the Territory of the Former Yugoslavia,* Report on the 49th Session, February 1–March 12, 1993, Economic and Social Council Suppl. No. 3, E/CN4/1993/122: e.g., "Rape and abuse of women and children in the former Yugoslavia which, *in the circumstances,* constitutes a war crime." (emphasis added). Likewise, the Vienna Conference limited its condemnation to "systematic rape" (Vienna Declaration, *supra* n. 10). See also Meron, *supra* n. 28.

35. Article 2 of the statute identifies as grave breaches "(a) willful killing; (b) torture or inhuman treatment, including biological experiments; (c) willfully causing great

suffering or serious bodily injury to body or health." United Nations, *Report of the Secretary-General, supra* n. 11, art. 2, paras. 37–40, pp. 10–11.

36. *Report of the Secretary-General, supra* n. 11, art. 5, paras. 47–49, p. 13.

37. Khusalini, *supra* n. 18, p. 23; see discussion therein, pp. 13–38.

38. *Report of the Secretary-General, supra* n. 11, para. 48, p. 13.

39. Idem, art. 7(3), p. 15.

40. America's Watch and Women's Rights Project, *Untold Terror, supra* n. 6; Swiss and Giller, *supra* n. 6.

41. Sajor, *supra* n. 2. Testimony of Bok Dong Kim before the Global Tribunal on Violations of Women's Human Rights, NGO Parallel Activities, 1993 World Conference on Human Rights, Vienna, June 15, 1993. See also *Hearings before the United Nations Secretary-General* (February 25, 1993) (testimonies of Hyo-chai Lee, MA; Soon-Kum Park, and Chung-Ok Yum, MFA, Korean Council for the Women Drafted for Military Sexual Service in Japan).

42. Brownmiller, *supra* n. 1, pp. 86–113.

43. See, e.g., Stiglmayer, *supra,* n. 5.

44. Angela Y. Davis, *Women, Race and Class* (New York: Vintage, 1983), p. 172.

45. See Anne Tierney Goldstein, "Recognizing Forced Impregnation as a War Crime Under International Law," Special Report of the Center for Reproductive Law and Policy (1993).

46. Conversation with D.B., New Haven, CT, April 1993.

47. See Brownmiller, *supra* n. 1, pp. 48–78, for the unrecognized sexual violence against women on the part of Allied as well as Axis forces. See also Erwin J. Haeberle, "Swastika, Pink Triangle, and Yellow Star: The Destruction of Sexology and the Persecution of Homosexuals in Nazi Germany," in *Hidden from History: Reclaiming the Gay and Lesbian Past,* edited by Martin Duberman, Martha Vicinus, and George Channcez, Jr., pp. 365–79 (New York: Meridian, 1990) (noting the gender aspect of the Nazi attacks on homosexuals reflected in the use of the pink triangle and charges of emasculation).

48. The *Convention Relating to the Status of Refugees* recognizes persecution based on race, religion, nationality, membership in a particular social group, or political opinion. The "social group" category is currently being expanded to encompass gender claims, but this is not enough. See Pamela Goldberg, "Anyplace But Home: Asylum in the United States for Women Fleeing Intimate Violence." *Cornell International Law Journal* 26:565 (Symposium 1993).

49. Two lawsuits have been filed against the Bosnian-Serbian leader, Radovan Karadzic. *Jane Doe v. Radovan Karadzic,* Civil Action No. 93 Civ. 0878 (PKL) (U.S. Southern District of New York, filed 1993); *S. Kadic v. Radovan Karadzic,* Civil Action No. 93 Civ. 1163 (PKL) (U.S. Southern District of New York, filed 1993). The Center for Constitutional Rights in New York City has a number of cases, including *Doe v. Karadzic,* and is the leading source of information on this strategy for domestic implementation of international law.

50. Amnesty International, *Report on Torture, supra* n. 27; Scarry, *supra* n. 32; Herman, *supra* n. 32; Finkelhor and Yllö, *supra* n. 32; Russell, *supra* n. 32.

51. See Charlotte Bunch, "Women's Rights as Human Rights: Towards a Re-Vision of Human Rights," *Human Rights Quarterly* 12 (1990); Celina Romany, "State Responsibility Goes 'Private': A Feminist Critique of the Public/Private Distinction in International Human Rights Law," in *The Human Rights of Women*, edited by Rebecca Cook (Philadelphia: Univ. of Pennsylvania Press, 1994); Copelon, *supra* n. 27.

52. Herman, *supra* n. 32.

This article is a shortened and updated version of "Surfacing Gender: Reconceptualizing Crimes Against Women in Time of War," in *Mass Rape: The War Against Women in Bosnia-Herzegovina*, edited by Alexandra Stiglmayer. By permission of Univ. of Nebraska Press. Copyright 1994 by U. of N. Press.

22

AIDS and Gender Violence: The Enslavement of Burmese Women in the Thai Sex Industry

Hnin Hnin Pyne

When I met Aye Aye, she had just been rescued during a brothel raid, along with eighteen other women. Aye Aye's image has stayed with me, because she was suffering from AIDS. The non-governmental organization (NGO) that ran the shelter where the women were placed had taken them to a clinic, where it was discovered that seventeen of the nineteen were HIV-positive, and all had some other form of sexually transmitted disease. Aye Aye's shoulder-length hair was pulled back by a barrette, and her gaunt face exaggerated her large, deep-set eyes. She was coughing and shivering as I sat next to her and her older sister. Aye Aye was seventeen years old. She had lived in Mathila, a major city in Central Burma, where her father mended pots and her mother sold food. As a young girl, she'd helped support her family by washing clothes for wealthy households. When she was only fourteen, a woman known in the community for her business in border trade and her frequent visits to Thailand proposed to Aye Aye's sister that she work as a maid in Bangkok. The girls' parents allowed the woman to take both sisters on her next trip, and two of Aye Aye's best friends also joined the party. Posing as merchants, they were smuggled across the border. Once in Thailand, the woman handed Aye Aye and the others over to a group of men, who took them to Bangkok and sold them into a brothel.

Aye Aye had been kept in Thailand for three years at two different brothels. When rescued, she was living on the fifth floor of the brothel, which had a pool hall and a bar on the first two floors. The building housed approximately one hundred women. From noon until two in the morning, Aye Aye, wearing a numbered button, would sit behind a glass partition, while men ogled her and the others from across the room. She would watch television while waiting for her number to be called. She served about twelve to twenty men a day. Customers paid the brothel Baht 150 (about $6 U.S.) for one-half hour; Aye Aye received only Baht 25 ($1 U.S.) per day. Because she looked young and inexperienced, Aye Aye's price was higher than that of her sister and two friends. The clients were mostly Thai and Chinese, although Aye Aye said that sometimes, when they were Burmese, the brothel owner threatened the girls, warning them not to murmur a word of Burmese.

The people from the shelter planned to take all the women back to the border the day after the raid. Aye Aye was thrilled about the prospect of going home—a month's trip during the rainy season. But she was upset by the shelter supervisor's request that she not take any luggage, since doing so might arouse suspicion and could lead to arrest, and she refused to leave her belongings. "I am not going home empty-handed! I have to take my things," she shouted. I listened to her with puzzlement. I was frustrated by not being able to persuade her that she might be risking her freedom and attempted once more to convince her. She was stubborn and repeatedly asserted, "I cannot go home empty-handed." It dawned on me that she needed to preserve her pride and dignity. She had been away from home for three years in a country that, for most Burmese, is a land of opportunity. Thailand may have taken away her virginity and her freedom, but she was determined to show her family and friends in Mathila that she had lived up to their expectations.

Aye Aye is just one of many who have been enslaved in the Thai sex industry. This enslavement—yet one more form of violence against women—has permanently marked her life with AIDS. This paper explores the intersection of AIDS and the trafficking of women into prostitution by analyzing the case of Burmese women in the Thai sex industry. The first part briefly describes the forces driving the trafficking of women across the Thai-Burmese border. The second part examines the conditions and experiences of these women, and the third part analyzes the linkage between AIDS and the trafficking of Burmese women into Thailand. This linkage urgently needs to be further understood and addressed by public health workers, feminists, and human rights activists.

Over the past three decades, Burma has suffered from severe economic decline, achieving in 1987 the United Nation's status of Least Developed Country. The "rice bowl" of Asia has become the most impoverished nation in the region, and, as the price of staple foods rises, more and more people struggle to survive. The ruling junta, known as the State Law and Order Restoration Council (SLORC), has concentrated all its resources on maintaining its 300,000-strong army and on purchasing arms to extinguish democratic and ethnic resistance. Burma today has experienced the disintegration of its educational and health-care systems, the latter of which suffers not only from insufficient numbers of clinics and physicians but also from inadequate supplies, including hypodermic needles; this is the case even in Rangoon hospitals, where health workers routinely share needles among patients.

The political and economic crisis in Burma has resulted in an exodus of refugees, prodemocracy activists, and many people simply searching for a way out. Increasing numbers of Burmese women have been persuaded to go to the border areas by promises of good wages paid in Thai currency. Burmese agents, who have connections in Thailand and with the military along trade routes, have taken advantage of the women's desperate situations to coerce them into prostitution. Although men have always had the option of joining the army or entering a monastery, poor women in Burma are presented with very few viable economic opportunities. Historically, rural women have migrated to cities to work as domestic servants, their move facilitated by a network of friends or agents (Khaing 1984). Today, however, the "prostitution" agents have tapped into this acceptable means by which poor women acquire employment and transformed the network into the basis of the trade in Burmese women.

The Thai sex industry also drives the trafficking of women and girls from other countries and remote villages. Because of a common belief among Thai-Chinese that sex with virgins enhances men's virility, brothel owners charge Baht 5,000–10,000 ($200–400 U.S.) for virgins or girls who have been with only one or two men. The AIDS epidemic has also spurred the demand for young girls from remote areas, because they are believed to be untouched by infections and diseases. There also exists a noted preference among Thai men for light-skinned girls, such as those from the hill tribes.

The dire political and economic situation in Burma, coupled with the flourishing Thai sex industry, propels the trafficking of Burmese women and girls into forced prostitution. It is difficult to know how many Burmese women have been forced into the sex industry; since the official numbers do not indicate the ethnicity or national origin of the prostitutes, there is no official estimate. In most cases, the owners of sex establishments identify the nationality only of Thai women, because others are considered illegal immigrants. There are, however, several ways to verify the presence of Burmese women in significant numbers. In 1991, the *Bangkok Post* reported nine brothel raids, in which more than 200 of the 342 women discovered came from Burma. The director of the Centre for Protection of Children's Rights (CPCR), which maintains a shelter for many women and children rescued from brothels, estimates that 30 to 40 percent of the prostitutes they assist are from Burma (Asia Watch 1993, 31). In the first six months of 1992, the Crime Suppression Police found about 300 Burmese girls and women in the brothels of Ranong (Asia Watch 1993, p. 31).

My fieldwork led me to forty-three Burmese women who were in the brothels in Ranong, situated in the south of Thailand across from the southernmost point of Burma, about 350 miles from Bangkok. The women I interviewed belonged to many different ethnic groups—Mon, Karen, Pa-O, and Shan—although the majority (83.7 percent) were (ethnic) Burmese. They all spoke the Central Burmese dialect, which is the official language of the country. They came from towns as near to Ranong as Mergui (180 miles) and as far away as Taung Gyi (1,000 miles). One-third of the women originated from Rangoon, Burma's capital. Their ages ranged from eighteen to thirty-seven, although the majority (72.1 percent) were in their late teens and early twenties. Nearly half the women (44.2 percent) had had no formal education, while 18.6 percent had continued beyond primary school. Their time in Thailand spanned from two weeks to over two years. About half (48.8 percent) of them had been in Ranong for six to eight months. It was only in Thailand that they had become involved in prostitution. They came from very poor families, and two-thirds of the women had children of their own to care for. Twenty-six percent of the women stated they had never worked before; in Burma, they had helped take care of the home and attended to parents; these women had very little experience with currency and commercial transactions and were, therefore, especially vulnerable to deceit by brothel owners concerning wages and "debt." About one-third of the women had earned a living selling food or other goods, in either their own or their parents' stalls. Other types of work included domestic help and farming.

The Burmese women came to the brothels of Ranong either by themselves or with a middle-person/agent. Only two women asserted that they approached the brothel owner/managers themselves; the rest contended that they had been tricked and sold into the brothel. There were different types of agents: three women had been sold by their husbands or boyfriends (in one case, a twenty-year old woman was sold by the man with whom she had just eloped), ten by a "friend", and twenty-eight by a stranger who, in most cases, enticed the women by promising them high wages as waitresses, maids, and food vendors. Some indicated that agents, who are of Burmese nationality, brought them to Thailand in groups of two to five. In each of the cases where women were sold, the brothel owner paid the agent Baht 3,000–5,000 ($120–200 U.S.) per woman. None of that money went to the women, who were not to be released until they had paid back the amount the brothel owner had paid the agent. The accounting of this debt was exclusively in the hands of the brothel owner, and the women had to rely solely on his or her words.

The working and living conditions of the women varied slightly from one place to the next. The forty-three women I met came from four brothels, one of which was disguised behind a coffee shop. The brothels housed from 16 to 100 prostitutes. In the three smaller brothels (with 16, 20, and 30 women), the women had individual rooms, whereas in the largest they lived two to a room. Two brothels employed a cook, while at the other two food was brought in from the outside or the women cooked for themselves. The women bought clothes from the owner or from vendors who came to the brothel. Expenditures for food and clothing were added to their total debt. The establishments were isolated, and the women had very limited access to media. Only one of the four brothels owned a radio. For entertainment, the women usually listened to music from a jukebox or a tape recorder or read magazines. In all four brothels, the women were forbidden to leave the area unless accompanied by a guard, motorcycle taxi driver, or *mamasan*.

Three of the brothels had waiting rooms in which the women, wearing numbered buttons, sat behind glass or a low partition. The men looked at them from the other side of the glass, then selected them by number. The women had to work every day, unless they were ill or menstruating. At one of the brothels, however, the women were required to provide sexual services even during menstruation and the early months of pregnancy. The establishments did not place quotas on the number of clients, but the women were prohibited from rejecting customers—they had no choice but to accept the men who selected them.

The clients in these brothels were predominantly Thai and Burmese fishermen. The number of customers varied from one place to another: the women at three of the brothels (with 16, 30, and 100 prostitutes) had about four to ten customers per day, while the women at the fourth brothel each had about fifteen to twenty customers per day. The men paid Baht 50–100 ($2–4 U.S.) for 30 to 45 minutes, depending on the woman, and Baht 200 ($8) for overnight stays. The amount of money that reached the women—if any—was minimal. In one brothel, women received no wages other than tips from customers. One brothel paid Baht 300 ($12 U.S.) a month and another the same amount for three months. It was difficult, however, to determine the women's official wages, since most had been informed of their salaries but had not seen a single Baht since they had been there.

All the brothels dispensed medication for minor illnesses and infections. Three of the four supplied injectable contraceptives. The other provided only condoms, and, at the time of my interviews, six of the twenty-four women from that brothel were pregnant. These twenty-four women had never been to a clinic for a check-up or blood test. The brothel provided them with antibiotic cream for friction sores and infections. The brothel owner permitted medical assistance only in the case of abortions; two women from that group had recently had abortions at a local hospital—for one of the women, it was the third. Less than one-third of the women from the three other brothels said they had received check-ups for sexually transmitted diseases. They mentioned, however, that "doctors" had come to the brothel to give them injections and to talk about diseases like syphillis and AIDS.

Most shook their heads in bewilderment and smiled in embarrassment when the subject of AIDS (which they call A-I-D-S) was raised. A few said they had never heard of the disease, but those who had heard of it had very little knowledge, if any, about means of transmission and protection. One group of women explained that the virus has little horns and is very "quick" and "strong." Another added that it cannot be killed, even in boiling water. The women were, however, afraid of AIDS, but not only because they considered themselves at risk. One woman conveyed her dread of seeing others contract the virus but did not believe it was communicable. Many related that they had heard stories of HIV-positive prostitutes who were taken away by the police and then killed.

Some women believed they were protected from the virus because they had received injections every three months. (It is a common belief among most Burmese villagers that a "shot in the arm" is a cure-all.) But those injections were for the prevention of pregnancy. All the women had rituals in which they cleaned themselves after sex. The majority used soap and water, but others used toothpaste or *kunyar se* (lime water). One woman mentioned that she used laxatives as a way of cleansing herself.

Condoms were perceived both as protection against diseases and as a cause of infection. Despite some women's favorable attitude toward condoms, usage rates were low. One prostitute stated that she had never had a client who used a condom, though she had been in the brothel for four months and had had about six clients per day. Another added that during her seven months in prostitution, she had used condoms with two (at most) of her eight daily customers. The clients routinely refused to wear condoms: "Burmese men never used condoms. Shan (Thai) men are better about that." "What can I do if he will not use a condom?" "It's up to the guests." The women had absolutely no power to bargain with the customers.

One group of women proclaimed their dislike for condoms, which they asserted were the cause of infections. Clients using condoms took more time to reach orgasm and would, therefore, spend more time with the prostitute. The length of time, when multiplied by a large number of clients, resulted in pain and exhaustion for the women. And the friction sores and vaginal irritations from which they suffered did, in fact, increase the risk of contracting HIV, confirming the women's view that condom use increases the risk of infection. Information on AIDS and other sexually transmitted diseases was limited, and access to health care, if any, sporadic. With the high number of clients, including fishermen (among whom intravenous drug use is common), the women are at great risk of contracting HIV.

As of a 1993 Ministry of Public Health study, Thailand's HIV cases numbered between 400,000 and 500,000, with sexual contact and needle sharing the primary modes of HIV transmission. In recent years the rate of infection in the female population has increased significantly, with especially high numbers seen in prostitute populations. The male-to-female ratio of people infected in Thailand has shifted drastically from 17:1 in 1986 to 3.1:1 in 1991 (MOPH 1991). The National Sentinel surveillance classifies female sex workers into two groups: women who work in brothels and who are specifically procured for sex; and those who work in massage parlors, bars, and escort agencies, and who provide other services in addition to sex. In June of 1993, Sentinel surveillance indicated that, among brothel prostitutes, the prevalence range was 5 to 64 percent and the HIV prevalence rate was 28.7 (i.e., 28.7% of brothel prostitutes tested for HIV were found to be positive). Among nonbrothel prostitutes, the range was 0 to 37 percent and the rate 7.6 percent (MOPH 1993). A 1992 study in Khon Kaen found that women working in the brothels were 7.4 times more likely than other sex workers to become infected with the AIDS virus (Brinkmann). Public health workers have tied the higher rates found among brothel prostitues to their larger number of clients as well as to those clients' low socio-economic backgrounds. This, however, overlooks other critical issues that help explain the high rates of HIV infection among women in the Thai brothels.

In order to prevent escapes by women who have been trafficked into prostitution for sale into brothels (where they both work and live), brothel owner/managers control the women's freedom of movement. Mobility and access to health care are intricately linked: Because the women in Ranong were forbidden to leave the vicinity of the brothel unless accompanied by a "hired" guard or someone else trusted by the owner, they could not freely visit the health center when they contracted infections or became ill. Many brothels arrange check-ups for a few women at a time, but access to health care rests entirely in the hands of the owner. This, of course, limits the amount and type of information (about AIDS and other sexually transmitted diseases) that reaches the women. Information through other sources is also insufficient, since many brothels do not own radios or televisions. Furthermore, the Burmese women do not understand AIDS education messages they might receive because almost none of them speak Thai. Their inability to communicate also limits their access to women's groups and other support networks.

Consideration of a prostitute's bargaining position with customers is critical to understanding her vulnerability to HIV. The decision as to whether to use a condom is ultimately made by the male client; that most prostitutes have little bargaining power is a reflection of the general status of women and of gender relations in Thai and Burmese society. Women in the brothels have still less bargaining power than women in other kinds of establishments, because they can neither choose nor reject clients. A woman who has been coerced into prostitution is in the worst bargaining position of all, as she holds no power either among the women or with respect to the owner.

The bargaining position of a prostitute, however, is located not only within her immediate situation in a sex establishment (relations between herself and owner/manager or *mamasan*), but also within a larger structure of gender relations. The bargaining may occur in a brothel, but it does not take place in a vacuum. The power relations between prostitute and client are constructed by social definitions of gender and sexuality. As in the case of Burmese women, it is not merely that a client may refuse a prostitute's request that he wear a condom, but that she may not even ask. Feeling powerless, many women remain in their traditionally defined roles, respecting and accepting the male's superior position and spiritual status.

Women in forced prostitution also have to endure threats and abuse. One woman I met had been caught in an attempted escape; to punish her and set an example for the others, the brothel owner tied barbed wire around her neck and hit her with a steel pipe. The women also reported they were beaten if they did not comply with clients' wishes. They were often threatened that, since they were in the country illegally, they would be jailed by the Thai police if they tried to escape. In this context, protection from HIV and other sexually transmitted diseases seemed a minor dimension of the daily struggle to survive.

Vulnerability to HIV/AIDS may be aggravated by the women's loss of dignity and low self-esteem. Unlike Aye Aye, many of the rescued Burmese women felt they could not go back home; they were too humiliated to face their parents or afraid they would disgrace them if the village or community discovered they had been prostitutes. Believing their lives had been ruined and that they deserved whatever happened to them, these women had no incentive to protect themselves from infection.

The HIV/AIDS pandemic has given a new urgency to the problem of trafficking women and girls into prostitution. The women lack access to health care, information, and support networks. They possess no bargaining power with either brothel owners or clients and live in constant fear of torture and psychological abuse. All these factors place the Burmese women who have been trafficked across the Thai-Burmese border into sexual slavery in a position of extreme vulnerability to the AIDS virus.

Bibliography

Asia Watch and Women's Rights Project. 1993. *A Modern Form of Slavery.* Washington, DC: Human Rights Watch.

Brinkmann, Uwe K., et al. 1993. "Risk Factors of HIV–1 Infection among Female Prostitutes in Khon Kaen, Northeast Thailand." Project commissioned by the Ministry of Economic Cooperation, Federal Republic of Germany.

Khaing, Mi Mi. 1984. *The World of Burmese Women.* London: Zed.

Ministry of Public Health. 1991. "HIV Infected Persons in Thailand by Year of Diagnosis." June 30.

Ministry of Public Health. 1993. "HIV/AIDS Situation in Thailand." December 31.

23

Female Genital Mutilation
Nahid Toubia

> The memory of their screams calling for mercy, gasping for breath, pleading that those parts of their bodies that it pleases God to give them be spared. . . . "Why Mum? Why did you let them do this to me?" Those words continue to haunt me. My blood runs cold whenever the memory comes back. It's now four years . . . and my children still suffer [its] effects.
>
> —Testimony of Miami (Gambia)[1]

Globally, at least 2 million girls a year are at risk of female genital mutilation (FGM)—approximately 6,000 per day. Overall an estimated 85 to 114 million girls and women in the world are genitally mutilated.[2] At present FGM is reportedly practiced in at least twenty-six African countries, among a few groups in Asia, and (increasingly) among immigrant populations in North and South America, Australia, and Europe. These women and girls experience pain, trauma, and (frequently) severe physical problems, such as bleeding, infections, or even death. Long-term physical complications are numerous, and there appear to be substantial psychological effects on women's self-images and sexual lives.

Female genital mutilation—also known as female circumcision—is an extreme example of efforts common to societies around the world to suppress women's sexuality, ensure their subjugation, and control their reproductive functions. Voices are being raised, both in Africa and abroad by women and men who want to eradicate FGM. This fight, however, is not new. Courageous individuals and small groups of intellectuals were among the early African pioneers who dared to pierce the social sanctity surrounding FGM. Professional organizations, most often those of doctors and nurses, helped gather much of the information, particularly on health complications, now used to fight FGM. Today, many African and Asian communities are sifting through their cultures and revising some traditions while holding onto others.

The attention of the world community on this issue has, so far, produced mixed results. When Western feminists in the 1970s and 1980s expressed their empathy by making public statements, undertaking studies, or pressing for national laws on international resolutions, they were helpful in exposing the issue and removing the shroud of silence surrounding it. But others, particularly the less responsible elements of the popular press, mishandled the issue by sensationalizing it and treating African and Asian women in a condescending manner. Unfortunately, this crude approach to a complex issue has created a defensive reaction among many people involved with the practice who might otherwise be allies in the fight for eradication.

Recent efforts at the official international level, particularly by the United Nations agencies, have successfully put FGM on women's health and human rights agendas as a health hazard and a form of violence against women. At the national level, many governments and national leaders have publicly denounced the practice, but few have translated their concern into laws prohibiting FGM or into programs to persuade people to abandon it. At the moment, there is a sense of bewilderment, both at the official level and among grassroots organizers, as to what can be done. The current high level of concern runs the risk of being reduced to indifference unless there is effective action.

What Is Female Genital Mutilation?

Female genital mutilation is the collective name given to several different traditional practices that involve the cutting of female genitals. It was practiced by many ancient cultures, including the Phoenicians, Hittites, and the ancient Egyptians. It was also used by modern physicians in England and the United States as recently as the 1940s and 1950s to "treat" hysteria, lesbianism, masturbation, and other so-called female deviances. In this text, FGM is not used to refer to minor forms of genital rituals, which may involve washing the tip of the clitoris, pricking it with a pin, or separating and cleaning the foreskin (prepuce). The term FGM is reserved to describe practices where the actual cutting and removal of sexual organs takes place.

FGM is one of the traditional rituals that prepare girls for woman-hood, although the age at which it is practiced varies widely. In some cultures, girls experience genital mutilation as early as infancy, while in others the ceremony may not occur until the girl is of marriageable age—approximately fourteen to sixteen years old. Most commonly, however, girls experience FGM between four and eight years of age, at a time when they can be made aware of the social role expected of them as women.

In the communities where FGM takes place, it is referred to as "female circumcision." This term, however, implies a fallacious anal-ogy to nonmutilating male circumcision, in which the foreskin is cut off from the tip of the penis without damaging the organ itself. The degree of cutting in female circumcision is anatomically much more extensive. The male equivalent of clitoridectomy (in which all or part of the clitoris is removed) would be the amputation of most of the penis. The male equivalent of infibulation (which involves not only clitoridectomy but also the removal or closing off of the sensitive tissue around the vagina) would be removal of all the penis, its roots of soft tissue, and part of the scrotal skin. Despite the imprecision of the term female circumcision, it is used in this text as a recognition of the terms of reference of the communities in which it occurs, and as a starting point from which to initiate the process of change.

Although studies refer to many different types of female genital mutilation, the different operations can be incorporated into two broad categories:

• Clitoridectomy (reduction operations): In this set of operations, one or more parts of the external genitals are removed. These include partial or total removal of the clitoris (called clitoridectomy and sometimes also known as Sunna circumcision)[3] or removal of both the clitoris and the inner lips (also known as excision). Even when the entire clitoris is not removed, its most sexually sensitive part is cut away. Approximately 85 percent of all women who undergo FGM have clitoridectomies.
• Infibulation (covering operations): An estimated 15 percent of all women who experience FGM have covering operations, also known as infibulation or Pharonic circumcision. In this group of operations, the clitoris is removed, some or all of the labia minora are cut off, and incisions are made in the labia majora to create raw surfaces. These raw surfaces are either stitched together or kept in contact by pressure

until they heal as a "hood of skin," which covers the urethra and most of the vagina.

Since a physical barrier to intercourse has been created, a small opening must be reconstructed for the flow of urine and menstrual blood. It is surrounded by skin and tough scar tissue and is sometimes as small as the head of a match stick or the tip of the little finger. If the opening is more generous, sexual intercourse can take place after gradual dilation, which may take days, weeks, or even months: If the opening is too small to start the dilation, recutting has to take place before intercourse. Recutting also occurs with each childbirth to allow exit of the fetal head without tearing the tough tissue. After birth the raw edges are sutured again—often to the same size as existed before marriage to recreate the illusion of virginal tightness.

In countries like Sudan, Somalia, and Djibouti, 80 to 90 percent of all FGM is infibulation. It is also practiced on a smaller scale in parts of Mali, Ethiopia, Eritrea, Gambia, and Egypt, and may be occurring in other communities where information is incomplete. A new practice, known as intermediate circumcision, has come into use in recent years. The term describes a variety of operations more severe than clitoridectomy and only slightly less damaging than infibulation. Intermediate circumcision was developed in countries where infibulation has been outlawed (such as Sudan) or where the impact of infibulation on women's health has been criticized. Nevertheless, this category of operation is quite similar to infibulation and the effects and complications are more or less the same; for this reason, these procedures are not considered a separate category in this text.

Complications and Effects of FGM

It is important to remember that FGM is neither a disease nor a reproductive risk. It is a socially driven surgical procedure that causes grave damage to women. Both clitoridectomy and infibulation can have serious physical complications, although those resulting from infibulation generally occur more frequently and are more severe and long lasting. With clitoridectomy, hemorrhage may occur, and protracted bleeding commonly leads to anemia. If bleeding is very severe and uncontrolled, it can result in death. Infection is very common, caused by unsterile cutting instruments or occurring within a few days as the area becomes soaked in urine and contaminated by feces. If not treated promptly, general toxic infection or tetanus infection usually leads to death.

The majority of operations are done without anesthetic. Even when doctors or midwives use local anesthesia (which can itself involve considerable pain, due to the dense concentration of nerve endings in the clitoris), pain in the highly sensitive area of the clitoris returns within two to three hours of the operation. Although general anesthesia is rarely used, it poses a considerable risk for children in countries with few specialized anesthetists. Damage to the urethra or anus may be caused by an inexperienced circumciser or may occur if the girl moves suddenly. Pain, swelling, and inflammation of the front of the vulva usually result in an inability to pass urine for hours or days. Urine retention increases pain and discomfort and can also cause urinary infection and back pain from pressure on the kidneys. For some women, it can become an ongoing nightmare: girls may suffer repeated infections, soreness, and intermittent bleeding; they may develop an abscess; a nerve ending may be scarred, leading to the formation of a benign tumor of the nerve, which causes intense pain; the scar over the clitoris may split open during childbirth.

With infibulation, the complications of clitoridectomy are compounded by extensive cutting and stitching: bleeding (and risk of hemorrhage), infection, and abscess are greater; pain is more severe and less likely to be dulled with local anesthesia; urine retention is more common, since the skin is stitched over the urethra. The health problems of infibulation rarely disappear after the first healing. The following are frequent: repeated urinary tract infection; stones in the urethra and bladder due to obstruction and repeated infections; excessive growth of scar tissue at the site, which may become disfiguring; the development of dermoid cysts, which can be as large as a grapefruit and must be removed by surgery.

If the false vaginal opening is very small, the menstrual flow is also obstructed, leading to frequent reproductive tract infections. Chronic pelvic infection follows, with constant back and menstrual pain, irregularity, and vaginal discharge. Pain during sexual intercourse is common (the physical and psychological trauma reinforcing each other). Often, the operation leads to infertility, which has devastating repercussions in a society in which a woman's reproductive capacity is central to her existence. Obstructed labor can cause life-threatening complications for both mother and child, as can the recurring de- and reinfibulation for intercourse and repeated childbirth (often ten to fifteen births).

Clitoridectomy is often promoted as a safer alternative to infibulation. But recent attempts to promote milder forms of FGM are regressive, as they tend to legitimize it. The ultimate question is not which procedure should take place, but what kind of medical system or public health policy condones the cutting away of part of the human body for no other reason than gender subjugation.

Sexual and Psychological Effects

With FGM, the delicate area where female genitals once existed is turned into tough scar tissue that bears more resemblance to cured hide than to human tissue. Removal of the clitoris takes away the primary specialized female sexual organ, dense with nerve endings and dedicated only to pleasure. The vagina is an organ of reproduction with minimal sensory capacity for sexual response. In other words, FGM removes the woman's sexual organ and leaves her reproductive organs intact.

Most circumcisions take place when a girl is already receiving multiple messages about her position in society in general, and in regard to boys and men in particular, linking the operation and a girl's experience of her social feminization (in some places accomplished through aggressive gender training and even threats of torture). It would be difficult for any child above infancy not to associate circumcision with some diminution of sexual desire; the message and the act appear to be interrelated. With infibulation, in particular, the radical shaving off of all sensitive tissue plus the folding away of the vagina can be seen as a metaphor for the more abstract denial of a woman's sexuality: her reproductive capacity is locked up with a chastity belt made of her own flesh. The "protective hood" is allowed to be cut open or dilated only to permit the husband his lawful access to the vagina in return for his bride price. Women who are sexually frustrated may no longer seek sexual contact with their partners and ultimately become sexual objects and reproductive vehicles for men.

Most of the attention given to the health problems associated with FGM concentrate on the physical aspect, with little attention to the psychological problems, since the psychological complications of FGM may be submerged (appearing only later in life) and are not, in any case, taken seriously, even when they are severe and incapacitating. There are very few qualified psychologists and psychotherapists available to analyze these problems, nor is psychological illness readily recognized in poor people. Psychological symptoms are often interpreted as the work of evil spirits, and traditional remedies and rituals are offered as cures. Repressed and untreated, such conditions can progress to psychopathological levels. As a clinician in public hospitals in Sudan, I have observed thousands of women who come in with vague symptoms of general fatigue, loss of sleep, backache, headache, pelvic congestion—women who, with a little probing, talk about fear of sex, the threat of infertility after infection, and fears about the state of their genitals. These symptoms of anxiety depression syndrome are labelled hysterical, and the women's feelings dismissed as those of malingerers.

The Cultural Significance of FGM

Although FGM is a practice of culture (not religion), it is often strongly associated with Islam because some African Muslim communities cite religion as the reason for performing it and because Westerners have mistakenly related FGM to Islam. When Islam entered Africa, it is most likely that newly converted leaders, seeking to continue the practice, linked it with Islam. But FGM is not a requirement of any religion: it is practiced by some Catholic groups (some Catholic missionaries condoned it as a means of preserving women's purity) and many Coptic Christians, as well as by Ethiopian Falasha Jews now living in Israel; it is not practiced in many predominantly Islamic countries such as Saudi Arabia, Iraq, the Gulf States, Kuwait, Algeria, and Pakistan. There is no major Islamic citation that makes female genital mutilation a religious requirement. Neither the Quran nor the "hadith" (collections of the sayings of the Prophet Mohammed) includes a direct call for FGM.[4]

FGM was spread by dominant tribes and civilizations, often as a result of tribal, ethnic, and cultural allegiances. For example, it was not known in western Sudan among the Furs and the residents of the Nuba mountains until the 1950s. After independence in 1956, local government, education, and health services were introduced in the region by professionals from the educated middle classes of the north where FGM was practiced. In the next twenty years, the cultural influences of the northern elites prevailed. A survey conducted in 1979 reported that in Fur and Nuba families, mothers were not circumcised, but most daughters were.

To combat FGM, those who are fighting for change must understand the deeply felt beliefs of the people who practice it. In Sierra Leone, for example, circumcisers are women leaders who control the secret societies and who, to their followers, are priestesses. The eradication

of FGM would mean loss of prestige and money for most practitioners—traditional birth attendants or medically trained midwives
and nurses; these women, drawing on their knowledge of antisepsis,
local anesthesia, and sterile suturing and their access to medical supplies provided to them by ministries of health or UNICEF programs,
have played an important role in legitimizing the practice. But more
powerful in claims for the preservation of FGM are arguments not
only that the ritual serves important values (adolescent initiation rites
produce responsible adults for the community, for instance) but also
that the few traditional practices that remain after colonialism must be
preserved. African opponents of FGM, however, believe that initiations
have been so altered in the modern world that in many areas they
have been reduced to the symbolic act. The challenge for Africans
now is to struggle to save the positive aspects of initiation rites while
eliminating damaging practices that subjugate women.

Unfortunately, views on FGM are also used to stir up the historic
rivalry between the European/American Christian culture and the
African/Arab Muslim civilizations. But the battle is, in reality, about
power and dominance—about finding a way to justify the abuse of
women. In the few studies conducted on the subject, when researchers
asked men and women why they performed genital mutilation, the
answers were surprisingly clear about the patriarchal underpinnings
of the practice and the ways in which women come to accept their
secondary status. A constantly reiterated theme is the inferiority of
women—a fact that women and men both seem to accept.

Following are some of the reasons given for FGM:

- Beauty/Cleanliness: Female genitals are unhygienic and need to be
  cleaned; female genitals are ugly and will grow to become unwieldy
  if they are not cut back; circumcision is the fashionable thing to do
  to become a real woman.
- Male Protection/Approval: Circumcision is an initiation into womanhood and into the tribe; the noncircumcised cannot be married;
  circumcision enhances the husband's sexual pleasure; circumcision
  makes vaginal intercourse more desirable than clitoral stimulation.
- Health: Circumcision improves fertility and prevents maternal and
  infant mortality.
- Religion: God sanctifies circumcision.
- Morality: Circumcision safeguards virginity; circumcision cures
  "sexual deviance" (i.e., frigidity lesbianism, and excessive sexual
  arousal).

The rising movement against FGM among African women is proof
that when women get rid of their psychological pain and fear—when
they throw off the denial mechanisms they have used for survival—they
are able to speak out against this inhuman and unnecessary suffering.
To understand why many women defend a practice that risks their
health and damages their sexuality, we have to understand that even
the most highly educated individuals become defensive when they feel
their culture and personal identity are being attacked. The fear of
losing the psychological, moral, and material benefits of "belonging"
is one of the greatest motivations to conformity. Africans who love and
cherish the positive aspects of their cultures and have been wounded by
colonialism fear that actions against FGM will be used as another
excuse to invade and humiliate them. We must, therefore, identify
FGM as part of the global subordination of women. None of the
underlying messages and language used to justify FGM is unique to
Africa. These messages reflect a universal language used to perpetuate
women's second-class status and are reminiscent of reasons given for
slavery, colonialism, and racism.

A Global Call to Action

The eradication of FGM requires global action. There are many
people the world over who would like to see genital mutilation of
women stopped. Their concerns and efforts must be linked so that
resources and knowledge can be shared, and so women are not forced
to fight isolated battles against their own social and economic powerlessness—a powerlessness that allows FGM to continue. We must learn
more: get exact information on prevalence, physical and psychological
effects, and religious requirements. Most of all, this information must
be accessible to a broad range of people and disseminated on a
wide scale.

The notion that FGM has a religious basis must be defeated, while
efforts to preserve cultural integrity must be honored. Both the message
and the facts about FGM will be lost if they use the language of
colonialism. The people of the countries where FGM is practiced resent
references to "barbaric practices imposed on women by male-dominated primitive societies," especially when they look at the Western
world and see women undergoing their own feminization rites intended
to increase sexual desirability: medically dangerous forms of cosmetic
plastic surgery, for instance, or high heels. Comparing FGM to cos-

metic surgery is not meant to trivialize the enormous physical and psychological damage FGM causes but to relate it back to the ways all women suffer from false ideals of "femininity."

There is, however, one very important difference between FGM and the ways in which women alter their bodies in other cultures: FGM is mainly performed on children, with or without their consent. The conflict of feelings created in the child prior to her operation must be considerable. On the one hand, there is the desire to please parents, grandparents, and relatives by doing something that is highly valued and approved of. Before the event, there is the desire to be "normal"— that is, to be like other members of society, particularly the peer group. This feeling is juxtaposed to the girl's expectation of pain, the stories of suffering, and the sheer terror of hearing the screaming of other children being circumcised. Finally there is the experience itself: being held down by force while part of the body is cut off.

A global action would unite local knowledge and sensibility with international technical and financial resources to create a multitude of programs. FGM would be linked not only to human rights but also to women's economic development, health, family planning, child development, education, and religion. The work of indigenous activists, scholars, and sympathetic religious leaders, among others, could serve as important sources of valuable information. The common link among these efforts would be the extensive use of indigenous mass information, popular art, and culture to create a multidirectional campaign.

International standards applicable to the issue of female genital mutilation are already in place. In addition to various pertinent international and regional human rights conventions and declarations, most affected countries have ratified the United Nations' *Convention on the Elimination of All Forms of Discrimination Against Women* (CEDAW) as well as the Children's Rights Convention (CRC). FGM directly contravenes several provisions of the CRC, among them: articles requiring nations to take measures that abolish traditional practices prejudicial to the health of children; articles against child abuse, the subjection of children to torture or cruel, inhuman, or degrading treatment; the article protecting the child's right to privacy. The *African Charter on the Rights and Welfare of the Child,* adopted by the Organization of African Unity in 1990, promotes gender equality among children. CEDAW calls on governments to modify or abolish customs and practices that constitute discrimination against women or are based on the idea of female inferiority or stereotyped roles for men and women.

It is clear that there must be legal action against FGM within affected countries. The question then becomes: at what point and what kind of action is appropriate? Although legislation may be effective toward the prevention of FGM in countries where only a small minority are practitioners (such as Western countries with African immigrants), the problem is altogether different in places where a majority follows the tradition. In these instances, the socio-cultural nature of the act as well as practitioners' ignorance of its consequences point to the greater need for public information campaigns about the effect of the practice on children, and private counseling of parents whenever possible. Clear policy declarations by governmental and professional bodies are essential to send a strong message of disapproval, but if the majority of the society is still convinced that FGM serves the common good, legal sanctions that incriminate practitioners and families may be counterproductive. Criminalization and regulations are effective only once a substantial body of public opinion has been raised against the practice.

In the African context, most anti-FGM legislation was passed by colonial governments who looked upon the indigenous culture with disdain. These laws were decidedly ineffective. Most countries have been independent for several decades now, and it is necessary to reassess the relationship between governments and their people on this issue. Only a few African countries have specific legislation against FGM. Sudan has had a law on its books for many years, although it was omitted from the 1991 legal revisions, as were many other laws, making their current status unclear. Egypt has had a Ministry of Health decree since 1959 that prohibits the practice of FGM by trained health personnel. Kenya banned FGM in 1990. In 1991, a representative of the Côte d'Ivoire told the United Nations that existing provisions of the nation's criminal code could be used to prohibit FGM. Burkina Faso has incorporated into its draft constitution a prohibition of female circumcision.

In some Western countries, such as the United Kingdom and France, FGM has already been criminalized. In the UK, anti-FGM legislation is supplemented by the Children's Act of 1989, which provides for investigation of suspected violations of the FGM prohibition as well as for removal of a child from her home in extreme cases where there is no better way to protect the child. The Children's Act also enables the courts to prohibit parents from removing their children from the country to have the operation performed elsewhere. Other countries with immigrant populations have applied existing laws to prohibit FGM within the provisions of the criminal code that prohibits violence against and mutilation of children. Both parents and practitioners have been convicted and sentenced under the laws, receiving suspended sentences in most cases. Government officials in Canada, Italy, and Australia have also said that existing legislation concerning assault or battery, violence against a person's physical integrity, mutilation, and child abuse are applicable to FGM.

Although laws alone will not eradicate FGM, legal measures must be pursued in all countries at the appropriate time. International human rights bodies and organizations must declare FGM to be violence against women and children and a violation of their rights. They should press for the explicit inclusion of FGM in international and regional conventions and treaties, and concerned governments must be persuaded to sign and act on them. Governments must then be monitored for compliance and the results published in a clear and widely accessible format. All relevant organizations should be involved: public health agencies; women's and children's health and family planning programs; organizations and programs dealing with women's economic development; doctors', nurses', and midwives' professional associations; professional legal associations at the international, regional, and national levels; media groups; educational institutions; research bodies.

The overriding consideration for all activities is that they be guided by the knowledge and wisdom of individuals from the communities involved, with special attention paid to the concerns of women. Unguided or patronizing interference from outsiders can create a backlash in favor of FGM, as has happened in the past. Finally, it is important to emphasize that FGM is a part of a persistent global situation in which women remain powerless because they lack access to resources, jobs, and education and in which women's bodies are controlled by a male-dominated social ideology. A global action against FGM cannot undertake to abolish this one violation of women's rights without placing it firmly within the context of efforts to address the social and economic injustice women face the world over. If women are to be considered as equal and responsible members of society, no aspect of their physical, psychological, or sexual integrity can be compromised.

Notes

1. Saffiatou K. Singhateh, "Female Circumcision in Gambia," *Female Circumcision: Strategies to Bring About Change,* The Somali Women's Democratic Organization.

2. Based on an analysis of trends from the Sudan DHS, and using four years as the intial age of risk, the number of girls at risk per year was calculated using the United Nations projections of female population in the affected African countries in 1965. If there is no decline from the current prevalence, 2.5 million girls will be at risk per year. This crude estimate assumes that all concerned societies have the same age distribution for FGM and will experience the same socio-economic, educational, and urbanization influences as Sudan, which was used as the standard for calculations because it is the only nation with detailed statistics. There are no comprehensive, country-by-country data collections on FGM. United Nations agencies do not collect statistics. The most extensive anecdotal estimates have been reported by an American, Fran Hosken (1983), whose latest estimates were published in 1992. Although it is not clear how these estimates were calculated, they are the most comprehensive figures available to date.

3. "Sunna" refers to any practice regularly required of Muslims. The belief that female circumcision is required of Muslims is a serious misunderstanding in the interpretation of Islam, and has contributed to the spread of the practice. (see note 4).

4. The directive most often cited as a reason for circumcision is from a question of Mohammed during a speech and is classified as a *makrama,* or nonessential practice. Even here, when Mohammed was asked what he thought of female circumcision, his answer was, in essence, an attempt to deter the practice. He is said to have told his listeners to circumcise but not to destroy (or mutilate), for not destroying the clitoris would be better for the man and would make the woman's face glow. Many people believe this describes a male-type circumcision where the prepuce is removed, making the clitoris even more sensitive to touch.

Reprinted in part with permission from *Female Genital Mutilation: A Call for Global Action* by Nahid Toubia, 1993. Women Inc.

Bibliography

A'Haleem, Asma M. 1992. "Claiming Our Bodies and Our Rights: Exploring Female Circumcision as an Act of Violence." *Freedom from Violence,* edited by Margaret Schuler. OEF International. Available from United Nations/UNIFEM.

Abdalla, Raqiya H.D. 1982. *Sisters in Affliction: Circumcision and Infibulation of Women in Africa.* London: Zed.

An-Na'im, Abdullahi. 1990. *Toward an Islamic Reformation: Civil Liberties, Human Rights, and International Law.* Syracuse, NY: Syracuse Univ. Press.

Assaad, Marie B. 1980. "Female Circumcision in Egypt: Social Implications, Current Research, and Prospects for Change." *Studies in Family Planning* 11(1) (January): pp. 3–16.

Balk, Deborah, Lindy Williams, and Zeinab Khadr. 1993. "Female Genital Mutilation in the Sudan: Demographic Correlates, 'Causes,' and Consequences." Paper presented at the Population Association of America Annual Meeting.

Dorkenoo, Efua, and Scilla Elworthy. 1992. *FGM: Proposals for Change.* London: Minority Rights Group International.

El Dareer, Asma. 1982. *Woman, Why Do You Weep?* London: Zed.

El Saadawi, Nawal. *Hidden Face of Eve: Women in the Arab World.* London: Zed, 1980.

Gevins, A. 1987. "Tackling Tradition: African Women Speak Out Against Female Circumcision." In *Third World, Second Sex,* edited by Miranda Davis. London: Zed.

Hosken, Fran. 1983 *The Hosken Report.* 3rd ed. Lexington, MA: WIN NEWS.

Koso-Thomas, Olayinka. 1992. *The Circumcision of Women: A Study for Eradication.* London: Zed.

Lowry, Thomas et al. 1976. *The Clitoris.* St. Louis, MO: Warren Green.

Skramstad, Heidi. 1990. *The Fluid Meanings of Female Circumcision in a Multiethnic Context in Gambia.* Bergen, Norway: DERAP, Chr. Michelsen Institute.

Somali Women's Democratic Organization. 1988. *Female Circumcision: Strategies to Bring about Change.* Proceedings of the International Seminar on Female Circumcision. 13–16 June. Available from Italian Association for Women in Development, Rome, Italy.

Thiam, Awa. 1986. *Black Sisters Speak Out: Feminism and Oppression in Black Africa.* London: Pluto.

Toubia, Nahid. 1985. "The Social and Political Implications of Female Circumcision: The Case of the Sudan." In *Women and the Family in the Middle East,* edited by E. Fernea. Texas Univ. Press.

Women of the Arab World, 1988. London: Zed.

Warzazi, Halima E. 1991. "Report of the United Nations Seminar on Traditional Practices Affecting the Health of Women and Children." Economic and Social Council, 5 July 1991.

WIN News. 18 (4) (Autumn 1992.)

World Health Organization, Eastern Mediterranean Regional Office. 1979. "Traditional Practices Affecting the Health of Women and Children." Report on a seminar, Khartoum, February 10–15. WHO/EMRO Technical Publications, No. 2.

24

Freedom Close to Home: The Impact of Violence Against Women on Reproductive Rights

Lori L. Heise

> There isn't much understanding in some marriages. My sister has six [children] and another has eight. I said to one of them that she shouldn't have any more. And she said "What can I do? When my husband comes home drunk, he forces me to sleep with him." And that is what happens to a lot of women. And if the women don't do it, the men hit them, or treat them badly. Or the men get jealous and think their wives are with other men.
>
> —Rene, a 29-year old Peruvian woman[1]

Gender violence is a major yet often underrecognized obstacle to reproductive choice. In both the abortion rights movement in the United States and the reproductive health movement globally, the "enemy" of self-determination and choice is usually seen as imposed from the top down. In the North, it is the government—through the courts, the legislature, and bureaucratic rulemaking—that threatens to rob women of reproductive autonomy. The image is one of the public sphere invading that which is private, of the state interfering with a woman's right to control her own body.

In the South, activism has focused on resisting programs and technologies imported from the North that are seen as emphasizing population control and contraceptive efficacy over the health and autonomy of women. Instead, women's health advocates have argued for a woman-centered approach to reproductive care that emphasizes choice, safety, and services that address the full range of women's reproductive health needs.

Nonetheless, there is an enemy of choice that exists at the level of our most personal relationships, one that does not often enter into official discussions on reproductive choice: male violence. Violence, in the form of rape, sexual abuse, or battering affects women's ability to protect themselves from unwanted pregnancy and sexually transmitted diseases (STDs), including AIDS. Even where violence is not used to control women's behavior, the possibility of violence helps ensure female deference to male decision making regarding sexual behavior and contraceptive use. These interpersonal barriers to women's reproductive autonomy can be as significant as government policy, if not more so.

In 1958, Eleanor Roosevelt observed that human rights begin "in the small places, close to home . . . the neighborhood, the school or college, the factory, farm or office. . . . Unless these rights have meaning here, they have little meaning anywhere."[2] Indeed, unless a woman's right to control her own body has meaning within the personal sphere of relationships, reproductive freedom will remain a distant goal.

Violence and Violation

Rape is undoubtedly the most direct breach of choice a woman can face. Sexual assault removes any semblance of control a woman has over when, where, and with whom she will have sex. A country may have excellent reproductive health services and laws guaranteeing access to safe, legal abortion, but a man still has the power to violate a woman's body and effectively abrogate her right to sexual self-determination. In effect, rape gives men the ability to "undo," in a single act, all the reproductive freedom and autonomy women's rights activists have fought so hard to guarantee.

Regrettably, statistics around the world suggest that rape is an all-too-common reality in the lives of women and girls. In the United States, for example, six well-designed studies suggest that between one in five and one in seven American women has been the victim of a completed rape.[3] Studies also demonstrate a remarkable consistency in the demographics of sexual assault. Contrary to popular perception, the majority of rape survivors know their assailants, a reality confirmed by studies in Malaysia, Mexico, Panama, Peru, Chile and the United States. Also, a large percentage of rapes (36–58 percent) are perpetrated

Table 1   Statistics on Sexual Crimes, Selected Countries

	Percent of perpetrators known to victim	Percent of victims fifteen years and under	Percent of victims ten years and under
Lima, Peru	60	—	18[a]
Malaysia	68	58	18[b]
Mexico City	67[c]	36	23
Panama City	63	40	—
Papua New Guinea	—	47	13[d]
Santiago, Chile[e]	72	58	32[a]
United States	78	62[f]	29

Note: Studies include rape and sexual assaults such as attempted rape and molestation except for U.S data, which includes only completed rapes.
[a]Percentage of survivors age nine and younger.
[b]Percentage of survivors age six and younger.
[c]Data from *Carpeta Basica,* (Mexico City: Procurador de Justicia del Distrito Federal de Mexico, 1990).
[d]Percentage of survivors age seven and younger.
[e]Based on five-year averages derived from crimes reported to the Legal Medicine Service, 1987–91; Anuario Estadisticio del Servicio Medico Legal de Chile.
[f]Percentage of survivors age seventeen and younger.
Sources: Malaysia;[4] Panama City;[5] Peru;[6] Papua New Guinea;[7] Chile;[8] Mexico City;[9] United States.[10]

against girls fifteen years and under, with a shocking percentage against girls younger than ten (see Table 1).

In addition to violating a woman's bodily integrity, rape can have serious consequences for her reproductive health. Along with physical injury and emotional trauma, rape survivors run the risk of becoming pregnant or contracting STDs, including AIDS. A support center for rape victims in Bangkok, Thailand, for example, reports that 10 percent of its clients contract a sexually transmitted disease as a result of the rape.[11] There are increasing reports both in the United States and abroad, of women and children who have contracted HIV through sexual abuse or rape. In Cape Town, South Africa, for example, two men were jailed in 1992 for raping an eleven-year-old girl. The girl contracted HIV through the attack and subsequently died.[12]

For Third World women, the possibility of pregnancy is also quite high. Mexican rape crisis centers report that 15–18 percent of their clients become pregnant because of rape, a figure consistent with data from Thailand and Korea.[13] A relatively new law in Mexico requires judges to rule promptly on a victim's request to abort, giving Mexican women more options than most. Thousands of others who live in countries where abortion is unavailable, unaffordable, or illegal in cases of rape must suffer the double humiliation of being raped and then having to bear the rapist's child.

Often those who must endure such humiliation are the very young: children made pregnant by a parent or another close relative. In the Maternity Hospital of Lima, Peru, for example, 90 percent of the young mothers ages twelve to sixteen have been raped by their father, stepfather, or another close relative.[14] An organization that works with young mothers in Costa Rica reports similar findings: 95 percent of their pregnant clients under fifteen are victims of incest.[15] These young women have not only been victims of sexual violence but have also had their reproductive rights transgressed.

Elsewhere in the world, rape—a form of violence itself—can beget more violence due to the stigma surrounding loss of virginity in unwed girls. In parts of Asia and the Middle East, the stain of rape is so great that victims are sometimes killed by family members who believe they are cleansing the family honor. While the vast majority of honor killings are against women suspected of adultery or fornication, even rape victims may be targets. In a study of women murdered in Alexandria, Egypt, 47 percent were victims of rape who had been killed by a relative.[16]

Barriers to Reproductive Control

It is generally assumed that women in consensual unions have greater say over their sexual lives than victims of rape. But here, too, gender power relations—often enforced through violence—greatly shape women's sexual and reproductive decision making.

Women's decisions regarding family planning use is a case in point. The family planning literature documents that for many women, fear of male reprisal greatly limits their ability to use contraception.[17] Men in many cultures react negatively to birth control because they think it signals a woman's intentions to be unfaithful (the logic being that protection against pregnancy allows a woman to be promiscuous). Where children are signs of male virility, a woman's attempt to use contraception may be interpreted as an affront to her partner's masculinity.[18] While male approval is not always the deciding factor, studies from countries as diverse as Mexico, South Africa, and Bangladesh have found that partner approval is the single greatest predictor of women's contraceptive use.[19] When partners disapprove, women either forgo contraception, leaving themselves open to the risks of incessant childbearing, or resort to family planning methods—such as injectibles, Norplant, or IUDs—they can use without their partners' knowledge.

The unspoken reality behind this subterfuge is that women can be beaten if they do not comply with men's sexual and childbearing demands. Hope Mwesigye of FIDA-Uganda, a nonprofit legal aid organization for women in Kampala, recounted the story of a young married mother who was running from a husband who regularly beat her. Despite earning a decent wage, the woman's husband refused to maintain her and their two children. To avoid bringing into the world more children she could not feed, the woman began using birth control without her partner's consent; the beatings began when she failed to bring forth more children, and became more brutal when he learned of her family planning use.[20]

In other countries, legal provisions requiring spousal permission before dispensing birth control can actually put women at increased risk of violence. According to Pamela Onyango of Family Planning International Assistance, women in Kenya have been known to forge their partners' signatures rather than open themselves to violence or abandonment by requesting permission to use family planning services.[21] Nor are Kenyan women alone in their fear of such consequences. Researchers conducting focus groups on sexuality in Mexico and Peru found that women had similar concerns about bringing up birth control: fear of violence, desertion, or accusations of infidelity.[22] Not surprisingly, when family planning clinics in Ethiopia removed their requirement for spousal consent, clinic use rose 26 percent in just a few months.[23]

Ironically, not all women who fear violence are necessarily at risk of abuse. In fact, some recent studies suggest that men may be more willing to consider family planning than most women suspect.[24] Communication in marriage, however, is often so limited that spouses frequently have no idea of what their partners' views of family planning might be. Women thus assume that their husbands' attitudes will mirror the cultural norm, which frequently says that men want large families and distrust women who use birth control. The discrepancy between women's perceptions and reality also speaks to the power of violence to induce fear by means of example.

In Sufferance and in Silence

Often women who are married have even less to say about their sexual lives than about birth control. Far from an act of mutual love and respect, sexual intercourse for many women is an unpleasant duty they tolerate rather than enjoy. In focus group discussions with Mexican women about men, sex, and marriage, many women expressed deep resentment about how men treated them in sexual relationships.[25] Women in particular mentioned:

- physical abuse by husbands to coerce the wife's sexual compliance
- widespread male infidelity
- men's authoritarian attitudes toward their wives
- threats of abandonment if wives failed to meet their husbands' sexual demands or their demands for more children
- an abiding sense of depersonalization, humiliation, and physical dissatisfaction during sex

Perhaps more than anything, the Spanish phrase women commonly use for sex captures their sentiment: "el me usa" (he uses me). Fortunately, the women in this study did not appear resigned to their fate. Most felt it was both appropriate and necessary for women to struggle for fairer and more considerate treatment.

Men's superior strength and their control over economic resources, however, makes women's struggle for dignity and sexual self-determination difficult. In this paper's opening quote, Rene alluded to what is a disturbingly common phenomenon for women around the world: marital rape. For women who live with violent or alcoholic partners, the possibility of rape is even more pronounced. Whereas 10–14 percent of all U.S. wives report being raped, the prevalence among battered women is at least 40 percent.[26] (In Bolivia and Puerto Rico, 58 percent of battered wives report being sexually assaulted by their partners, and in Colombia, the reported rate is 46 percent.[27])

Studies evaluating natural family planning in the Philippines and sexual attitudes among the women in Guatemala also emphasize forced sex by partners, especially when the men arrive home drunk.[28] The summary document of the Guatemalan focus groups observes, "It is clear from the replies the women gave . . . that being forced through violence to have sex by their partner is not an uncommon experience for Guatemalan women."[29] When asked if a wife could refuse sex to her husband, most women said they could not because their husbands were physically stronger.

An Issue of Self-Defense

The specter of AIDS adds a new critical dimension to gender power relations and reproductive rights. So far, most AIDS prevention programs have been based on three strategies: encouraging individuals to reduce their number of partners, promoting condom use, and treating traditional STDs. But women's economic dependence on men and men's physical strength greatly limit women's ability to utilize these strategies for their own protection.

Strategies based on "negotiating" condom use, for example, assume an equity of power between women and men that simply does not exist in many relationships. As Anke Ehrardt, director of an AIDS research project at the New York State Psychiatric Clinic, observes, "We have not only ignored the fact that women do not control condom use, but we have also rushed into prevention efforts aimed at getting women to insist on condom use without taking into account that they may risk severe repercussions, such as violence and other serious threats to their economic and social support."[30] The potential costs of ever discussing condom use can be stark: a woman from Buwnunga, Uganda observed recently in a village discussion on AIDS, "If you advise your husband to use a condom, he may beat you and send you away. Where will you go then?"[31]

Similar fears plague low-income and minority women in the United States. According to Dooley Worth, an anthropologist working with an AIDS education project in New York City, "Women engage in sexual risk taking mainly because of perceived threats to their social and economic survival, and a lack of power in sexual decision making."[32] Three-quarters of the women Worth surveyed have been physically abused as adults, primarily by their sexual partners. "Asking them to introduce condoms into their relationship," notes Worth, "can mean asking them to risk further abuse."[33]

The problem is that, given today's options, negotiating condom use is the only self-preservation strategy available to women. Clearly, things can and should be done to help empower women and strengthen their negotiating position. Women need independent sources of income and training in how best to broach the subject of condom use. And AIDS programs must begin drawing on women's demonstrated capacity for collective action. But women desperately need a new option for protecting themselves against sexually transmitted diseases—one that puts control of the technology into women's hands.

In this regard, women are uniquely vulnerable. AIDS activists are empowering men by giving them information, and men have a technology—condoms—to use on their own behalf. Advocates are reaching IV drug users as well, and they have protective technologies—namely clean needles and bleach—that are within their power. Only women, who are up against centuries of social conditioning that grants sexual license to men, are being asked to defend themselves without a method that they control.

Recently, after pressure from women's organizations and other health nonprofits, there has been increased interest among mainstream research institutions and scientists in developing female controlled options of HIV prevention. In March, the Population Council in New York published "The Development of Microbicide: A New Method of HIV Prevention for Women," which argues that it is indeed possible to develop a vaginal product women could use to protect themselves from HIV without their partner's knowledge. (The paper also evaluates the potential of other female controlled methods such as the female condom.) As the paper concludes: "Only a persistent and conscious neglect of women's needs will explain continued inattention to this important area of research."[34]

The Impact Lives On

Recently, a new link between violence and reproductive health has begun to emerge—namely the relationship between childhood sexual abuse and high-risk sexual behavior and drug use by adults. The full contours of the relationship are yet undefined, but a growing body of literature suggests that sexual victimization, especially in childhood, may play a role in some of the most intractable problems of our time: teenage pregnancy, STDs, prostitution, and AIDS.

In a recent study of 535 adolescent mothers in Washington state, for example, researchers Debra Boyer and David Fine found that, compared with teens who became pregnant but were not abused, sexually victimized adolescents began intercourse a year earlier, were more likely to have used drugs and alcohol, and were less likely to practice contraception.[35] Abused adolescents were also more likely to have been battered by an intimate partner and to have exchanged sex for money, drugs, or a place to stay. The differences were even more pronounced when victimized teens were compared to adolescents who were sexually active but did not get pregnant. The average age at first intercourse for abused women was 13.8 years compared to the national (female) average of 16.2. Only 28 percent of the victimized teens used birth control at first intercourse, compared to 49 percent of their peers (sexually active women aged 15–19).

In discussing their results, the authors noted that, despite concerted effort to improve access to birth control and sex education for teens, the level of adolescent pregnancy has remained relatively steady for the past twenty years. "We suggest," they conclude, "that a key factor in the conundrum of adolescent high-risk sexual behavior and adolescent pregnancy and repeat pregnancies—sexual victimization and abuse—has been overlooked."[36]

Childhood sexual abuse also appears to play a role in other behaviors that put individuals at increased risk of STDs, including AIDS. Several studies, for example, link sexual abuse with a high risk of entering prostitution.[37] Researchers from Brown University found that men and women who had been raped or forced to have sex in either childhood or adolescence were four times more likely than nonabused individuals to have worked in prostitution. They were also twice as likely to have multiple partners in any single year and to engage in casual sex with partners they did not know. Women survivors of childhood sexual assault were twice as likely to be heavy consumers of alcohol and nearly three times more likely to become pregnant before the age of 18. These behaviors did not translate directly into higher rates of HIV among women, but men who experienced childhood sexual abuse were twice as likely to be HIV-positive as men who did not. (The higher prevalence of HIV among male survivors could not be explained by a history of intravenous drug use.[38])

The impact of sexual abuse on sexual risk taking has also been documented in a developing country: Barbados. Based on an island-wide random survey of 407 men and women in Barbados, anthropologist Penn Handwerker has shown that sexual abuse is the single most important determinant of high-risk sexual activity during adolescence for both men and women.[39] (One woman in 3 and 1–2 men in 100 reported behavior constituting childhood or adolescent sexual abuse.) After controlling for a wide range of socio-economic and home-environment variables (e.g., absent father), sexual abuse remains strongly linked both to the number of partners adolescents have and to their age at first intercourse. Further analysis shows that direct effects of childhood sexual abuse on partner change remain significant into the respondent's mid-thirties. For men, physical, emotional, and/or sexual abuse in childhood is also highly correlated (after controlling for many other variables) with lack of condom use in adulthood.[40]

Collectively, these studies suggest a profound link between early sexual victimization and future behavior that puts individuals at risk of unwanted pregnancy, traditional STDs, and AIDS. This new line of research makes a powerful case for increased collaboration between advocates working on violence issues and those committed to women's reproductive health and autonomy.

First Do No Harm

Reproductive health activists, especially women from the South, have also been instrumental in identifying and challenging violence within the reproductive health system itself. Contrary to the organizing ethic of all medical care—first do no harm—there is ample evidence that "health care" as practiced in some parts of the world exposes women to increased risk instead of improving their health and well being.

Perhaps the most notorious example of "medical violence" is forced sterilization. During the 1970s, a series of scandals involving sterilization came to light in places as diverse as the United States, Puerto Rico, and India.[41] In the United States, for example, the involuntary sterilization of poor, minority, and mentally retarded young women during the early 1970s led to the enactment of more stringent sterilization regulations in 1978. The incident that galvanized attention around the issue was the now infamous Relf case, in which two black teenagers in Alabama were sterilized without their consent or knowledge. Ruling against the government, a federal district court judge found

> uncontroverted evidence in the record that minors and other incompetents have been sterilized with federal funds and that an indefinite number of poor people have been improperly coerced into accepting a sterilization operation under the threat that various federally supported welfare benefits would be withdrawn unless they submitted to irreversible sterilization.[42]

Recent talk in state legislatures of linking certain welfare benefits to a woman's willingness to submit to surgical implantation of Norplant harkens back to the logic and rationale of this earlier sterilization abuse.

While today there are few instances of direct coercion in cases of sterilization, women's health advocates still worry that various forms of "structural coercion" lead women to choose sterilization when some other form of birth control may better suit their needs. In Puerto Rico and Brazil, for example, government policies severely limit access to reversible contraceptives such as condoms, diaphragms, and IUDs. As a result, 60 percent of Puerto Rican female contraceptive users and 41 percent of those from Brazil are sterilized.[43] According to a World Bank report on women's reproductive health in Brazil, "many women resort to sterilization despite its irreversibility because of the lack of alternative methods."[44]

Clearly, sterilization as a method is not inherently bad. Many women who have completed their childbearing welcome sterilization as a way to put aside permanently concerns of unwanted pregnancy. But sterilization must be offered without pressure or incentives and accepted with the full knowledge and consent of the woman. As reproductive rights activist Betsy Hartman observes, "In the right hands [sterilization] can be a powerful tool of reproductive freedom. In the wrong hands it is an intrusive act of physical violence, no matter how clean the surgeon's gloves."[45]

Elsewhere, women's health activists have begun to challenge the brutish, humiliating treatment women sometimes endure at the hands of the professional health care system. Women's treatment during pregnancy and birth are areas of particular concern. In Sao Paulo, Brazil, for example, the hospital system has so few beds reserved for poor people that pregnant women in labor often have to go from hospital to hospital to find an institution willing to accept them. A recent maternal mortality survey documents a case in which a low-income woman in labor had to go to eleven different hospitals before one agreed to admit her.[46]

Once in a hospital, a woman's treatment does not necessarily improve. According to Dr. Simone Grilo Dinez of the Sexuality and Health Collective of Sao Paulo, a woman hospitalized in that city for labor is not allowed contact with anyone she knows, has a 50–50 chance of having a cesarean section, and a 15–40 percent chance of contracting an infection. Childbirth is largely orchestrated for the convenience of doctors, which explains in part why Sao Paulo's cesarean rate is more than three times that which is considered medically necessary.[47] Women in Brazil and elsewhere recount stories of crying out during childbirth and being ridiculed with degrading comments such as, "I wonder how loud you were screaming when you were lying with your husband." One Mexican woman recalls, "It all resembled torture . . . it seemed they were punishing us all the way, for a great sin, the sin of having enjoyed some past moment of pleasure."[48] Dr. Grilo Dinez says that Brazilian doctors withhold anesthesia when performing D&Cs after illegal abortions for the same reason—to make women pay; similar accusations have been waged against physicians operating on native women in Canada.[49]

Many activists have come to see such treatment as violence perpetrated by the medical system itself. The examples single out Brazil not because it is the only country where women are mistreated, but because the country has such a well-organized and vocal women's health movement. But dehumanizing treatment by health care workers is so widespread internationally that even mainstream population and health groups have begun to take up the issue under the rubric of "quality of care." Progressive policy makers have come to realize that the success or failure of different health programs hinges in part on how clients are treated by service providers.[50]

A final link between violence and the reproductive health care system itself is the growing use of violence by antiabortion forces in the United States. Between 1984 and 1993, there were 73 reported arson attacks on abortion clinics, 29 bombings, 59 attempted bombings or arson attacks, 150 death threats to providers, 1 murder, 1 attempted murder, 26 burglaries, and 473 instances of invasion or vandalism.[51] More recently, the antichoice fundamentalist group, Operation Rescue, has taken to blocking women's access to clinics by physically barring their way. Since 1988, at least 590 clinics have been blockaded by prolife demonstrators, and 32,978 arrests have been made for assault, trespass, and invasion.[52] Perhaps no other example better illustrates the implications of violence for reproductive freedom than the use of physical force to prevent women from exercising their constitutional right to abortion.[53]

Moving Forward: Potential for Joint Action

Even this cursory review of violence and reproductive health suggests that the two movements could better exploit their potential to serve as natural allies. Legal changes related to domestic violence or rape, for example, are centrally important to many women's reproductive freedom. The women's health movement can help mobilize its constituency to provide crucial political support on important initiatives regarding violence. Likewise, on issues of reproductive rights and health, advocates working in the field of violence should recognize that the ability to control one's own body is often the prerequisite to taking control of one's life.

On a programmatic level, there is much that the reproductive health/rights community can do to bring to life the reality of violence in many women's lives. First, the existence of forced sex and violence should be openly acknowledged in the rhetoric and demands of the reproductive health movement. Calls for reproductive autonomy should condemn negation of choice at the individual level (e.g., through marital rape) as well as at the level of the state.

Further, advocates' positions on various reproductive technologies should acknowledge that some women need methods they can use without their partners' cooperation or consent. In their zeal to protect women from potentially harmful methods—such as Depo Provera and other injectables—reproductive rights activists have at times found themselves at odds with the very women they are attempting to serve. Experience has shown that, for women living with partners who object to contraceptive use (especially violent partners), the ability to use a method surreptitiously may override other long-term safety concerns in the minds of some women. Indian feminist doctor Hari John, for example, defends her use of Depo Provera in South India on the basis of male opposition to contraception: "Using Depo Provera," she contends, "is the only way these women can have any control over any aspect of their lives."[54] This is not to say that dangerous methods should be approved just because they are convenient. Rather, it is a plea that health activists respect the primacy of "safety from violence" in some women's sexual and reproductive decision making.

Reproductive health care providers can also play an important role in identifying and referring survivors of sexual assault, child sexual abuse, and battering to counselors. By virtue of their ongoing contact with women throughout their lives, family planning providers, nurses, and prenatal care clinicians are especially well positioned to identify and counsel victims of abuse. Studies in the United States demonstrate that women are remarkably willing to identify themselves as battered, especially when questioned in private by an understanding individual. When Planned Parenthood of Houston and Southeast Texas added four abuse-assessment questions to their standard intake form, 8.2 percent of women identified themselves as physically abused. When asked the same questions in person by a provider, 29 percent of women reported abuse.[55]

The cooperation of reproductive health workers is especially important in politically repressive countries where women are unlikely to seek help from the police or other governmental authorities. These same women may admit abuse, however, when questioned in private by a supportive health care provider. Providers can emphasize that no one deserves to be beaten or raped, and help a woman think through options for protecting herself in the future (e.g., seeking safety at a friend's). Over thirty-five developing countries also have women's crisis centers to which providers can refer women for legal or psychological support.[56] But even where no external support exists, having a sympathetic individual acknowledge and denounce the violence in a woman's life offers considerable relief from isolation and self-blame.

At the same time, advocates working to combat violence must fight for alternatives that grant women as much reproductive autonomy as possible, given the presence of violence in many women's lives. The top priority on this front would be for these advocates to join forces with women's health advocates and AIDS activists to demand the development of a safe, effective, female-controlled microbicide that women could use vaginally to protect themselves from HIV and other STDs.

Finally, we need more and better research into the impact that sexual victimization appears to have on individuals' sexual risk-taking behavior as adults. This new line of research suggests that some of the most intractable reproductive health issues of our time may be linked to unresolved issues around sexual victimization. Like it or not, the intersection of violence and reproductive decision making is showing up in the realities of women's lives. Both movements had better organize to confront it.

Notes

1. Perdita Huston, *Third World Women Speak Out* (New York: Praeger, 1979).

2. Eleanor Roosevelt. 1958. From her speech, "The Great Question." Cited in Elaine Partnow, *The New Quotable Woman* (New York: Meridian Books, 1993) p. 279.

3. M. Koss, "Detecting the Scope of Rape: A Review of Prevalence Research Methods," *Journal of Interpersonal Violence* (1993) 8: 198–222. Dean Kilpatrick, C.N. Edmundo, and A.K. Seymour, "Rape in America: A Report to the Nation" (Charleston, SC: Crime Victims Research and Treatment Center, 1992).

4. Consumers Association of Penang, *Rape in Malaysia* (Penang, Malaysia: Consumers Association of Penang, 1988).

5. Amelia Marquez Perez, "Aproximacion Diagnostica a Las Violaciones de Mujeres en Los Distritos de Panama y San Miguelito" (Panama City: Centro Para el Desarrollo de la Mujer, Universidad de Panama, 1990).

6. Ana Maria Portugal, "Cronica de una Violacion Provocada?" in *Revista Mujer/ Fempress: Contraviolencia* (Santiago, Chile: FEMPRESS-ILET, 1988).

7. Christine Bradley, "Why Male Violence Against Women is a Development Issue: Reflections from Papua New Guinea." Occasional Paper. (New York: United Nations Fund for Women [UNIFEM], 1990).

8. Cited in Cecilia Avendano and Jorge Ivan Vergara, "La Violencia en Chile, Dimensiones: Colectivo, Cultura y Politica" (Santiago, Chile: Servicio Nacional de la Mujer).

9. COVAC, "Evaluacion de Proyecto para Educacion, Capacitacion, y Atencion a Mujeres y Menores de Edad en Materia de Violencia Sexual, Enero a Diciembre 1990," unpublished report (Mexico City: Asociacion Mexicana Contra la Violencia a las Mujeres, A.C. [COVAC], 1990).

10. Dean Kilpatrick, C.N. Edmundo, and A.K. Seymour, *Rape in America: A Report to the Nation* (Charleston, SC: Crime Victims Research and Treatment Center, 1992).

11. Data from Ban Thanom Rak, a home for rape survivors run by the Friends of Women, Bangkok, Thailand as quoted in K. Archavanitkui and A. Pramualratana, "Factors Affecting Women's Health in Thailand," paper presented at the Workshop on Women's Health in Southeast Asia, Population Council, Jakarta, October 29–31, 1990.

12. Private communication with Dr. Bonnie Dattel, Medical Director of the San Francisco Rape Crisis Center and Associate Professor of OB-Gyn at the University of California, San Francisco, March 4, 1992. See also Sue Armstrong, "South Africa's Rape Epidemic Fuels HIV," *World AIDS* 27, (May 1993), Panos Institute, London.

13. COVAC, "Evaluacion de Proyecto para Educacion, Capacitacion, y Atencion a Mujeres y Menores de Edad en Materia de Violencia Sexual, Enero a Diciembre 1990" (Mexico City: Asociacion Mexicana Contra la Violencia a las Mujeres, 1990); CAMVAC, "Carpeta de Informacion Basica Para la Atencion Solidaria y Feminista a Mujeres Violadas" (Mexico City: Centro de Apoyo A Mujeres Violadas [CAMVAC], 1985); K. Archavanitkui and A. Pramualratana, "Factors Affecting Women's Health in Thailand," paper presented at the Workshop on Women's Health in Southeast Asia, Population Council, Jakarta, October 29–31, 1990;

Korea data from Young-Hee Shim, "Sexual Violence Against Women: A Victimization Survey of Seoul Women," paper presented at the conference on International Perspective: Crime, Justice and Public Order, St. Petersburg, Russia, June 21–27, 1992.

14. M. Isabel Rosas, "Violencia Sexual y Politica Criminal," CLADEM Informativo No. 6., Lima, April 1992.

15. Tatiana Treguear L. and Carmen Carro B., *Niñas Madres: Recuento de una Experiencia* (San Jose, Costa Rica: PROCAL, 1991) as cited in Elizabeth Shrader-Cox, "Violence Against Women in Central America and its Impact on Reproductive Health," paper presented at the Safe Motherhood Central America Conference, Guatemala City, January 27–31, 1992.

16. Philip Graitcer and Z. Youssef, eds., *Injury in Egypt: An Analysis of Injuries as a Health Problem* (Cairo: Ministry of Health; and Washington DC: U.S. Agency for International Development, 1993).

17. Ruth Dixon-Mueller, "The Sexuality Connection in Reproductive Health," *Studies in Family Planning* 24 (5) (1993): 269–82.

18. Chris Elias, and Lori Heise, "The Development of Microbicide: A New Method of HIV Prevention for Women," working paper no. 6. The Population Council, (New York, 1993).

19. By no means is male approval always the greatest determinant of contraceptive use. For studies indicating where it is, see "Men—New Focus for Family Planning Programs," *Population Reports,* Series J, No. 33, 1986. Bangladesh data from D. Lawrence Kincaid, et. al. "Family Planning and the Empowerment of Women in Bangladesh," paper presented at the 119th Annual Meeting of the American Public Health Association, Atlanta, GA, November 13, 1991.

20. Suzanna Stout Banwell, *Law, Status of Women and Family Planning in Sub-Saharan Africa: A Suggestion for Action* (Nairobi: Pathfinder Fund, 1990).

21. Ibid., p. 14.

22. Mexico example from Evelyn Folch-Lyon, Luis Macorra, and S. Bruce Schearer, "Focus Group and Survey Research on Family Planning in Mexico," *Studies in Family Planning* 12 (12) (1981): 409–432; Peru example from Alfredo Fort, "Investigating the Social Context of Fertility and Family Planning: A Qualitative Study in Peru," *International Family Planning Perspectives* 15 (3) (1989): 88–94.

23. Rebeccca Cook, and Deborah Maine, "Spousal Veto over Family Planning Services," *American Journal of Public Health* 77 (3) (1987): 339–44.

24. *Population Reports* p. J-891.

25. Folch-Lyon, Macorra, and Schearer, *supra* n. 21.

26. U.S. figures from Jacqueline Campbell and Peggy Alford, "The Dark Consequences of Marital Rape," *American Journal of Nursing* (July 1989), p. 946–48.

27. Fifty-eight percent refers to studies in Puerto Rico and Bolivia as cited in "Campaña sobre la Violencia en contra de la Mujer," *Boletin* 16–17, Santiago, Chile: Red de Salud de las Mujeres Latinoamericanas y del Caribe, Isis International (April 1988). Colombia data from "Estudio sobre la Violencia Contra la Mujer en la Familia Basado en la Encuesta Realizada a las Mujeres Maltratadas Que Acudieron Al Servicio Juridico de ProFamilia Entre El 15 de Marzo de 1989 y El 30 de Marzo

de 1990," *La Violencia y Los Derechos Humanos de la Mujer,* (Bogota, Colombia: Profamilia, 1992).

28. Philippines data cited in Laurie Liskin, "Periodic Abstinence: How Well Do New Approaches Work?" *Population Reports,* Population Information Program, Johns Hopkins University, Baltimore, MD, 1981.

29. Preliminary report (1991) "Guatemala City Women: Empowering a Vulnerable Group for HIV Prevention," DataPro SA and the Asociacion Guatemalteca para la Prevencion y Control del SIDA, Guatemala City, 1991.

30. Peter Freiberg, "Condom Use: Burden Shouldn't Be Woman's," *Christian Science Monitor* (1991).

31. Jane Perlez, "For the Oppressed Sex, Brave Words to Live By," *New York Times,* June 6, 1990.

32. Dooley Worth, "Sexual Decision-Making and AIDS: Why Condom Promotion among Vulnerable Women Is Likely to Fail," *Studies in Family Planning* 20 (6) (1989): 304.

33. Ibid. p. 305.

34. Chris Elias and Lori Heise, "The Development of Microbicide: A New Method of HIV Prevention for Women," working paper no. 6, Population Council, New York, 1993.

35. Debra Boyer and David Fine, "Sexual Abuse as a Factor in Adolescent Pregnancy and Child Maltreatment," *Studies in Family Planning* 24 (1), (1992):4–10.

36. Ibid. p. 11.

37. See D. Finkelhor, (1987) "The Sexual Abuse of Children: Current Research Reviewed," *Psychiatric Annals* 17 (1987): 233–241; and J. James and J. Meyerding, "Early Sexual Experience and Prostitution," *American Journal of Psychiatry* 134 (1977): 1381–85.

38. Sally Zierler, Lisa Feingold, Deborah Laufer, Priscilla Velentgas, Ira Gordon-Kantrowitz and Kenneth Mayer "Adult Survivors of Childhood Sexual Abuse and Subsequent Risk of HIV Infection," 81 (5) (1991): 572–75.

39. Penn Handwerker, "Gender Power Differences Between Parents and High Risk Sexual Behavior by their Children: AIDS/STD Risk Factors extend to a Prior Generation," *Journal of Women's Health* 2 (3) (1993): 301.

40. Variables controlled for include years in legal or common-law union during previous five years; raised in lower-class home; education of mother; education of father; raised in stable nuclear family; raised solely by mother; raised with a stepfather; degree of affection mother's partner showed her; degree of physical and emotional abuse to mother; degree of affection mother showed son; degree of affection mother's partner showed son; degree mother's partner physically and emotionally abused son; man's educational status; man's occupational status.

41. Rosalind Petchesky, *Abortion and Woman's Choice: The State, Sexuality, and Reproductive Freedom* (Boston: Northeastern Univ. Press, 1990).

42. Rosalind Petchesky, quoted in Betsy Hartmann, *Reproductive Rights and Wrongs: The Global Politics of Population Control and Contraceptive Choice* (New York: Harper and Row, 1987), p. 241.

43. Jodi Jacobson, *Women's Reproductive Health: The Silent Emergency* (Washington, DC: Worldwatch Institute, 1991).

44. Helen Saxenian, "Brazil: Women's Reproductive Health," Population and Human Resources Operations Division, Report # 8215-BR, Washington, DC, August 23, 1991.

45. Betsy Hartman, *Reproductive Rights and Wrongs.* p. 242.

46. Dr. Simone Grilo Dinez, personal communication, June 7, 1991.

47. Brazil has the highest rate of cesarean section deliveries in the world. In 1981 an estimated 31 percent of all births were by cesarean, compared with under 10 percent in the Netherlands, 15 percent in England and Wales, 20 percent in Canada, and 25 percent in the United States. Rates continue to rise in most countries despite evidence that the increased use of cesarean sections has not reduced infant (or maternal) mortality. In the United States, one highly successful program aimed at eliminating unnecessary cesareans reduced the cesarean rate from 17.5 percent to 11.5 percent, without adverse effects for the mother or infant. A recent review of the literature estimates that perhaps 15 percent of cesareans are medically justified. See Helen Saxenian, *Brazil: Women's Reproductive Health* (draft) (Washington, DC: World Bank, 1989).

48. "Health Services and Maternity in Mexico," *Women's Global Network for Reproductive Rights,* 36 (July–September 1991).

49. Mary Eberts, "Emerging Legal Issues in Health Care," paper presented at the 6th International Conference of the Society of Law and Medicine, Toronto, Ontario, July 1992.

50. Barbara Mensch, "Quality of Care: A Neglected Dimension," In *Women's Health: A Global Perspective,* ed. Marge Koblinsky, Judith Timyan, and Jill Gay (Boulder, CO: Westview, 1993).

51. "Incidents of Violence and Disruption Against Abortion Providers," (1993), National Abortion Federation, Washington, DC data as of November 12, 1993.

52. Ibid.

53. In 1994, President Clinton signed the Clinic Access Bill, which bars such blockades; pro-life forces, however, are presenting challenges to the new law.

54. "Depo Provera: Control of Fertility—Two Feminist Views," *Spare Rib* (London), no. 116, March 1982, as quoted in Betsy Hartman, *supra* n. 41, p. 194.

55. Linda Bullock, and Judith McFarlane, "The Prevalence and Characteristics of Battered Women in a Primary Care Setting," *Nurse Practitioner* 14 (1989): 47–54.

56. See Lori Heise, "Violence Against Women: The Missing Agenda," In *Women's Health: A Global Perspective*, ed. Marge Koblinsky, Judith Timyan, and Jill Gay (Boulder, Co: Westview, 1992).

Reprinted with permission from Lori L. Heise, "Reproductive Freedom and Violence Against Women: Where Are the Intersections?" *The Journal of Law, Medicine & Ethics,* 21 no. 2 (1991): 206–16.

25

International Human Rights and Women's Reproductive Health

Rebecca J. Cook

Protection of women's reproductive health has not been a high priority in the value systems of governments and the laws they have created. The principal duty of women historically was to bear men's children, particularly sons, and to serve as the foundation of families. The cost to women's health of discharging this duty went unrecognized. Ill health, influenced by early and excessive childbearing, and women's premature deaths (in labor/birth or from weakness or exhaustion due to pregnancy and close birth spacing) were explained through fate, destiny, and divine will rather than through governmental neglect of reproductive health services. Maternal mortality and morbidity were not considered amenable to human control through comprehensive reproductive health services, education, and laws.

Women's reproductive health raises sensitive issues in many legal traditions because it relates to human sexuality and affects the moral order. The moral belief was that if women could enjoy sexual relations and have recourse to methods to prevent pregnancy and sexually trans-mitted diseases, sexual morality and family security would be in jeopardy. This traditional morality is reflected in laws that attempt to control women's behavior by limiting, conditioning, or denying women's access to reproductive health services.

Many women die or are chronically disabled from pregnancy-related causes because of neglect of women's reproductive health.[1] Maternal deaths are defined as deaths among women who are pregnant or who have been pregnant during the previous forty-two days.[2] The World Health Organization has estimated that each year 500,000 women die from pregnancy-related causes.[3] This startling and distressing statistic becomes even more dramatic when it is realized that unsafe abortion associated with unwanted pregnancy "causes some 25–50% of [maternal] deaths, simply because women do not have access to family planning services they want and need, or have no access to safe procedures or to humane treatment for the complications of abortion."[4] These statistics, albeit the most dramatic, are only one indication of how countries have neglected women's reproductive health and well-being.

Epidemiological studies can indicate which women have limited access to care and are therefore at higher risk of maternal mortality and morbidity.[5] The universal risk factor is simply the fact of being female. "The cause of maternal death often has some of its roots in a woman's life before the pregnancy," writes H. Mahler, then Director General of the World Health Organization:

> It may lie in infancy, or even before her birth, when deficiencies of calcium, vitamin D, or iron begin. . . . The train of negative factors goes on throughout the woman's life: the special risks of adolescent pregnancy; the maternal depletion from pregnancy too closely spaced; the burdens of heavy physical labor in the reproductive period; the renewed high risk of childbearing after 35 and, worse, after 40; and, running through all this the ghastly dangers of illegal abortion to which sheer desperation may drive her. All these are links in a chain from which only the grave or menopause offer hope of escape.[6]

Thus, there are many causes that contribute to maternal deaths, and some combine with others to compound the risk of death faced by pregnant women.[7]

Paternalistic control of women's sexual and reproductive behavior manifests itself in laws and policies that condition women's access to necessary medical services. For example, the availability of voluntary sterilization services in some countries is contingent on the number of cesarean sections that a woman has undergone.[8] Disregard of women is also apparent in the lack of laws and policies that facilitate women's reproductive health that, even when they exist, are rarely and inadequately enforced. In countries where there is no legal age of marriage, or where it is low or not enforced, adolescent girls often face the consequences of adolescent pregnancy. Childbearing at an early age is associated with high obstetrical risk and leads to a high incidence of maternal mortality in the adolescent age group.[9] In Nigeria, where there is no legal minimum age of marriage, one-quarter of all women are married by the age of 14, one-half by the age of 16, and three-quarters by the age of 18.[10] The work of Kelsey Harrison and others indicates the dimensions of high rates of adolescent pregnancy in Zaria,

Nigeria. Teenage girls under 15 constitute 30 percent of the maternal deaths. A high proportion of teenage pregnancies end in fetal loss, embryotomy (infant death), and death or severely harmful consequences to the adolescent girl, such as vesicovaginal fistulas (VVF)—an injury to the bladder, urethra, and even the lower end of the bowel causing constant leakage of urine and sometimes vaginal excretion of feces. The adolescent VVF victims suffer the medical consequences of infection and/or the social consequences of infertility, often becoming social outcasts through divorce or by being forced into prostitution.[11]

Throughout the world, major abuses of women's dignity and autonomy occur in the delivery of reproductive health services that are available, in part because of lack of enforcement and misapplication of the legal doctrine of informed consent.[12] For example, the rate of cesarean sections is unnecessarily high in both developed and developing countries in part because women are "encouraged" to undergo the procedure without being given adequate information to make an informed choice between cesarean and vaginal deliveries.[13]

In contrast to this traditional neglect, a humane view is emerging that women's reproductive health

> implies that people have the *ability* to reproduce, to regulate their fertility and to practice and enjoy sexual relationships. It further implies that reproduction is carried to a *successful outcome* through infant and child survival, growth, and healthy development. It finally implies that women can go *safely* through pregnancy and childbirth, that fertility regulation can be achieved without health hazards and that people are safe in having sex.[14]

Services to promote and maximize reproductive health include appropriate sex education; counseling; and the means to prevent unintended pregnancy, to treat unwanted pregnancy, and to prevent sexually transmitted diseases and other manifestations of sexual and reproductive dysfunctions, including infertility.[15] Epidemiological and related data show how reproductive health services can reduce maternal mortality and morbidity and contribute significantly to women's reproductive health.[16] Epidemiological data also demonstrate life and health risks from pregnancies that come too early, too late, too often, or too rapidly in a woman's reproductive years.[17]

An emerging analysis assesses governmental neglect of preventable causes of women's mortality and morbidity as part of a larger social phenomenon of systemic discrimination against women. Laws that deny, obstruct, or condition availability of and access to reproductive health services are being challenged as violating women's basic human rights protected by international human rights conventions. The *Convention on the Elimination of All Forms of Discrimination Against Women* (The Women's Convention) obliges countries that have ratified it, known as states parties, "to pursue by all appropriate means and without delay a policy of eliminating discrimination against women,"[18] and in particular "to eliminate discrimination against women in the field of health care in order to ensure . . . access to health care services, including those related to family planning."[19] States parties assume obligations reliably to determine risks to women's reproductive health. The means chosen by states parties to attack dangers to reproductive health will be determined by national considerations, such as patterns of reproductive health service delivery and the epidemiology of reproductive disability. The emerging international imperative is that the means chosen by states should lead to the reduction of maternal mortality and morbidity and enhance the dignity of women and their reproductive self-determination.

If international human rights law is to be truly universal, it has to be applied so as to require states to take effective preventive and curative measures to protect women's reproductive health and to afford women the capacity for reproductive self-determination. International human rights treaties require international and domestic application in order to secure women's rights to: be free from all forms of discrimination; achieve their rights to liberty and security, to marriage and foundation of families, to private and family life, and to information and education; and to have access to health care and the benefits of scientific progress. Women's reproductive freedom under international human rights law is a composite right founded on these separate rights.[20]

Methods of national protection of women's reproductive rights will in the long run be more effective than methods of international protection, because the international methods are too limited in number and scope to deal with the particular complexities of violations in different community contexts. National protection of international human rights derives its legal force from incorporation of international human rights treaties into domestic law through national legislation and through judicial application.

The following analysis starts with the right to be free from all forms of discrimination, and then proceeds to an analysis of rights to life, liberty, and security of the person; the right to marry and found a family; the right to private and family life; rights regarding information and education; the right to reproductive health and health care; and the right to the benefits of scientific progress. Women's reproductive health interests often cross the boundaries that separate one legally described right from another. Advocates tend to invoke several rights that are alleged to have been jointly violated. They must identify the specific articles of conventions that they claim have been violated, and tribunals will distinguish one right from another in their judgments, but approaches to reproductive health must refer to all of the different rights implicated in particular grievances.

The Women's Convention, in prohibiting all forms of discrimination, including private discrimination, is intended to be comprehensive. It recognizes that women are not only subject to specific inequalities but that they are also subject to pervasive forms of discrimination that are woven into the political, cultural, and religious fabric of societies. In addressing "all forms" of discrimination that women suffer, the Women's Convention requires states to confront the social causes of women's inequality. Article 5(a) requires states parties to take all appropriate measures:

> [t]o modify the social and cultural patterns of conduct of men and women, with a view to achieving the elimination of prejudices and customary and all other practices which are based on the idea of the inferiority or the superiority of either of the sexes or on stereotyped roles for men and women.

Female circumcision, for instance, arises from the stereotypical perception that women are the principal guardians of a community's sexual morality and also the primary initiators of unchastity. Article 5(a) points more widely to the need to examine such customary practices, and might be used to require states to educate those condoning and practicing female circumcision about the empirical data of its harmful effects[21] and to use legal sanctions where appropriate.[22]

Included in the goal of eliminating all forms of discrimination is the elimination of marital status discrimination. This objective is shown in the provision in the Article 1 definition of offensive conduct as that which distinguishes on the basis of sex and which has the effect or purpose of denying women "irrespective of their marital status" their human rights and fundamental freedoms in the "civil or any other field". For example, a practice of health clinics to require a wife, but not an unmarried adult woman, to secure the authorization of a man, namely her husband, in order to receive health care constitutes marital status discrimination that violates the Convention and would accordingly have to be changed.

UN documentation draws on extensive worldwide evidence to reach the conclusion that "the ability to regulate the timing and number of births is one central means of freeing women to exercise the full range of human rights to which they are entitled."[23] Women's right to control their fertility through invoking the prohibition of all forms of discrimination against women may therefore be considered a fundamental key that opens up women's capacity to enjoy other human rights. Article 12 of the Women's Convention prohibits all forms of discrimination against women in the delivery of health care:

1. States Parties shall take all appropriate measures to eliminate discrimination against women in the field of health care in order to ensure, on a basis of equality of men and women, access to health care services, including those related to family planning.
2. Notwithstanding the provisions of paragraph 1 of this article, States Parties shall ensure to women appropriate services in connection with pregnancy, confinement and the post-natal period, granting free services where necessary, as well as adequate nutrition during pregnancy and lactation.

In considering whether a restrictive abortion law offends this article, two questions must be asked:[24]

a. Does the law have a significant impact in perpetuating either the oppression of women or culturally imposed sex-role constraints on individual freedom?

A restrictive abortion law does have a significant impact in perpetuating women's oppression. It exacerbates the inequality resulting from the biological fact that women carry the exclusive health burden of contraceptive failure. Contraceptive failure is defined as "counts of unintended pregnancies occurring during the practice of contraceptive and the number of months spent at risk." It is estimated that the rates of contraceptive failure range from 6 percent of women using the pill experiencing failure during the first 12 months of use, to 14–16 percent for the condom, diaphragm, and rhythm methods to 26 percent for spermicides.[25] Moreover, a restrictive abortion law requires a woman with an unwanted pregnancy to carry that pregnancy to term with all the consequent moral, social, and legal responsibilities of gestation and parenthood.

b. Since the law does have this impact, is it justified as the best means
    of serving a compelling state purpose?

The state purpose in a restrictive abortion law is to serve the state's
interest in the protection of prenatal life, which becomes more compelling as the pregnancy advances. A restrictive abortion law is only one
means of protecting prenatal life, and the question has to be asked
whether it is the *best* means. Other means include sex and reproductive
health education and wide availability of contraceptive services to
maximize the prospects of women achieving only wanted pregnancies,
reducing the need for abortion services and thus the overall abortion rate.

In 1987, legal abortion rates "ranged from a high of at least 112
per 1,000 women of reproductive age in the Soviet Union to a low of
5 per 1,000 in the Netherlands."[26] The Netherlands has a liberal abortion law as well as public accommodation of sex education and accessible contraceptive information and services, resulting in low and
declining abortion rates. Dutch law enables postcoital treatment in
the event of contraceptive failure; consistent with the medical definition
of pregnancy,[27] this law characterizes as contraception (and not as
abortion) interceptive methods used before the pre-embryo has
implanted in the uterus. The Dutch approach presents the best means
of serving a compelling state purpose in the protection of prenatal life
that is consistent with the right to be free from all forms of discrimination.

The most obvious human right violated by avoidable death in pregnancy or childbirth is a woman's right to life itself. Article 6.1 of the
International Covenant on Civil and Political Rights (the Political
Covenant) provides that "every human being has the inherent right
to life. This right shall be protected by law. No one shall be arbitrarily
deprived of his life."[28] This right is traditionally referred to in the
immediate context of the obligation of states parties to ensure that
courts observe due process of law before capital punishment is
imposed.[29] This understanding of the right to life is essentially male
oriented, since men consider state execution more immediate to them
than death from pregnancy or labor. Feminist legal approaches would
suggest that this interpretation ignores the historic reality of women,
which persists in regions of the world from which almost all of the
500,000 women who die each year from pregnancy-related causes
come. The Human Rights Committee has noted that "the right to life
has been too often narrowly interpreted. The expression 'inherent right

to life' cannot be properly understood in a restrictive manner, and the protection of this right requires that States adopt positive measures."[30]

The Committee considers it desirable that states parties to the Political Covenant take all possible measures to reduce infant mortality and to increase life expectancy. A compatible goal is reduction of maternal mortality, for instance by promoting methods of birth spacing that would improve both infant and maternal survival.

An argument that a woman's right to life entitles her to have access to basic reproductive health services, and that legislation obstructing such access violates international human rights provisions, can be made in regard to an individual woman. The argument must be expanded, however, where the threat to a woman's survival of pregnancy is indicated not by her medical condition but by her membership in a group at high risk of maternal mortality or morbidity due to pregnancy. The collective right to life of women in groups at risk raises the question whether states have a positive obligation to offer appropriate reproductive health services to them, or at least education and counseling services that alert them both to risks and to means to minimize risks. The *African Charter on Human and Peoples' Rights,* given its emphasis on collective rights in its preamble, might well be invoked to impose obligations on African governments to service rights of groups of individuals who are at highest risk of death through unintended pregnancies.

The strongest defense of individual integrity under the Political Covenant exists in article 9(1), which provides that "[e]veryone has the right to liberty and security of the person. . . . No one shall be deprived of his liberty except on such grounds and in accordance with such procedures as are established by law."[31] This right would seem to serve the negative interest in noninterference by the state in individual pursuit of means to limit, or to promote, fertility. The right transcends that of a woman to protect her life and health, and recognizes her right to reproductive choice as an element of her personal integrity and autonomy not dependent on health justifications.

Under international human rights law, states cannot compel women to conceive children against their will nor force men to impregnate women. A violation of liberty and security occurs when the state denies women access to means of fertility control, leaving them to risk unintended pregnancy. For example, in El Salvador the lack of availability of contraceptives causes women to have about twice as many children as they want.[32] Further violation occurs when a state's laws allow husbands or partners to veto wives' or girlfriends' use of birth control. Courts in at least eight countries, and a regional human rights tribunal, have rejected applications by husbands or boyfriends to prohibit abortions.[33] Parental veto laws may be condemned when they obstruct personal choices by mature or emancipated minors who are able to make their own sexual decisions and to bear the consequences of their choices.[34]

The limitations imposed by international human rights instruments on restrictive laws against women's choices have not been explored in any comprehensive or even adequate way. A special case for the protection of liberty and security concerns women who are imprisoned for terminating their own pregnancies. In Nepal, women are often convicted of the crime of self-abortion, punishable by up to life imprisonment.[35] The offense is necessarily applicable only to women, and may constitute discrimination on the basis of sex. Article 2(g) of the Women's Convention requires states parties "to repeal all national provisions which constitute discrimination against women." Women may be inappropriately charged for this offense, particularly if they had no access to contraceptive services, and be denied access to legal representation in court proceedings.

Article 19 of the *Convention on the Rights of the Child* (The Children's Convention) requires states "to protect the child from all forms of physical or mental violence, injury or abuse, neglect or negligent treatment, maltreatment or exploitation, including sexual abuse." This article furnishes grounds to question the "neglect" of states that results in high rates of adolescent pregnancy and such treatment of children as female circumcision. States ignoring the consequences for adolescent women of lack of availability of contraceptives and female circumcision should be found in violation of article 19 of the Children's Convention.

Article 23 of the Political Covenant and article 10 of the *International Covenant on Economic, Social and Cultural Rights* (the Economic Covenant) both recognize the family as the "natural and fundamental group unit of society." The former states that "the right of men and women of marriageable age to marry and found a family shall be recognized."[36] The latter recognizes that "special protection should be accorded to mothers during a reasonable period before and after childbirth. During such period working mothers should be accorded paid leave or leave with adequate social security benefits."[37]

The Human Rights Committee's General Comments to article 23 of the Political Covenant explain that the right to found a family implies, in principle, the possibility to procreate and live together. When States Parties adopt family planning policies, they should be compatible with the provisions of the Covenant and should, in particular, not be discriminatory or compulsory.[38]

The right to found a family is inadequately observed if it amounts to no more than the right to conceive, gestate, and deliver a child. An act of "foundation" goes beyond a passive submission to biology to involve the right of a woman positively to plan, time, and space the births of children to maximize their health and her own. Accordingly, article 16(1)(e) of the Women's Convention requires states parties to ensure that women enjoy "rights to decide freely and responsibly on the number and spacing of their children and to have access to the information, education and means to enable them to exercise these rights."[39]

Maria Isabel Plata has explained[40] that when Colombia adopted the Women's Convention into Colombian law,[41] this article became part of the new 1991 Constitution.[42] The Colombian Ministry of Public Health has interpreted the Women's Convention to establish a gender perspective in national health policies that considers "the social discrimination of women as an element which contributes to the ill-health of women."[43] A new Ministerial resolution orders all health institutions to ensure women the right to decide on all issues that affect their health, their life, and their sexuality; and guarantees rights "to information and orientation to allow the exercise of free, gratifying, responsible sexuality which cannot be tied to maternity."[44] The new policy requires provision of a full range of reproductive health services, including infertility services, safe and effective contraception, integrated treatment for incomplete abortion, and treatment for menopausal women. The policy emphasizes the need for special attention to high risk women, such as adolescents and victims of violence.

In some parts of the world, the right to found a family is most threatened by reproductive tract infections. In Africa, for example, it is the cause of up to 50 percent of infertility.[45] Government inaction that violates this right constitutes a basis of state political accountability, whether or not the right is classified in law as a positive right (i.e., a right that governments must service through positive action). If the right is negative (i.e., a state must not obstruct its exercise by those who are capable), legal liability of the state might nevertheless arise not because of infertility itself but because of the differential impact infertility has on the lives of women.[46]

The right to found a family incorporates the right to maximize the survival prospects of a conceived or existing child through birth spacing by contraception or abortion. This right is complementary to the right of a woman herself to survive pregnancy, for instance by delaying a first pregnancy. State laws that do not provide a minimum age of marriage, and practices that do not enforce such laws, permit young girls to marry, not uncommonly with questionably free consent, and to conceive children before they are physiologically mature, with consequently high rates of maternal and infant mortality and high levels of morbidity. The right to marry and to found a family can be limited by laws that are reasonably related to a family-based objective. Laws requiring a minimum age of marriage are not incompatible with rights to marry and to found families. The right to marry and to be a parent is a right of adults rather than of those who are themselves children or young adolescents.

The right to private and family life is distinguishable from the right to found a family, although for some purposes the latter right may be considered to be part of the former. The right to private and family life contains liberty interests. Article 17 of the Political Covenant provides that "no one shall be subjected to arbitrary or unlawful interference with his privacy, family, home or correspondence, nor to unlawful attacks on his honour and reputation."[47]

The *European Convention on Human Rights* (the European Convention) specifies conditions under which private and family life may be compromised or sacrificed to higher interests of the state. Article 8 provides that:

1. Everyone has the right to respect for his private and family life, his home and his correspondence.
2. There shall be no interference by a public authority with the exercise of this right except such as is in accordance with the law and is necessary in a democratic society in the interests of national security, public safety or the economic well-being of the country, for the prevention of disorder or crime, for the protection of health or morals, or for the protection of the rights and freedoms of others.

This article was held to have been violated in the case of *Bruggemann & Scheuten v. Federal Republic of Germany*.[48] Two West German women claimed that a 1976 restrictive abortion law interfered with respect for their private lives contrary to this article in that they were not permitted privately and alone to decide to terminate their unwanted pregnancies. The majority of the European Commission of Human Rights rejected the applicants' claims and found that the restrictive laws did not constitute an interference with private life.

Greater scope was given to a women's right to private life in the case of *Paton v. United Kingdom*.[49] The European Commission upheld a British decision preventing a woman from being coerced to continue an unwanted pregnancy through her husband's veto of her abortion. The Commission gave priority to respect for a wife's private life in her decision on childbearing over her husband's right to respect for his family life in birth of his child, and found that the husband's right could not be interpreted to embrace even a right to be consulted on his wife's decision. A state's interest in an unborn life is not greater than that of the biological father, so that preclusion of his right necessarily precludes the state's right to prevail. Rights to seek, receive, and impart information are protected by all the basic human rights conventions[50] and are essential to the realization of reproductive health. The Women's Convention explicitly requires that women have the right to information and counseling on health and family planning.[51]

Article 10 (1) of the European Convention protects "the right to freedom of expression that shall include freedom . . . to receive and impart information and ideas without interference by public authority and regardless of frontiers." The European Court of Human Rights in the recent case of *Open Door and Dublin Well Women v. Ireland*[52] found that the Irish government's ban on counseling women where to find abortions abroad violates this article. In order to comply with this decision, the Irish government can no longer ban such counseling. This decision also applies to other countries that are members of the European Convention in the event that they try to restrict the counseling of women seeking services in other countries.

The right to education[53] serves the goal of individual and reproductive health. Women have access to contraception more easily when they are literate, and can read and understand the risks to their health and the health of their children presented by close birth spacing.[54] Education affecting sexual matters can raise issues, however, of rights to freedom of thought and religion.[55] Conflicts have arisen when public school systems have introduced health-oriented programs of instruction on sexual matters to which parents have objected on grounds of their religious convictions.

In the *Danish Sex Education* case,[56] some Danish parents objected to compulsory sex education in state schools. They complained that it violated the state's duty to respect "the right of parents to ensure such education and teaching in conformity with their own religious and philosophical convictions,"[57] and either jointly or alternatively it violated their right to religious nondiscrimination; rights to private and family life; and the right to freedom of thought, conscience, and religion set out in the European Convention. The European Court held that compulsory sex-education classes in Danish schools violated none of these duties or rights because they were primarily intended to convey useful and corrective information that, though unavoidably concerned with considerations of a moral nature, did not exceed "the bounds of what a democratic state may regard as in the public interest."[58]

By article 12(1) of the Economic Covenant, states parties "recognize the right of everyone to the enjoyment of the highest attainable standard of physical and mental health." Article 12(2) provides that the steps to achieve the full realization of this right

> shall include those necessary for: a) The provision for the reduction of the stillbirth-rate and of infant mortality and for the healthy development of the child. . . . d) The creation of conditions which would assure to all medical service and medical attention in the event of sickness.[59]

Article 12 addresses reproductive health services indirectly, in that multiple pregnancies and short birth intervals endanger infant survival and health. This article is reinforced by article 24(f) of the Children's Convention, which requires that states parties "develop preventive health care, guidance for parents and family planning education and services." Epidemiological evidence demonstrates the significance of birth spacing to this goal.

The breadth of the concept of "health" is apparent in the preamble to the Constitution of the World Health Organization, which describes health as "a state of complete physical, mental and social well-being and not merely the absence of disease or infirmity."[60] In this sense, idealistic or ambitious though it may appear, the right to seek the highest attainable standard of health is inherent in every human being. Because mental and social well-being are components of health, unwanted pregnancy that endangers mental or social well-being is as much a threat to women's health as is pregnancy that endangers survival, longevity or physical health.

States parties may be called upon to explain their protective failures to such bodies as the Economic Committee.[61] The Economic Committee may want to seek assistance from WHO and UNFPA in the development of a General Recommendation for reporting on the progress made in improving women's reproductive health, according to the WHO Indicators for Health For All By the Year 2000.[62] WHO indicators now include the reduction of maternal mortality by half by the year 2000.[63] Countries that are not moving progressively to meet this goal may *prima facie* be found in breach of their human rights responsibilities to protect the lives and well-being of women. If, for instance, epidemiological or other evidence indicates that rates of maternal mortality or morbidity are rising without justified cause, the country will become liable to be asked to give enforceable undertakings of improved performance. In most cases, enforcement will not be through means such as economic sanctions, but through, for instance, the international sanctions of embarrassment generated by nongovernmental organizations.

Article 15(1)(b) of the Economic Covenant recognizes the right of everyone "to enjoy the benefits of scientific progress and its applications." Further, by article 15(3), states parties "undertake to respect the freedom indispensable for scientific research."[64] Freedom of research requires states parties to tolerate and accommodate research on new techniques of fertility control and enhancement, and may create states' responsibilities actively to facilitate such research and development, particularly from women's perspectives.[65] Access to scientific advances is significant, since so many of the modern techniques of fertility control and promotion and of assisted reproduction are the results of scientific progress, which has resulted in women's freedom from unwanted pregnancy through safe, effective and convenient contraception.[66] Male fertility regulating methods,[67] contraceptive implants,[68] nonsurgical abortion,[69] and fertility regulating vaccines[70] are all parts of a new and emerging range of fertility-regulating methods achieved by advances in science.

The right to the benefits of scientific progress requires states parties to facilitate the use of methods that are proven to be safe and effective and to favor interpretations of existing law that would facilitate their use. For example, some Islamic schools of thought allow abortion up to 120 days of pregnancy, but abortion laws in some Islamic countries are not implemented accordingly.[71] Where abortion is already lawful, the right to the benefits of scientific progress and its applications requires governments to facilitate the availability of nonsurgical abortion, as was recently done in the United Kingdom by an amendment to the British Abortion Act 1967.[72] Patent laws, such as the French patent law,[73] facilitating the introduction of therapeutic products for the protection of women's health are also necessary.[74] Laws and practices obstructing drug approval and drug importation of safe and effective methods violate this right.[75]

States parties to the Economic Covenant are obliged to ensure that health professionals apply appropriate scientific knowledge according to the wishes and interests of their patients. When states delegate legal control of health professionals to self-regulating professional authorities that fail in this responsibility, the question arises of state responsibility in international law for treaty violation. An example of failed responsibility can be seen in the high rates of abortion conducted by less safe methods than are in fact available. Suction abortion is safer than dilatation and evacuation, but in many parts of the world the medical profession has not moved to require physicians' retraining in the suction method.[76] State responsibility might require the passage of laws similar to an Italian law that requires "the use of modern techniques of pregnancy termination, which are physically and mentally less damaging to the woman and are less hazardous."[77]

The widespread disadvantage that women suffer through neglect of their reproductive rights, under laws and practices perpetuated by states, denies them more than their enjoyment of health. Women's reproductive functions have been an agent of control of women themselves. States have advanced their chosen social, economic, and, for instance, population agendas through implementing laws and employing practices that control women's reproduction. Governments must be made accountable not only for their acts of discrimination and omissions but also for the effects of their conduct on the status of women within their countries. Family planning and women's associations are beginning to provide legal services to women in order to protect their reproductive rights.[78] Rights are worth very little to women where there are no corresponding duties on the part of governments, organizations, and individuals to respect those rights. Violations of rights will go unrecognized and unremedied where there is no understanding of those rights or no legal services to advocate for those remedies.

International governmental agencies and NGOs have an important role in monitoring states' conduct. CEDAW can be a catalyst for advancing women's reproductive rights by developing General Recommendations on standards against which countries' performances can be measured. For example, such Recommendations might include reducing maternal mortality, establishing minimum legal ages of marriage, and healthy birth spacing. CEDAW can also hold states parties to strict account through national reports and receive assistance in scrutinizing reports from international agencies and NGOs.

Great potential exists to enforce state responsibility for the observance of women's reproductive rights by employing the resources of international law. These include mechanisms of account under the Women's Convention, the Political and Economic Covenants, and the regional human rights treaties. Of the human rights to which women are entitled, the right whose observance is frequently the precondition to the enjoyment of others is the right to reproductive self-determination. This transcends the rights to reproductive health and to reproductive health care and the right to sexual nondiscrimination. It concerns the fundamental principle of respect for "the inherent dignity and . . . the equal and inalienable rights of members of the human family," which the *Universal Declaration of Human Rights* observes to be the foundation of freedom, justice, and peace in the world.[79]

Notes

1. C. AbouZahr and E. Royston, *Maternal Mortality: A Global Factbook* (Geneva: World Health Organization, 1991).

2. World Health Organization, *Prevention of Maternal Mortality: A Report of a WHO Interregional Meeting* (Geneva: WHO, 1985), p. 5.

3. Safe Motherhood Conference Conclusions, *Lancet* 1 (1987): 670.

4. Id.

5. B. Winikoff and M. Sullivan, "Assessing the Role of Family Planning in Reducing Maternal Mortality," *Studies in Family Planning* 18 (1987): 128–42.

6. H. Mahler, "The Safe Motherhood Initiative: A Call to Action!" *Lancet* 1 (1987): 668–70.

7. M. Fathalla, "The Long Road to Maternal Death" *People* (IPPF) 14 (1987): 8.

8. Brazilian Medical Code of Ethics, chapter 6, article 52 (1965), cited in T. Merrick, "Fertility and Family Planning in Brazil," *International Family Planning Perspectives* 9 (1983): 110.

9. Population Information Program, "Youth in the 1980s: Social and Health Concerns," *Population Reports*, Series M, No. 9 (1985).

10. See "Digest," *International Family Planning Perspectives* 11 (1985): 98, summarizing National Population Bureau, *The Nigeria Fertility Survey 1981/82*, principal report, 1984.

11. K. Harrison, et al., "The Influence of Maternal Age and Parity on Child-bearing with Special Reference to Primigravidae Aged 15 and Under," *British Journal of Obstetrics and Gynaecology*, Supp. 5 (1985): 23–31.

12. B.M. Dickens, "Reproduction Law and Medical Consent," *Univ. of Toronto Law Journal* 35 (1985): 255–86.

13. C. Notzon, et al., "Comparisons of National Caesarian-Section Rates," *New England Journal of Medicine* 316 (7) (1987): 386; F. Barros, et al., "Epidemic of Caesarean Sections in Brazil," *Lancet* 338 (20 July 1991): 167.

14. M. Fathalla, "Reproductive Health: A Global Overview," *Annals of the New York Academy of Sciences* 626 (1991): 1–10.

15. F. Sai and J. Nassim, "The Need for a Reproductive Health Approach," *International Journal of Gynecology and Obstetrics,* Supp. 3 (1989): 103–114.

16. D. Maine, *Safe Motherhood Programs: Options and Issues* (New York: Columbia Univ. Center for Population and Family Health, 1991).

17. E. Royston and S. Armstrong, eds., *Preventing Maternal Deaths* (Geneva: World Health Organization, 1989).

18. Article 2 of the Women's Convention.

19. Article 12(1) of the Women's Convention.

20. R.J. Cook, "International Protection of Women's Reproductive Rights," *New York University Journal of International Law and Politics* 24 (1992): 645–727.

21. Inter-African Committee on Traditional Practices Affecting the Health of Women and Children, *Report on the Regional Seminar on Traditional Practices Affecting the Health of Women and Children in Africa* (1987); United Nations, *Report of the Working Group on Traditional Practices Affecting the Health of Women and Children,* E/CN.4/Sub.2/1991/6.

22. Judgment of 10 July 1987, Case of Fofana Dala Traore, Cour d'Appel (convicted of circumcising her daughter contrary to French law) *Le Monde,* 13 July 1987; *Annual Review of Law and Population* (1987), p. 205.

23. *Status of Women and Family Planning,* UN Doc. E/CN.6/575/Rev.1 (1975).

24. S. Law, "Rethinking Sex and the Constitution," *University of Pennsylvania Law Review* 132 (1984): 955–1040.

25. E. Jones and J. Forrest, "Contraceptive Failure in the United States: Revised Estimates from the 1982 National Survey of Family Growth," *Family Planning Perspectives* 21 (1989): 103–109.

26. S. Henshaw, "Induced Abortion: A World Review," *Family Planning Perspectives* 22 (1990): 76–89.

27. E.C. Hughes, ed., "Committee on Terminology of the American College of Obstetrics and Gynecologist," *Obstetric-Gynecologic Terminology* (1972), pp. 299, 327.

28. This article reflects the Universal Declaration's article 3 and is given further effect in, for instance, the European Convention's art. 2, the American Convention's art. 4, and the African Charter's art. 4.

29. P. Sieghart, *The International Law of Human Rights,* (Oxford: Oxford Univ. Press, 1983): pp. 128–34.

30. United Nations document CCPR/C/21/rev.1 at para. 5, 19 May 1989.

31. This article reflects the Universal Declaration's art. 3 and is given further effect in, for instance, the European Convention's art. 2, the American Convention's art. 4, and the African Charter's art. 4. This right, protected in art. 7 of the Canadian *Charter of Rights and Freedoms,* was held by the Supreme Court of

Canada to be violated by the restrictive criminal abortion law in *R. v. Morgentaler* (1988), 44 D.L.R. (4th) 385 (S.C. Can).

32. A.I. Garcia, "Situacion General de las Mujeres en Centro America y Panama," in *Las Juezas en Centro America y Panama,* ed. T. Rivera Bustamente (San Jose, Costa Rica: Center for the Administration of Justice, Florida International Univ. 1991): pp. 15–40, cited in C. Medina, "Towards a More Effective Guarantee of the Enjoyment of Human Rights by Women in the Inter-American System," in *Human Rights of Women: National and International Perspectives* ed. R. Cook (Philadelphia: Univ. of Pennsylvania Press, 1994).

33. R.J. Cook and D. Maine, "Spousal Veto over Family Planning Services," *American Journal of Public Health* 77 (1987): 339–44.

34. B.M. Knoppers, I. Brault and E. Sloss, "Abortion Law in Francophone Countries," *American Journal of Comparative Law* 38 (1990): 889–922; J. Paxman and J. Zuckerman, *Laws and Policies Affecting Adolescent Health* (Geneva: World Health Organization, 1987).

35. Women's Legal Service Project, *Female Inmates of Prisons in Nepal* (Kathmandu, Nepal: Women's Legal Service Project, 1989), p. 13.

36. This article reflects the Universal Declaration's art. 16 and is given further effect in, for instance, the European Convention's art. 12, the American Convention's art. 17, and the African Charter's art. 18.

37. Article 10(2).

38. United Nations document CCPR/C/21/rev. 1/add.2, 19 Sept 1990.

39. This is the first time this right is established in international law. The origins of this legal right date at least to a 1966 UN General Assembly Resolution on Population Growth and Economic Development, which recognized the principle that "the size of the family should be the free choice of each individual family" (UNGA Res. [xxii] [1966]); See generally, UN, *Population and Human Rights: Proceedings of the Expert Group Meeting on Population and Human Rights,* Geneva, 3–6 April 1989, pp. 54–74.

40. M.I. Plata, "Reproductive Rights as Human Rights: The Colombian Case," *Human Rights of Women: National and International Perspectives,* ed. R.J. Cook (Philadelphia: Univ. of Pennsylvania Press, 1994).

41. The *Colombian Presidential Decree* No. 1398 of 3 July 1990; *Colombian Law* 51 of 1981.

42. 1991 *Colombian Constitution,* article 42.

43. *Salud para la Mujer, Mujer para la Salud* (Health for Women, Women for Health) (Bogota, Colombia: Ministry of Public Health, 1992).

44. *Colombian Ministry of Public Health Resolution* 1531 of 6 March 1992.

45. J.N. Wasserheit, "The Significance and Scope of Reproductive Tract Infections among Third World Women," *International Journal of Gynecology & Obstetrics,* Supp. 3 (1989): 145–168; A. Germain, K.K. Holmes, P. Piot, and J.N. Wasserheit, eds., *Reproductive Tract Infections: Global Impact and Priorities for Women's Reproductive Health* (New York: Plenum Press, 1992).

46. International Women's Health Coalition, *Reproductive Tract Infections in Women in the Third World* (New York: International Women's Health Coalition, 1991): pp. 3–6.

47. This article reflects the Universal Declaration's art. 12 and is given further effect in, for instance, the American Convention's art. 11 and the African Charter's arts. 4 and 5.

48. 3 Eur. H.R. Rep. 244 (1977).

49. 3 Eur. H.R. Rep. 408 (1980).

50. The Universal Declaration' art. 19, the Political Covenant's art. 19, the European Convention's art. 10, the American Convention's art. 13, and the African Charter's art. 9.

51. See arts. 14(b) and 16(e).

52. 14 Eur. H.R. Rep. 131 (1993).

53. Universal Declaration's art. 26, the Economic Covenant's art. 13, art. 2 of Protocol 1 of the European Convention, the American Convention's art. 26, the African Charter's art. 17 and the Women's Convention's art. 10(e).

54. J. Casterline, S. Singh, J. Cleland, and H. Ashurst, "The Proximate Determinants of Fertility," *World Fertility Survey Comparative Studies,* No. 39, London, 1984.

55. Universal Declaration's art. 18, the Political Covenant's art. 18, the European Convention's art. 9, the American Convention's arts. 12–13, the African Charter's art. 8.

56. 1 Eur. H.R. Rep. 711 (1976).

57. Art. 2 of Protocol No. 1 of the European Convention.

58. N. 78, Para. 54.

59. This article reflects the Universal Declaration's art. 25 and is given further effect in, for instance, the European Social Charter's art. 13; the American Convention's art. 26, and art. 10 of its Additional Protocol in the Area of Economic, Social and Cultural Rights, signed in San Salvador, El Salvador, "Protocol of San Salvador," *OEA Documentos Oficiales* OEA-Ser. A-44 (SEPF), 28 I.L.M. 156 (1989); the African Charter's art. 16, and the Children's Convention's art. 24.

60. The Preamble to the Constitution of the World Health Organization, *Official Records of the World Health Organization* 2:100 (June 1948).

61. S. Leckie, "An Overview and Appraisal of the Fifth Session of the UN Committee on Economic Social and Cultural Rights," *Human Rights Quarterly* 13 (1991): 545–72.

62. World Health Organization, *Global Strategy for Health for All by the Year 2000,* "Health for All" Series No. 4 (1981).

63. A. Starrs, *Preventing the Tragedy of Maternal Deaths: A Report on the International Safe Motherhood Conference* (Nairobi, Kenya and Washington DC: World Bank, 1987), p. 8.

64. This article reflects the Universal Declaration's art. 27(2).

65. World Health Organization and International Women's Health Coalition, *Creating Common Ground: Women's Perspectives on the Selection and Introduction of Fertility Regulation Technologies,* WHO/HRP/ITT/91 (1991).

66. World Health Organization *Annual Technical Report 1991 of the Special Programme of Research, Development and Research Training in Human Reproduction*, WHO/HRP/ATR/91/92 (1992).

67. Id., pp. 59–76.

68. B. Dorig and F. Greenslade, eds., *Norplant Contraceptive Subdermal Implants* (Geneva: World Health Organization, 1990).

69. P. Van Look and M. Bygdeman, "Antigestational Steroids: A New dimension in Human Fertility Regulation," Edited by SR. Milligan, *Oxford Review of Reproductive Biology,* vol. 11, Oxford, UK: Oxford Univ. Press, 1989): pp. 1–61.

70. G.L. Ada and P.D. Griffin, eds., *Vaccines for Fertility Regulation: The Assessment of their Safety and Efficacy* (Cambridge, UK: Cambridge University Press, 1991).

71. Z. Sachedina, "Islam, Procreation and the Law," *International Family Planning Perspectives* 16 (1990): 109–110.

72. The UK *Human Fertilisation and Embryology Act,* 1990, U.K. Stats 1990, c. 37.

73. Code de Commerce, *Brevets d'Invention,* arts. 37–40, January 2, 1968.

74. R. Boland, "RU 486 in France and England: Corporate Ethics and Compulsory Licensing," *Law, Medicine and Health Care* 20 (1992): 226–34; R. Cook, "Antiprogestin Drugs: Medical and Legal Issues," *Family Planning Perspectives* 21 (1989): 271.

75. R. Pine, "*Benten v. Kessler:* The RU 486 Import Case," *Law, Medicine and Health Care* 20 (1992): 238–42.

76. K.E. McLaurin, C.E. Hand, and M. Wolf, "Health Systems' Role in Abortion Care: The Need for a Pro-Active Approach," *Issues in Abortion Care* 1 (1991): 5.

77. Sec. 15 of Law 194 of 22 May 1978 (Italy).

78. M.I. Plata, "Family Law and Family Planning in Colombia," *International Family Planning Perspectives* 14 (1988): 109–111.

79. Para. 1 of preamble.

A longer version of this article was originally published in *Studies in Family Planning* 24: 73–86 (1993) and is reprinted here with the permission of the Population Council.

Development and The Socio-Economy

26

Women's Access to Productive Resources: The Need for Legal Instruments to Protect Women's Development Rights

Nadia H. Youssef

Contextual Background

The past thirty years have witnessed three interrelated struggles to bring women's rights to the foreground of social and political movements. These have been directed at (a) mobilizing action around distinctively women-centered issues and working toward the empowerment of women as a world political force (the Feminist Movement); (b) ensuring universal recognition of the principle of equality between men and women (the 1979 *Convention on the Elimination of All Forms of Discrimination Against Women*); and (c) securing women's socio-economic rights through the full integration of women into development (the 1985 *Nairobi Forward Looking Strategies*).[1] What has been absent, however, is the articulation of the ways in which these movements may be integral to a consolidated struggle for human rights.[2]

This paper addresses in brief form one problematic aspect of the human rights agenda: women's rights in the context of socio-economic development. Whereas men in developing regions have, at times, been left out of the development process, women—as the literature on women in development so well documents—have often been denied entry altogether. Where such violations have prevailed, they have been upheld by a patriarchal mentality rooted not only in traditional cultures but also in the heart of national and international agents of development as well. In countries undergoing social and economic moderniza-

279

tion, rural women who are heads of household often constitute a group particularly vulnerable to economic burdens that have been thrust upon them as the sole supporters of self or family. These burdens are aggravated by the marginality of their status (divorced, widowed, abandoned) in the community and, in many instances, by their advanced age.

Focus on the economics of such households reveals that income is irrelevant as a measure of economic status in rural economies where cash income is restricted. Rather, the access such households have to productive resources—principally land, credit, cattle, and technical know-how—is the central indicator of their economic position. In this essay, I focus on Africa because information is more readily available about that region, but that focus should offer a paradigm for understanding the violation of women's socio-economic rights elsewhere and should in no way imply that such violations are exclusively African. Rather, I would like to suggest that such violations are a global problem, even if particulars vary from region to region.

The Relationship of Women to Land

In Africa, women's limited legal and customary rights to land through usufruct ownership clearly affect the ability of rural women heads of household to provide for themselves and their dependents by means of agricultural production. Rural systems of land tenure and inheritance are undergoing the stresses of modernization that too often further restrict women's customary rights of access to tribal "public" land under usufruct systems. The influence of European laws that elaborate individual rights and remedies, as opposed to public rights and duties, were heavily drawn upon in national efforts to reform civil laws. In that process, customary rights and the traditional usufruct system were undermined. The "victims" of the resulting legal pluralism have almost always been women, whose access to and power to own land has remained minimal.

Under customary law, land was "owned" collectively in the limited sense that a group of people had a certain right to its use and were responsible for its care. Usually, some land remained for collective use and was never identified with an individual: common pastures, village common areas, and certain water and forest areas were available to all. Individuals raising specific food crops or animals had the right to use specific plots of land. When the individual ceased to use those plots, the land returned to the collective group for use by someone else.

Though men controlled decisions related to land use, customary rights have traditionally granted women indirect access through their relationship—by blood ties or marriage—with men. Today, both customary and religious laws continue to limit women's direct access to land, reflecting assumptions that land will be provided to women by their male kin. As land has increased in value as a marketable commodity in itself, women's traditional rights of access to land have diminished. Even when kinsmen continue to grant women land to cultivate, the quality and size of plots are reduced. Overcropping, soil erosion, and overgrazing have further diminished soil fertility, and, without adequate fertilizer, women farmers have been forced to let what little land they do have lie fallow for extended periods. The justification for such restrictions on women engaged in farming is that women do not produce crops for cash or export sales. In the context of economic development priorities, women farmers have no ecological or economic niche.

In many instances, land reform laws have discriminated against women. Similarly, resettlement programs have also failed to include women, other than as wives and daughters. Excluding women from the bases of rural productivity has been achieved by: (1) denying women rights to land ownership; (2) stipulating "exceptions" for women in cases where full ownership of land is granted irrespective of sex; and, most important, (3) "masculinizing" the head of household concept on the premise that all families contain an adult male economically responsible for maintaining women and children. Exclusion from property rights deprives women of access to credit and membership in cooperatives. Land ownership continues to be the most important form of collateral for credit and a requirement for participation in cooperative organizations, both income generating and producer oriented.

It would not be useful to propose a single list of recommendations for the reform of existing land ownership laws, not only because of the heterogeneity of conditions but also because the application of some suggestions might raise the need for others. Overall, it is necessary to find common points between land reform legislation and civil/religious inheritance and property laws. Land reform—which can be more easily effected than changes in civil/religious inheritance and property laws—can be effective only if and when it is coupled with legislation and effective enforcement procedures stemming from the executive and the judicial systems. International endorsement of land ownership rights for women and a call for necessary legislation occurred at the 1979 World Conference on Agrarian Reform and Rural Development (sponsored by the UN's Food and Agricultural Organizations), in which strong recommendations on female and joint access to land ownership were approved.[3]

Lack of Livestock for Cash and Draft Power

The significance of access to ownership of cattle may vary from one setting to another, for not all arable agriculture is equally suited for, or as strongly dependent upon, raising livestock. In certain circumstances, however, lacking livestock has been shown to have serious consequences for women's productivity and their ability to purchase services. Cattle are not only critical to the use of draft power (which refers to the force needed or animal used for pulling heavy loads) but also represent a capital asset with the potential for conversion to cash.

Lack of access to cattle ownership has been shown to be a major constraint on women's successful arable production; without owning cattle they are unable to take advantage of rainfall patterns by plowing at the optimal time. Cattle ownership and not sex determines who can plow and when one can plow. Those women who own draft power are not only the first to plow; they plow more than women who borrow, exchange, or hire draft power.

Very little research has been done on sex differences in the ownership of cattle. The general impression is that cattle ownership by women is as restricted as land ownership. It is difficult to quantify actual access because statistics register ownership/holdership, concepts that may be very loosely interpreted in societies in which women claim, by virtue of kinship ties, the use of cattle they do not own.

Detailed data from 1980 on cattle ownership, identifying the sex of the head of household, are available for Botswana, where agriculture is a very high-risk occupation and cattle ownership is of strategic importance. In rural Botswana, 50 percent of all women surveyed who were heads of households owned cattle; the average herd size was below that considered necessary to make up a team of oxen (seven and more). Measuring access to draft power instead of ownership, surveys found that 59 percent of women household heads surveyed had no access to draft power, compared to 28 percent of the males. Of the 41 percent who had access, 12 percent did not have the necessary number of oxen needed for plowing. Effectively, 71 *percent of women heads of household surveyed did not have access to draft power.*[4]

The fact that women own fewer cattle than do men also reduces their profit-making potential as compared with that of men who are household heads, because they are forced to incur more cash expenditures (which they are ill equipped to afford) than men in order to hire draft power, including tractors. When such costs are subtracted from their gross profits, the net gain is considerably reduced. (There are some cases, however, in which women continue managing plowing operations their husbands had started before migrating.)

Cattle ownership also represents one of the few means available to rural women by which cash income can be raised. This is a particularly crucial point for woman-headed households, because their cash expenditures for hiring labor and draft power are often greater than those of male-headed households and their income-earning potential, via work and assets, is considerably lower. The assumption that cash remittances sent home from male relatives who work as migrant laborers outside Botswana compensate for women's lack of access to productive resources in the village has not been borne out.

Lack of Access to Credit

Due to conventional collateral requirements, rural commercial banks in Third World countries have, in the past, typically catered to the requirements of landowners and larger lenders, allowing them further to improve their economic positions at the expense of small farmers. The small farmer was dependent for credit needs on moneylenders and small traders. This situation has been somewhat rectified, in that formal institutions have begun to extend credit to small farmers for farm activities and, increasingly, for rural industry and petty trade activities. Yet institutional credit continues to be biased in that it is based on security and property rights, and, in general, poor groups still face restrictions on access to formal financial institutions that hinder their potential productivity. In many countries small holders, tenants, and share-farmers who have no registered title to land are mostly barred from access to cheap credit. Steps taken to make credit available to the poor have mostly benefited males, leaving poor women little access to financial markets, both because they are poor and because they are women. Such class and sex discrimination can be rectified if committed governments and international multilateral agencies, through their extension of credit programs, make provisions to insure loans for women. (This has indeed been done in Bangladesh, Indonesia, and other countries.)

Women small farmers in Africa, particularly those heading independent households, desperately need access to credit. They are, however, subject to more obstacles in obtaining loans than are male farmers because sex-specific constraints inhibit their participation in the formal lending system. These constraints include high levels of illiteracy, lack of information about the availability of loans, lack of collateral or surety for loans, and the unwillingness of many credit institutions to deal with new and small-scale borrowers who, in most cases, are women.

Cooperatives

Because of the obstacles inhibiting women's access to formal banks, cooperatives can perform an essential intermediary function in facilitating women's access to credit. Cooperatives (1) reduce transaction costs for both lenders and borrowers, (2) perform important functions by removing the obstacles of inexperience and lack of credit-worthiness faced by borrowers, and (3) provide the vehicle for eventual direct contact with formal banks.

Women's experiences with rural formal cooperatives have not, in general, been successful. Even as members, women often find themselves without equal access to credit resources. Males dominate opportunities for agricultural credit, and the cooperative organizations through which such credit is channelled seem to be largely male controlled. In Africa, the cooperative movement has often failed to involve women because women's multiple economic roles as farm producer/manager and head of household do not carry institutional recognition. The attribute associated with the terms "producer" and "cultivator" is ownership of land, which, in legal terms, is reserved to men. The result has been all-male cooperative membership. Only widows of deceased members can join cooperatives as administrators of their husbands' land; how many actually do so is not known.

Sex Bias in the Delivery System

Built into the structure of the agricultural extension system is a sex-segregated division of labor under which male extension workers deliver technical knowledge to a male clientele, (as though rural women have little part to play in agricultural production and farm management), while female home economists concentrate on teaching women to perfect domestic roles. Several priorities established within most agricultural delivery systems also coalesce to exclude a female clientele. Foremost is the fact that such services are delivered by male staff members who make assumptions about the sexual division of labor on the farm and, accordingly, structure the flow of information toward men. Second, innovations in agricultural methods are directed toward cash crops (thereby excluding women, as they are less often involved in cash-crop farming). Third, extension curriculums omit activities in which women play important roles (e.g., the harvest). Last, when extension agents contact and exchange information with farmers, they tend to select the more wealthy and influential class of farmers. Women agriculturists are associated with traditional subsistence and low-yield food crops, poverty, lack of influence, and the inability to adopt crop and husbandry innovations. Even wealthy and innovative women farm managers, however, experience bias in the receipt of agricultural services. It is presumed erroneously that what information women might need about crop production will be communicated to them either by their husbands, other males, or informally by other women. The situation is most critical for women who become heads of household and/or are managers of farms. The absence (usually through death or migration) of an adult resident male in the household cancels the presence of a link between the extension agent and the woman who runs her own farm. In some cases, widows of former cooperative members are contacted by extension agents, but others, such as women farm managers, are likely to be excluded from the mainstream of agricultural delivery services. In some regions of Kenya, for example, where one-third of all farms are managed by women, extension agents have expressed candidly their preference for dealing with farms jointly managed by men and women or managed by men alone.

Underlying the basic inequity in service delivery are the assumptions among extension workers that (1) all households are intact and are headed by resident males; (2) men are the main agricultural productive agents and are interested and fully involved in farm work; (3) information and benefits derived by men from the delivery system will trickle down to women within the household; and (4) women will necessarily adopt the practices transmitted to them by male kin. Such assumptions are untenable when one considers: (a) the increasing number of farm households with no resident male in which women assume the major responsibility, whether on a permanent or temporary basis, and (b) the resistance among resident males in the household to share information with their women.

Women's Exclusion from Skill Training

The potentially limiting factors that operate to "exclude" or "discourage" women from access to productive skills training have to do with the content of training programs available to them and with related conditions that discourage women from using and/or investing in what limited opportunities there are. These factors can be seen as explicit and implicit exclusion. All are closely interrelated in agricultural planning, design, and implementation processes.

Women's exclusion from technically oriented training programs occurs across regions and independent of international funding. In Africa, where women's major responsibilities for agricultural production and animal husbandry are acknowledged, nonformal rural education programs pertaining to agricultural techniques have managed virtually to exclude women from attendance. This is done often simply by neglecting to consider some of the constraints women face with respect to transportation, freedom of movement, time availability, and level of education. Implicit exclusion in the design and planning of programs occurs when schedules are not modified to reflect women's additional responsibilities. In other cases, women are left out of training programs because of traditional views about the segregation of the sexes. In rural areas, community organizations with exclusively male membership are often selected as locations for training, resulting in de facto exclusion of women. Some cooperative organizations provide training separately for men and women and serve single-sex interests; in others, membership is based on land ownership and may exclude women—particularly those who are divorced, separated, or abandoned—who do not have title or land. The latter restriction hurts women heads of households.

Rural training programs running under the banner of "Small Industry Development Training" teach women sewing, embroidery, and handicrafts—all low in marketability and profit—instead of carpentry, electrical wiring, bicycle/home appliance repair, machine maintenance, animal husbandry, accounting, etc. This is very frustrating for women who desire or need to compete effectively in the marketplace; it results in women investing their time and resources unproductively, and leads planners to believe that training for women is not cost effective.

An Agenda for Action

Several lines of action need to be pursued to rectify effectively the gender inequities identified, all of which run counter to the letter and spirit of the *Convention on the Elimination of All Forms of Discrimination Against Women* (see articles 2, 3, and 6.1). To do so will necessitate bold movement on the part of national governments and strong commitment on the part of national and international development organizations.

It is vital that the link between development processes and human rights in the Third World be emphasized, and that the right to benefit from socio-economic development be acknowledged as a human rights issue. New legal mechanisms are needed to ensure that women's socio-economic rights be protected by international human rights instruments. Without such protection, it is difficult to mobilize resources for women effectively and/or invoke human rights standards in the face of discriminatory action against women. In this regard, it is vital that women in Africa organize and that they use those legal resources that promote the development of self-reliance, participatory decision making, and grassroots power. Women's organizations exist in Africa, but most are not the kind through which women can become empowered to use law or to effect changes in the law to secure their rights. Meanwhile, legislative efforts to reform rural bureaucracies have not been favorable to guaranteeing women access to productive resources.

The kinds of action to be taken on behalf of women touch at the cornerstones of agrarian reform law, family law, rural employment strategy, and a deeply embedded patriarchal mentality. Hence, it is imperative that women find mechanisms for addressing such issues as a whole through self-reliant, participatory, collective initiatives, in which these issues are addressed as fundamental to women's human rights. Two principal issues need to be raised in this respect: (1) Do existing activist movements in Africa have the potential to address the question of women's legal access to productive resources *within the context of the human rights framework?* Is there a need to create new movements and, if so, how can women be encouraged to do so? and (2) What is the best way to mobilize the social consciousness of international funding agencies involved in development support programs to extend support primarily to those movements that encourage women to develop self-reliance, that promote participatory decision making, and that lay groundwork for the empowerment of grassroots groups?

Notes

1. *Nairobi Forward Looking Strategies for the Advancement of Women,* adopted by the World Conference to Review and Appraise the Achievements of the UN Decade for Women, Nairobi, Kenya, 1985. Endorsed by the General Assembly, Resolution 40/108, 13 December 1985.

2. I am indebted to Charlotte Bunch for her insightful discussion of the difficulty of connecting women's rights to human rights: "Women's Rights as Human Rights: Toward a Re-Vision of Human Rights," *Human Rights Quarterly* 12 (1990):586–498.

3. For an excellent review of the legal aspects of women's restricted access to land, see Lisa Bennet, "Legal Status of Rural Women: A Review of Those Aspects of Legal Status Which Limit the Economic Participation of Women in Rural Development," Food and Agricultural Organization, Human Resource Institutions and Agrarian Reform Division, Rome (1979).

4. F.M. Bettles, "Women's Access to Agricultural Extension Services in Botswana," paper prepared for the Ford Foundation Workshop on Women in Agricultural Production in Eastern and Southern Africa, Nairobi, Kenya, April 9–11, 1980.

This essay is a revised version of "Need for Legal Resources to Ensure Women's Access to Productive Resources: The Problem of the Woman-Headed Household in African Society," which appeared in *Third World Legal Studies-1987: The Application of Law and Development Theory: Some Case Studies* (Indiana: Valparaiso Univ. School of Law).

27

Contextualizing Gender and Labor: Class, Ethnicity, and Global Politics in the Yemeni Socio-Economy

Huda A. Seif

Literature on feminist theory, labor, and gender relations often classifies gender roles in broad terms: "Women in the Third World" (or "Women in Islam" or "Women in Arab Society"), conjuring up a "Third World" or an "Arab World" that is a monolithic "other," with a single undifferentiated history, timeless and fixed, and a single set of experiences common to all women. But a close contextual look at different locales shows the reductiveness of such categories—the complexity, multiplicity, and variability of any given place and time, and any gender role in that place and time. For those who recognize the necessity of going beyond the male/female duality (in which all differentials are reduced to gender difference), it is crucial to recognize the innumerable variables that shape a woman's life and work, among them environment (rural, urban); class, race, and ethnicity; the global politics of the historical moment. Any argument for the protection of women's economic rights—even if such protection were at the international level—would have to be flexible enough to respond to these particular conditions. To use broad categorizations in explaining the place of gender (and the gendering of labor) in a given socio-economy—to perceive those categorizations as static and resistant to reform—is to renounce the possibility of change.

While it is part of my argument that geographical and historical conditions are unique, that argument is applicable globally. But I would like to focus my discussion of the variables that may determine gender roles in the economy by using the example of Yemen, basing this on my fieldwork there and my general knowledge of the country.[1] In Yemen, neither Islam as a religion nor the "Moslem World" as a common historic entity is the determinant of women's status. Gender relations and gender roles have been neither static nor immune to global influences, nor has the hegemony of "patriarchy" alone been culpable in the subordination of women. Within Yemeni society, gender relations and gender roles have been shaped and reshaped by other factors, internal and external, including severe labor migration, nationalist struggles against local religio-political autocratic rulers and colonial powers, radical social revolutions, and hierarchical caste-like social classes.[2]

What it means to be a woman in Yemen is more heavily influenced by class, race, and labor role than by biological difference. Marginalization is the result not only of attitudes toward gender but also toward class and race as they have been configured through Yemen's history. (My own biography offers an instance of the complexity of the interrelationships among the legacy of migration, gender, class, ethnicity, and race.) The products of Yemeni fathers and African (Ethiopian, Sudanese, or, as in my case, Somali) mothers belong to an entirely different class known as *Muwalliddin,* i.e., hybrids, and this brings a different kind of discrimination and, necessarily, a radically different sense of what it is to be female.

I. Agents of Change

Since the 1960s, external and internal factors have converged to create an ambiance that allows gender roles and gender relations to be renegotiated, integrating women into the newly established Yemeni nations. Radical social, political, and economic changes have coalesced to challenge deeply ingrained prejudices against women, especially in urban areas, where women were previously confined to the domestic sphere. The transformations experienced by women in Yemen have less in common with those of women in other "Moslem" societies and more with those of women in societies that share a recent history of revolutionary social and economic upheavals with concomitant nations of nation-state building.

The most important catalysts for change in social relations in Yemen have been two social revolutions and the emigration of nearly one-third of Yemen's male work force to neighboring oil-producing countries, especially Saudi Arabia. The outflow, which affected urban and rural areas, was so severe that the region's economy became heavily dependent on the remittances the migrant workers sent back from abroad, and at the same time created a vacuum in the labor force. Meanwhile, the two revolutions brought accelerated social reforms in the process of constructing "modern" nation-states. In Yemen, a combination of factors—revolutionary ideas, a shortage in the labor force, and remittances from labor migration—came together as agents of change that reshaped Yemeni society. Central to this reshaping were practical considerations and ideological commitments stemming from various sources. On the one hand, as was the case in the North, large male labor migration called for the recognition of women as a labor force, making inevitable their integration into the process of economic "development" in the postrevolutionary era. On the other hand, as was the case in the South, redefining gender roles and relations was part of a revolutionary ideological commitment to eradicating social inequalities.

II. Two Revolutions and "The Woman Question"

Such redefinition of gender roles was not monolithic; it varied in urban and rural areas and, most significantly, in South and North Yemen. The division of Yemen into two distinct political entities started to take shape around the 1800s under the influence of British and Ottoman colonial expansions in the region. As a result, the southern part of Yemen was seized by the British in 1839 and eventually became a directly ruled British colony. The region remained under British rule until it gained its independence through the 1967 revolution, and subsequently the People's Democratic Republic of Yemen (PDRY) was established in South Yemen. In a similar fashion, the northern part of Yemen fell to the Ottoman Empire in the 1870s and remained partially ruled throughout the early 1900s by the Ottomans along with a local theocratic regime, the Zaidi Imamat. Following the withdrawal of the Ottomans by the end of World War I, Northern Yemen was claimed in its entirety by this Imamat, with its despotic, isolationist regime. A succesful overthrow of the Imamat came, after several failed attempts in the revolution of 1962, when the Yemen Arab Republic was established, ending a millennium of theocracy. Over the years, however, the northern Republic moved toward conservatism, whereas the regime in South Yemen moved from an identification with Arab nationalism to a more radical identification with worldwide socialist and Marxist revolutionary movements such as those of Cuba and Ethiopia. The two Yemen states remained separate until their unification in 1990.

Recent events such as the May 1994 civil war threaten this unification. The economic aftermath in both states was chaotic, and severe male labor migration to the neighboring oil-producing countries as well as to the United States and Britain increased dramatically. Many of the repercussions of this war on women's status remain to be seen.

The postrevolutionary states' efforts to transform gender roles and relations showed a consciousness of the roots of their eeconomic problems. Mobilizing women as a potential labor force outside the home became important to the process of building both a "civil society" and a "modern" revolutionary nation-state amidst the economic turmoil and civil dissatisfaction with earlier regimes. Training women and educating both male and female children became urgent national priorities.

III. After the Revolution: Redefining Gender Roles

A. South Yemen

Reform in gender relations and roles in postrevolutionary South Yemen has to be seen, then, as part of a broader socialist social and economic reform that targeted not just gender inequalities but also class-related inequities. The establishment of a revolutionary state after independence was accompanied not only by massive labor migration but also by general economic underdevelopment. Central to economic and social transformations were socialist ideological commitments that tried to restructure all existing social relations. Measures to improve women's status and their subsequent integration into the work force were seen as inevitable parts of the nation's welfare.[3] Various institutions such as education and health services, training programs, and campaigns against adult illiteracy were launched. These programs were considered prerequisites for tapping the new nation's potential. Constitutional articles were drawn up to advance women's social status by guaranteeing them full rights and access to education, employment, training in technical skills, paid maternity leave, and day care for working mothers. "The state," declared Article 36 of the Constitution, "shall ensure equal rights for men and women in all fields of life. . . . It shall also work for the creation of circumstances that will enable women to combine participation in productive and social work with their role within the family sphere."[4]

By demanding of men and women equal responsibility, the socialist government challenged the preexisting gender-based division of labor that confined urban women to the private sphere of the home. In theory, women were guaranteed full economic, political and social rights, and were provided an equal opportunity to pursue these rights. These rights were accompanied by radical reforms in family law—the locus of gender asymmetries in Yemen. The 1974 Family Law challenged many of these asymmetries by making polygynous marriages virtually unattainable, by outlawing attempts to force women into unwanted marriages, and by prohibiting female child marriage. The most radical reforms were the ones that stipulated equal rights in marriage contracts and responsibilities in family affairs, divorce decisions, and settlements, while at the same time giving women full rights to the custody of children in the case of divorce.

Although one should not underestimate the emancipatory potential of these constitutional rights and Family Laws, for many women much of this potential was never realized. In practice, the power of the patriarchal family overrode the realization of such rights. Although many of the reforms were pushed forward by women who operated within the state apparatus, they cannot be taken as the work of a feminist-nationalist alliance against the patriarchal family structure. They were, rather, part of an ongoing nationalist struggle against colonialism and imperialism. Revolutionary idioms and discourses of nationalist struggle against global inequality kept the ferment alive and allowed the socialist state's reforms to be seen as neither disloyal to Islamic culture nor as a threat to the patriarchal family, and therefore they obtained allegiance from both women and men.

B. North Yemen

The integration of women into the public arena in the postrevolutionary state came mainly as a practical response to social and economic crises following the defeat of the Imamat. The enthusiasm with which gender equality was promoted, however, had far less to do with ideological commitments than with practical considerations. Indeed, it was the growth of state offices and institutions (educational facilities, hospitals in urban areas) amidst a culture of male migration that quickly directed the government's attention to the need to mobilize the labor potential of the female population. One could argue that there was an element of desire to integrate women for the sake of "modernism,"[5] which required changes in perceptions about women's presence in the previously exclusively male public sphere. Unlike in southern Yemen, with its socialist ideology, there were no radical commitments or overall projects for changing asymmetries in Family Law so as to redress gender inequalities. Instead, double-edged discourses defining the importance of women's participation in the nationalist struggle became the state's devices for changing popular attitudes toward women's work outside the house. These discourses were meant to allow the state apparatus to mobilize female labor while at the same time keeping a cozy relationship with conservative groups.

Idioms such as *Al-Nisa' Shaqa'iq Al Rijal* (women are the sisters of men) and *Al-Jannah Taht-Aqdam Al-Ummahat* (heavens are located under mothers' feet), which are Islamic in origin, were revived and popularized to "normalize" women's employment and their presence in urban public domains such as government offices, schools, and hospitals, while at the same time emphasizing women's domesticity and their roles as homemakers and mothers. These idioms were usually accompanied by huge posters showing women wearing headcovers in public areas and holding a child by the hand, presumably taking the child to school before going to work. The revival of the term *Shaqa-iq* (sisters) is an interesting one because it refers to full sisters, unlike *Ukht,* which also means "sister" but could also mean "half-sister." *Shaqa'iq* and its plural masculine form (*Ashiqa,* brothers) connote "fullness" or "wholeness" in sisterhood and brotherhood, and hence became gender equalizers. The use of such idioms may sound banal to the outsider, but within the Yemeni context their revival and ritualistic deployment were ingenious devices for mobilizing women into the labor force outside the house while simultaneously perpetuating "traditional" role expectations and norms of conduct.

To speak in such terms, then, became a way of launching a nationalistic discourse that demanded equal participation from men and women in the construction of a "modern" nation-state while at the same invoking Islamic sentiments and historicity through the recalling of centuries-old Islamic idioms. Many educated women negotiated their way to positions in the General People's Congress, on town councils, in trade unions, and other governing bodies. The National Charter, "*Al-Mithaq Al-Watani,*" drawn up in 1982, gave women equal political rights.

Not all integration meant better conditions for women. Many women were absorbed into employment sectors, such as government-owned food and textile factories, that required few skills and paid very little. Nevertheless, the advantages of such integration far outweighed the disadvantages. Apart from generating income that gave women autonomy, working outside the house also provided opportunities to interact with women's networks and associations that provided social support as well as marriage and personal crisis counseling.

IV. The Unified Yemen and the Position of Women

Since the unification of the two Yemens in 1990, several major developments have directly or indirectly affected gender roles and women's place in the work force. The Gulf War and the expulsion of Yemeni immigrants from Kuwait and Saudi Arabia cut remittances from abroad as well as aid from Persian Gulf countries. This led to the disruption of several programs that integrated women into the larger society. High inflation and unemployment have soared, making many women unable to live on low-paying jobs. Furthermore, with the presence of the returned male migrants, many of whom have acquired several skills abroad, competition in job markets has grown fiercer, making women with lesser skills less appealing in the labor market.

This puts constraints on progress in women's political representation. Today only two of the 302 members of the General People's Congress are female, although women occupy many important lower-level political posts. The disturbing growth of the fundamentalist party, which argues strongly against women's emancipation, is not unrelated to the recent surge in the unemployment rate. Not surprisingly, this party has recently received support from the neighboring Saudis, becoming the vehicle through which the Saudi kingdom exerts its influences on the course of Yemeni politics. Women, however, retain the full right to vote, and may well continue using this power to keep the conservative party at bay, as they did in the 1993 major elections.[6]

V. Migration, Remittances, Commodities: Gender Roles and Labor in Rural Yemen

If revolutionary ferment was minimal in most rural areas of Yemen, these areas were nevertheless affected by the region's history of emigration.[7] It was estimated that more than 1 million out of a total population of 5 million in the North emigrated during the 1970s oil boom in the Gulf countries.[8] The impact of this emigration on Yemen's rural population (which makes up a large percent of the total population) was devastating. Huge remittances were helpful in offsetting economic losses caused by the ensuing labor shortages and concomitant decreases in food production, but labor shortages could not be remedied by mobilizing rural women (as was done in the urban sector), because women were already major contributors to the agricultural labor force. The situation did, however, encourage a wider participation of women in the informal sector, both as wage earners in the fields and as entrepreneurs in the weekly food markets. Such large-scale male labor migration was thus effective in introducing women to new domains, allowing them to take on previously male roles such as decision making in both family and financial matters.

Given the hierarchical class structure of Yemeni society, the social changes that resulted were hardly uniform. In the Tihama region, for instance, where land ownership tends to be largely concentrated in the hands of a few tribal (*quaba'il*) groups, the repercussions varied depending on the social and economic status of the group affected by the changes. In rural Yemen, a dualistic male-female division does not pervade the entire society, since class is an everyday life differential that subdivides gender categories more radically. To be a woman of the dominant social classes, such as the *Qaba'il* or the *Sada,* is not the same as to be a woman from the *Akhdam* or *'Abid,* subordinate caste-like classes. Gender identities in this context are constructed and consolidated not by sex difference but (mainly) through genealogies and activities in everyday life. The fact that the lower caste-like classes are people of African descent conflates the class system with race, thus making gender categories in Yemen meaningless if they are not contextualized within class and race categories and ideologies. Despite the postrevolutionary state's constitutional guarantee of equal rights to all "citizens," the class system and the disenfranchisement of the minority lower classes still prevail in rural Yemen, where privileges and access to economic activities are allocated accordingly.

The effects of male labor migration, then, meant different things for different classes. For poor women with little land, the absence of a husband meant an added workload of arduous chores such as fetching water and wood for cooking. For large landowners, the absence of husband or brothers provided women with the opportunity to become decision makers in matters previously beyond their domain, such as supervising production and marketing produce, hiring a labor force to help work the land, and making overall daily decisions.[9]

Remittances from abroad meant that some large landowners either let their fields lie fallow or engaged exclusively in trade, completely abandoning the use of land for food production. For those dependent on selling their labor for seasonal sharecropping, such decisions often meant the loss of livelihood and the fragmentation of families through migration to urban centers such as Al-Hodeidah, Ta'iz, and San'a'. As wage laborers they became (at best) part of the informally employed sector, which is not regulated by the government. Often, women and children stayed behind to work for daily wages or small shares of crop production with small landholders or to participate in marketing activities. A large number of the women who sell in rural markets today were once agricultural wage laborers.

Unlike *Akhdam* and *'Abid* men, who are categorically confined to menial and manual labor, *Akhdam* and *'Abid* women have more flexibility and hence participate in different—though mostly devalued—activities.[10] When husbands migrate to urban areas, either for economic reasons or to protest their social status, *Akhdam* and *'Abid* woman may stay behind and become wage laborers or join the households of higher status families to work as *Khaddama* (servants). This may involve assisting women of the household in doing activities (such as the weekly marketing of agricultural products) that require mobility and in which women of higher status are not allowed to engage.

The indifferent social attitudes toward *Akhdam* and *'Abid* women and the absence of cultural "expectations" that they remain "chaste" allow them to engage vigorously in outdoor activities. This involves interaction, such as sharing market space, with men from higher strata, who are usually the only ones who can conduct business transactions requiring contracts. In most rural markets, transactions and contracts—business or otherwise—fall into informal categories where there is no governmental regulation. It is taken for granted that tribal names ensure adherence to agreements, and hence these names become facilitators of exchange relations in the absence of any written legal documents. Since it is assumed that persons of lower status lack a "name" to protect or honor, they are excluded from participation in transactions requiring contracts.

Taking advantage of the ambivalence of their social position (which allows them relative freedom), many women from the subordinate groups actively participate in market activities that do not involve the use of contracts, such as selling homemade goods or agricultural products on a small scale (either independently or for women of higher strata). Processed foodstuffs, biscuits, candies, chocolates, Coca Cola, and assorted fruit juices from the neighboring oil-producing countries are creeping into local markets, where they compete with the home-made goods and agricultural products these women sell in the weekly and small daily markets.

But commodities from Saudi Arabia, such as ready-made dresses and colorful costume jewelry, threaten the livelihood of subordinate groups, which produce handmade clothing and jewelry locally. These changes in commodity flow, production, and marketing are pushing women further, leading them to migrate to urban shanty towns, where they live in destitute conditions. Usually, there are two options for such women; at best, they become employed by the municipality as street sweepers, a job people from no other Yemeni social group would engage in, or they become beggars and live off the streets. Either way, they live at the margins of the larger society.

The presence of women in urban streets who do not adhere to any dress code does not seem to draw the attention of male passersby, since these women are *Akhdam;* nor, for that matter, are these women perceived as invading male domains when they beg or sweep the streets uncovered. Even the rising fundamentalist party, which would send women in urban areas back to the domestic domain, seems little con-cerned with these women's activities, legal or illegal.

Conclusion

Akhdam and *'Abid* women appear to be exempt from observing some of the dominant social and sexual mores, such as chastity, honor, dignity, and modesty. To ask whether this is liberation or marginaliza-tion would be reductive, just as it would be reductive to ask whether the revolution meant better or worse conditions for women in the workforce. As we have seen, the rhetoric of liberation and the ostensi-bly equal employment rights it brings does not always mean better conditions for women. It may mean that women in upper classes are granted greater opportunities, only to have those opportunities taken away when the needs of the state change. It may mean that women in some lower classes are forced to do double duty without real com-pensation. It may mean that women in the lowest of classes gain a mobility and freedom of dress that make them only more invisible. Women's rights have historically been granted only in the service of the state's need for workers, and only as a result of shifts in extrana-tional conditions.

For gender roles in the socio-economy to change in a more fundamental way—for women of all classes and races to be granted truly
equal rights—a more profound change in cultural perceptions and
attitudes has to take place. I argued at the beginning of this paper
that gender and labor roles have more to do with demands of global
economic factors, class, ethnicity, race, and the "national economy"
than with broad categories like "the Third World," "the Middle East,"
or "Islam." I am skeptical about the efficacy of using even broader
categories—women universally, for instance—in an effort to impose
changes on a global scale. International legislation on women's rights
is incapable of accounting for and responding to the deeply entrenched
particularities of a given culture, its class demarcations, and its inter-
woven socio-economic complexities of inequalities and prejudices. And
yet to recognize the radical historical changes that a country like Yemen
has undergone over the course of the last half-century is to recognize
the possibility of change: in the kinds of work women do, in the ways
they are made to feel about that work, in their participation in the
improvement of the conditions of their lives.

Notes

1. For a comparative analysis of the processes of social changes related to women's
   participation in the labor force in many Arab societies, see Hijab (1988).

2. My approach to the dynamics of gender in Yemen is not new, but rather is
   reminiscent of approaches taken by other anthropologists who place local transformations into a larger global context. I am referring here to M.E. Combs-Schilling,
   in *Sacred Performances: Islam, Sexuality and Sacrifice* and Roger Lancaster, in
   Life Is Hard, who place their analyses of sexuality and gender relations in a context
   of global transformations. I use the word "gender" to refer to those categorizations
   of social subjects that draw not just on sexual difference but also on the ways in
   which such difference constructs perceptions about the nature of social relations.
   As such, gender is a function of culture, class, and ideology. This definition is an
   amalgam of Strathern's and de Lauretis's definitions of gender.

3. An account of the first ten years of state policies toward women's work in South
   Yemen is well detailed in Molyneux (1982).

4. Article 36 of the 1978 Constitutional Law of the former South Yemen.

5. Such ideas were not independent from the influences that the late Egyptian leader,
   Jamal Abdulnasser, had on the North Yemeni revolutionary elites. Abdulnasser
   denounced categorically any form of "backwardness," of which he considered
   veiling to be an example.

6. The May 1990 Constitution of the unified Yemen defines rights pertaining to
   gender equalities in a broad manner. Articles 9 and 21 state, respectively, "The
   state shall guarantee to all its *citizens* equal political, economic, social and cultural

opportunities" and "Every *citizen* has the right to seek and practice the job he chooses within the law" (*emphasis added*).

7. The following ethnographic account is based mainly on my own fieldwork in Northern Yemen during the past eight years.

8. Manfred Wenner points out that in 1975, the estimates of total migrants including those who migrated to Western Europe and North America were about 1.23 million (1991).

9. For a detailed analysis of the impact of male migration on women's roles, see Adra (1983).

10. For a succinct account and analysis of social and economic activities pertaining to social inequalities, see Walters (1987).

Works Cited

Adra, Najwa. 1983. "The Impact of Male Migration on Women's Roles in Agriculture in the Yemen Arab Republic." Paper prepared for Inter-Country Experts Meeting on Women In Food Production. Amman, Jordan, October 22–26, 1983, p. 33.

Combs-Schilling, E.M. 1989. *Sacred Performances: Islam, Sexuality and Sacrifice.* New York: Columbia Univ. Press.

de Lauretis, Teresa. 1987. *Technologies of Gender: Essays on Theory, Film and Fiction.* Bloomington: Indiana Univ. Press.

Hijab, Nadia. 1988. *Womanpower* Cambridge: Cambridge Univ. Press.

Lancaster, Roger N. 1992. *Life Is Hard.* Berkeley and Los Angeles: Univ. of California Press.

Molyneux, Maxine. 1982. *State Policies and the Position of Women Workers in The People's Democratic Republic of Yemen,* 1967–77. Geneva, ILO.

Strathern, Marilyn. 1988. *The Gender of the Gift.* Berkeley and Los Angeles: Univ. of California Press.

Walters, Delores. 1987. "Social Inequality in the Yemen Arab Republic." Unpublished Ph.D. dissertation, New York University.

Wenner, Manfred. 1991. *The Yemen Arab Republic.* Boulder, CO: Westview.

28

Women's Rights and the Right to Development

Rhoda E. Howard

Women and Development

This paper discusses potential incompatibilities between women's rights and the right to development in sub-Saharan Africa. Capitalist development undermines the status of African women, putting control of the national economy into elite male hands and control of the family into the hands of its male members. Women's rights cannot be realized without changes in the political and ideological, as well as the economic, spheres. Recent preoccupation with the economic dimension of African women's status deflects analytical attention from these other crucial realms. The task of achieving women's rights is not synonymous with the task of "integrating women into development"; the latter requires more efficient use of female labor power, while the former requires political empowerment of women.

Women have the same human rights as men. The international consensus on human rights is represented by the 1948 *Universal Declaration of Human Rights,* which outlaws discrimination based on sex. Most African states have agreed in principle to this document, and many African constitutions make specific reference to it. In 1979, the United Nations proclaimed the *Convention on the Elimination of All Forms of Discrimination Against Women* (CEDAW), which specifically addresses the rights of women in development, and in particular the rights of rural women, acknowledging "the significant roles which rural women play in the economic survival of their families" (Article 14[1]). Women are promised *inter alia* the right "to have access to agricultural credit and loans, marketing facilities, appropriate technol-

301

ogy and equal treatment in land and agrarian reform as well as in land resettlement schemes" (Article 14[g]). These concerns reflect the detrimental effects of capitalist development on women; in Africa, these include loss of land, discriminatory denial of credit, and discrimination in land resettlement schemes.

By December 31, 1992, CEDAW had been ratified or signed by thirty-eight African governments, but the establishment of these rights for women has been predominantly a normative exercise. United Nations Declarations are not necessarily enforceable in law; nevertheless, they do provide a standard of comparison by which activists who favor rights for women can assess their governments, especially when governments have ratified these documents or included reference to them in their own constitutions.

Strengthening these norms, an African *Charter on Human and Peoples' Rights* was adopted by the Organization of African Unity in 1981 (Hamalengwa, Flinterman, and Dankwa 1988, 5–19). Women's rights are ambiguously addressed in this Charter. Article 2 guarantees rights without discrimination as to sex, but Article 18 stresses the family as the "natural unit and basis of society," and Article 17(3) also mandates that the state should protect "morals and traditional values recognized by the community." Traditional values frequently reflect deeply held ideological beliefs that include an entrenched notion of the moral inferiority of women to men and of the need to subordinate women to men's familial and political authority. Nevertheless, the formal recognition of the equality of women in this Charter provides African women activists with a stronger normative standard than does mere reference to international documents.

If the status of women in Africa is to improve, women's rights must be conceived as far more than an aspect of the right to development. In Africa, the notion of economic development as pure growth has, in general, been rejected. Development is now usually taken to mean some combination of growth, self-reliance, and equitable distribution of resources to all citizens; frequently, political participation is also included as an ingredient of development. This change in conceptualization has been reflected at the United Nations, which, in 1986, approved a *Declaration on the Right to Development.* In this Declaration, development was defined somewhat redundantly as the right of "every human person and all peoples . . . to participate in, contribute to and enjoy economic, social, cultural and political development, in which all human rights and fundamental freedoms can be fully realized."

But despite this broader conceptualization of development, it can be argued that, from the points of view of both African governments and aid donors, the primary criterion of success is still pure growth (Howard 1989). There is a practical reason for this: while in the 1970s growth without development was criticized, in the 1980s and 1990s, development without growth is under even more severe attack. A country cannot sustain equity or self-reliance in a stagnant economy or in one that has negative growth rates, as has, tragically, been the case in many African countries in the 1980s and '90s.

Given that, in practice, the primary criterion of success is still growth, why is so much effort devoted to promotion of the right to development? This effort is part of the larger enterprise of ideological legitimation in which both weak African states and their donor countries are engaged. For African governments, promotion of the right to development indicates concern for the basic needs of ordinary citizens. In the recent past, such promotion was frequently used as justification for ignoring basic civil and political rights in the name of the higher goal of economic progress, although the stress on democratization in Africa that has emerged in the 1990s now undermines this argument. For donor countries, publicly articulated political concern about development helps to mask the more pragmatic reasons for aid, such as trade promotion, employment generation, and political influence in recipient countries.

Thus development and the right to it, both originally proposed as radical counterparts to the preoccupation with growth, have now been incorporated into statist ideologies. Women's rights, like civil and political rights, are in danger of subordination to the development ideology, whose very absorption of all other rights implies their irrelevance. Proponents of the ideal, rights-protective version of development often do not recognize that, in practice, development is a political, frequently a coercive, activity. The international development community of the late twentieth century views development as planned, nonpolitical social change. But human rights standards are necessary precisely because nonpolitical social change is impossible. Women are one among many social groups that frequently suffer severe economic and social dislocation as a result of development plans and projects. "Women in development" (WID), which demanded sensitivity to women's development needs, was originally an idea critical of the effect on women of technocratic, growth-oriented development projects. But increasingly, WID is part of the depoliticized, planned social change that the development establishment in general espouses. The cooptation of WID ideology can be viewed as part of the effort by Western states to satisfy mainstream liberal feminist demands without addressing either structures of inequality or the deep ideological causes of the subordination of women. This is not to say that the adverse effects on women of individual development projects are not noted or that remedies are not attempted. But the assumption of planned, nonpolitical social change still obtains, and the systemic material, political, and ideological biases against women cannot be addressed by project-oriented models of development. WID has become an effi-ciency-oriented goal. Integration of women into development projects now fits nicely into state-centric plans for economic growth, but it is not necessarily true that integrating women into development projects improves their overall status.

A combination of certain strands of feminism and of dependency theory also encourages the absorption of WID ideology into planned depoliticized social change. Dependency theory was originally a critical argument that Africa's poverty is rooted in its dependent integration into the world capitalist system. It is now, however, sometimes used as an excuse to externalize the causes of economic and political abuses in Africa. In this ideological version of dependency theory, Africa is a blameless victim of imperialism. This approach accords well with some strands of the newer literature on human rights, in which Africa is presented as a morally superior continent, rejecting the individualism and selfish acquisitiveness of the West. Similarly, in certain strands of feminist thought, women are presented not only as the blameless vic-tims of male power and authority but also as morally superior persons. This perspective presupposes that women are essentially different from men; they are supposed to be more cooperative, more committed to the family and community, less acquisitive and less interested in power than men. Thus both Africa and women are the innocent victims of Western male acquisitiveness and aggression.

Such essentialist beliefs about differences between men and women fit nicely into the male-dominated African ideology of women's role as guardians of the family and the indigenous culture. Specific griev-ances of African women against both the African state and African men are lost. African women, like Africa in general, become the inno-cent victims of Western imperialism and, like Africa in general, their primary rights-claim is for the right to development. Thus we come full circle: the rights of women *in* development become the right of women *to* development, defined not by them but by the development establishment, both in their own country and without.

To break this circle requires the assertion of women's human rights that are separate from development, possibly against the development establishment, and not necessarily compatible with the development enterprise. The political empowerment of women implies confrontation with men. In practice, "development" frequently means capitalist entrenchment that deprives women of their access to, and control of, land, use-values, and indigenous marketing systems. This process is facilitated by men's political, ideological, and familial domination of women, in Africa as elsewhere. Yet within the development establishment there is little, if any, concern about these noneconomic dimensions of male control over women. Indeed, since one of the important latent objectives of development is to depoliticize social change, there is not likely to be interest in the politicization of gender relations that women's rights require.

Misogyny and the Necessity for Cultural Change

In contemporary Africa, rural women work in both subsistence and cash-crop agriculture, yet men are frequently considered the legal owners of both the land and the income it generates. Urban and industrial jobs are very rarely available to women, and when they are, women are paid far less than men. Most women in the cities earn their living through petty trade or the offer of sexual or other domestic services. They cannot rely on men—whose own employment is usually sporadic and low paid—to support them. Thus the material stakes are high in Africa, and conflict between men and women over resources and jobs can be expected to intensify.

Such conflicts are mediated in legal and political arenas controlled by men. Men in Africa are influenced by, *inter alia,* their traditional cultural beliefs about the proper role of women in society. Thus, to understand why development may not be compatible with women's rights in Africa, one must also analyze the ideological dimension of women's subordinate status.

Rogers (1982) has written that, in Tanzania, "the failure of various development efforts to substantially improve the conditions of rural women's lives can be traced to a refusal to confront the basic structures of gender relations. . . . [T]he object of analysis . . . must be relations between women and men" (26). There is a significant ideological component to women's subordination in sub-Saharan Africa that predates the entry of the colonial powers and is rooted in indigenous norms of appropriate gender-specific behavior. These norms in turn appear to defend on world-ordering dichotomizing concepts that denigrate women (concepts that are not, of course, unique to Africa). "In many African societies, there are ideological oppositions associating women with left rather than right, crooked rather than straight, and a whole host of negative, inferior qualities" (Robertson 1987, 112).

Puberty rituals in Africa frequently teach females to defer to men. In the Rufiji valley in Tanzania the young girl is taught that "on going to her husband she must remain quiet and bear her lot; she must not use words or behavior that would offend him; she must not be stubborn; . . . and [she must] in all ways conduct herself as an obedient subservient wife" (Swantz 1985, 34). Women's fertility arouses very ambiguous emotions. Fertile women are honored, yet in eight of the thirteen indigenous religions surveyed by Kilson, menstruating and pregnant women were considered to be religiously impure (Kilson 1976, 136). Among the Luguru of Tanzania, pubescent girls have been confined to dark huts for one to three years, during which time they are considered sacred but unclean (Brain 1978, 180). Childless women are humiliated: barrenness is grounds for divorce, and barren women are often considered to be victims of witchcraft (Knipp and Cohen 1981, 12).

Thus, in contemporary Africa an ideology of fear and hatred of women can still be found. In Ghana, popular songs include such lyrics as "obey your husband in all respects . . . the glory of a home lies in the woman, and the glory of a woman lies in the husband" (Asante-Darko and van der Geest 1983, 249). In Tanzania popular songs and short stories about women contain themes of "prostitutes preventing men from fulfilling their kinship obligations back home . . . unfaithful wives . . . wayward girls . . . unfortunate and nasty wives who dare to question their husbands' rule over household and checkbook" (Rogers 1982, 39 n. 5).

Women in Africa, as elsewhere, are divided clearly into "good" and "bad." This division is reflected in the belief that all single, unattached women in the cities are prostitutes; in the frequent attempts by governments to expel single women back to rural areas, sometimes with orders to get married; and in physical attacks on urban women (Howard 1986, 194). Touring Yoruba theatre companies in Nigeria have five predominant roles for town women, "the prostitute, the co-wife, the witch, the half human/half animal, and the transvestite" (Strobel 1984, 99). Successful Yoruba businesswomen are often regarded as witches who possess strong psychic powers with which to attack men (Robertson 1987, 112).

Misogyny extends to the indigenous division of labor. It is extremely humiliating for men to do "women's work," even when they have no work of their own; thus one finds the village phenomenon of depressed, unemployed men sitting idle while their wives collect wood, fetch water, care for children, and engage in subsistence cultivation. Among the Mbum of Chad, "men who live alone without wives sometimes prepare their own meals, but because of the shame of doing women's work they cook only inside the house" (O'Laughlin 1974, 305). In Tanzania, "women are apt to assume many jobs once considered to be men's but few men will undertake chores considered women's work" (Mbilinyi 1972, 373).

The misogynistic beliefs found in indigenous African societies have been reinforced by several centuries of foreign influence and colonialism. Both Christian and Islamic traditions preach female subservience and withdrawal from the public sphere. Wealthy Muslim women in Nigeria, for example, retreat into *purdah* (the practice of segregating the sexes by keeping women in seclusion) as a symbol of their husbands' success. This practice is increasingly spreading to the poor; in Kano in the early 1980s, 95 percent of all married Muslim women were in *purdah* (Callaway 1984, 431). Elite women in coastal Tanzania also stayed at home, "enjoying prestige but condemned to silence in the presence of their male superiors and living a life circumscribed by rules and deprived of personal rights" (Swantz 1985, 37).

Where belief systems include the notion that women are untrustworthy and must be subordinate to men, the integration of women into development is a difficult task. As elsewhere, such beliefs characterize both ordinary male householders and elite male decision makers in Africa. But since it is intellectually and ideologically illegitimate for politicians on the world stage to oppose women's rights, members of the elite frequently mask their beliefs. This masking is often done either by accusing Western feminist critics of ideological imperialism or by asserting the necessity of defending African culture. Women are bound up, in many male Africans' eyes, with home, family, and community. Women are expected to preserve culture and tradition while men migrate, move outward, and increasingly assert their individuality (Obbo 1980, 143). Insofar as there is much more fear that women will abandon their culturally prescribed roles than that men will, discriminatory ideologies of the proper place of the two sexes limit women's capacity to take advantage of the new opportunities offered by developing capitalist society.

Women's rights require cultural change in all societies. Respect for cultural differences should not obscure the fact that, in most cultures, women are subordinate to men. If African women are to organize in defense of their own rights, they may well articulate their struggle in ways that differ from those of Western women. But African feminists, like Western feminists, are aware that they must confront the ideological and political, as well as the material, bases of their subordination before they can obtain equal rights with men.

Women's Activism and Rights for Women

In the struggle to organize themselves for political change, African women do have one strong advantage, namely the existence of an international feminist movement and an influential official ideology of women's rights. The international feminist movement will assist in the articulation of specifically feminist demands in Africa. To say this is not to prescribe that African women make the same feminist demands upon the state, development agencies, or male members of their own families that women in the West make. An indigenously articulated African feminism is already evolving as the gender-based economic, ideological, and political blocks to women's participation in the direction of their own, their children's, and their countries' futures are identified more clearly.

African women have one other slight advantage, a heritage of the liberal constitutional models negotiated at independence: unlike Western women, they have not had to struggle to obtain the vote and the right to participate in politics. The existence of military regimes and personalist dictatorships, however, frequently obviates women's (and most men's) political participation in practice. The current round of multiparty political competition has not significantly enhanced women's overall powers, although it has permitted more women to play a role in the formal political sphere.

Until the 1990s, there were very few voluntary organizations in Africa concerned with human rights and even fewer concerned specifically with women's rights. In the last few years, many women's rights organizations have sprung up; women are active participants in the new civil society that is blossoming in sub-Saharan Africa. There are also many other types of women's organizations, some of which may well be interested in human rights even if human rights are not their main focus. These include secret societies of various sorts, market-women's organizations, occupational societies such as prostitutes' organizations, savings and credit societies, church groups, communal labor groups, and female members of "hometown" or ethnic associations (Wipper 1984).

Such organizations ought not to be romanticized; they are subject to the same fissiparous splits as any other organizations. Women are not an undifferentiated social category; like men, they are divided by ethnicity, caste, class, and many other variables. Many African women who engage in politics are not interested in women's rights, instead focusing on their own family, clan, or ethnic claims or safeguarding their own economic privilege. For example, in the 1970s elite women used Kenya's Maendeleo Wa Wanawake organization to further their own political or status-oriented goals (Wipper 1975).

Nevertheless, as part of the contemporary surge of interest in democratization and the establishment of an independent civil society in Africa, women's rights groups have been multiplying. Thus, despite the continent's current economic crisis, African women are now preoccupied with defending their rights and are themselves undertaking social action in defense of those rights. But this requires an agenda separate from that of "development."

The Role of Foreign Aid in African Women's Rights

In Africa, then, development aid can play only a minor role in realizing women's rights. Women's rights, like men's rights, must be wrested from below, and are primarily a matter of internal social change. Even if Africa's position in the world economy were to improve, women would not necessarily benefit. Rather, gendered economic stratification would probably intensify. There is nothing inherent in the development process that impels a parallel promotion and protection of women's rights. Women's rights must be viewed as an objective separate from, and not necessarily compatible with, development.

Given this difficulty, is there then any role for foreign aid in promoting women's rights in Africa at the broad societal level, as opposed to offering a project-oriented approach that attempts to "integrate" women into development where appropriate? There is such a role *if* the aid is clearly intended for women's rights and if it is accepted that such aid might not have any demonstrable development (growth) effect.

If African women are to protect themselves from the intensified gender inequality that capitalist development usually entails, then the main focus of aid directed to women's rights in Africa must be to assist African women in organizing themselves to become effective actors in national politics, especially through the exercise of freedom of speech, press, and association. Such participation is necessary to insure that the development enterprise does not undermine the economic rights women already have and that the ideological and political, as well as the economic, bases of women's subordination are addressed. These participatory freedoms are in their turn dependent upon judicial protection. They are also dependent upon a reasonably high degree of education, which is necessary so that women can articulate their rights-claims both against male members of their own families and against the state. In education, law, and the judiciary, and in safe-guarding freedom of speech, the press, and association, foreign aid can play a role in the empowerment of African women.

With regard to education, what is needed is not more token African women in science or engineering but more in the humanities, social sciences, and law whose primary object of study is gender relations. Better access to knowledge about gender relations in their own societies can empower African women. Further, certain social issues key to the abolition of patriarchy—such as violence against women—are now routinely discussed in Western universities where African women on scholarships might train, whereas in Africa itself the dominant ideology often still denies that such violence exists or that, if it does exist, it is illegitimate.

Aside from education, a rights-focused aid package could assist women to pressure for changes in laws in Africa. Laws do not automatically change social structure, especially when they are improperly enforced or subject to the executive control of the state, but they do have a normative, standard-setting impact. With regard to the key political rights of freedom of speech, the press, and association, there is also room for foreign assistance. Supplies can be purchased and journalists trained to set up or sustain women's newsletters and networks. Organizations specifically interested in acquiring civil and political rights or in struggling for equality with men must be as eligible for assistance as more "development" (i.e., economically)-oriented organizations such as women's agricultural cooperatives.

All of the above suggestions are offered to indicate that foreign aid in the area of women's rights is possible, but it should be expected to have very limited impact on development (read "economic growth") in the short to medium run. Women's newsletters, for example, might focus more on family violence than on development projects. Moreover, in the short to medium run, immediate beneficiaries will more likely be upper- or middle-class African women than poor women. But in the long run, human rights established in principle can be claimed by the less, as well as the more, privileged.

It could be objected that to allocate scarce foreign aid dollars to projects specifically concerned with women's rights is not a sensible strategy, since women are not unanimous in their views of their needs. In Africa as elsewhere, women are influenced by far more than their own gender-based subordination, and in Africa as elsewhere, associations of women who favor traditional ideologies and family-based roles may well emerge. To note these internal disagreements is not, however, to refute the claim that, in the long run, human rights and women's rights benefit even those ostensibly opposed to them. In practice, of course, both Western aid establishments and Western feminist organizations should be guided in their activities in Africa by requests for assistance made by African actors themselves, oriented to projects that African women deem priorities.

The foreign aid measures supported above are not in accord with standard notions of economic development. But that is precisely the point of making them. Protection of women's rights is a separate matter from development. Women's rights are not necessarily a path to what development actually means in practice: that is, state-centric economic growth. Nor is such state-centric economic growth—however benignly camouflaged as concern for self-reliance and equitable distribution—necessarily a path to women's rights.

The ideological pacification of the originally critical feminist concern with women in development has obscured the need for specifically gender-based rights claims against the family, the kin group, and the state in both underdeveloped and developed economies. Women, like men, need civil and political rights in order to make these claims. Democratic action by a free citizenry is the best path to both development and human rights, but the absorption of women's rights into the "women-in-development" ideology may well hinder, not help, the eventual emergence of such democratic actions.

Note

This essay is a radically shortened and somewhat revised version of my "Women's Rights and the Right to Development," which appeared previously in *Human Rights* and Governance in Africa, ed. Ronald Cohen, Goran Hyden, and Winston P. Nagan, pp. 111–38 (Gainesville: Univ. of Florida Press.) I am grateful to the Univ. of Florida Press for permission to reprint it.

Works Cited

Asante-Darko, Nimrod, and Sjaak van der Geest. 1983. "Male Chauvinism: Men and Women in Ghanaian Highlife Songs," *Female and Male in West Africa*. ed. Christine Oppong. London: Allen and Unwin: pp. 242–55.

Brain, James L. 1978. "Symbolic Rebirth: The *Mwali* Rite Among the Luguru of Eastern Tanzania." *Africa* 48 (2):176–88.

Callaway, Barbara J. 1984. "Ambiguous Consequences of the Socialisation and Seclusion of Hausa Women." *Journal of Modern African Studies* 22 (3): 429–50.

Hamalengwa, M., C. Flinterman, and E. V. O. Dankwa. 1988. *The International Law of Human Rights in Africa: Basic Documents and Annotated Bibliography*. Boston: Martinus Nijhoff and United Nations Institute for Training and Research.

Howard, Rhoda E. 1989. "Economic Rights and Foreign Policy." *Human Rights and Development: International Views*, ed. David P. Forsythe. London: Macmillan.

Human Rights in Commonwealth Africa. 1986. Totowa, NJ: Rowman and Littlefield.

Kilson, Marion. 1976. "Women in African Traditional Religions." *Journal of Religion in Africa* 8 (2): 133–43.

Knipp, Margaret M., and Ronald Cohen. 1981. "Women and Change in West Africa: A Synthesis." *Southern Association of Africanists' Bulletin* 9: 7–18.

Mbilinyi, Marjorie J. 1972. "The Status of Women in Tanzania." *Canadian Journal of African Studies* 6 (2): 371–77.

Obbo, Christine. 1980. *African Women: Their Struggle for Economic Independence*. London: Zed.

O'Laughlin, Bridget. 1974. "Mediation of Contradiction: Why Mbum Women Do Not Eat Chicken." *Woman, Culture and Society*, ed. Michelle Zimbalist Rosaldo and Louise Lamphere. Stanford, CA: Stanford Univ. Press: pp. 301–18.

Robertson, Claire. 1987. "Developing Economic Awareness: Changing Perspectives in Studies of African Women, 1976–1985." *Feminist Studies* 13 (1): 97–135.

Rogers, Susan G. 1982. "Efforts Towards Women's Development in Tanzania: Gender Rhetoric vs. Gender Realities." *Women and Politics* 2 (4): 23–41.

Strobel, Margaret. 1984. "Women in Religion and in Secular Ideology." *African Women South of the Sahara*, ed. Margaret Jean Hay and Sharon Stichter. New York: Longman: pp. 87–101.

Swantz, Marta-Liisa. 1985. *Women in Development, A Creative Role Denied: The Case of Tanzania*. New York: St. Martin's.

United Nations. 1987. *Resolutions and Decisions Adopted by The General Assembly During the First Part of Its Forty-First Session, from 16 September to 19 December 1986*. New York: United Nations Press Section, Department of Information, Press Release GA 17463, 12 January 1987.

Wipper, Audrey. 1984. "Women's Voluntary Associations." *African Women South of the Sahara,* ed. Margaret Jean Hay and Sharon Stichter. New York: Longman: pp. 69–85.

"The Maendeleo Wa Wanawake Organization: The Co-optation of Leadership." 1975. *African Studies Review* 18 (3): 99–120.

The Persecuted, The Voiceless

29

Women and the Word: The Silencing of the Feminine

Siobhan Dowd

International PEN (Poets, Playwrights, Editors, Essayists and Novelists), the world's only international association of writers, is dedicated
to fighting censorship wherever and however it occurs. To this end,
the organization's researchers attempt to keep on computer files details
of every writer and journalist in the world who encounters a serious
form of harassment in the course of carrying out her or his profession.
The list of writers is a sad litany of assaults on freedom of expression
worldwide, containing information about people who have been ostra-
cized, banned, sacked, confined to their homes or towns, imprisoned,
tortured, tormented with death threats, and murdered. PEN's list is
proof, if ever proof were needed, that writing can be quite literally a
fatal occupation.

In the early 1990s, PEN's list typically contained up to nine hundred
cases of people around the world who have been victimized for what
they have written. Of these, only about one-seventeenth of them were
women. One of the questions asked most frequently regarding the list
of imperilled writers and journalists is why there are so few women.
Some people assume that PEN's research is not comprehensive enough;
that perhaps, through no immediate fault of any of the researchers,
PEN is simply failing to discover, let alone do anything about, the
many courageous women writers who have been silenced. Others conclude that there are fewer female than male writers in the world, and
that the list simply reflects this fact.

Both theories contain some elements of truth. Women *are* being
silenced every minute of the day, and their names do not appear on
the PEN list. Usually, these women are not silenced by jailers, assassins,

or official censors—the methods of censorship of which the PEN list *does* take account. A different mechanism is responsible for keeping even more women than men silenced on a day-to-day basis. The fact that the work of undeniably fewer female than male writers is known around the world is a direct reflection of this mechanism: For every man in the world who has not learned to write, there are at least two women.[1]

Illiteracy has never been regarded, traditionally, as a mechanism of censorship. It is a fact, however, that many of the world's women are deprived of the ability to read and write, and thus of the ability to reach beyond or even learn about events outside of their immediate sphere. International literacy rates yield interesting discoveries.[2] For example, literacy rates are generally shown to be lower in francophone African countries than in their anglophone neighbors, and in South Korea, where the illiteracy rate is a modest 3 percent, the female/male breakdown is 6.5 percent for women as against 1 percent for men—one of the highest differentials anywhere. Guatemala's official literacy rates indicate that 53 percent of women as against 37 percent of men are illiterate. However, activists among Guatemala's indigenous population (which accounts for some 65 percent, possibly even 75 percent, of the whole population) estimate that in reality 80–90 percent of indigenous women are illiterate. Further, figures in some countries may count those unable to read or write in any language, where in other countries they count those unable to read or write in the official language. In any configuration, however, literacy figures indicate a disturbing discrepancy between the sexes, as is shown in the following table:

Country	Illiteracy Rates (% of total population)	
	Women	Men
Brazil	20	17
China	32	16
Saudi Arabia	52	27
Guatemala	53	37
Iran	56	36
Senegal	80	48
Nepal	87	62
Sudan	88	57

Of great concern is the extent to which illiteracy is aggravated or deliberately perpetuated by governments whose hold on the reins of power depends on keeping silenced and powerless a majority underclass. One obvious motivation for maintaining such an underclass is that the illiterate usually do not vote. In Guatemala, where the indigenous population has the right to vote, many indigenous people who live in rural communities do not read newspapers, may not understand how elections work, and have no one to assist them in filling out ballots, and so are not likely (or even able) to vote. The resulting de facto disenfranchisement means that a large portion of the electorate is unable to exercise its most basic civil right, and thus has no role in determining how the country should be governed.

An illiterate underclass is attractive to autocratic rule for other reasons. Although they may have access to local radio stations (and, in Guatemala, these play an increasingly important role in servicing the needs of indigenous communities), the illiterate have no access to print media. While some socially conscious members of the literate class champion the cause of the illiterate, such actions can prove dangerous. Myrna Mack, a noted social anthropologist whose writings were instrumental in focusing world attention on the massacres, displacement, and torture of members of indigenous communities in Guatemala's highlands at the hands of the Guatemalan military, was murdered on September 11, 1990 by two men who stabbed her seventeen times as she left her office at the Association for the Advancement of the Social Sciences in Guatemala. Her colleagues have no doubt that her brutal murder was directly related to her commitment to being a voice for the voiceless.

Foreign aid is often aimed at development programs that teach literacy in rural communities, but, as many studies have shown, such aid is often diverted and ends up in the pockets of government officials or heads of states.[3] A global study is urgently needed to investigate diversion of aid money, but it is obvious that when such diversion takes place it serves a dual purpose: not only does it line the pockets of the leadership, but it helps to strengthen their position as leaders by depriving the poorer population of the programs it needs to improve its lot. Aid money is not the only source of funds thus diverted: often, a nation's entire gross national product is squandered similarly. This means that both national leaders and community customs may be complicitous in the effective censorship of women.

If illiteracy is the single most common method of silencing the female half of society, equally worthy of examination is the freedom with which the literate portion of the female population expresses itself. If, for argument's sake, one happens to be one of the 25 percent of women in Togo who has learned the basics of reading and writing, does that mean that one also has the necessary skills and opportunities to work on a top newspaper, or even a local community newsletter—if such a thing even exists? Could one string together enough sentences to make a short story? In between pregnancies, breastfeeding, shopping, working the fields, farming, and cleaning, can one find time to write a feature article or novel? A Kenyan publisher attributes the fact that he receives very few manuscripts written by women to lack of education and spare time, noting that many women, in addition to full responsibility for running the home, hold full-time jobs.[4]

The problem does not apply solely to women from developing countries. A well-known woman writer who lives in the United States, the mother of two young children, says, "I *know* why I can't write great books—I keep being interrupted." She was referring to the demands of her two young children. Many people assume that writing, which on the face of it can be done in the home as easily as anywhere else, is the ideal pursuit for the wife and mother. But the concentration and sustained attention writing requires demands an environment free of interruption and distraction. Men who write in the home are frequently accorded insulation from the rest of the household. All too often, women are not given or do not insist upon the same. It may be hard enough for them to insist upon the shared childcare responsibilities that would free them to write.

If women from the North have such difficulty making space in their lives to write, women of the South, who frequently live in circumstances of far greater exigency, have little hope, even if they are literate, of succeeding. Most women employed by the world's newspapers work in clerical positions, not on editorial teams. Those who do work as journalists and editors usually have little chance of being promoted to positions of prominence. Considering, then, how few women have the means or opportunity to make their views heard, it should come as little surprise that there are only fifty women in PEN's list of imprisoned writers.

Yet another factor explaining the disparity between women and men on the PEN list is that women who have the courage to speak out may be brutally targeted by their countries' male leadership. While men who are arrested frequently face beatings, sleep deprivation, starvation, and other methods of torture, women face all these threats as well as one of the worst forms of torture: sexual humiliation and rape.

This additional component makes the prospect of arrest all the more terrifying for women.

Women may further silence themselves because imprisonment would put their families at risk. What, they may wonder, would become of their elderly relatives and young children while they are being detained for having expressed their political views? For many women the dilemma is acute: Although they would like to do something about the injustices they see around them, they feel that their first duty must be toward their families. It comes as little surprise that, of the fifty women on PEN's list, the vast majority are single or have families who have long since grown up and left home. There are, or course, those who have been victimized despite the fact that they have families who rely on them. Martha Kumsa, a journalist of Oromo origin in Ethiopia, was held from 1980 to 1988 without charge or trial despite the fact that she was raising four young children on her own and breastfeeding the youngest at the time of her arrest. But most of those who would risk their lives are reluctant to risk those of their children or elderly relatives.

Those who, like the prize-winning Cuban poet Maria Elena Cruz Varela, do speak out pay a heavy price. After becoming active in an opposition group, Cruz was expelled by the Writers' Union and labeled in the official press as a CIA agent. When a foreign journalist asked how she felt about the risks she was taking, she replied, "Between a terrifying end and terror without end, I choose the former."[5] Her fears proved justified: On November 19, 1991, a mob of demonstrators (who, it is believed, had been hired by the government) broke into her home, dragged her by her hair down four flights of stairs, beat her, and stuffed her writings into her mouth. Two days later she was arrested and served eighteen months in prison for "defamation" and "illegal association." The symbolism of the incident, in which Cruz's attackers tried to gag her with her own words, is highly unusual, but perhaps sent a particularly powerful (and, importantly, nonverbal) message to women who dare to speak out: If you speak out, the very words you have produced will be part of the punishment which you have called upon yourself.

Alaida Foppa, one of Guatemala's great poets, was abducted by the military in 1980 and was never seen alive again. Foppa's words are especially moving because they acknowledge her special relationship with the written word, which is both precious and dangerous:

> *Poets always speak to someone . . .*
> *but in my dark retreat*

I bear poetry
like a secret disease,
a hidden,
illicit fruit.

Foppa was sixty-two years old and the mother of five grown children when she disappeared. A respected art critic, producer of a radio program called *Women's Forum,* and the cofounder of *FEM,* Latin America's first feminist journal, Foppa had returned from self-imposed exile in Mexico to see her ailing mother a few weeks after having conducted a series of radio interviews in which Quiché women had testified to the brutal killings carried out by the Guatemalan military. The resulting documentary was broadcast the week she disappeared.

Tang Min is a Chinese writer of fiction whose articles on government-enforced artificially induced miscarriage (the euphemism for "abortion" in Chinese), which Tang charged was used to control and degrade women, caused controversy in her country. Eventually, after publishing a short story based on her experiences in the village where she was sent to work as an "educated youth" during the Cultural Revolution, Tang was prosecuted and convicted of libel. Although the judge who sentenced her noted that the facts of her story were true, Tang spent a year in prison. At the time of her arrest, she was pregnant. She had a miscarriage soon afterwards.

On the island of Sri Lanka, perhaps as many as 75,000 people have lost their lives as a result of ethnic conflict between the Tamils and the Sinhalese. Thiagarajah Selvanithy was a student at Jaffna University, where she cofounded the feminist magazine, *Tholi.* Selvi, as she was known to friends, was an outspoken critic (in both writing and conversation) of the Liberation Tigers of Tamil Eelam (or Tamil Tigers), who are believed to be responsible for her arrest on August 30, 1991. At the time of her arrest, Selvi was producing two plays about the role of Sri Lankan women in the search for peace. As of May 1994, she was still in custody.

One of Bangladesh's most famous writers, Taslima Nasrin, a poet, novelist, and journalist, was threatened with death in September 1993 by the Council of Soldiers of Islam, a Muslim fundamentalist group. The call for Nasrin's execution was a response to articles in which she criticized certain fundamentalist policies toward women, including violent punishment by what she terms "extremist interpreters of Islamic law." Her novel, *Lajja (Shame,)* which told the story of a Hindu family persecuted by Muslims after the destruction of the Ayodhya Mosque in India, was banned by the government. Although the Bangladeshi government supplied her with twenty-four–hour protection, it had earlier confiscated her passport, leaving her with no way to leave the country to escape the danger. Nasrin's passport was finally returned to her in April 1994, after an International Campaign had been mounted on her behalf.

These are just a few of the women who have paid a heavy price for the decision to speak out for human rights. There are many more. Women may be silenced behind prison bars or by censors' blue pencils, but more often they are silenced by being deprived of the skills they need in order to be heard in the first place. It is perhaps impossible to assess what loss society sustains by the silencing of women. However, it is often in those societies in which women's views on public issues are most slighted that the most harrowing problems occur. Taslima Nasrin eloquently expresses the tragedy of this situation:

> But I will not be silenced. Everywhere I look I see women being mistreated, and their oppression justified in the name of religion. Is it not my moral responsibility to protest? Some men would keep women in chains—veiled, illiterate and in the kitchen. There are 60 million women in my country. Not more than fifteen percent of them can read and write. How can Bangladesh become a modern country and find its place in the world when it is dragged backward by reactionary attitudes toward half its people?[6]

Notes

1. This is a rough approximation based on country by country literacy statistics, which have been supplied by the *UNESCO Statistical Year Book 1990.*

2. Available statistics should be taken as a rough guide only; all too often, government studies, which may be manipulated for political purposes, are the sole sources of figures on literacy.

3. The U.S.-based Fund for Free Expression's report, *Off Limits—Censorship and Corruption* (New York: Human Rights Watch, July 1991), has documented clearly the ways in which such officials then punish those who try to expose them.

4. See the PEN mission to Kenya report, *"The Rhetoric of Repression"* (New York: PEN American Center, April 1992).

5. Ana E. Santiago, "Cuban Dissident Writer Says She Walks 'Razor's Edge,' " *Miami Herald.* August 8, 1991.

6. Taslima Nasrin, "Sentenced to Death" (op-ed) *New York Times,* November 30, 1993.

30

Discrimination and the Tolerance of Difference: International Lesbian Human Rights

Julie Dorf
Gloria Careaga Pérez

In 1993 in the United States, Sharon Bottoms lost custody of her two–year-old child after the judge in the case deemed her an unfit mother because she is a lesbian.[1] In Brazil, a seventeen–year-old girl was expelled from her high school for kissing another girl, and twenty-nine–year-old Alice Dias do Amaral was brutally murdered by her lover's brothers after they found out about their sister's lesbianism.[2] In Meghrai, India, Gita Darji and Kishora Shah hung themselves from a ceiling fan in 1989 after their families attempted to force them apart.[3] In 1991, Irene Petropoulou, the lesbian editor of the Greek lesbian and gay magazine *AMPHI,* was sentenced to five months in prison and fined 50,000 drachma for publishing "indecent materials."[4] These are just a few examples of the ways in which lesbians are denied their basic human rights.

In many countries, female homosexual practice is considered unnatural, abnormal, immoral, horrifying, criminal, or worse. This perception has led governments not only to restrict lesbian rights but also to produce criminal statutes that legitimize the brutal persecution of lesbians, persecution that (unlike that of many other groups) governments hardly feel obliged to defend.[5] Lesbians are denied their basic right to freedom from torture, punitive psychiatry, arbitrary arrest, and incarceration, their right to have children, and even their basic right to life with hardly a word of public remonstrance.

But discriminatory legislation and other repressive measures are not the only threats to the human rights of people who engage in same-sex sexual relations. Homosexuals are subjected to the vigilance of a heterosexist society that stigmatizes that which it perceives as questioning, exceeding, or subverting social limitations.[6] Societies are, in a sense, threatened less by the fact of same-sex individuals having erotic sexual relations than they are by homosexuality's capacity to acknowledge and demonstrate the existence of different lifestyles, different ways of liberating oneself from established norms.[7] Homosexuality's power to shake up or even rupture the social structure inspires the implementation of measures intended to marginalize those who manifest "differentness."

When repression against lesbians is in direct violation of human rights norms, as traditionally defined by the *Universal Declaration of Human Rights* and the international conventions and treaties, state actors often justify themselves by arguing that exceptional means may be necessary to achieve legitimate social ends, and that such means themselves protect the "human rights" of others, or protect the "public morals and values" of society. States sometimes invoke the cultural relativist argument, claiming that the regulation of sexual norms (like other cultural practices—clitoridectomy, the marriage of young girls, or the sex trade, for instance) is a fundamental part of the local culture, and that the imposition of "homosexual rights" is a Western (neoimperialist) concept. For example, at the United Nations Conference on Human Rights in Vienna in 1993, representatives of the government of Singapore mentioned gay rights in a laundry list of "Western-imposed" rights that should not be considered universal.[8] Indeed, state officials often claim that homosexuality simply does not exist in their culture, and so the extension of rights to homosexuals is meaningless for them. For example one of India's top scientists, Dr. A.S. Paintal, insists that "homosexuality is alien to Indian culture—there is no homosexuality in India because there is a law against it."[9]

The Oppression of Lesbians Parallels the Oppression of Gay Men

Some persecution of lesbians, then, is not dissimilar to that of gay men, and some countries have legal statutes that are parallel for male and female homosexuality. In Iran, for example, where a lesbian or gay man is to be executed after the fourth sexual offense,[10] the only legal distinction between gay men and lesbians is that sodomy is defined as uniquely male and lesbianism is defined as "the homosexuality of women by genitals."[11] In countries like Romania and Nicaragua, antihomosexuality laws that apply equally to women and men have been introduced as recently as 1993. For instance, Article 205 of Nicaragua's penal code (passed in 1992) mandates one to three years' imprisonment for "anyone who induces, promotes, propagandizes or practices sex among persons of the same sex in a scandalous manner."[12] In Romania, a recently proposed antihomosexuality law calls for prison terms of up to five years.[13]

Even in countries in which criminal laws against lesbians are minimal or nonexistent, laws against gay male sex may at times be used against lesbians, as in the case of cogender political organizing. In 1991 and 1992, for example, authorities in Leningrad used the existence of the (male) antisodomy law as justification for rejecting the official registration of two lesbian and gay organizations whose members, the ruling stated, would be gathering with the intention to commit criminal acts.[14] More recently, in the United States, local citizens in Mississippi attempted to use the state's sodomy law to force two lesbians from their land, and the United States Attorney General had to intervene.[15] The vague language of laws in some countries (Russia and Romania, for instance) leaves them open to broad interpretation, which means broad applicability and dangerously low standards of evidence for prosecution.

But if legal interpretation is not used for controlling homosexual men and women, psychological interpretation may be—the punitive psychiatry that is a frequent form of persecution and that is used more often against lesbians than against gay men. In Russia, where lesbianism is considered a form of schizophrenia, accepted medical treatment includes the administration of mind-altering medications.[16] According to reports from the former Soviet Union, it is not unusual for the discovery (say, by a teacher or parent) of lesbian relationships between very young women to result in institutionalization.[17] Following hospitalization or institutionalization, lesbians or gay men have been forced to remain registered with local psychiatric institutions and can be barred from certain jobs or other civic privileges, such as holding a driver's license.[18] Other reports of forced "medical treatment" include the use of electroshock and "aversion" therapy in China.[19]

Violence against sexual minorities, rampant in many parts of Latin America, North America, and Eastern Europe, is often condoned or tolerated by government authorities and in some cases even perpetrated by government actors. In either case, perpetrators of violence against lesbians, bisexuals, gay men, and transvestites are rarely held accountable for their crimes. It is even rarer that sexual minorities are specifically protected from hate crimes. Reports of inadequate judicial responses to the murders of lesbians, gay men, and transvestites have come from numerous countries including Russia, Mexico, Colombia, Ecuador, and Peru.[20] Other forms of violence against sexual minorities are so common that, for example, the U.S. government has had to formally legislate the gathering of statistics on antigay hate crimes.[21]

Many laws effectively criminalize not only the sexual behavior of gay men and lesbians but also their association, speech, and use of the press. The denial of freedom of expression can take both legal and extralegal forms and include closing down lesbian and gay publications, denial of registration to political and social groups, harassment of lesbian and gay (formal or informal) organizations, and the closing of such organizations' meeting places. Raids on bars frequented by lesbians or gay men are common practice in many countries. Following a raid on a lesbian bar in Peru in 1987, approximately seventy women were detained and questioned by police, then forced out of the station after the official curfew. The raid was staged in cooperation with a local television station so that, as the women were forced one by one out of a small door, the entire country was able to watch the incident on the evening news. As a result, many women lost their jobs, some are reported to have been beaten by their families, and at least two were raped on their way home from the police station.[22]

In the area of family rights, discrimination against lesbians can often parallel discrimination against gay men. The *Universal Declaration of [Heterosexual] Human Rights* guarantees all persons the right to marry and found a family, and calls the family a "fundamental group unit of society which is entitled to protection by society and the State."[23] But in no country are homosexual couples afforded the same benefits as married heterosexual couples. Although partnership laws in Norway and Denmark do provide many legal and economic benefits for gay male and lesbian couples, and some cities in the United States provide some partnership benefits to lesbian and gay city employees, these are the exceptions, and most lesbian and gay male partnerships do not enjoy the economic, social, cultural, and legal rights and benefits afforded heterosexual partnerships.

Such discrimination has numerous adverse affects on the lives of lesbians and gay men. Couples are separated and families broken apart because immigration laws do not recognize lesbian and gay family units. In medical emergency and guardianship situations, lesbians and gay men may be denied access to their partners by biological family members, hospital officials, or the state. For example, in the United States, Karen Thompson had to fight for years to gain custody of her quadriplegic partner, Sharon Kowalski, after Kowalski's disabling car accident in 1988.[24]

Lesbians and gay men are frequently denied the right to have children through alternative insemination and adoption or to retain custody of biological children. In most countries, adoption is restricted to heterosexual couples, and lesbians are even denied the right to adopt their partners' biological offspring. As governmental regulation becomes more common in response to the need to test sperm for HIV infection, lesbians have increasingly restricted access to insemination: In France and the United Kingdom, legislation has been introduced that would restrict official (HIV-tested) insemination to heterosexual married women.[25]

Women in many countries report having lost, or battled desperately to retain, custody of their children because of their sexual orientation. In 1993, in the United States, a judge denied Sharon Bottoms custody of her child, referring to the state of Virginia's criminal sodomy statute and calling Bottoms an "unfit parent" because she is a lesbian. In Argentina, Mariela Elcira Muoz, the mother of three children, lost custody of her adopted twins because it became known that she is a (male-to-female) transsexual.[26] A recent study of lesbian visibility in the former European Community, now European Union, revealed that lesbians are engaged in custody battles in seven member states.[27]

In such areas as employment, housing, and education, discrimination against lesbians is often parallel to that against gay men. But many violations of lesbians' human rights (such as rape, sexual abuse, and unfair and inadequate trials) are gender based and are therefore less similar to those of gay men than to those of women in general. In some cultures (in Mexico, for example), sexual harassment and assault are practiced with the intention of forcing lesbians to "recognize" our "repressed" desire to be dominated by men, and to "set us on the road to rehabilitation."

If there exist far more laws that criminalize gay male sex than lesbian sex, this should not be interpreted as a reflection of greater tolerance of lesbianism, but rather of the inherent sexism of lawmakers and their failure to understand female sexuality. An underlying assumption of many sex crime laws is that "sex" necessarily involves a man's penis. Intimate acts between two women, then, do not constitute sex. In a related area, consent laws often set higher ages for gay male sex than for heterosexual sex, while lesbian sex may not be addressed at all. While such an omission may indeed be to our benefit, the absence of antilesbian laws means merely that governments—failing formally to recognize lesbianism—use other laws to incarcerate lesbians. In many countries, more general laws—such as those regulating decency and public morality or loitering and hooliganism—are invoked against lesbians.[28]

Lesbian-specific human rights abuses (those that are different from the abuses of either heterosexual women's or gay men's human rights) are sometimes entirely concealed by cultural expectations or by more ordinary abuses of women. If girls are married in their early teens, as they are in many countries, or forced into the sex trade—two forms of coercion that are often interchangeable—they have no opportunity to discover their sexual identity. But far more pervasive is the general repression of lesbian sexual identity. This is often internalized in a self-directed homophobia, and can lead to extreme isolation, passive acceptance of persecution, exile, and even suicide. Here, it is impossible to separate the political from the personal. In the words of a young lesbian from India:

> In our case, the most traumatic thing is that the world is neither aware of our "marriage" or of the end. I had to face the pain more or less by myself. Many other women like me must have attempted suicide and even succumbed to such attempts. How many more must undergo this trauma silently? And why?

In Russia, there are reports of young women committing themselves to psychiatric institutions to be "cured" of this "personality disturbance" because they have never met another lesbian and have no reference to lesbianism as anything other than an illness.

Bowing to cultural pressure to keep the private and public spheres separate, lesbians sometimes find it easier to deny their sexual identity. This denial means not only lies, secrecy, and destruction—the wounding of integrity and the negation of identity—but also a kind of collaboration in the preservation of the status quo. This means becoming an agent of one's own oppression, adopting heterosexist values for survival. When we accede to these values, we accede to the cultural requirements that have been fundamental to the oppression of not only lesbians but of women in general: submission to authority and its institutions, denial of female sexuality (and especially of its pleasures), necessary maternity, the role of being mere vessels for the continuation of the male species.

Even within the feminist movement, lesbians are often marginalized, isolated, and limited by homophobic assumptions. There are very few countries in the world that can claim that their feminist movement's institutions, structures, and theories have openly welcomed lesbian activists or included lesbian issues. In fact, lesbians who come out in their feminist communities often face painful struggles for legitimacy. For example, at the first "Forum for Independent Women" in the former Soviet Union, organizers tried to bar lesbian workshops because they feared repercussions against the conference, which had been threatened with closure by the authorities because of lesbian participation. Lesbian activists from the Philippines, Thailand, India, Germany, the United States, United Kingdom, Italy, and elsewhere have reported serious barriers to advancing lesbian rights within their feminist movements.

It is necessary, then, to question the "universal" female identity that is imagined by mainstream feminism, just as it is necessary to question the "universality" of international human rights doctrines and institutions and even of the "universality" of a lesbian and gay identity. It is necessary not only for the sake of lesbians but also for the sake of the women's human rights movement in general, for limiting the rights of lesbians has repercussions for all women and, indeed, for all of society. The right to decide the fate of one's own body, for instance, is a primary issue for women of any sexual orientation. Inversely, the positive assertion of lesbian rights may be beneficial for women in general. By establishing supportive communities of single women who, living and working with other women, share energy and lend support, lesbians help legitimate a more tolerant attitude not only toward sexual preference but also toward sexuality itself, offering a model for identifying sexuality not primarily with procreation but rather with pleasure. If, in the midst of the struggle for recognition and social reform, the lesbian finds herself in the position of being discriminated against as both a woman and a homosexual, she may also find herself in a position of opening pathways for both women's and lesbians' human rights.

Significant progress has been made in traditional human rights institutions, particularly in international human rights non-governmental organizations (NGOs) and in inter-governmental organizations. Three lesbian and gay groups were accredited to attend the 1993 World Conference on Human Rights in Vienna, and a few lesbians and gay men participated in the plenary sessions and in the main committee, finding widespread support among NGOs. Visible lesbian organizing took place within the NGO sections of the Vienna conference and involved lesbians from many parts of the world, which has resulted in organized, visible participation in the preparatory process for the

1995 UN Conference on Women in Beijing.[29] In July 1993, the Economic and Social Council of the United Nations (ECOSOC) approved the admission of the International Lesbian and Gay Association (ILGA), an umbrella organization of more than 350 gay and lesbian groups from more than 50 countries, as an NGO with consultative status to the ECOSOC. Surprisingly, ILGA obtained votes from countries in which homosexuality is legal but in which lesbians and gay men are frequently persecuted, and even from countries in which homosexuality is illegal. While there was heated debate about ILGA's admission, twenty-two countries voted for admission, seventeen abstained, and only four voted against.

If lesbians and gay men constitute, at present, no more than a plurality of fragmented groups that enjoy little, if any, recognition as political subjects, international bodies may now be one way to offer a forum for the education of officials who can make public the violation of homosexual rights internationally. Homophobic governments may be singled out at the UN as human rights violators. For example, after Irene Petropolou was sentenced for publication of "indecent materials," a petition was submitted to the UN, and the UNESCO executive board took a formal decision on her case. Similarly, the Tasmanian Gay and Lesbian Support Group received a significant response from the United Nations Human Rights Committee in a challenge to their country's antigay law. In its historic reply, the Committee called on the Australian government to repeal the law in the state of Tasmania because it violated the fundamental right to privacy as guaranteed in the *International Covenant on Civil and Political Rights*. Although the Tasmanian government has yet to comply, this is the first time the United Nations has clearly stated that homosexual sex is protected by an international treaty. Other intergovernmental bodies such as the European Court of Human Rights and the Council of Europe have made significant decisions and resolutions regarding the rights of homosexuals.[30] Three legal cases in particular, *Dudgeon v. Great Britain, Norris v. Ireland,* and *Modinos v. Cyprus,* have proved the influence and importance of an intergovernmental body, which can have the power to force the repeal the antisodomy laws in those countries.

Other regional and intergovernmental institutions—the Inter-American Commission on Human Rights, the Organization of American States, the Organization of African Unity, and the UN Committee on the Elimination of Discrimination Against Women, among others— could be challenged to uphold the rights and freedoms of lesbians and gay men. In the non-governmental sphere, Amnesty International's recognition of individuals incarcerated for homosexuality as prisoners of conscience constitutes another important step toward the formal demand for the respect of homosexual rights. Amnesty's recently published report, *Breaking the Silence: Human Rights Violations Based on Sexual Orientation,* discusses execution, torture, imprisonment, and other forms of persecution of lesbians and gay men.

Ever more countries in the world are beginning to recognize lesbians and gay men as a particular social group deserving of the rights of asylum. Australia, Canada, Germany, the Netherlands, Sweden, Finland, Denmark, the United States, and New Zealand have all granted asylum or humanitarian refugee status to individuals because of their fear of persecution as lesbians or gay men. Even the United Nations High Commissioner for Refugees has submitted supporting evidence that there is a need for viewing lesbians and gay men as a particular social group that is the target of persecution.

More important, the grassroots lesbian movements that exist all over the world are taking steps locally to fight oppression based on sexual identity and practice. In places as varied as Mexico, Ecuador, Russia, and Taiwan, lesbian organizations are a growing part of social movements. A gay rights group in Japan, OCCUR, won a discrimination case against the City of Tokyo because the group was barred from using public educational facilities to hold its meetings. In Malaysia, Pink Triangle (the only lesbian and gay rights organization in a Muslim-dominated country) has so far been allowed to exist and function, publicly distributing condoms and safer-sex materials. A Latin American and Caribbean-wide network of lesbians and lesbian groups has been holding regular meetings for over seven years; a similar network of Asian lesbians has been meeting annually for four years. Newly emerging lesbian groups in the former Soviet Union and Eastern European countries are creating correspondence networks and other publications to help develop a sense of community. Openly lesbian politicians have run for and been elected to political office in Mexico, the United States, and the Netherlands, among other countries.

While these steps are significant, they are only a beginning. If we are to construct a feminist international law that adequately addresses the human rights of all women—that allows for the construction of identities different from the norm—it must respond far more fully to the abuse of lesbians. It must confront not only abuses similar to those directed at gay men or at women in general but also abuses of the kind uniquely directed at lesbians. Lesbians must now seek not merely tolerance but full acceptance: a full part in the construction of both a feminist international law and a genuine declaration of human rights for all people.

Notes

1. "Appeal Goes Well for Virginia Lesbian Mom," *Washington Blade,* February 18, 1994, 25 (7): 1. "Grandmother Appealing Decision Giving Lesbian Custody of Son," *New York Times,* June 26, 1994, p. 22. In April 1993, a Virginia judge awarded custody of Bottoms's son to Bottoms's mother, P. Kay Bottoms. In June 1994, that ruling was reversed by the Virginia Court of Appeals. P. Kay Bottoms has decided to appeal that decision, and so retains custody of the child at least until the case is heard (or rejected) by the Virginia Supreme Court.

2. OPOVO (newsletter), Rio de Janeiro, Brazil, January 30, 1991, p. 1.

3. "Macabre Suicide," *India Today,* 1989.

4. *Action Alert* (International Gay and Lesbian Human Rights Commission publication), February 1992; "Greek Editor Sentenced to 5 Months in Prison," *Gay and Lesbian Times* (London) March, 1992.

5. We use the term "lesbian" throughout this paper for the contemporary practice of female homosexuality, although we acknowledge that some, perhaps many, women identify otherwise and construct their sexualities differently; the limitations of this paper prohibit a more respectful, sophisticated approach. We have also chosen to focus on the human rights abuses afforded women who engage in sexual acts with other women or who identify as such women rather than explore a more accurate description of their local sexualities.

6. Xabier Lizárraga, "El Clóset Roto: Distancias y Desencuentros," *Del Otro Lado, La Revista Gay de México y América Latina* no. 2–3 (1992): 16.

7. Patria Jiménez and Gloria Careaga, "Homosexualidad y Sociedad. Juicios y Prejuicios," Speech presented at the Panel Sexualidad y Democracia en Tiempos de Elecciones (Sexuality and Democracy at Election Time), Coordinadora Feminista del Distrito Federal, Mexico 1991.

8. A similar debate ensued about the Human Freedom Index developed by the United National Development Programme, which included discrimination against homosexuals as an indicator.

9. *Less than Gay,* p. 42.

10. *Islamic Penal Law,* approved by the Islamic Consultancy Parliament, 1991.

11. Ibid., article 127.

12. *Washington Post,* August 6, 1992, A34.

13. *Romanian Senate Penal Code Modification of Article 200,* February 3, 1994.

14. "Tchaikovsky Fund Denied Registration," *Baltiski Vremya,* no. 48 (December 11, 1990); "Gays Versus Leningrad City Council," *Nash Dom,* March 1, 1991.

15. Sheila Walsh, "Mississippi Harassment, Residents Using Sodomy Law to Oust Women from Home," *Washington Blade,* December 10, 1992.

16. Gessen, *The Rights of Lesbians and Gay Men in the Russian Federation,* a report of the International Gay and Lesbian Human Rights Commission, 1994, p. 17.

17. Ibid

18. Ibid., p. 18.

19. "China Using Electrodes to 'Cure' Homosexuals," *New York Times,* January 29, 1990.

20. *Action Alerts* (International Gay and Lesbian Human Rights Commission publication), February 1992; March 1992; September 1992; December 1992.

21. *Hate Crimes Statistics Act,* April 1990.

22. Videotape of news from Peruvian television channel 2 (June 1987), and reports by Peruvian lesbian survivors of the incident.

23. *Universal Declaration of Human Rights,* article 16.

24. Karen Thompson and Julie Andrzyeski, "Why Can't Sharon Kowalski Come Home?" *Spinsters/Aunt Lute,* 1988.

25. British journalist Diane Bailey to the International Gay and Lesbian Human Rights Commission, June 1, 1993.

26. Information from Sociedad de Integración Gay-Lesbica Argentina.

27. Vibeke Nissen and Inge-Lise Paulsen, *Lesbian Visibility,* a pilot study carried out for the Commission of the European Communities by the National Danish Association of Gays and Lesbians and the International Lesbian and Gay Association, November 1993, pp. 88–90.

28. It is not unreasonable to believe that violent attacks and extrajudicial killings of transvestites are based in both misogynist and homophobic attitudes. Although this is not a "lesbian-specific" issue, it is important to take note of violations in which both gender and sexual orientation are clearly at issue. In Brazil, Grupo Gay de Bahia has documented over 1,200 murders of lesbians, gay men, and transvestites. Newspaper coverage of the murders of transvestites is by far the most sensational, sometimes including descriptions of lingerie worn by victims, and even showing pictures the victims' mutilated and dismembered bodies.

29. Such participation has occurred, for instance, in the Asian and Latin American prepcom meetings.

30. Evert van der Veen, Aart Hendriks, and Astrid Mattijssen, "Lesbian and Gay Rights in Europe: Homosexuality and the Law," *The Third Pink Book,* (Buffalo, NY: Prometheus, 1993).

31

Human Rights for Refugee and Displaced Women

Sima Wali

> The traditional system for protecting refugees has come dangerously close to breaking down. The massive number of people on the move has weakened international solidarity and endangered, at times seriously, the time-honored tradition of granting asylum to those in genuine need of protection.
> —United Nations High Commissioner for Refugees (1993)

As this paper is being written, a rising wave of xenophobia in Europe and the example of the forced return of Haitians to zones of civil strife are threatening the safety of refugees, immigrants, and asylum seekers. Disturbing as these events are, they are but two manifestations of a cataclysmic tide of conflict that is erupting throughout the world and threatening basic human rights. As states allow their political and economic fears to override humanitarian concerns, the rights to protection and asylum come under serious attack. The world community's pledge that the atrocities of the Holocaust will "never again" be allowed to happen rings hollow, as torture and widespread human rights violations are committed. In place of outrage, "compassion fatigue" appears to have become the normal response to grotesque inhumanity.

The post-Cold War world is witnessing a forced displacement of humanity unprecedented in number and scope. Major political and religious upheavals and ethnic warfare and genocide, spawned in the wake of the Cold War's end, have created a refugee and displaced population totaling some 45 million people. In the past decade, the number of refugees fleeing their countries to seek asylum elsewhere has risen dramatically, from fewer than 10 million to more than 18 million (and this number does not even include those internally displaced within the borders of their homelands). In the coming decade, the world community has mandated that the United Nations High Commissioner for Refugees (UNHCR) return between 7 and 10 million refugees to their home countries—countries no safer now than they were when the returnees fled.[1]

An estimated 75 percent of all refugees and displaced persons are female.[2] As women, as girls, as mothers, they bear the brunt of the most egregious forms of human rights abuse, from mass rape and torture to the sale of children. Human rights abuses against refugee women and girls do not abate upon flight or resettlement in neighboring countries. Vietnamese, Cambodian, and Laotian refugee women, for example, often fall prey to pirates who have been known to rape girls as young as 9 and women over 50. Often, female refugees are subjected to multiple rapes, including vicious gang rapes, and are held apart from their families in inhumane conditions that are isolated from international refugee practitioners and advocates.

For women and girls who join the international flow of forced migration, the failure of political and legal institutions to uphold their human rights at all stages of flight and in countries of first asylum is particularly devastating. Because of the world's view of state sovereignty, those displaced within their own countries have no legal recourse outside of their own governments, which often sanction or ignore the violence perpetrated against them. The UNHCR, the major international entity entrusted with the protection of refugees, is dependent upon individual states to carry out its mandate and, as a consequence, is incapable of protecting refugees adequately.

The narrow and strictly legal definition of refugee protection used by the UNHCR is a contributing factor to the difficult task of ensuring physical protection. For example, states that ostensibly accept the principle of *refoulement,* which bars them from forcibly returning asylum seekers to zones of conflict, nevertheless do so with impunity because they define *refoulement* so narrowly. Despite valiant efforts by the UNHCR, such flagrant violations occur frequently, as in cases of the forced return of women and children across mine-infested lands by resistance movements and by governments determined to curb the flow of "illegal" migrants into their territories.

This paper discusses the principal issues and problems affecting human rights for refugee and displaced women and children and delineates the steps international bodies and relief organizations must take to address them. Developing adequate standards of human rights and assisting the victims of civil, economic, and political strife are not only necessary for meeting the challenges posed by a dramatically changing world order, they are a political imperative. Demographics, gender equity, and humanitarian considerations all dictate that attention be paid to those made most vulnerable to socio-political unrest.

Trauma and Its Impact on Refugee and Displaced Women

Several years ago, in preparation for the UN Decade for Women, Refugee Women in Development (RefWID), Inc., an international non-profit agency based in Washington, DC, initiated a dialogue with refugee and undocumented women in the United States, asking them to identify issues of primary concern to themselves and their families. Overwhelmingly, they responded by expressing concern for their physical and legal protection. For the first time, refugee women addressed publicly the issue of sexual abuse as a human rights issue.

Since then, RefWID has documented the following extreme forms of violence against refugee women: multiple and/or gang rapes; abduction, trafficking, and forced prostitution of women and children; the demand for sexual favors in exchange for food, relief assistance, and documentation; sale of children; domestic violence; murder; torture; and forced childbearing. Forced childbearing is prevalent in refugee and displaced communities, as refugee women—though malnourished and heavily traumatized—are expected to bear numerous children to replenish male populations lost to war.

In the camps in countries of first asylum, the priority accorded to male refugees means that the needs of rape victims, widows, and the handicapped are especially ignored because men do not regard them as valuable or because they lack male protection. Women are often malnourished because they receive less food than male refugees. They are last to receive medical attention, and are among the first to starve to death. Rendered voiceless and powerless, refugee and displaced women are expected to defer their needs to the political and religious dictates of the male hierarchy. Unfortunately, Western and international assistance agencies often perpetuate this condition by granting food, relief assistance, and protection to male refugees. Often, they justify such action by claiming it "culturally appropriate."

Women are often used as pawns in political bargaining or in settling scores with the enemy in their countries of origin or in countries of asylum. For example, the rape of Vietnamese women in front of family members is a strategy used by Thai forces to humiliate the victims; tradition dictates that the shame of a rape victim is ineradicable, even in death. The perpetrators of sexual violence against refugee women fleeing across borders are frequently those assigned to protect them—border and military guards and camp administrators—as well as refugee men.

The crisis faced by victims of sexual assault is intensified because community attitudes often mean blaming the victim and subjecting her to forced isolation from her community and even her immediate family. In an effort to "cleanse" themselves of members who threaten their "virtue," many communities sanction "honor" killings of rape victims. In such a hostile environment, female victims of sexual assault fear reporting such violations and usually choose to remain silent.

An analysis of the profound psychological impact of the more serious human rights violations suffered by women is beyond the scope of this paper. However, a survey of Southeast Asian refugee women conducted by RefWID revealed that the lingering trauma can destroy the victims' abilities to rebuild their shattered lives. Many who work with refugee and displaced people make the common mistake of focusing primarily on the traumatic experience rather than on the political, economic, and social institutions that cause and perpetuate the injustice, causing victims to relive the experience and doing nothing to alleviate self-blame.

It is imperative to reformulate the issue of violence against female war victims in the broader societal and institutional context, shifting the blame from the refugee victim to the underlying causes of the victimization of women. RefWID is a major advocate for the recognition that violence against refugee, returnee, and displaced Third World women and girls constitutes a human rights abuse. It has long called for the recognition of the rape of these women and girls as a form of political torture.

Prioritizing Refugee and Displaced Women in the Human Rights Agenda

It has become clear over the past decade that refugee and displaced women and girls are no longer by-products of war but, rather, specific objects of warfare. Reports of ethnic breeding in former Yugoslavia and frequent attacks against women in Muslim societies are merely two cases in point. Female refugees and their dependents are the most vulnerable of all groups not only to violence but also to hunger and hunger-related illnesses. The suffering they endure over the loss of home and forced migration is made even more unbearable by inequitable food distribution, which exacts a high toll in infant and maternal deaths among refugee populations. Afghan war widows in refugee camps in Pakistan relate that they have gone hungry for weeks at a time because of food distribution systems that favor men.[3]

The time has come when women and their families' right to survival must become a priority, and society and its institutions must take serious measures to develop appropriate policies and programs that can protect women from the effects of persecution, civil strife, and war. Human rights agendas and guidelines must focus on the rights of refugee, displaced, and returnee women.

No Mechanisms to Address Abuse

The world community lacks the mechanisms necessary to combat the systematic genocide of Third World women, which has reached the scale of a global holocaust. This is evident even at the most basic level of information sharing in connection with violence. Despite the pervasiveness of brutality against female refugees, little information is passed on to policy makers. What violence is reported is typically viewed as isolated transgressions that bear little or no relationship to larger political and conflict-resolution issues.

At both national and international levels, only crises seem to drive the work done in the fields of violence and human rights abuses against refugee and displaced populations. Practitioners and decision makers have focused on short-term priorities instead of developing long-range strategies to cope with the deeper causes of social and economic inequity. Female refugees often have contact only with refugee counselors of victims of torture, and it is crucial, therefore, that such counselors assume a significant role in developing and implementing protection programs and policies.

Institutions that Perpetuate Human Rights Abuses Against Refugee and Displaced Women

Those close to refugee populations can offer a clear view of human rights abuses to counter claims for traditional norms and religious

practices fostered by patriarchal social institutions, which often camou-
flage gross human rights violations. Since such abuse has profound
political and economic roots, it is no coincidence that culture serves
to perpetuate it. The resurgence of religious revivalist movements,
especially in the Islamic world, has fueled the zeal to use "cultural"
and sociopolitical practices as weapons to keep Muslim women isolated and cut off from resources. At the same time, the practice of
veiling and the consequent denial of education and training to female
refugees have had a crippling impact on the countless women widowed
as a result of war, women who have no traditional family support to
fall back on. Not surprisingly, statistics reveal that the numbers of
Muslim refugee and displaced women are dramatically increasing the
feminization of migration and poverty.

In the United States in recent years, terrorist attacks allegedly insti-
gated by "Muslim fundamentalists" precipitated a revision of immigration law. The fervor to appease xenophobes, however, has resulted in
legislation that could severely restrict the claims of genuine asylum
seekers. Women and human rights advocates are concerned about the
impact of the revised law on women seeking asylum from gender-
based persecution, and are pressuring the United States to recognize
gender-based kinds of persecution.

Proposals for Change

This section discusses priorities for introducing changes to promote
the human rights of female refugee, displaced, and returnee populations.

(a) The international community and the United Nations must
demand that governments that create refugee populations or provide
refuge for them recognize and uphold universal human rights norms.
Furthermore, the international community and the United Nations
must support platforms of leadership that respect democracy, pluralism, and human rights for both male and female citizens.

(b) Repatriation can occur only if peace processes initiated and
supported by the United Nations are successful. Currently, more than
45 million refugees and displaced people await the return of peace
and the reconstruction of their war-torn countries. Repatriation has
been initiated in Cambodia, South Africa, and El Salvador, with
Afghanistan and other regions to follow. It is imperative that the
governments of these emerging democracies commit themselves to the

development of equitable societies by including women's rights in their constitutions. Human rights bodies, which have not been involved in this critical process, must now become active in protecting women's basic human rights by developing appropriate constitutional and legislative models that can be adopted by emerging democracies. Without such safeguards at the outset of nation building, women's rights will not be respected.

(c) Some refugee populations have considered demanding war reparations from parties that have committed genocide against their own or other people. Though this may appear unrealistic in the wake of the end of the Cold War and strained global economies, political instruments should be developed to hold warring factions and forces of invasion responsible for their actions.

(d) In a changing world, the concept of human rights must be reexamined and expanded. In this regard, it is of the utmost importance that domestic and international mental health practitioners and human rights activists, who are often the only official links to refugees, redefine their roles as human rights advocates. If they fail to do so, serious violations will continue unabated and will be addressed only on the personal level, if at all. This strictly individual approach to the suffering inflicted on women fails to condemn the perpetrators of human rights violations and does not expose the larger systemic structures that support such abuses.

A redefinition of human rights abuse should include such issues as the raping of refugee women not only by men who are connected with the military or government but by any men; forced migration over treacherous routes of escape that are rife with land mines and grenades; the disguising of grenades as toys; and the kidnapping of children for forced servitude or military and ideological training. Governments that prey on the young should be held accountable for committing such flagrant acts of violence against them.

(e) Generally, refugees and Third World women need to be trained to serve as human rights advocates. To this end, they must be involved as equal partners in defining and developing an appropriate human rights framework that responds to their needs.

(f) Repatriation presents an opportunity to solve the short- and long-term development concerns of refugee populations. It is an incentive for introducing positive change and advancing strategies that provide women access to land, credit, and technology. In this context, development is fundamentally a human rights issue. But repatriation will succeed only if the international community attends to the development concerns of women and girls.

(g) The physical protection of women and children upon return to their homes must be guaranteed. In order to ensure the safety of at-risk populations, it is important to assign joint teams of international agencies and female returnees to develop workable protection plans and monitor their implementation. It is especially important to monitor reintegration and safety in rural regions upon the departure of international peacekeeping troops.

The current deficit of human rights monitors in refugee camps—due in large part to the reluctance of international organizations to get involved, since in so doing they risk being expelled from host countries—increases the probability that violations will occur. Monitoring to reduce human rights violations will succeed only when all parties, including refugee service providers and refugees themselves, work together.

(h) It is important to clearly identify as human rights violations those oppressive cultural and ideological norms and practices that contribute, at best, to the subjugation of women and girls and, at worst, to their mutilation or murder. The world community and international agencies must support refugee women who challenge such practices by sponsoring educational and awareness-training programs directed at changing the attitudes of uprooted women and men.

In particular, the international relief and development community must desist from using culture as an excuse to exclude women from development programs. Instead, they must establish direct liaisons with female community organizers and support a gender-responsive policy that calls for refugee women, rather than male political and religious leaders, to represent their own issues in their own voices. Attention must be focused on empowering refugee and displaced women and supporting their rehabilitation to prepare them for repatriation and the reconstruction of their war-torn homelands. By actively participating in decision-making processes, empowered women will themselves define culture and cultural practices in a just and equitable manner.

Conclusion

The number of refugees and displaced persons has increased almost twofold during the last decade. We are entering an age in which refugees and forced migrants are becoming permanent populations. Unless the changes recommended here are implemented, refugees and displaced people will continue to linger in camps, victimized by ongoing brutal violations of their rights. And the women and children in these camps will continue to suffer the most egregious abuse.

This human tragedy, afflicting the most at-risk members of society, will change only when it is addressed at the systemic level. State violence against displaced and refugee populations is the real issue. Strategies and mechanisms must be developed to hold governments accountable for the forced international migration caused by their policies and practices. The oppressive actions and organized brutality of states that condemn asylum seekers as "illegals" and sanction inhumane treatment of their own displaced citizens must be condemned. As widespread human rights atrocities against women and children mount, there is an urgent need to redefine the universal human rights agenda and move the discussion from the private sphere into the public realm where action can be taken.

Finally, in the twenty-first century political activity must center on building civil societies and supporting the expansion of human rights and democracy. The rehabilitation of countries whose social structures and value systems have been shattered by chronic warfare cannot be separated from the need to support infrastructure development in newly emerging societies. Women, who have the responsibility in most traditional cultures of building and maintaining the social fabric of their communities, must be included in this process if it is to have any meaningful and lasting effect.

Notes

1. According to the United States Committee for Refugees, the total number of refugees to date is 16,255,000, and there are currently at least 26 million internally displaced people. These are conservative figures based on country-by-country assessments, United Nations High Commissioner for Refugees statistics, and U.S. Department of State figures. In late 1993, UNHCR quoted a figure of 18 million refugees, which includes internally displaced Bosnians and refugees who have already been repatriated, but does not include refugees from or people internally displaced by the 1994 Rwandan conflict.

2. This is a widely accepted, though probably conservative, estimate. For further discussion of refugee populations and demographics, see Susan Forbes-Martin, *Refugee Women* (London: Zed, 1992); and Women's Commission for Refugee Women and Children, New York.

3. The distribution of refugee food rations is handled by UNHCR and its implementing partners (host governments, international NGOs), usually in public places easily

accessible to men who have ration cards. Ration cards are issued to male family members; this of course is a problem for widowed women and women who cannot appear in public places. Furthermore, male family members make decisions about food distribution, an additional problem for widowed women who have to rely on male members of the extended family.

32

Where in the World Is There Safety for Me?: Women Fleeing Gender-Based Persecution

Pamela Goldberg

As the world's refugee population is increasingly made up of women and children, the intersection between women suffering gender-specific human rights abuses and those who flee because of such abuses is gaining international attention. Of the estimated 18 million refugees worldwide,[1] 80 percent are women and children.[2] All refugees face difficult and painful circumstances in their struggle for safety from fear and tragedy.

Internal strife, brutal dictatorships, extreme economic hardship, starvation, severe discrimination, and abuse—all are reasons people flee their homelands to seek refuge elsewhere. For women such circumstances often have an especially tragic impact. Frequently during times of great hardship, women are left alone to care for themselves and their children while husbands, fathers, or other male support are fighting, in prison, in hiding, or away seeking work, leaving women at once vulnerable and faced with tremendous burdens. When there is a lack of food due to drought or other causes, women and female children are often the first to do without. When there is a natural disaster, women are expected to maintain the family, to care for their needs, to search for water, to find food. Rape and other forms of sexual assault often accompany war. Torture, including sexual and physical violence, goes hand-in-hand with brutal dictatorships and political oppression. In some countries, or under certain circumstances—even in the absence of internal strife or other kinds of extreme hardship—women may face rape, sexual assault, intimate violence, forced marriage, forced sterilization or abortion, forced prostitution, genital mutilation, rigorous imposition of restrictive religious or customary practices such as wearing the veil or not being allowed in public unless in the company of a male relative.

When the decision to flee is made, women and their children are especially vulnerable. Often traveling without men, women are subject to rape, assault, robbery, harassment, and other cruel treatment. They may be separated from their children. Money may be taken from them, and food denied them by those "assisting" them in their passage. Often, they arrive at their destination beleaguered, lacking funds or resources, and suffering from exhaustion and perhaps physical abuse after the treacherous journey to safe haven.

A very small number of the women who flee find their way to distant countries, far from home, family, and friends. These women are forced to undergo a rigorous process to determine whether they will be eligible to remain in the country of safety. Yet many of the specific conditions that cause women to flee are seldom recognized as legitimate reasons for granting asylum. For many women, however, the ability to remain outside the homeland is a grave matter, and forced return can mean persecution in the form of abuse, extreme ridicule, ostracism, and even death.

Obtaining refugee status is difficult, and the procedures are often insensitive to the human dimension of asylum seeking. The substantive law applied in evaluating whether an individual is eligible for refugee status is generally narrowly construed and does not usually recognize the full panoply of issues shaping an individual's reasons for seeking safe haven. This is particularly true in regard to claims presented by women.

The universal definition of a refugee is contained in the 1951 *Convention Relating to the Status of Refugees* (The Refugee Convention), as modified by the 1967 *Protocol Relating to the Status of Refugees*, which was established for the purpose of affording protection to those persons fleeing persecution in their homelands. Under the Refugee Convention, a refugee is a person who, "owing to a well-founded fear of being persecuted for reasons of race, religion, nationality, membership of a particular social group or political opinion, is outside the country of his [sic] nationality and is unable or, owing to such fear, is unwilling to avail himself of the protection of that country."[3] Signatory states, although bound by this definition, are free to enact their own laws and regulations concerning the determination of refugee status.[4]

Persecution is not defined in the Refugee Convention but is generally viewed as encompassing serious violations of an individual's human rights. The United Nations *Handbook on Procedures and Criteria for*

Determining Refugee Status,[5] an important source internationally for interpreting refugee and asylum laws, offers a broad definition of persecution that includes "serious violations of human rights."[6] The Convention names five grounds for legitimate fear of persecution: race, religion, nationality, membership in a particular social group, or political opinion. No international or regional convention or national statute includes recognition of gender as one of the categories. This means that to be eligible for refugee status under the Convention, a woman must show she is afraid she will be persecuted because of, for example, her religion or political opinion. Although this omission creates a limitation in gaining recognition of the claims of women, it is not an insurmountable obstacle. The greater difficulty lies not in the legal definition but rather in how that definition is interpreted and applied. As with the common understanding of what constitutes human rights violations, the traditional view of what constitutes persecution reflects a male consideration of "normal" or acceptable conduct.[7]

Historically, international human rights law has created a divide between acts that are considered to be in the public realm (such as the detention and torture of political prisoners) and those that occur in the private realm, between "private" individuals, particularly in the home. More recently, there is increasing recognition by scholars and international human rights monitoring bodies that, under some circumstances, states may be held accountable for human rights violations even where the perpetrator of the abuse is a nonstate actor.

Where a state refuses to intervene to protect against human rights violations, to investigate charges, or to prosecute and punish perpetrators of harmful acts, it does, in effect, condone those acts.[8] According to the interpretation of refugee law by the United Nations High Commissioner for Refugees (the international organization whose function it is to assist and protect refugees throughout the world), the persecutor may be either the state or a force that the government cannot or will not control: it does not have to be a governmental actor.[9] Thus, human rights violations of a woman's physical security and bodily integrity, for example—even those occurring in the home or workplace—could theoretically be protected under asylum and refugee law.[10]

Recently, great strides have been made toward recognizing abuses perpetrated against women as violations of women's human rights.[11] The arguments used to promote that recognition are equally critical for promoting the legitimacy of claims for refugee status due to gender-based persecution. Despite an international climate that grows increasingly hostile to refugees, there is some movement toward the recognition of gender-based persecution as a legitimate basis for granting protected status.

What is gender-based persecution? Certainly the most notorious recent example is the widespread rape of women in former Yugoslavia. Few of these women will ever reach safety in a third country like France, Germany, or the United States. Of those who do, fewer still will actually be granted refugee status. Although there is some hope that the claims of those who are able and willing to come forward will be recognized, whether they actually receive the protection of refugee and asylum law remains to be seen.[12]

The mass rapes in former Yugoslavia have received a certain amount of attention. But there are many, many forms of gender-based persecution, from the forced marriage of an underage Zimbabwean woman to a man many years her senior (a man who repeatedly beats and rapes her and forces her to bear his children), to a woman in China who fears being forced to undergo an abortion and perhaps even sterilization because she already has one child, to an Iranian woman who flees her country because she cannot follow the restrictive religious and social practices mandated by law and fears severe punishment should she return. These are just a few of the many forms of violence and persecution perpetrated virtually exclusively against women. While efforts to expand human rights doctrines to include the recognition of such acts as human rights violations continue, in the realm of asylum and refugee law, complaints from women about gender-based abuse are being heard with increasing insistence.

Of course, women do also make claims for refugee status based clearly on one of the five existing grounds: race, religion, nationality, membership in a particular social group, or political opinion. For those women, protection comes if they are able to show their fear to be well founded and based on the grounds alleged. But for many, the persecution experienced or feared is of a type not traditionally recognized under the Refugee Convention or under most countries' asylum eligibility laws.

One of the first efforts to recognize the legitimacy of gender-based persecution claims in the Western/Northern world occurred as early as 1984, when the European Community admitted that such claims might be recognized under the category of membership in a particular social group.[13] On the heels of this recommendation, the Executive Committee (EC) of the Office of the UNHCR issued its own similar recommendation in 1985. In the first UNHCR statement of its kind, the EC acknowledged that states may recognize claims of gender-based persecution under the "particular social group" category.[14]

This was a significant, if limited, breakthrough. As the internationally recognized body for overseeing refugee matters, the UNHCR's interpretations of the Refugee Convention are not only widely respected but also often followed. As such, the 1985 conclusion set the stage for greater recognition of gender-based persecution claims. At the same time, by specifically recommending that these claims be understood to fall within the "particular social group" category, it failed to acknowledge other potential bases for establishing gender-based persecution and made no mention of the need for gender itself to be included as a category in order more fully to accord protection to women fearing or experiencing persecution on account of gender.

In 1991 the UNHCR adopted *Guidelines on the Protection of Refugee Women*.[15] These groundbreaking Guidelines confirmed the need to address gender-based persecution and the need for states to recognize claims for asylum and refugee status by women fleeing such persecution. The Guidelines surpassed the EC Conclusion of 1985 in that, although they specifically name the social group category as a likely basis for gender-based persecution, they also recognize that such claims may be classified as persecution on the grounds of political opinion or religious affiliation. The UNHCR Guidelines mark a significant advance in the recognition of gender-based persecution, and recommend that evaluators be trained to respond sensitively to the particular problems and requirements of refugee women when conducting interviews and determining refugee status eligibility.

Most recently, the Executive Committee issued a Conclusion on violence against women[16] that specifically recognizes sexual violence as a violation of the "Fundamental right to personal security as recognized in international human rights and humanitarian law" and "strongly condemns persecution through sexual violence." The Conclusion further "urges States to respect and ensure the fundamental right of all individuals . . . to personal security." Perhaps one of the most significant recommendations in the Conclusion is that which calls for the "development by States of appropriate guidelines on women asylum-seekers, in recognition of the fact that *women refugees often experience persecution differently from refugee men*."[17]

In March 1993, Canada enacted its own set of comprehensive guidelines for determining the validity of asylum claims by refugee women.[18] The Canada *Guidelines on Women Refugee Claimants Fearing Gender-Related Persecution* reflect a comprehensive understanding of such claims and offer a range of recommendations for effectively evaluating them. The Canada Guidelines are more expansive than the UNHCR Guidelines, allowing for the assessment of gender-based persecution claims under any of the five grounds that may be applicable: race, religion, nationality, membership in a particular social group, or political opinion. In addition to laying out a systematic method for evaluating claims, the Guidelines also call for recognition of and sensitivity to the particular difficulties women face in the asylum and refugee adjudication process.

The Canada guidelines do not exist in a vacuum, but come out of and are followed by a body of individual decisions in which women's claims of gender-based persecution have been recognized. The case of "Nada," a Saudi Arabian woman who was viciously attacked by community members and religious leaders for not wearing the veil, is only one example.[19] The 1987 Incirciyan case, which involved a Turkish woman and her three children, was pivotal in the development of Canadian law.[20]

Ms. Incirciyan, a widow, and her three children (especially her twenty one–year-old daughter) were repeatedly harassed, assaulted, and threatened. Although as Christian Armenians living in Turkey they raised their claim of persecution on the grounds of religion and nationality, the Canadian Appeals Board expanded the claim and granted them refugee status based on their membership in the "social group made up of single women living in a Moslem country without the protection of a male relative (father, brother, husband, adult son)."[21] Since this decision, there have been a growing number of decisions recognizing women's gender-based claims, among them the recent decision granting refugee status to an Ecuadorian woman fleeing her violent husband.[22] In that case the Board, identifying the applicant as a member of the particular social group of "Ecuadorian women subject to wife abuse," compared her treatment to that of political prisoners subjected to detention and torture.[23]

Other countries are gradually making inroads in granting asylum protection to women fleeing gender-based persecution. Sometimes, as in the "Nada" case in Canada, refugee status is denied but the claimant is allowed to remain, having been granted status on other grounds. Aminata Diop, who as a young Mali woman was to be married by family arrangement and forced to undergo genital mutilation, fled to France, where she sought asylum. Denied refugee status, she was nevertheless allowed to remain in France and given lawful resident status.[24]

Nor is Canada alone in recognizing claims of gender-based persecution as a basis for granting asylum—at least in individual cases; Germany has, on occasion, granted asylum on such grounds. In a 1988 decision, the Federal Office found five Iranians had established eligibility for asylum based on their political activities,[25] and went on to add that one of them, the woman, was a member of a "specific social group"—Iranian women—and as such was subject to persecution specific to women. The decision stated that "the ideologically based power of men over women results in a general political repression of women in defiance of their individual liberties and human rights." In a later decision, however, although the Administrative Court granted an asylum claim to an Iranian woman, it did so based on the fact that the Iranian government, which was actively seeking her husband, had interrogated her several times in an attempt to discover his whereabouts.[26] In that case, no mention was made of the "political repression of women" or the "ideological power base of men over women."

The United States has yet to recognize gender-based persecution claims and has declined to accept such claims under one of the other existing categories. The few reported cases that have been decided by the administrative immigration bodies and the courts have, with little exception, been denied. One notable example is the case of a Salvadoran woman who was repeatedly raped and brutalized by the armed opposition.[27] The Federal Court of Appeals denied her claim, finding that she had not established that she was persecuted on account of one of the five grounds. The Court did not accept her argument that she was a member of the particular social group of young women who had been repeatedly raped and assaulted, arguing that gender and age are categories too broad to constitute a social group. The Court ruled that the reason the woman was raped was not identifiable and, as such, refused to accept rape as a basis for fearing future persecution.[28]

In a fascinating early case, a woman who had been repeatedly raped and forced to perform menial labor for a sergeant in the Salvadoran armed forces was granted asylum in the United States.[29] The court found that, by resisting her assailant, the woman was expressing a political opinion that men did not have the right to dominate women. The Court also found that by her actions she had expressed the political opinion that the government of El Salvador was responsible for lawlessness and would not protect her from her persecutor. Finally, the Court based its actual decision on the fact that the sergeant constantly threatened to expose her as a subversive if she did not do exactly as he said. The fact that he knew she was not a subversive did not minimize her claim because, as a member of the armed forces, he had power over her. Although this case is unique in its logic and language, as well as in its outcome,[30] it nevertheless represents hope for the direction future decisions might take.[31]

Women fleeing gender-based persecution are entitled to the full protection of international refugee and asylum laws. In bringing their claims forward, case by case, country by country, women are ever so gradually beginning to receive needed recognition and protection. The law moves slowly, but the immediacy of their situation does not allow refugee women to wait before seeking safety. It is only as more and more claims of gender-based persecution are raised whenever and wherever the abuses occur that the world will begin to recognize the legitimacy of those claims as the basis for granting asylum.

Notes

1. U.S. Committee for Refugees, *1993 World Refugee Survey* (Washington, DC: 1993). This does not include the estimated additional 20 million internally displaced persons who have had to flee their homes and are either unwilling or unable to leave their country of origin, or the estimated 5 million persons in "refugee-like situations." Nor does it include those 5 million who have been granted asylum status or have been repatriated. Id., p. 54.

2. See, e.g., Susan Forbes-Martin, *Refugee Women* (London Zed, 1991). Exact figures are unavailable due to the fluidity of refugee populations, the instability of the living conditions of many refugees throughout the world, lack of resources, and a general disinclination to derive breakdowns of refugee populations based on gender or age.

3. *Convention Relating to the Status of Refugees,* opened for signature July 28, 1951, 19 U.S.T. 6260, T.I.A.S. No. 6577, 189 U.N.T.S. 137.

4. For example, the Organization of African Unity in its 1969 *Convention on Refugees in Africa* expanded its definition of a refugee to include any person who "owing to external aggression, occupation, foreign domination or events seriously disturbing public order in either part of or the whole country, is compelled to seek refuge outside his [sic] country of origin." Article 1, para. 2 1001 United Nations *Treaty Series* at 47.

5. Office of the United Nations High Commissioner for Refugees, *Handbook on Procedures and Criteria for Determining Refugee Status Under the 1951 Convention* (U.N.T.S. vol. 89, p. 167) and the *1967 Protocol Relating to the Status of Refugees,* (U.N.T.S. vol. 606, p. 267) Geneva, January 1988 (hereafter "*Handbook*"). This *Handbook* has been widely recognized as an important guide in interpreting refugee laws in a given country. See, e.g., *Immigration and Naturalization Service v. Cardoza-Fonseca,* 480 U.S. 421 (1987), where the United States Supreme Court recognized the influence of the *Handbook* in interpreting United States asylum law.

6. The *Handbook* states that it may be inferred that any threat to life or freedom on account of race, religion, nationality, political opinion, or membership of a particular social group is always persecution.

> Other serious violations of human rights—for the same reasons—would also constitute persecution. Whether other prejudicial actions or threats would amount to persecution will depend on the circumstances of each case . . . An applicant may have been subjected to various measures not in themselves amounting to persecution (e.g. discrimination in different forms), in some cases combined with other diverse factors (e.g. general atmosphere of insecurity in the country of origin). In such situations, the various elements involved may, if taken together, produce an effect on the mind of the applicant that can reasonably justify a claim to well-founded fear of persecution on "cumulative grounds." (*Handbook*, paras. 51–53, pp. 14–15).

7. See, e.g., Judy A. Mayotte, *Disposable People? The Plight of Refugees* (Maryknoll, NY 1992) citing Anders Johnson, Deputy UN High Commissioner for Refugees who observed that the *1951 Convention Relating to the Status of Refugees* was written with male refugees in mind, stating that "not a single woman was to be found amongst the plenipotentiaries who met in Geneva in 1951 to draw up the Convention" (Mayotte, p. 186). On state accountability for violations by nonstate actors, see, e.g., Celina Romany, "Women as Aliens: A Feminist Critique of the Public/Private Distinction in International Human Rights Law," Harvard H.R.J. 6 (Spring 1993): 87; Sharon Hom, "Female Infanticide in China: The Human Rights Specter and Thoughts Towards (AN)Other Vision," *Col. H.R.L.R.* 23 (Summer 1992). 249, Hilary Charlesworth, "The Public/Private Distinction and the Right to Development in International Law," *Australian Year Book of International Law*, (1992) p. 190.

8. This principle stems from various international treaties and covenants, including the *International Covenant on Civil and Political Rights*, as well as from an instrumental decision rendered by the Organization of American States Human Rights Court, *Velasquez-Rodriguez*, which has been interpreted to stand for just this proposition.

9. *Handbook*, para. 65, p. 17.

10. See, e.g., Pamela Goldberg, "Anyplace but Home: Women Fleeing Intimate Violence," *Cornell International L.J.* 26 (Symposium 1993):3; Felicite Stairs and Lori Pope, "No Place Like Home: Assaulted Migrant Women's Claims to Refugee Status and Landings on Humanitarian and Compassionate Grounds," *Journal of Law and Social Policy* 6: (1990) 148. A landmark human rights report examined the Brazilian legal system's response to violence against women with a focus on spousal violence and recognized violence against women as a human rights issue. *Criminal Injustice: Violence Against Women in Brazil* (Americas Watch and Women's Rights Project of Human Rights Watch, 1991).

11. See, e.g., World Conference on Human Rights, *The Vienna Declaration and Programme of Action, June 1993*, United Nations Dept. of Public Information DPI/1394-39399-August 1993-20M (hereafter, *"Vienna Declaration"*). The

groundbreaking 1991 Amnesty International Report, *Women in the Front Line: Human Rights Violations Against Women* (New York: Amnesty International, 1991), marks one of the first instances in which rape is recognized by an international human rights monitoring body as a form of torture.

12. The distinction between refuge and asylum varies from country to country. The end result sought is essentially the same: permission to remain in a country in which one has asked for protection from a country where one fears persecution. This permission may be temporary, long-term, or permanent and may be renewable or not, but the core is the granting of some form of protection from forced return to a place where the refugee fears persecution.

13. Cited in Felicite Stairs and Lori Pope, "No Place Like Home: Assaulted Migrant Women's Claims to Refugee Status and Landings on Humanitarian and Compassionate Grounds," *Journal of Law and Social Policy* 6: (1992) 167.

14. *Conclusion No. 39 (XXXVI), Refugee Women and International Protection,* UN Doc. HRC/IP/2/Rev. 1986 (July 8, 1985).

15. *Information Note on UNHCR's Guidelines on the Protection of Refugee Women,* UN High Commissioner for Refugees, 42nd Sess., UN Doc. ES/SCP/67 (1991).

16. United Nations High Commissioner for Refugees, Executive Committee, 44th Sess. *Refugee Protection and Sexual Violence,* Conclusion 2, A/AC.96/XLIV/CRP.3 (1993).

17. Id. (emphasis added).

18. Chairperson, Canadian Immigration and Refugee Board, *Guidelines on Women Refugee Claimants Fearing Gender-Related Persecution* (1993).

19. Although the "Nada" case is widely viewed as an important breakthrough in asylum claims for women in Canada, in fact, "Nada" was not granted asylum. Her claim was denied but she was allowed to remain in Canada under a grant of humanitarian grounds.

20. *Incirciyan v. Minister of Employment and Immigration,* Immigration Appeal Board Decision M87-1541X, August 10, 1987 (Canada).

21. Id., p. 1.

22. File U92-087 Immigration and Refugee Board (Refugee Division), June 4, 1993 (Canada).

23. Id., p. 7.

24. Ms. Diop's lawyer, Linda Weil Cureil, believes that although the Court did not want to set a precedent granting refugee status under such circumstances, the serious reasons for her flight and the potentially highly charged claim she was making caused immigration officials to grant her status in an effort to defuse the issue (information based on personal conversation with Ms. Diop and Ms. Weil Cureil in June 1993).

25. AN 19K 88.35346, Bundesamt für die Anerkennung Auslandischer Fluchtlinge (Federal Office for the Recognition of Foreign Refugees), November 24, 1988 (Germany, Fed. Rep.) p. 6.

26. AN 19K 88.35346 Bayerisches Verwaltungsgericht Ansbach (Bavarian Administrative Court at Ansbach), 1989 (Germany, Fed. Rep.)

27. *Gomez v. I.N.S., (Immigration and Naturalization Service)* 947 F.2d 660 (2d Cir. 1991).

28. Id.

29. *Lazo-Majano v. I.N.S.*, 813 F.2d 1432 (9th Cir. 1987).

30. This is the only U.S. decision to date rendered by a Federal Court of Appeals that grants asylum where the claim concerns gender-based persecution. A groundbreaking decision by the Third Circuit Court of Appeals, while denying an Iranian woman's claim for asylum (finding that she failed to establish sufficiently her fear of persecution), ruled that a fear of persecution on account of gender could be a basis for granting asylum. *Fatin v. I.N.S.*, F.3d (3rd Cir. 1993)

31. Currently there is an effort in the United States to introduce guidelines similar to those promulgated by Canada concerning the asylum claims of women. Draft Guidelines have been circulated and are being presented to the I.N.S. Central Asylum Office for review. There is hope that the guidelines will be accepted and, if they are, will ultimately lead to a change in the way decisions about women's persecution claims are made.

Conclusion
Dorothy Q. Thomas

In and between the lines of *Women's Rights, Human Rights* is a declaration of intent: women's human rights activists, scattered across the globe, have gathered in dialogue to change fundamentally not only the content but also the form of international human rights work. This collection could, of course, serve as an educational tool alone, essential reading for any student of the development and dilemmas of the field of women's human rights. It provides a detailed map of pressing issues and emerging concerns in women's human rights; a guide to gendered theories of international human rights law; a systematic account of the persistent exclusion of certain classes of women's issues, and of certain activists, from international human rights work. But informing its readers is only half the book's aim. While it may serve as a useful primer, it is also a powerful manifesto.

In this sense, the essays compiled here are not simply *descriptive* (designed to explain "the women's human rights issue" in its various aspects): they also are *transformative*. They propose a fundamental reenvisioning of human rights that encompasses the experience of women, and they call on the reader to act against gender-based human rights violations.

As you read this book, the transformative character of the emerging international women's human rights movement itself begins to take shape. It begins, as Elisabeth Friedman points out, with "women's organizing on local, national, regional and international levels around issues that affect their daily lives." As such—and unlike many other social movements in the world today—the women's human rights movement is inherently diverse, created and led by women of many different cultures, countries, regions, ages, races, classes, and sexual orientations. Its vitality, and ultimately its power, lie in its capacity to affirm this distinctive variety and still find ways for women to connect with one another in order to make fundamental changes in their lives and the lives of other women.

Balancing difference and commonality is no easy task. The human rights movement in general has often suffered from over-emphasizing one of these areas at the expense of the other. What is striking about the growing women's human rights movement is its resistance to polarization and, therefore, its dynamism. Both within and between the essays collected here, there is constant movement from the particular experiences of women to the commonalities and affinities that arise from those experiences. The particular and the general constantly interrogate and inform one another. The goal is a politics of difference that has already begun to give rise to a rejuvenated conception of universality as the foundation for human rights at the local, national, regional, and international levels, a rejuvenation from which the entire human rights movement stands to benefit.

The dynamism of the women's human rights movement serves to counter what Arati Rao refers to as "reductionism, essentialism, and rhetorical rigidity." As was evident in much of the government rhetoric at the UN World Conference on Human Rights in Vienna in June of 1993, the uncritical affirmation of difference *per se* can have disastrous results. Notions of race, gender, class, nationality, or (as at the Vienna conference) culture can become static and unyielding, easily deployed to justify the denial or curtailment of universally recognized human rights.

The attempt to transcend specific differences and identify commonalities, however, runs the risk of producing token universality devoid of content, particularly where the experience of women is concerned. Much has been written in this volume and elsewhere about the risk of false or faceless universalism. As Mallika Dutt of the Center for Women's Global Leadership points out, "one of the biggest problems with universality as it has existed in the past is that [in] the process that led to universal articulation, a lot of people did not participate."

Rigid concepts of culture, coupled with formulaic notions of universality, have led to a false antagonism between human rights and cultural difference. As Rao points out here, current human rights discourse is permeated by an "overly simple notion of the relationship between culture and human rights in our world of difference [that] has emerged in a dichotomous form with the universalists on one side and the cultural relativists on the other."

The women's human rights movement, however, is transforming this debate by demonstrating that universal human rights and the principle of difference can readily accommodate each other. At a regional meeting in preparation for the Vienna conference, Asian women's rights activists struck this balance well by affirming cultural pluralism while rejecting the use of notions of cultural difference to deny any fundamental human rights—women's human rights included.

Yet even as the women's human rights movement challenges dichotomies that have left human rights discourse more generally in a stalemate, the articulation of women's human rights is always in danger of replicating those same dichotomies within itself. Depending on where we are situated, each of us is at risk of replicating unexamined divisions of North and South, East and West, Black and White, rich and poor, grassroots and elite, gay and straight—sometimes merely by invoking such categories. The power of the movement lies in resisting these (and other) ancient polarizations and instead engaging in constant self-interrogation in the interest of creating a movement that can avoid reduplicating the very hierarchies it seeks to challenge, a movement that, as a result, has the potential to achieve fundamental change in women's lives. The fundamental challenge for the movement for women's human rights is that it not become a reformist project: its recipe should not read, "Add women and stir," but "Add women and alter."

Thus, both within and outside the movement, even as these writers and other thinkers and activists affirm women's specific and various experiences, they continually and critically evaluate the notion of difference itself, not only from within various particularities (e.g., of nationality, race, class, gender, and sexual orientation) but also in relation to emerging commonalities. At the same time, they simultaneously affirm and interrogate the principle of universality. While striking such a balance is no easy task, the very process of doing so is at the heart of women's human rights movement's transformative power. As Audre Lorde once wrote, "We sharpen self-definition by exposing self in work and struggle together with those whom we define as different from ourselves. For Black and white, old and young, lesbian and heterosexual women alike, this can mean new paths to our survival."[1]

Most of the world's predominant forces are arrayed against the global women's human rights project that this book describes and of which it is part. The lure of long-standing parochialisms like those described above is strong, both within and outside the movement. Moreover, the influence of opposing international economic, political, and social trends is pervasive. The economic gains to be had from maintaining women's subordination, for example, are immense, as Liza Largoza-Maza notes when she describes the "export-oriented/import-dependent debt-driven economic program" that continues to "intensify the exploitation of Filipino women as a source of cheap, docile labor and as sexual commodities."

Resistance to forces such as these depends on persisting in the kind of discussion—simultaneous analysis and outcry—that this book represents. It depends on persistently unveiling those circumstances that provide the content of women's human rights work and, at the same time, examining and reexamining that content and its consequences. Ultimately, the measure of the success of the women's human rights movement will be the extent to which, in Maria Suarez' words, it makes "a tangible difference in women's lives."

Note

1. Audre Lourde, *Sister Outsider* (CA: Crossing Press Feminist Series, 1984), p. 123.

Contributors

Charlotte Bunch is Director of the Douglass College Center for Women's Global Leadership at Rutgers University (which recently coordinated the Global Campaign for Women's Human Rights at the 1993 United Nations World Conference on Human Rights in Vienna) and a Professor in the Bloustein School of Planning and Public Policy at Rutgers University. A feminist author and organizer for over two decades, she worked on global feminism and the UN Decade for Women with a variety of organizations during the 1980s, and was a founder of D.C. Women's Liberation and of *Quest: A Feminist Quarterly*. She has edited seven anthologies. Her latest book is *Passionate Politics: Feminist Theory in Action*.

Gloria Careaga Pérez, who was born in Guadalajara, is the founder of the Gender Studies Department at the National Autonomous University of Mexico (UNAM). Her first degree was in psychology and education, and she did a masters in social psychology. She is a feminist activist who has worked to promote respect for lesbians and to increase the visibility of the lesbian rights movement. She is a member of the lesbian group, Sor Juana's Closet.

Hilary Charlesworth is Professor of Law at the University of Adelaide in South Australia. She holds a B.A. and LL.B from the University of Melbourne and an SJD from Harvard Law School. She teaches and writes primarily on international and human rights law and feminist legal analysis. She is a Commissioner with the Australian Law Reform Commission on its reference on Equality and the Law and is also a member of the Australian Council of Women, a body established to advise the Australian government on its preparations for the Fourth World Conference on Women to be held in Beijing in September 1995.

Rebecca J. Cook, M.A., M.P.A., J.D., LL.M., and a member of the Bar of Washington, DC, teaches at the University of Toronto, where she is Associate Professor and Director of the International Human Rights Programme in the Faculty of Law, and Associate Professor in the Department of Health Administration in the Faculty of Medicine. She is a member of the Ethics Committee of the International Federation of Gynaecology and Obstetrics and of the Scientific and Ethical Review Group of the World Health Organization's Human Reproduction Programme. Her principal teaching and research interests relate to international human rights, sex discrimination, and health law and ethics.

360

Rhonda Copelon is a Professor of Law at the City University of New York School of Law, and Co-Director of its International Women's Human Rights Law Clinic. As a feminist attorney and activist with the Center for Constitutional Rights in New York City since 1971, she has also been involved in a broad range of human rights litigation and advocacy in the United States and has argued several cases before the U.S. Supreme Court. She has developed courses in gender and law, has written numerous articles, and is coauthor of a forthcoming study of sex discrimination. She works with the Programa de las Mujeres of the International American Institute of Human Rights and the Programa Mujer y Justicia of the United Nations Latin American Institute for the Prevention of Crime and Treatment of Delinquency (ILANUD) in Costa Rica.

Julie Dorf is the founder and Executive Director of the International Gay and Lesbian Human Rights Commission (IGLHRC), a nonprofit, San Francisco–based organization that monitors, documents, and mobilizes responses to human rights violations based on sexual orientation and HIV status. She spent eight years involved with dissident movements in the Soviet Union. Her work and the work of IGLHRC have been featured in *Time, Newsweek,* the *Los Angeles Times,* the *New York Times,* the *San Francisco Chronicle, Ms. Magazine,* and on the BBC, NPR, and *Larry King Live.*

Siobhan Dowd is Program Director of the Freedom-to-Write Committee of American PEN, which campaigns against abuses of the right to freedom of expression around the globe and protests infringements of the First Amendment in the United States. She is Irish, but was raised in London and did a degree in Classics at Oxford. The author of some eighty articles, book reviews, and travel pieces for various anthologies and journals including *The Literary Review* and *Poets and Writers,* she is coordinator of the Rushdie Defense Committee USA and has been frequently interviewed on the topic of censorship.

Marsha Freeman is Deputy Director of International Women's Rights Action Watch and a Senior Fellow at the Humphrey Institute of Public Affairs at the University of Minnesota. She received her J.D. from the University of Minnesota and her Ph.D. from the University of Pennsylvania. In 1987 she was appointed by the Supreme Court of Minnesota to serve as Reporter for the Task Force for Gender Fairness in the Courts and to oversee preparation of its final report. She has been a member of the Minnesota State Bar Association's Committee on Women in the Legal Profession and President of Minnesota Women Lawyers and Co-Chair of its Task Force on the Status of Women in the Legal Profession. She has written widely on women's human rights, development, and reproductive law.

Elisabeth Friedman is a Ph.D. candidate in political science at Stanford University, concentrating in comparative politics with an emphasis on Latin America and feminist political theory. She is presently working on her dissertation, "*¿Nuestra Democracia?* Venezuelan Women's Political Participation, 1948–1994.*"

Pamela Goldberg is full-time Adjunct Professor of Law and Co-Director of the Immigrant and Refugee Rights Clinic at the City University of New York School of Law. She has a J.D. from New York Law School. At the World Conference on

Human Rights in Vienna, she coorganized and presented a paper at an NGO Forum on Human Rights Issues for Refugee and Migrant Women. She was a participant/observer at the United Nations Expert Group Meeting on Violence Against Women, convened by the Commission on the Status of Women in October 1993, and has written and spoken on a variety of topics including women and human rights and refugee and migrant women.

Lori Heise directs the Violence, Sexuality and Health Rights Program of the Pacific Institute for Women's Health. A long-time advocate for women's health internationally, she has worked extensively in the area of gender-based violence, women and HIV issues, and sexuality education. She lives and works in Washington, DC.

Rhoda E. Howard is Professor of Sociology at McMaster University, Hamilton, Ontario, and Director of McMaster's undergraduate Theme School on International Justice and Human Rights. She holds a Ph.D. in Sociology from McGill University and is a Fellow of the Royal Society of Canada. She is the author of *Colonialism and Underdevelopment in Ghana, Human Rights in Commonwealth Africa,* and *Human Rights and the Search for Community,* and is coauthor (with Jack Donnelly) of the *International Handbook of Human Rights.*

Indira Jaising is a Senior Advocate of the Supreme Court of India. She is the founding member of the Lawyer's Collective, an organization of lawyers and students involved in providing legal services to the community, and the editor of a monthly magazine, *The Lawyers.* She has argued several cases relating to the rights of women and the rights of the homeless, and she represented the victims of the Bhopal tragedy.

Natalie Hevener Kaufman is Professor of Government and International Studies at the University of South Carolina. She is the author of *International Law and the Status of Women* and *Human Rights Treaties and the Senate,* and the editor of *The Dynamics of Human Rights in U.S. Foreign Policy* and *Diplomacy in a Dangerous World.* Her articles have appeared in *Human Rights Quarterly, Harvard Women's Law Journal, International and Comparative Law Quarterly,* and the *International Journal of Women's Studies.*

Jasmina Kuzmanović is chief correspondent for the Associated Press in Zagreb and one of two section editors for Croatia in the Budapest-based periodical, *East European Reporter.* She studied English and comparative literature at Zagreb University, and has been a regular contributor to the weekly news magazine, *Novi Danas;* a columnist/media watcher for the cultural supplement, *Profil* (in the weekly *Nedjeljna Dalmacija,* based in Split); and a contributor to the U.S. daily economic bulletin, the *Eastern Europe Report.* In 1988 she won the Alfred Friendly Press Fellowship and spent six months working for the *Nashville Tennessean* and *USA Today,* for which she became the war correspondent in 1991. She has also been the chief stringer in Croatia for *Time* magazine.

Liza Largoza-Maza is the Secretary General of GABRIELA, the National Alliance of women's organizations in the Philippines. She received her B.S. in business economics from the University of the Philippines (where she was also a student activist) and, after graduation, worked as a researcher at the Philippine Center for Advanced Studies and the President's Center for Strategic Studies. She is also a founding member of the Women's International League for Peace and Freedom (Philippine Section), and is on the editorial board of *Laya Feminist Journal.*

Stefanie A. Lindquist graduated from the Temple University School of Law in 1988, where she was editor in chief of the Temple Law Review. Following graduation, she clerked for a judge on the U.S. Court of Appeals for the Third Circuit in Philadelphia. She also practiced law for a private firm in Washington, DC, where she specialized in the areas of corporate tax and tax litigation. She is now a Ph.D. candidate in the Department of Government and International Studies at the University of South Carolina.

Brigitte Mabandla is a South African human rights activist who is currently Coordinator of the Gender Project and Senior Research Fellow at the Community Law Centre at the University of the Western Cape. She has an LL.B. from the University of Zambia and is the African National Congress advisor on gender. She is a member of the ANC Constitutional Committee, the ANC Women's League, and the South African Women's Coalition Legal Working Group.

Ann Elizabeth Mayer is Associate Professor of Legal Studies at the Wharton School of the University of Pennsylvania and is a member of the Pennsylvania Bar. She has a Ph.D. in Modern Middle Eastern History from the University of Michigan and a J.D. from the University of Pennsylvania and has also pursued advanced study in Islamic and comparative law at the School of Oriental and African Studies of the University of London. She has written on various aspects of Islamic Law in contemporary Middle Eastern legal systems and human rights issues in the Middle East and is the author of *Islam and Human Rights, Tradition and Politics.*

Julie Mertus is Counsel for Helsinki Watch/Human Rights Watch, where she focuses exclusively on human rights issues in former Yugoslavia. She is an adjunct Professor of Political Science and Women's Studies at New York University and has worked for the American Civil Liberties Union. She writes and lectures widely on human rights issues, and is the author of a monograph, "The Health Care Needs of Women Survivors of the Balkan Conflict," and was principal author of of *Open Wounds,* a book on human rights abuses in Kosovo. Since mid-1994, she has been working with women's and human rights groups in Belgrade. She is a graduate of Cornell University and received her J.D. from Yale Law School.

Akram Mirhosseini is the Founder and President of the Paris-based League of Iranian Women (affiliated with the Organization for Human Rights in Iran). She did her M.A. in law and completed her Ph.D. thesis in Political Economics at Tehran University. She held a number of positions in the Iranian government (the State Organization for Administration and Employment Affairs and the Ministry of Water and Power), as well as teaching public and business administration. Her publications include *Women's Rights Discrimination in the Islamic Republic of Iran* and *Moving Tribes in Confrontation with Economic Development,* as well as several studies in political economics.

Koki Muli is an Advocate of the High Court of Kenya. She has been Editor of the *Nairobi Law Monthly Journal,* and was a Visiting Scholar in the International Human Rights Advocates Program at the Center for the Study of Human Rights at Columbia University in 1992. Currently Legal/Programs Officer of the International Commission of Jurists, Kenya Section (and Assistant Editor of the *Kenya Jurist Magazine),* she was recently appointed joint secretary of the National Task Force on Press Law by Kenya's Attorney General.

Ilka Tanya Payan, a native of the Dominican Republic, is a New York City Human Rights Commissioner and a specialist in immigration law, as well as an actor. She received her J.D. in 1981 from the People's College of Law and became a member of the California Bar, where she was admitted to the Federal Appeals Court. She is an advocate for women's health and health care reform, and has lobbied for immigrants with AIDS since the beginning of the epidemic. An HIV-positive immigrant herself, she has received recognition from colleagues, the media, and educational institutions around the country for her work in AIDS education. She writes two weekly columns on immigration and human rights issues for *El Diario La Prensa* (New York City's largest circulation Spanish-language newspaper).

Hnin Hnin Pyne was born in Rangoon, Burma, and grew up in Bangkok, Thailand. After receiving her B.A. from Wellesley College, she returned to Thailand to work with Burmese refugees. Interested in international development and gender issues, she earned a masters degree in Planning at the Massachusetts Institute of Technology, returning to Southeast Asia to do research for her thesis on AIDS and prostitution and continuing to concentrate on women's reproductive health and rights as a David E. Bell/MacArthur Fellow at the Harvard Center for Population and Development Studies in 1992–93. She is currently a consultant on HIV/AIDS issues in the Asia Technical Department of the World Bank.

Arati Rao, who was born and studied in India, received her Ph.D. in Political Science at Columbia University and is Assistant Professor of Political Science at Wellesley College. In addition to her specialization in feminist political theory, she teaches courses in human rights theory, the politics of identity, and the comparative politics of race and ethnicity. Her current research is on the conceptual contradictions in international human rights that constrain the field's responsiveness to women's concerns, with a focus on power, violence, and state-citizen relations.

Huda A. Seif was born in Mogadiscio to a Yemeni father and Somali mother, and has lived in Yemen, Kuwait, and Somalia. She has done research in rural northern Yemen and worked with Somali women in refugee camps near Aden, southern Yemen. She studied Anthropology and Economics at the City University of New York and is currently working toward her Ph.D. in Anthropology at Columbia University.

Carmel Shalev is a senior legislation officer at the Israeli Ministry of Justice (where her areas of responsibility include women's rights, family law, and constitutional law), and a lecturer in feminist legal theory at the Tel Aviv University Faculty of Law. In February 1994, she was elected to be a member of the United Nations Committee on the Elimination of Discrimination Against Women (CEDAW). She is a graduate of the Faculty of Law of the Hebrew University, Jerusalem and earned her doctoral degree from Yale Law School. She is the author of *Birth Power: the Case for Surrogacy* and various other publications in English and Hebrew on reproductive law, women in Israeli law, and human rights.

Elissavet Stamatopoulou is Chief of the New York Office of the United Nations Centre for Human Rights. Born in Athens, Greece, she is a member of the Athens Bar Association. She earned a master's degree in the Administration of Criminal Justice from Northeastern University in Boston, Massachusetts, and received her doctorate in International Law from the Institute of Graduate International Studies of the University of Geneva, Switzerland. She began working for the UN in Vienna in 1979, joined the Centre for Human Rights in Geneva in 1980, and has been with the New York office since 1984.

Maria Suarez Toro, a Costa Rican and Puerto Rican teacher and activist, is the producer of *FIRE (Feminist International Radio Endeavor)* at Radio for Peace International in Costa Rica. She was the coordinator of the Human Rights Popular Education Program at the Central American Human Rights Commission from 1988 to 1991, where she initiated the Women's Human Rights Project. She was a member of the Latin American and Caribbean Linking Committee for the 1993 UN World Conference on Human Rights, of UNIFEM's Caucus, and of the coalition that organized the Global Tribunal on Violations of Women's Human Rights at the NGO Forum in Vienna. She is part of a team working on the Women's Human Rights Education Campaign of the People's Decade on Human Rights Education, 1991–2001

Donna Sullivan, J.D., is Director of the Women in Law Project of the International Human Rights Law Group. She is an expert on women's rights in international law and, in particular, on potential conflicts between women's rights and other rights protected by international law. As head of the Women's Rights Project of the International League for Human Rights from 1991–92, she worked closely with the UN Committee on the Elimination of Discrimination Against Women to draft its General Recommendation on violence against women. She teaches a course on Gender, Cultural Difference and International Human Rights Law at the Washington College of Law of American University (Washington, DC)

Dorothy Q. Thomas is Founder/Director of the Women's Rights Project of Human Rights Watch. Since its inception in 1990, the Project has released numerous reports documenting severe abuses of women's human rights in all five regions monitored by Human Rights Watch. Originally from New York City, Thomas has a masters degree in women's studies and literary theory from Georgetown University and has begun a second masters in international political economy at Columbia University. She has traveled to Brazil, Pakistan, India, and Russia to investigate violations of women's rights; at the World Conference on Human Rights in Vienna, she played a key role in highlighting abuses of women's rights. She has appeared on the BBC, PBS, and NPR, and been interviewed by major news organizations including the *New York Times,* the *Boston Globe,* and the *Washington Post.* She is the author of several books and articles including *Criminal Injustice: Violence Against Women in Brazil, Double Jeopardy: Police Abuse of Women in Pakistan,* and

"Domestic Violence as a Human Rights Issue." On September 27, 1993, she testified about women's human rights abuses and U.S. foreign policy before Congressman Tom Lantos's Sub-Committee on International Security.

Nahid Toubia was the first woman surgeon in Sudan. She has been active in women's health and rights issues for the past twenty years, both in her own country and internationally. She is an advisor to the World Health Organization and other United Nations agencies, and the Vice-Chair of the Women's Rights Project of Human Rights Watch. She is currently the director of the Global Action Against FGM Project at the Columbia University School of Public Health in New York City. In addition, she is the editor of *Women in the Arab World* and the author of *FGM: A Call for Global Action.*

Sima Wali, who is a native of Afghanistan, is Executive Director of Refugee Women in Development (RefWID), a nonprofit organization in Washington, DC. Previously, she was Communications Officer of the Secretariat for Women in Development at the New TransCentury Foundation. In Afghanistan, she worked at the U.S. Embassy and, in Washington, served as an advisor to the U.S. Office on Refugee Resettlement's Task Force on Refugee Women. She sits on several boards and advisory committees, and has been the recipient of several awards, including a distinguished service award for her work with the Peace Corps.

Nadia H. Youssef, an Egyptian national, received her B.A. and M.A. from the American University in Cairo and her Ph.D. in Sociology from the University of California, Berkeley, and has taught at California State University, Hayward, and at the University of Southern California. She has been Research Director of the International Center for Research on Women, Senior Policy Specialist for the Program and Policy Division of UNICEF, and Senior Demographer at the Center for Immigrant and Population Studies at the City University of New York. She is the author of three books and numerous journal articles and research papers. She is currently conducting research on cross-national variations in the social status of widows and widowers.

Zhu Hong is Research Professor at the Institute of Foreign Literature, Chinese Academy of Social Sciences in Beijing. She is currently a Visiting Professor at Boston University, where she teaches a course on Chinese women's writing. She has translated two volumes of contemporary Chinese short stories (both published in the United States): *The Chinese Western* and *The Serenity of Whiteness.*

Index